Semantic Web Technologies and E-Business:

Toward the Integrated Virtual Organization and Business Process Automation

A.F. Salam
The University of North Carolina at Greensboro, USA

Jason R. Stevens
The University of North Carolina at Greensboro, USA

IDEA GROUP PUBLISHING
Hershey • London • Melbourne • Singapore

Acquisitions Editor:	Kristin Klinger
Development Editor:	Kristin Roth
Senior Managing Editor:	Jennifer Neidig
Managing Editor:	Sara Reed
Assistant Managing Editor:	Sharon Berger
Copy Editor:	Holly Powell
Typesetter:	Cindy L. Consonery
Cover Design:	Lisa Tosheff
Printed at:	Integrated Book Technology

Published in the United States of America by
Idea Group Publishing (an imprint of Idea Group Inc.)
701 E. Chocolate Avenue
Hershey PA 17033
Tel: 717-533-8845
Fax: 717-533-8661
E-mail: cust@idea-group.com
Web site: http://www.idea-group.com

and in the United Kingdom by
Idea Group Publishing (an imprint of Idea Group Inc.)
3 Henrietta Street
Covent Garden
London WC2E 8LU
Tel: 44 20 7240 0856
Fax: 44 20 7379 0609
Web site: http://www.eurospanonline.com

Library of Congress Cataloging-in-Publication Data

Semantic web technologies and e-business : toward the integrated virtual organization and business process automation / A. F. Salam and Jason R. Stevens, editors.
p. cm.
Summary: "This book presents research related to the application of semantic Web technologies, including semantic service-oriented architecture, semantic content management, and semantic knowledge sharing in e-business processes. It compiles research from experts around the globe to bring to the forefront the many issues surrounding the application of semantic Web technologies in e-business"--Provided by publisher.
Includes bibliographical references and index.
ISBN 1-59904-192-8 (hardcover) -- ISBN 1-59904-193-6 (softcover) -- ISBN 1-59904-194-4 (ebook)
1. Electronic commerce. 2. Semantic Web. 3. Internet. 4. Business enterprises--Computer networks. I. Salam, A. F., 1966- II. Stevens, Jason R., 1976-
HF5548.32.S459 2007
658.4'03802854678--dc22

2006032159

British Cataloguing in Publication Data
A Cataloguing in Publication record for this book is available from the British Library.

Dedication

To my parents, Dr. K. N. Rahman and Dr. Salima Rahman, for their wisdom, foresight, and affection and to my loving wife Shima, for her constant love, support, and patience, and most importantly to my inspiration my son Sameen R. Salam for his insatiable curiosity.

A. F. Salam

I would like to dedicate this book to my family.

Jason R. Stevens

Semantic Web Technologies and E-Business:
Toward the Integrated Virtual Organization and Business Process Automation

Table of Contents

Preface vii

Section I: Semantic Representation, Business Processes, and Virtual Integration

Chapter I. Developing Dynamic Packaging Applications Using Semantic Web-Based Integration 1
Jorge Cardoso, Universidade da Madeira, Portugal

Chapter II. A Semantic Service-Oriented Architecture for Business Process Fusion 40
Athanasios Bouras, National Technical University of Athens, Greece
Panagiotis Gouvas, National Technical University of Athens, Greece
Gregoris Mentzas, National Technical University of Athens, Greece

Chapter III. A Design Tool for Business Process Design and Representation 77
Roberto Paiano, Università di Lecce, Italy
Anna Lisa Guido, Università di Lecce, Italy

Chapter IV. Automatically Extracting and Tagging Business Information for E-Business Systems Using Linguistic Analysis 101
Sumali J. Conlon, University of Mississippi, USA
Susan Lukose, University of Mississippi, USA
Jason G. Hale, University of Mississippi, USA
Anil Vinjamur, University of Mississippi, USA

Preface

Introduction

The Semantic Web vision of the World Wide Web Consortium (W3C) is comprised of four primary components: (1) expressing meaning, (2) knowledge representation, (3) ontology, and (4) agents. Expression of meaning is fundamental to the construction of the new "intelligent" Web. The current Web lacks mechanisms for expressing meaning and is therefore static. Knowledge representation provides the mechanism that allows meaning to be expressed in structured format allowing inference mechanism to be applied to arrive at useful conclusions. To make knowledge representation both meaningful and practical, the "meaning" behind the "data" has to be "shared." This can be accomplished using ontologies. Ontology refers to a shared vocabulary of some concept. The premise is that if the vocabulary is shared regarding a concept then the meaning behind the concept becomes apparent among those sharing the vocabulary. Once the ontology has been agreed upon by a community and if the ontology can then be captured in machine-readable form using resource description framework (RDF), RDF schema (RDFS), or Web ontology language (OWL) then software agents can be used to "reason" with the knowledge represented and captured using that ontology. There may be many such ontologies in use but by using a global standard such as OWL from the W3C, it is possible to create many ontologies which are interoperable—therefore amenable—to machine reasoning by software agents.

In this knowledge-based economy, businesses succeed or fail based on how well they are able to share knowledge and information to effectively respond to the changing demands in the marketplace. Semantic Web technology brings to the business world a set of tools that will help in the development of meaningful shared vocabulary or ontologies leading to standardization of terms and concepts related to the descriptions of products, processes, and coordination mechanisms both within and across enterprises. This will lead to the development of effective knowledge management systems that are tightly integrated to the business processes that they are designed to support. The primary purpose of this book is to highlight business, managerial, technological, and implementation issues surrounding the application of Semantic Web technologies to business process automation eventually leading to the new integrated knowledge-based virtual organizations.

Each and every single business process is enacted by human and/or software agents within a certain set of knowledge domains such as customer knowledge domain, supplier knowledge domain, financial knowledge domain, logistics knowledge domains, and so forth. Semantic technology enables us to capture and codify these knowledge domains in a practical and effective manner, thereby allowing the application of reasoning to be incorporated within these automated business processes thus paving the way towards the integrated knowledge-based virtual organizations.

Significant and in-depth research is needed to understand both the managerial and technological dimensions of how business enterprises may benefit from this promising technology—the Semantic Web. Additionally, business managers, IT professionals, students, and academics need to understand the potential of this technology and its application to the benefit of the consumers. This book is intended to fill this gap.

The audience of this book is MBA students, IT professionals, business executives, consultants, and seniors in undergraduate business degree programs

The scholarly value of this book and its contribution will be to the literature in the information systems/e-business discipline. Most of the publications are more focused toward the computer science audience and many are compilations of proceedings papers from conferences in computer science and artificial intelligence. This book is intended to bring a business perspective to this promising new technology—the Semantic Web.

Chapter Overview

Chapter I introduces an innovative semantic technology allowing for the automated online configuration and assembling of packaged travel products for individual customers. Dynamic packaging applications require a suitable integration of heterogeneous, autonomous, and distributed tourism information systems. This integration is a complex and difficult issue. The Semantic Web, a relatively new concept, brings a set of emerging technologies and models that need to be explored and evaluated to assert their use for the implementation of more integrated dynamic packaging applications. In this chapter, the author analyzes dynamic packaging application requirements and presents an architecture that enables the integration of tourism data sources and creation of dynamic packages using semantic annotation, semantic rules, ontologies, Web services, and Web processes.

Chapter II proposes a semantically enriched service-oriented business applications (SE-SOBA) framework that will provide a dynamically reconfigurable architecture enabling enterprises to respond quickly and flexibly to market changes. The authors also propose the development of a pure semantic-based implementation of the universal description, discovery, and integration (UDDI) specification, called pure semantic registry (PSR), which provides a flexible, extendable core architectural component allowing the deployment and exploitation of Semantic Web services. The implementation of PSR involves the development of a semantic-based repository and an embedded RDF-based reasoning engine, providing strong query and reasoning capabilities to support effective service discovery and composition. The authors claim that when SE-SOBAs are combined with PSR and rule-based formalizations of business scenarios and processes, they constitute a holistic business-driven semantic integration framework, called FUSION, applied to intra- and inter-organizational enterprise application integration (EAI) scenarios.

Chapter III focuses on business process design as middle point between requirement elicitation and implementation of a Web information system. The authors attempt to solve both the problem of the notation to adopt in order to represent in a simple way the business process and the problem of a formal representation, in a machine readable format, of the design. They adopt Semantic Web technology to represent process and explain how this technology has been used to achieve their goals.

Chapter IV contends that the Semantic Web will require semantic representation of information that computers can understand when they process business applications. Most Web content is currently represented in formats such as text, that facilitate human understanding, rather than in the more structured format, that allow automated processing by computer systems. This chapter explores how natural language processing principles, using linguistic analysis, can be employed to extract information from unstructured Web documents and translate it into extensible markup language (XML)—the enabling currency of today's e-business applications, and the foundation for the emerging Semantic Web languages of tomorrow. The authors developed a prototype system and tested the system with online financial documents.

Chapter V presents an emerging technology like business process execution language (BPEL), and its implementation in BPEL for Web services (BFEL4WS) as a rich set of possibilities in describing business processes. They contend that BPEL further adheres, as a technology, in a consistent way to the underlying Web service-based implementation technology and is a perfect fit for service oriented architectures as they are currently implemented in many business organizations as a successor to EAI. However, BPEL4WS, in its current implementation, will only serve in a static way for production workflows. In this chapter, the authors discuss how Semantic Web services through a semantic service-oriented architecture (SSOA) can be used to extend BPEL4WS to create ad hoc and collaborative workflows.

Chapter VI provides a vision that with the evolution of the next generation Web—the Semantic Web—e-business can be expected to grow into a more collaborative effort in which businesses compete with each other by collaborating to offer the best products to the consumers. Electronic collaboration involves data interchange with multimedia data being one of them. Digital multimedia data in various formats have increased tremendously in recent years on the Internet. An automated process that can represent multimedia data in a meaningful way for the Semantic Web is highly desired. In this chapter, the authors propose an automatic multimedia representation system for the Semantic Web.

Chapter VII addresses the issues of evolving software agents in e-commerce applications. Even though agent-based e-commerce has been booming with the development of the Internet and agent technologies, little effort has been devoted to exploring the learning and evolving capabilities of software agents. An agent structure with evolutionary features is proposed with a focus on internal hierarchical knowledge. The authors argue that the knowledge base of an intelligent agent should be the cornerstone for its evolution capabilities, and that the agent can enhance its knowledge base by exchanging knowledge with other agents. In this chapter, product ontology is chosen as an instance of a knowledge base. The authors propose a new approach to facilitate ontology exchange among e-commerce agents. The ontology exchange model and its formalities are elaborated. Product-brokering agents have been designed and implemented, which accomplish the ontology exchange process from request to integration.

Chapter VIII describes how Web services are self-contained, self-describing modular applications. Different from traditional distributed computing, Web services are more dynamic with regards to service discovery and run-time binding mechanisms. This chapter provides an in-depth discussion on research related to Web services discovery. The authors present some basis knowledge for the Web services discovery and their Semantic Web-based solution for quality of service (QoS)-aware discovery and measurement. It complements OWL-S to achieve better services discovery, composition, and measurement.

Chapter IX introduces how to effectively organize ontology languages and ontologies and how to efficiently process semantic information based on ontologies. In this chapter, the authors propose the hierarchies to organize ontology languages and ontologies. Based on the hierarchy of ontologies, the conflicts in different ontologies are resolved, thus the semantics in different ontologies are clear without ambiguities. These ontologies can be used to efficiently process the semantic information in Semantic Web and e-business.

Chapter X presents arguments in favor of an integrative, systems-based model of knowledge sharing that can provide a way of visualizing the interrelated elements that comprise a knowledge management system. This original model, building on a rhetorical process model of communication, includes both the objective and subjective elements within human cognition. In addition, it clarifies the purpose and method elements at the center for any effective knowledge system. The model centers on the purpose elements of intentions and audience, and the method elements of technical tools and human processes. The output of knowledge sharing includes objective products and subjective interpretations. Feedback verifies the timeliness and efficiency in the process of building both information and knowledge.

Chapter XI introduces a new approach named *semantic knowledge transparency,* which is defined as the dynamic on-demand and seamless flow of relevant and unambiguous, machine-interpretable knowledge resources within organizations and across inter-organizational systems of business partners engaged in collaborative processes. Semantic knowledge transparency is based on extant research in e-business, knowledge management, and Semantic Web. In addition, theoretical conceptualizations are formalized using description logics and ontological analysis. As a result, the ontology supports a common vocabulary for transparent knowledge exchange among inter-organizational systems of business partners of a value chain, so that semantic interoperability can be achieved. An example is furnished to illustrate how semantic knowledge transparency in the e-marketplace provides critical input to the supplier discovery and selection decision problem while reducing the transaction and search costs for the buyer organization.

Chapter XII introduces an application of the Semantic Web based on ontology to the tourism business. Tourism business is one promising area of Semantic Web applications. To realize the potential of the Semantic Web, we need to find a "killer" application of the Semantic Web in the knowledge management area. Finally, the authors discuss the relationship between the Semantic Web and knowledge management processes.

Chapter XIII presents an ontology-based query formation and information retrieval system under the m-commerce agent framework. A query formation approach that combines the usage of ontology and keywords is implemented. This approach takes advantage of the tree structure in ontology to form queries visually and efficiently. It also uses additional aids such as keywords to complete the query formation process more efficiently. The proposed information retrieval scheme focuses on using genetic algorithms to improve computational effectiveness.

Chapter XIV proposes a system that, when mature, should be able to support the needs of travelers in automatically composing and executing their travel arrangements using software agents. The authors argue and illustrate how Semantic Web technologies combined with software agents can be used in the proposed system. Finally, they show how RDF demarcated data is to be used to support personal information delivery. They conclude with the description of the current state of implementation and plans for further development of the system.

Chapter XV proposes an ontology using OWL for the Australian timber sector that can be used in conjunction with Semantic Web services to provide effective and cheap business-to-business (B2B) communications.

From the perspective of the timber industry sector, this study is important because supply chain efficiency is a key component in an organization's strategy to gain a competitive advantage in the marketplace. Strong improvement in supply chain performance is possible with improved B2B communication which is used both for building trust and providing real time marketing data.

Traditional methods such as electronic data interchange (EDI) used to facilitate B2B communication have a number of disadvantages, such as high implementation and running costs and a rigid and inflexible messaging standard. Information and communications technologies (ICT) have supported the emergence of Web-based EDI which maintains the advantages of the traditional paradigm while negating the disadvantages. This has been further extended by the advent of the Semantic Web which rests on the fundamental idea that Web resources should be annotated with semantic markup that captures information about their meaning and facilitates meaningful machine-to-machine communication.

Chapter XVI provides an illustration of how Semantic Web technologies can be used for searching medical information on the Web. There has been a paradigm shift in medical practice. More and more consumers are using the Internet as a source for medical information even before seeing a doctor. The well-known fact is that medical terms are often hard to spell. Despite advances in technology, the Internet is still producing futile searches when the search terms are misspelt. Often consumers are frustrated with irrelevant information they retrieve as a result of the wrong spelling. An ontology-based search is one way of assisting users in correcting their spelling errors when searching for medical information.

Chapter XVII discusses Semantic Web standards and ontologies in two areas: (1) the medical sciences field and (2) the healthcare industry. Semantic Web standards are important in the medical sciences since much of the medical research that is available needs an avenue to be shared across disparate computer systems. Ontologies can provide a basis for searching context-based medical research information so that it can be integrated and used as a foundation for future research. The healthcare industry will be examined specifically in its use of electronic health records (EHR), which need Semantic Web standards to be communicated across different EHR systems. The increased use of EHRs across healthcare organizations will also require ontologies to support context-sensitive searching of information, as well as creating context-based rules for appointments, procedures, and tests so that the quality of healthcare is improved. Literature in these areas has been combined in this chapter to provide a general view of how Semantic Web standards and ontologies are used and to give examples of applications in the areas of healthcare and the medical sciences.

Section I

Semantic Representation, Business Processes, and Virtual Integration

Chapter I

Developing Dynamic Packaging Applications Using Semantic Web-Based Integration

Jorge Cardoso, Universidade da Madeira, Portugal

Abstract

Dynamic packaging has been introduced as an innovative technology allowing for the automated online configuration and assembling of packaged travel products for individual customers. Dynamic packaging applications require a suitable integration of heterogeneous, autonomous, and distributed tourism information systems. This integration is a complex and difficult issue. The Semantic Web, a relatively new concept, brings a set of emerging technologies and models that need to be explored and evaluated to assert its use for the implementation of more integrated dynamic packaging applications. In this chapter, we analyze dynamic packaging application requirements and present an architecture that enables the integration of tourism data sources and creation of dynamic packages using semantic annotation, semantic rules, ontologies, Web services, and Web processes. We will recognize that the Semantic Web is a good candidate able to supply a solution for overcoming the interoperability problems that (current) dynamic packaging applications face.

Introduction

Tourism has become one of the world's largest industry players, and its growth shows a consistent year-to-year increase. The World Tourism Organization (2006) predicts that by 2020 tourist arrivals around the world will increase over 200%. Tourism has become a highly competitive business for tourism destinations all over the world. Competitive advantage is no longer natural, but increasingly driven by science, information technology, and innovation.

The continuing growth in the use of the Internet has transformed the world into a global village. For example, e-tourism-related Web sites provide a vast amount of rich information, maps, pictures, sounds, and services on destinations throughout the world. A study by Forrester (Forrester, 2005) estimates that business-to-business (B2B) revenues will reach $8.8 trillion in 2005 and business-to-customer (B2C) revenues in the U.S. will reach $229.9 billion by 2008.

The Internet is already the primary source of tourist destination information for travelers. About 95% of Web users use the Internet to gather travel-related information and about 93% indicate that they visited tourism Web sites when planning for vacations (Lake, 2001). The number of people turning to the Internet for vacation and travel planning has increased more than 300% over the past 5 years. It has outpaced traditional sources of information on tourist destinations within a short period of time. One major cause for the growth of e-tourism is that it extends existing business models, reduces costs, and expands and introduces new distribution channels.

Evidence indicates that the effective use of information technology is crucial for tourism businesses' competitiveness and prosperity, as it influences their ability to differentiate their offerings as well as their production and delivery costs. Tourism is an information-based industry and one of the leading industries on the Internet. For example, it is anticipated that most sectors in the travel industry throughout the world will have Web sites on the Internet. Thus, it is vital for every tourism destination and travel business to embrace the use of information technology and exploit its potential.

Barnett and Standing (2001) argue that the rapidly changing business environment brought on by the Internet requires organizations to quickly implement new business models, develop new networks and alliances, and be creative in their marketing. In order to compete in the electronic era, businesses must be prepared to use technology-mediated channels, create internal and external value, formulate technology convergent strategies, and organize resources around knowledge and relationships (Rayport & Jaworski, 2001).

Tourism information systems (TIS) are a new type of business system that serve and support e-tourism and e-travel, such as airlines, hoteliers, car rental companies, leisure suppliers, and travel agencies. These systems rely on travel-related information sources to create tourism products and services. The information present on these sources can serve as the springboard for the development of a variety of systems, including dynamic packaging applications, travel planning engines, and price comparison applications.

In this chapter we are particularly interested in studying the development and implementation of dynamic packaging applications. Dynamic packaging can be defined as the combination of different travel products, bundled and priced in real time, in response to the requests of the consumer or booking agent. In dynamic packaging applications, consumer requirements shape the response of the packaging system, the final price, and the products of travel packages. Our approach to the development of dynamic packaging applications encompasses the use of the latest information technologies such as the Semantic Web, Web services, Web processes, and semantic packaging rules.

E-tourism is a perfect application area for Semantic Web technologies since information integration, dissemination, and exchange are the key backbones of the travel industry. Therefore, the Semantic Web can considerably improve e-tourism applications (DERI International, 2005). Dynamic packaging application solutions deal with B2B integration and B2C transactions. While organizations have sought to apply semantics to manage and exploit data or content to support integration, Web processes are the means to exploit its application, increasingly made interoperable with Web services.

Web services and Web processes are defined as loosely coupled, reusable components that encapsulate functionality and are distributed and programmatically accessible over standard Internet protocols. They constitute one of the "hot" areas of the Web technology supporting the remote invocation of business functionality over the Internet through message exchange. They provide an "information" layer that allows integrating different data standards to exchange information seamlessly without having to change the proprietary data schemas of tourism organizations.

Semantics can also be used to formally specify the packaging rules that influence which products will be part of dynamic packages. The use of semantic packaging rules has several benefits for dynamic packaging applications since travel managers or travel agents, without programming experience, can manage and change packaging rules to reflect market conditions; packaging policies can be easily communicated and understood by all employees; and rules can be managed in isolation from the application code.

Dynamic Packaging Applications

Currently, with most tourism information systems, travelers need to visit multiple independent Web sites to plan their trip, register their personal information multiple times, spend hours or days waiting for response or confirmation, and make multiple payments by credit card. Consumers are discouraged by the lack of functionalities. Dynamic packaging applications are emerging in response to these limitations and have caught the attention of major worldwide online travel agencies.

The Dynamic Packaging Model

A dynamic packaging application allows consumers or travel agents to customize trips by bundling trip components. Customers can specify a set of preferences for a vacation, for example, a 5-day stay on Madeira Island, then the dynamic packaging application dynamically accesses and queries a set of tourism information sources to find products such as air fairs, hotel rates, car rental companies, and leisure activity suppliers in real time. In the off-line world, such packages used to be put together by tour operators in brochures. This new dynamic packaging technology includes the ability to combine multiple travel components on demand, in creating a reservation. The package that is created is handled seamlessly as one transaction and requires only one payment from the consumer, hiding the pricing of individual components.

Main Players: Expedia, Travelocity, and Orbitz

The travel industry's three most dominant online agencies—Expedia, Travelocity, and Orbitz—are leading the development of dynamic packaging technology, and they continue to put significant investment into providing an efficient and sophisticated booking experience. Travelers are given the opportunity to construct customized packages by choosing the airline carrier, their flight, the hotel location, the car rental company, their insurance, other travel products such as theme park passes, and even tours.

Expedia is the largest online travel agency. Expedia follows the merchant model, that is, it consigns hotel rooms at a wholesale rate and resells them to consumers. The key in the merchant model is to negotiate satisfactory agreements with providers. Expedia has stated that the popular durations requested by consumers are not the traditional 7/14 night model, but holidays of 3, 5, and 8 nights, a level of flexibility that is outside the costing model of most charter-based, mass-market tour operators. This is one of the strategies having lead to its top market position. From the customers' view point, the Expedia business model has two major drawbacks. When Expedia sells all of its allocated hotel rooms, it informs customers that no rooms are available for sale. This is misleading because there might be rooms available outside of Expedia's allocated share. Moreover, Expedia does not fully disclose the taxes and fees that will be added to the sale price. In some cases additional tax and service fees mean that consumers might actually pay more than if they had booked the room directly from the hotel.

Expedia's use of dynamic packaging is one of the best among the competition: Using Expedia's Web site, consumers can book airline tickets and hotel rooms, and also book a shuttle to pick them up at the airport and set up prepaid restaurant meals. In this way Expedia focuses on the total journey of consumers. Expedia pioneered dynamic packaging in 2002 and now gets almost 30% of revenue from package buyers (Mullaney, 2004).

Travelocity provides Internet and wireless reservation information for more than 700 airlines, more than 55,000 hotels, and more than 50 car rental companies (PRNewswire, 2002). In addition, Travelocity offers more than 6,500 vacation packages, tour and cruise departures, and a vast database of destination and interest information. It is now the second largest online travel agency. Travelocity launched a new merchant model hotel program offering advantages so compelling that more than 2,000 hotels signed agreements to participate. Travelocity can pull rates and availability directly from the hotel's central reservation system (CRS). This eliminates the time and costs associated with manually allocating blocks of rooms to a separate system for discounted sales. Travelocity can provide a "single view" of room inventory. This is an advantage compared to the merchant model of competitors. Also, Travelocity pays the hotels immediately upon checkout, eliminating the waiting period for payment that hotels experience with other merchant model distributors.

Travelocity made a strategic acquisition of Site59.com, whose dynamic packaging technology allows Travelocity to respond to the growing popularity of Expedia's dynamic packages. Travelocity dynamic vacation technology will be the first to allow users to book specific airline seats and hotel rooms themselves, in real time. Travelocity has included taxes and fees in its products and strives to only list flights and rooms still available.

Since launching its Web site to the general public in June 2001, **Orbitz** has become the third largest online travel site in the world. It was founded by five major airlines, American, Continental, Delta, Northwest, and United. The main objective was to compete with Expedia and online ticketing sales, hoping to take advantage of increase in ticket sales online. The launch of Orbitz, a $100 million joint venture (Hospitality, 2005), demonstrates the high cost of entry into the travel space. It is a costly undertaking that requires cooperation with existing industry players. Therefore, new entrants face enormous challenges.

Orbitz had a perceived advantage over Travelocity and Expedia because it had a deeper inventory of "Web fares," the heavily discounted tickets promoted on the carriers' own Internet sites (CBS NEWS, 2003). This advantage has drawn wide-ranging criticism from Expedia and Travelocity with the claim that the airline-backed ticketing operation is antithetical to competition in the industry and hurts consumers. Orbitz has lowered distribution costs for its suppliers by sharing a portion of the fees that global distribution systems (GDSs) pay to Orbitz as an incentive for booking travel on their systems. Orbitz further reduced distribution costs for several airlines through their participation in the Orbitz Supplier Link technology program, which allows Orbitz to sell some tickets without using a GDS.

Orbitz's Web site has already completed the implementation of its dynamic packaging engine. One major characteristic of Orbitz strategy is that the customer relationship does not end when a customer buys a travel product. Orbitz is the only travel site with a customer care team that monitors nationwide travel conditions for travelers. The care team gathers and interprets Federal Aviation Administration (FAA), National Weather Service, and other data providing the latest information on flight delays, weather conditions, gate changes, airport congestion, or any other event that might impact travel via mobile phone, pager, personal digital assistant (PDA), or e-mail.

Dynamic Packaging Application Architecture

The development of dynamic packaging applications is a complex issue since it requires the integration of distributed systems with infrastructures that are not frequently encountered in more traditional centralized systems. For dynamic packaging applications to be successful it is indispensable to studying their architecture. The study of architectural strategies has a critical impact on early decisions in system development; it is both cost effective and efficient to conduct analyses at the architecture level, before substantial resources have been committed to development (Bass, Clements, & Kazman, 1998). Therefore, we will undertake a study of our approach to dynamic packaging application development by presenting its architecture.

We propose an architecture for dynamic packaging applications composed of six layers: (1) tourism information systems, (2) tourism data sources, (3) data model mapping, (4) data consolidation, (5) shared global data model, and (6) dynamic packaging engine. The relationships between these layers are illustrated in Figure 1.

To better understand the purpose of each architectural layer, we will briefly describe them in this section and give a detailed presentation in the following sections.

Figure 1. Architecture of semantically enabled dynamic packaging applications

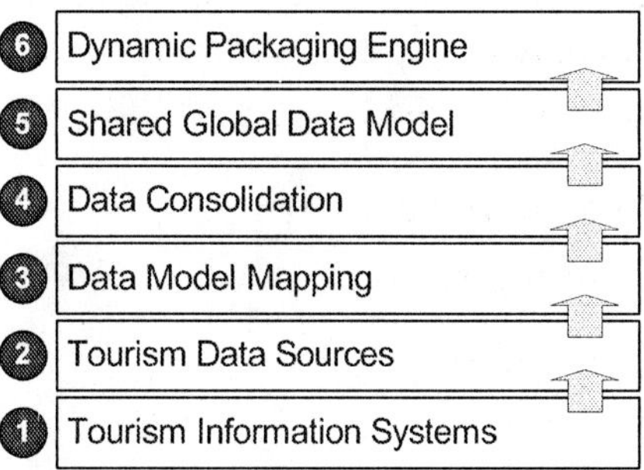

- **Tourism information systems.** The information needed to build dynamic packages is stored in tourism information systems, such as CRS, GDS, HDS, DMS, and Web sites.
- **Tourism data sources.** Each tourism information system makes travel data available through data sources in one or more formats, such as HTML, XML, RDF, flat files, relational model, and so forth.
- **Data model mapping.** In our architecture, data on data sources is mapped to the concepts of a common ontology to facilitate the integration of information.
- **Data consolidation.** The various segments of the common ontology constructed from individual data sources are consolidated using procedures described using an abstract business process model.
- **Shared global data model.** With the data consolidated in the previous level, we populated the shared global data model, represented with an e-tourism ontology, by creating instances.
- **Dynamic packaging engine.** Based on the information present in the e-tourism ontology, we extract knowledge to build dynamic packages.

Tourism Information System Integration

Tourism information systems provide travel agencies and customers with crucial information such as flight details, accommodations, prices, and the availability of services. Dedicated and specialized information systems are providing real time tourism data to travel agents, customers, and other organizations.

A few years ago, e-tourism applications were mainly focused on handling transactions and managing catalogs. Applications automated only a small portion of the

Figure 2. The various tourism information systems that need to be integrated

electronic transaction process, for example, taking orders, scheduling shipments, and providing customer service. E-tourism was held back by closed markets that could not use each other's services due to the use of incompatible protocols.

Business requirements of dynamic applications, however, are evolving beyond transaction support and include requirements for the interoperability and integration of heterogeneous, autonomous, and distributed tourism information systems. The objective is to provide a global and homogeneous logical view of travel products that are physically distributed over tourism data sources. However, in general, tourism information systems are not designed for integration. A considerable number of tourism information systems were developed in the 1960s when the integration of information systems was not a major concern.

One of the challenges that dynamic packaging applications face is the integration of the five tourism information systems most widespread in the tourism industry that are a fundamental infrastructure for providing access to tourism information, namely, computerized reservation systems (CRS), global distribution systems (GDS), hotel distribution systems (HDS), destination management systems (DMS), and Web sites (Figure 2).

Computerized Reservation System

A CRS is a travel supplier's own central reservation system (Inkpen, 1998). A CRS enables travel agencies to find what a customer is looking for and makes customer data storage and retrieval relatively simple. These systems contain information about airline schedules, availability, fares, and related services. Some systems provide services to make reservations and issue tickets. CRS were introduced in the 1950s as internal systems within individual organizations. With time and with the development of communication technologies they became available to travel agencies and other organizations. CRS are extremely popular and widespread, especially among airlines. It is estimated that 70% of all bookings are made through this channel (European Travel Agents' and Tour Operators' Associations, 2004).

Global Distribution System

A GDS is a super switch connecting several CRSs. A GDS integrates tourism information about airlines, hotels, car rentals, cruises, and other travel products. It is used almost exclusively by travel agents. The airline industry created the GDS concept in the 1960s. As with CRSs, the goal was to keep track of airline schedules, availability, fares, and related services. Prior to the introduction of GDSs, travel agents spent a considerable amount of time manually entering reservations. Since GDSs allowed automating the reservation process for travel agents, they were able to be productive and turn into an extension of the airline's sales force (HotelOnline, 2002). The use of these systems is expensive since they charge a fee for every segment of travel sold through the system. There are currently four major GDSs (Inkpen, 1998): Amadeus, Galileo, Sabre, and Worldspan. Today, 90% of all U.S. tickets are sold through these four global distribution systems (Riebeek, 2003).

Hotel Distribution System

An HDS works closely with GDSs to provide the hotel industry with automated sales and booking services. An HDS is tied into a GDS, allowing hotel bookings to be made in the same way as an airline reservation (Inkpen, 1998). HDSs may be categorized into two main types: (1) the HDS is linked directly to the hotel's own booking system and in turn linked with a GDS that can be accessed by booking agents, and (2) dedicated companies provide a reservation system linked to airline GDSs.

Destination Management Systems

DMSs supply interactively accessible information about a destination, enabling tourist destinations to disseminate information about products and services as well as to facilitate the planning, management, and marketing of regions as tourism entities or brands (Buhalis, 2002). These systems offer a guide to tourist attractions, festivals, and cultural events, coupled with online bookings for accommodation providers. They also feature weather reports, Web movies, and feed from Web cams positioned in popular tourist areas. One of the goals of DMS is to develop flexible, tailor-made, specialized, and integrated tourism products. Two of the most well known DMSs include Tiscover[1] (Austria) and Gulliver[2] (Ireland).

Direct Distribution Using Web Sites

The Internet is revolutionizing the distribution of tourism information and sales. Small and large companies can have Web sites with "equal Internet access" to international tourism markets. Previously, many companies had to use their booking systems as platforms from which to distribute their products via existing channels, such as GDSs. Recently, companies such as the airlines, have chosen the strategy to sell tickets on their own Web sites to avoid using a GDS (Dombey, 1998). This is the simplest and cheapest strategy to sell tickets since they do not have to pay a fee to the GDS. Small providers, such as local hotels, can use the Internet to supply information about their products and allow the automatic booking of rooms and other services. A recent survey (O'Connor, 2003) revealed that over 95% of hotel chains had a Web site, with almost 90% of these providing technology to allow customers to book directly.

Tourism Data Source Integration

Given the rapid growth and success of tourism data sources, it becomes increasingly attractive to extract data from these sources and make it available for dynamic packaging applications. Manually integrating multiple heterogeneous data sources into applications is a time-consuming, costly, and error-prone engineering task. According to industry estimates, as much as 70% of information technology spending may be allocated for integration-related activities. Consequently, many organizations are looking for solutions that can make the integration of information systems an easier task (Gorton, Almquist, Dorow, Gong, & Thurman, 2005).

Data source integration is a research topic of enormous practical importance for dynamic packaging. Integrating distributed, heterogeneous and autonomous tourism information systems, with different organizational levels, functions, and business processes to freely exchange information can be technologically difficult and costly.

Dynamic packaging applications need to access tourism data sources to query information about flights, car rentals, hotels, and leisure activities. Data sources can be accessed using the Internet as a communication medium. The sources can

Figure 3. The various tourism data sources to be integrated

contain hypertext markup language (HTML) pages present in Web sites, databases, or specific formatted files, such as extensible markup language (XML), resource description framework (RDF), or flat files. To develop a robust dynamic packaging application it is important to classify each data source according to its type of data since the type of data will influence our selection of a solution to achieve data integration. For dynamic packaging applications, tourism data sources can host three major types of data: (1) unstructured data, (2) semi-structured data, and (3) structured data.

Types of Data

Data can be broken down into three broad categories (Figure 4): (1) unstructured, (2) semi-structured, and (3) structured. Highly unstructured data comprises free-form documents or objects of arbitrary sizes and types. At the other end of the spectrum, structured data are what is typically found in databases. Every element of data has an assigned format and significance.

Unstructured Data

Unstructured data is what we find in text, files, video, e-mails, reports, PowerPoint presentations, voice mail, office memos, and images. Data can be of any type and do not necessarily follow any format, rules, or sequence. For example, the data present on HTML Web pages are unstructured and irregular.

Unstructured data does not readily fit into structured databases except as binary large objects (BLOBs). Although unstructured data can have some structure—for example, e-mails have addressees, subjects, bodies, and so forth, and HTML Web pages have a set of predefined tags—the information is not stored in a way that allows for easy manipulation by applications and computers.

Figure 4. Unstructured, semi-structured, and structured data

Unstructured data

The university has 5600 students. John's ID is number 1, he is 18 years old and already holds a B.Sc. degree. David's ID is number 2, he is 31 years old and holds a Ph.D. degree. Robert's ID is number 3, he is 51 years old and also holds the same degree as David, a Ph.D. degree.

Semi-structured data

```
<University>
  <Student ID="1">
    <Name>John</Name>
    <Age>18</Age>
    <Degree>B.Sc.</Degree>
  </Student>
  <Student ID="2">
    <Name>David</Name>
    <Age>31</Age>
    <Degree>Ph.D. </Degree>
  </Student>
....
</University>
```

Structured data

ID	Name	Age	Degree
1	John	18	B.Sc.
2	David	31	Ph.D.
3	Robert	51	Ph.D.
4	Rick	26	M.Sc.
5	Michael	19	B.Sc.

Semi-Structured Data

Semi-structured data lie in between unstructured and structured data. *Semi-structured data are data that has some structure, but are not rigidly structured.* This type of data include unstructured components arranged according to some predetermined structure that can be queried using general-purpose mechanisms.

Semi-structured data is organized into entities. Similar entities are grouped together, but entities in the same group may not have the same attributes. The order of attributes is not necessarily important and not all attributes may be required. The size and type of same attributes in a group may differ. An example of semi-structured data is a curriculum vita (CV). One person may have a section of previous employment, another person may have a section on research experience, and another may have a section on teaching experience. We can also find a CV that contains two or more of these sections.

A very good example of a semi-structured formalism is XML which is a de facto standard for describing documents that is becoming the universal data exchange model on the Web and for B2B transactions. XML supports the development of semi-structured documents that contain both metadata and formatted text. Metadata is specified using XML tags and defines the structure of documents. Without metadata, applications would not be able to understand and parse the content of XML documents. Compared to HTML, XML provides explicit data structuring using Document Type Declaration (DTD) (XML, 2005) or XML Schema Definition (XSD) (World Wide Web Consortium, 2005b) as schema definitions. Figure 4 shows the semi-structure of an XML document containing students' records of a university.

Structured Data

In contrast, structured data *is very rigid* and uses strongly typed attributes. Data is organized in entities and similar entities are grouped together using relations or classes. Entities (records or tuples) in the same group have the same attributes. Structured data have been very popular since the early days of computing, and many organizations rely on relational databases to maintain very large structured repositories. Recent systems, such as customer relationship management (CRM), enterprise resource planning (ERP), and content management systems (CMS) use structured data for their underlying data model.

What Tourism Data Sources Need to be Integrated?

Data sources contain tourism information which is fundamental for dynamic packaging applications. A data source includes both the source of data itself and the connection information necessary for accessing the data. Data sources are uniquely identifiable collections of stored data called data sets for which there exists programmatic access and for which it is possible to retrieve or infer a description of the structure of the data, that is, its schema. We have identified various tourism data sources that need to be considered when integrating tourism information systems: flat files; HTML Web pages; XML and RDF data sources; and relational databases.

Flat Files

A tourism data source can be a flat file that is accessible via the file system application program interface (API). A flat file is a generic term for text file formats such as comma separated value (CSV), tab delimited, fixed width, and so forth. Flat file formats are supported by a wide collection of tourism information systems because they can be used as an interoperable format for exchanging information between different applications. In practice, flat files have proven to be very useful for allowing users to share information.

However, though they are supported by many applications, flat files generally require additional processing to be integrated seamlessly with common data formats. Since tourism information can often be stored in flat files, dynamic packaging applications need to include methods to integrate these data into a common data model. This requires the development of specific software application modules to access and extract the necessary data.

Hyper Text Markup Language

With the growth of the Web, many tourism information providers already have Web sites for storing and advertising the description of tourism services and products. Almost all Web sites support static HTML pages accessible through a Web server via the HTTP protocol. Dynamic packaging applications require integrating Web-based data sources in an automated way for querying, in a uniform way, across multiple heterogeneous Web sites, containing tourism-related information.

Extensible Markup Language

XML (XML, 2005) is a semi-structured data model that promises to accelerate the construction of systems that integrate distributed and heterogeneous data. XML provides a common format for data across the network and is being supported by a vast number of data management tools. Unlike HTML, which controls how data is represented, XML allow organizations to define data schemas that relate XML tags with data content.

The travel industry has been adopting XML as a common format for data exchanged across travel partners. For example, the Open Travel Alliance (OTA)[3] provides a vocabulary and grammar for communicating travel-related information as tags implemented using XML across all travel industry segments. XML is well suited in this context since schema for defining the XML tags can differ among industries, and even within organizations. Furthermore, the three major worldwide online travel agencies—Expedia, Travelocity, and Orbitz—have also adopted the XML standard to enable the exchange of supplier information using XML-based exchange formats.

Resource Description Framework

The RDF (World Wide Web Consortium, 2005a) provides a standard way of referring to metadata elements and metadata content. RDF builds standards for XML applications so that they can interoperate and intercommunicate more easily, facilitating data and system integration and interoperability. RDF is a simple general-purpose, metadata language for representing information on the Web and provides a model for describing and creating relationships between resources. A resource can be a thing, such as a person, a song, or a Web page. With RDF it is possible to add predefined modeling primitives for expressing semantics of data to a document without making any assumptions about the structure of the document. In a first approach, it may seem that RDF is very similar to XML, but a closer analysis reveals that they are conceptually different. If we model the information present in an RDF model using XML, human readers would probably be able to infer the underlying semantic structure, but general purpose applications would not.

While XML is being widely used across all travel industry segments, RDF is a recent data model and its adoption is just starting in areas such as digital libraries, Web services, and bioinformatics. Nevertheless, as the number of organizations adhering to this standard starts growing, it is expected that the travel industry will also adopt it.

Databases

In modern tourism organizations, it is almost unavoidable to use databases to produce, store, and search for critical data. Yet, it is only by combining the information from various database systems that dynamic packaging applications can take a competitive advantage from the value of data. Different travel industry segments use distinct data sources. This diversity is caused by many factors including lack of coordination among organization units; different rates of adopting new technology; mergers and acquisitions; and geographic separation of collaborating groups.

To develop dynamic packaging applications, the most common form of data integration is achieved using special-purpose applications that access data sources of interest directly and combine the data retrieved with the application itself. While this approach always works, it is expensive in terms of both time and skills, fragile due to the changes to the underlying sources, and hard to extend since new data sources require new fragments of code to be written. In our architecture, the use of semantics and ontologies to construct a global view will make the integration process automatic, and there will be no requirement for a human integrator.

Tourism Data Source Integration

The technologies and infrastructures supporting the travel industry are complex and heterogeneous. The vision of a comprehensive solution to interconnect many applications and data sources based entirely on standards, such as the one provided by OTA (2004), that are universally supported on every computing platform, is not achieved in practice and far from reality.

Data integration is a challenge for dynamic packaging applications since they need to query across multiple heterogeneous, autonomous, and distributed (HAD) tourism data sources produced independently by multiple organizations in the travel industry. Integrating HAD data sources involves combining the concepts and knowledge in the individual tourism data sources into an integrated view of the data. The construction of an integrated view is complicated because organizations store different types of data, in varying formats, with different meanings, and reference them using different names (Lawrence & Barker, 2001).

To allow the seamless integration of HAD tourism data sources rely on the use of semantics. Semantic integration requires knowledge of the meaning of data within the tourism data sources, including integrity rules and the relationships across sources. Semantic technologies are designed to extend the capabilities of data sources allowing to unbind the representation of data and the data itself and to give context to data. The integration of tourism data sources requires thinking not of the data itself but rather the structure of those data: schemas, data types, relational database constructs, file formats, and so forth. Figure 5 illustrates the component in layer 3 of our architecture which carries out the mappings between different data models.

This layer can be seen as a middleware level that implements the interfaces to the data sources to be integrated. These interfaces must overcome the heterogeneities of communication protocols as well as the heterogeneities regarding programming languages. Since the results are typically returned in different formats, the interfaces should translate them into the reference data model which is used inside the middleware.

The *syntactic* data present in the tourism data source, such as databases, flat files, HTML and XML files, are extracted and transformed using extractors and wrappers. An important aspect of tourism data sources is that there is no single generic method to retrieve data source data. Additionally, the schema of the tourism data sources may or may not be available. In some data sources, such as XML documents, the data sets may be self-described and schema information may be embedded inside the

Figure 5. Mapping between different data models

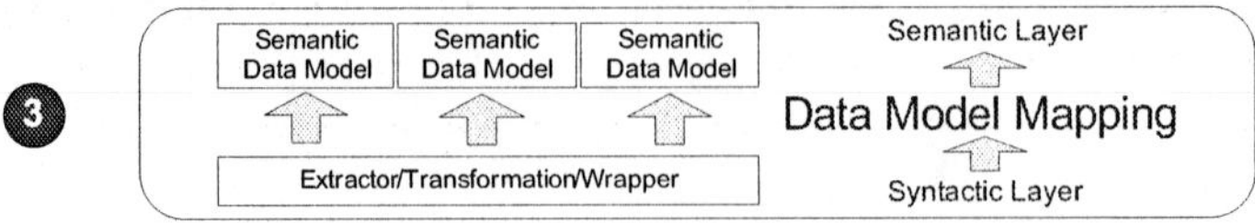

data sets. In other cases, such as with databases, the system may store and provide the schema as part of the data source itself but separately for the actual data. Finally, some sources may not provide any schema. This is the case of HTML Web pages. For this situation, methods need to be developed to analyze the data and extract its underlying structure.

Once the data has been extracted and transformed, we use metadata to link the data with tourism ontologies. Tourism ontologies are the backbone of semantic dynamic packaging applications and explicitly define a set of shared tourism concepts and their interconnections. They make explicit all concepts in a taxonomical structure, their attributes, and relations. Wrappers, information extraction, and text analysis combine information with ontologies and thereby create metadata. These tasks can be done automatically.

Putting a *semantic layer* on a syntactical architecture creates an environment where integration issues can be upgraded to an abstract level where graphical modeling allows a higher degree of flexibility when developing and maintaining semantic integration.

Data Integration using a Global Data Model

One simple approach to data integration is to implement each interface to data sources as part of individual development projects by hand coding the necessary data conversions. This approach is time consuming and error prone. It is necessary to implement N*(N–1) different translation interfaces to integrate N data sources. For dynamic packaging applications—where more than 100 tourism data sources may need to be integrated—this approach is not feasible.

A more advanced approach uses hubs or brokers to achieve data and process integration. With this approach it is necessary to have two translation interfaces per data source, one interface in and one out of the hub or broker. The number of required interfaces between systems is 2*N. The data is not translated directly from a source system to a destination system, but it is translated using a global data model present in the hubs or brokers.

Another solution is to map all data sources onto an expressive global data model and automatically deploy all the translation interfaces from these mappings. This approach requires N mappings and the use of ontologies to develop expressive global data models. In our architecture for dynamic packaging applications, we use this last approach.

Data Extraction and Transformation

To achieve tourism data source integration, extractors and wrappers can be used to extract the data that will be reconsolidated later. The extractors attempt to identify simple patterns in data sources and then export this information to be mapped through a wrapper. Since dynamic packaging applications use information stored in various HAD data sources, an extractor has to be implemented for each kind of data source to import. Therefore, a database extractor, an HTML extractor, an XML extractor, and an RDF extractor have to be implemented.

As an example, let us describe the structure of an HTML extractor. Dynamic packaging applications should be able to extract relevant information from an unstructured set of HTML Web pages describing tourism products and services. The role of the *HTML extractor* is to convert the information implicitly stored as an HTML document, which consists of plain text with some tags, into information explicitly stored as part of a data structure. This information is processed in order to provide meaning to it, so that dynamic packaging applications can "understand" the texts, extract, and infer knowledge from it. As will be shown later, this process of providing meaning to the unstructured texts is achieved using e-tourism ontologies. In the case of the Web, the extractor has to deal with the retrieving of data, via the HTTP protocol (through a GET or a POST method). An extractor is split into two separate layers:

1. retrieval layer
2. extraction layer

The retrieval layer deals with accessing the source through a GET or a POST method. This layer is in charge of building the correct URL to access a given resource and to pass the correct parameters. It should also handle redirections, failures, and authorizations.

The extraction layer is specific to the resource and deals with the actual extraction, taking advantage of the HTML grammar as well as regular expression patterns. Each extraction layer consists of a set of extraction rules and the code required to apply those rules. The extraction language should be expressive enough to capture the structure expressed by the resource or document. At this level the extracted information should be regarded as a string.

To program our extractors we have selected Compaq's Web language (formerly known as WebL) (Compaq Web Language, 2005). WebL is an imperative, interpreted scripting language for automating tasks on the Web that has built-in support for common Web protocols like HTTP and FTP, and popular formats such as HTML and XML.

A critical problem in developing dynamic packaging applications involves accessing information formatted for human use and transforming it into a structured data format (Werthner & Ricci, 2004). *Wrappers* are one of the most commonly used solutions to access information from data sources being in charge of transforming the extracted information into the target structure that has been specified according to the user's needs. Wrappers have to implement interfaces to data source and should take advantage of generic conversion tools that can directly map extracted strings into say dates, zip codes, or phone numbers. These interfaces must overcome the heterogeneities of communication protocols as well as the heterogeneities regarding programming languages.

Data Model Mapping

There are many factors that make data integration for dynamic packaging applications a difficult problem. However, the most notable challenge is the reconciliation of the semantic heterogeneity of the tourism data sources being integrated. For dynamic packaging applications one of the best solutions toward reconciling semantic heterogeneity is the use of languages for describing semantic *mappings*, expressions that relate the semantics of data expressed in different structures (Lenzerini, 2002). Figure 6 illustrates the mappings established between XML data sources and the semantic data model used by our dynamic packaging application. Our common data model is defined using an e-tourism ontology specified using the Web Ontology Language (OWL) (World Wide Web Consortium, 2004).

OWL offers a common open standard format capable of representing both structured data, semi-structured, and unstructured data. Thus, OWL can be used as a common interchange format. We will discuss the details of this approach in the "Ontology Language Selection" section. For each tourism data source type, that is, flat files, relational models, XML, HTML, or RDF, mappings need to be defined to reference concepts present in our e-tourism ontology.

Data Consolidation

Data consolidation focuses on the orchestration of interactions between multiple local data models, as illustrated in Figure 7. Local data models (layer 3) are combined to create a global data model (layer 5) using the data consolidation layer (layer 4).

Figure 6. Mapping between different data models

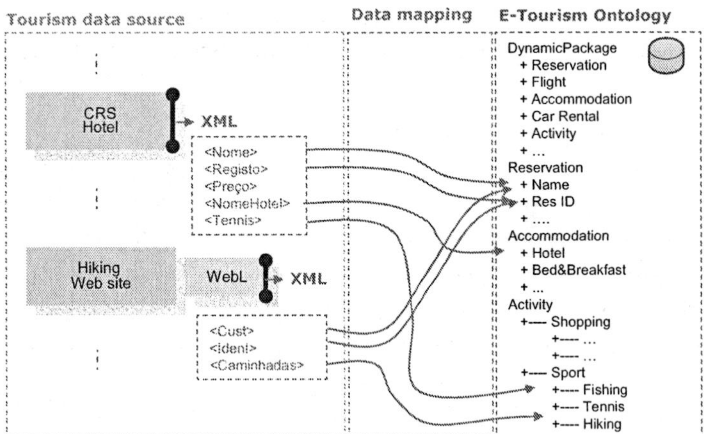

As explained previously, to facilitate the integration of data source and construct local and global data models, we have adopted OWL as the standard format for information exchange.

One of the key principles of our approach is the separation of the process being implemented from the data being manipulated. We consolidate the semantic data models using processes to subsequently create a shared global data model. To achieve this incorporation, we define processes using workflow management systems and technology. We use two main software components to consolidate data: process designer and workflow engine. The process designer permits graphically designing processes that will consolidate the semantic data models. This tool permits defining business rules representing the integration logic. The workflow engine is a state machine that executes the workflow activities that are part of a process. It supports the execution of decision nodes; subprocesses; exception handling; forks and joins; and loops.

The processes describing the activities that are necessary to construct our shared global data model, based on the semantic data models, are formally specified using the business process execution language for Web services (BPEL4WS) (BPEL4WS, 2003) and semantic data models are interfaced with Web services (Chinnici, Gudgin, Moreau, & Weerawarana, 2003). BPEL4WS provides a language for the formal specification of (business) processes by defining an integration model that facilitates the development of automated process integration in both intra-organization and B2B settings.

At runtime, as the processes are executed, their Web services are invoked. Web services present an efficient solution to reduce integration efforts and to quicken the

Figure 7. Integration with business processes

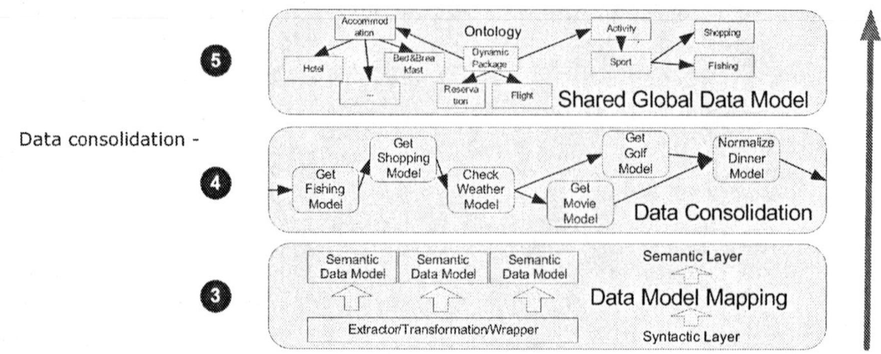

creation of interfaces that allow for communication with semantic data models. In dynamic packaging applications, Web service-based solutions have the following advantages:

- loosely coupled integration of tourism information systems leading to reduced development costs and more flexibility, and
- reduced dynamic packaging applications' complexity due to the use of standardized interfaces.

Web services are easier to design, implement, and deploy than any other traditional distributed technology, such as RPC and CORBA. At the foundation of Web services architecture are software standards and communication protocols such as XML; Simple Object Access Protocol (SOAP) (World Wide Web Consortium, 2002); Hyper Text Transfer Protocol (HTTP); Universal Description, Discovery, and Integration (UDDI) (UDDI, 2002); and Web Services Description Language (WSDL) (Christensen, Curbera, Meredith, & Weerawarana, 2001), which allow information to be accessed and exchanged easily among different programs. These technologies allow applications to communicate with each other regardless of the programming languages they were written in or the platform they were developed for. Web services are not used to build monolithic systems; they are a set of technologies with the objective of putting together existing applications to create newly distributed systems.

Shared Global Data Model

In order to develop efficient dynamic packaging applications, we believe that it is not required to adopt a common hardware platform or common database vendor. What is needed is a *shared global data model across participating tourism information systems.* Requiring the organizations of the tourism industry to have a common hardware platform or database is not realistic. Figure 8 shows the various approaches to data integration.

The use of a shared global data model is a cornerstone of the design of many applications that require data integration. It brings integration costs and efforts down to a minimum. With a shared global data model a dynamic packaging application can merge all the information made available by CRS, GDS, HDS, DMS, and travel agents' Web sites, thus allowing cross-departmental and cross-organizational integration. Our shared global data model is represented with an ontology providing a common understanding of tourism data and information (Figure 9).

In the following sections we discuss the semantic model and semantic language selected to represent our shared global data model, the problems that semantic data sources face when integrated, and the steps involved in the development of our e-tourism ontology.

Figure 8. Tight and loose coupling approaches to data integration (Robbins, 1996)

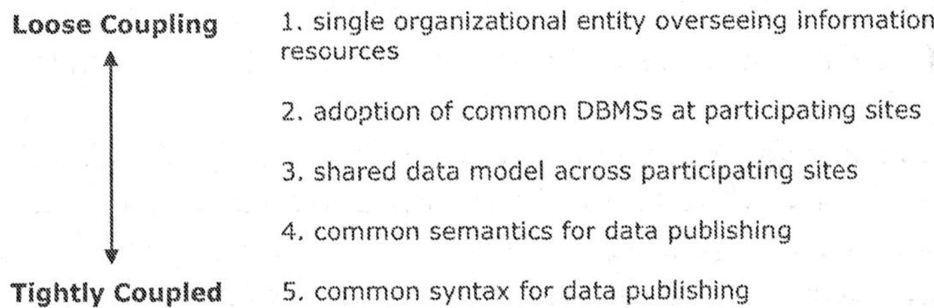

Loose Coupling
Tightly Coupled
1. single organizational entity overseeing information resources
2. adoption of common DBMSs at participating sites
3. shared data model across participating sites
4. common semantics for data publishing
5. common syntax for data publishing

Figure 9. Shared global data model defined using the e-tourism ontology

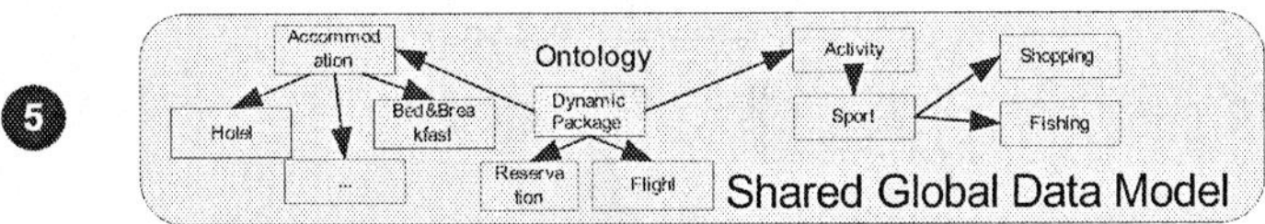

Shared Common Vocabulary

A shared global data model is not useful for data integration unless the sources being integrated share common vocabulary elements representing some shared conceptual model. Depending on the approach, different data models can be used to add semantics to terms—such as controlled vocabularies, *taxonomies,* thesaurus, and ontologies—and different degrees of semantics can be achieved.

Controlled vocabularies are at the weaker end of the semantic spectrum. A controlled vocabulary is a list of terms that have been enumerated explicitly with an unambiguous and non-redundant definition. A *taxonomy* is a subject-based classification that arranges the terms of a controlled vocabulary into a hierarchy without doing anything further. A thesaurus is a networked collection of controlled vocabulary terms with conceptual relationships between terms. It is an extension of a taxonomy by allowing terms to be arranged in a hierarchy and also allowing other statements and relationships to be established between terms, such as equivalence, homographic, hierarchical, and associative (National Information and Standards Organization, 2005).

Ontologies are similar to taxonomies but use richer semantic relationships among terms and attributes, as well as strict rules about how to specify terms and relationships. Compared to the other approaches, ontologies provide a higher degree of expressiveness. Furthermore, expressive standards have already been developed (for example, OWL [World Wide Web Consortium, 2004]) to construct ontologies and are being used in practical applications. For these reasons, we have selected ontologies for our dynamic packaging architecture to explicitly connect data from tourism information systems and to allow machine-processable interpretation of data.

Semantic Integration

To provide a dynamic packaging application for integrating disparate heterogeneous data sources, a common modeling language is needed to describe data, information, and knowledge. Since computers have no built-in mechanism for associating semantics to words and symbols, an ontology is required to allow dynamic packaging applications to determine semantically equivalent expressions and concepts residing in HAD tourism data sources. Agreeing on the terminology and sharing the same ontology for each tourism domain is a pre-condition for data sharing and integration (Wiederhold, 1994).

After studying several online travel, leisure, and transportation sites, we concluded that there is a lack of agreement on conventions in the tourism industry. The following are some of the differences found among several data sources:

- Web sites written in English use syntactically different words than Web sites written in Portuguese, but with the same semantics. For example, tennis/tenis, walking/caminhadas, and time/hora.
- The price of tourism products and services are expressed in many different currencies (euros, dollars, British pounds, etc.)
- The time specifications do not follow a standard format. Some Web sites state time in hours, others in minutes, others in hours and minutes, and so forth.
- The way of expressing time also varies. For example, 1 hour and 30 minutes, 1h and 30 min, 1:30 h, 90 min, one hour and thirty minutes, ninety minutes, 1:30 pm, and so forth.
- The keywords used to specify a date are not expressed in a normalized way. Some Web sites express a day of the week using the words Monday, Tuesday,..., Sunday, while other use the abbreviations M, T, ..., Su.
- The temperature unit scale is not standard. It can be expressed either in degrees centigrade or in degrees Celsius.
- Numerical values are not expressed in a normalized way. They can be expressed with numbers: 1, 2, and 3 or with words such as one, two, and three.

One big challenge for dynamic packaging applications is to find a solution to cope with the nonstandardized way of describing tourism products and services. There are no conventions or common criteria to express transportation vehicles, leisure activities, and weather conditions when planning for a vacation; several ways were found among all the tourism data sources consulted. Our objective is to find a solution to surpass this lack of standardization by automatically understanding the different ways of expressing tourism products and services. We argue that semantics and ontologies are good candidates for dynamic packaging information systems since they allow us to associate metadata to data sources making the data machine understandable and processable.

E-Tourism Ontologies

Ontologies are the key elements enabling the shift from a purely syntactic to a semantic integration and interoperability. An ontology can be defined as the explicit and formal descriptions of concepts and their relationships that exist in a certain universe of discourse. When a particular user group commits to an ontology, it has been proven to be a solution for data integration because it offers a shared, organized, and common understanding of data which allows for a better integration, communication, and interoperability of inter- and intra-organizational tourism information systems.

Ontologies describe the things that exist in a domain. This includes properties, concepts and rules, and how they relate to each other. For dynamic packaging applications, an ontology with the appropriate tourism concepts needs to be built for identifying destinations, activities, weather forecasts, places, dates, and relationships. We identify the need for two distinct types of ontologies: local ontologies and shared global ontologies. Local ontologies define the semantics of specific tourism data source domains, such as hotels, car rentals, and airlines. In addition, we also consider the notion of shared global ontologies, which are common semantics shared between all the tourism domains and tourism information systems, that is, these ontologies model the information that resides in many separate domains.

Our initial tasks were to select a semantic language to model our ontologies (local and shared global ontologies), select an ontology editor to construct, browse, and manage the ontologies under development, and adopt a methodology to develop the ontologies. These tasks are described in the following sections.

Ontology Language Selection

Several languages have been developed to support the Semantic Web. These structured languages can carry meaning besides giving structure to data. Some languages are more directed to providing meaning to data, while others go further and can make assertions and infer knowledge.

In this area, the major developments are being made by an international Semantic Web research activity, spearheaded by the World Wide Web Consortium (W3C) (www.w3.org) and the Defense Advanced Projects Research Agency (DARPA) Agent Markup Language (DAML, 2005) program. The newest languages are developed based on the progress from previous ones, evolving and improving their characteristics. The most relevant semantic languages that need to be considered for developing ontologies for e-tourism are the following:

- **RDF.** RDF (W3C, 2005) and RDF schema (RDFS) became a W3C recommendation in 1999. It is a general framework to describe the contents of Internet resources. RDFs can be used directly to describe an ontology by making objects, classes, and properties available to programmers.
- **DAML+OIL.** The DARPA agent markup language + ontology inference layer (DAML+OIL) (DAML, 2005) is an extension of XML and RDF. DAML+OIL aims at complete support for defining ontologies. It provides rich constructors for forming complex class expressions and axioms for enabling reasoning and inference on ontology data.

- **OWL.** OWL (W3C, 2004) is a semantic markup language for publishing and sharing ontologies on the Web. It is the newest Semantic Web standard and became a W3C recommendation in February 2004.

From the different Semantic Web languages available (e.g., RDF, RDFS, DAML+OIL, and OWL) we have selected OWL to develop our e-tourism ontologies. This decision was based on two reasons. Firstly, OWL is a standard developed as a vocabulary extension of RDF, RDFS, and is derived from DAML+OIL. The standardization of OWL by the W3C allows semantics to move out of the research and development community and into broad-based, commercial-grade platforms for building highly distributed and cross-enterprise applications. Secondly, OWL provides a sound theory of meaning from which to build highly expressive data models. It expresses and includes a large set of primitives that are indispensable to building expressive ontologies. Primitives include cardinality constraints, class expressions, data types, enumerations, equivalence, and inheritance. OWL language is particularly well suited to formalize ontologies for the tourism industry by defining classes and properties of those classes and defining individuals and asserting properties about them. Furthermore, it is possible to conduct advanced knowledge inference, compared to other approaches.

Editor Selection

Ontology editors are tools that enable viewing, browsing, codifying, and modifying ontologies. Choosing the right editor for our project can become a daunting task since many choices exist and an appropriate tool selection depends on the level of user experience, the languages supported, the architecture, and the scalability.

Examples of popular editors include OilEd, OntoEdit (n.d.), WebODE, and Protégé (n.d.). OntoEdit is an ontology engineering environment supporting the development and maintenance of ontologies using graphical means. The editor supports representations of F-Logic, RDF Schema, and OIL. OilEd (Bechhofer, Horrocks, Goble, & Stevens, 2001) is an ontology editor allowing the user to build ontologies using DAML+OIL. Unfortunately, the current version of OilEd does not provide a full ontology development environment. It does not support the development of large-scale ontologies, versioning, argumentation, and many other activities that are involved in ontology construction. WebODE (Arpírez, Corcho, Fernández-López, & Gómez-Pérez, 2003) is a scalable workbench for ontological engineering that provides services for editing, browsing, importing, and exporting ontologies to classical and Semantic Web languages. Protégé (n.d.) is an extensible, platform-independent environment for creating and editing ontologies and knowledge bases. It is a tool which allows users to construct domain ontologies, having various storage formats such as OWL, RDF, and XML.

After conducting an analysis of ontology editors, we have selected Protégé (n.d.) to construct our ontologies for the tourism industry for four main reasons: (1) it includes implementations for the major computing platforms (such as Mac OS X, AIS, Solaris, Linux, and Windows), (2) it allows the construction of ontologies using OWL, (3) it is supported by a strong community of developers, such as academic, government, and biomedicine, and (4) it is a free and open source tool.

Ontology Development Methodology

Tourism is a data rich domain. This data is stored in many hundreds of data sources and many of these sources need to be used in concert during the development of the dynamic package and its applications. Our e-tourism ontologies provide a way of viewing the world of tourism. They organize tourism-related information and concepts. It will become clear later how the ontologies will allow us to achieve integration and interoperability through the use of a shared vocabulary and meanings for terms with respect to other terms. It should be noted that this is a work in progress; our tourism ontologies are not complete yet. We are still gathering new concepts for the taxonomies and developing new axioms.

Our ontologies were built to answer three main questions (Figure 10) that can be asked when developing dynamic packages for a tourist: what, where, and when.

- **What.** What can a tourist see, visit, and what can he do while staying at a tourism destination?
- **Where.** Where are the interesting places to see and visit located?
- **When.** When can the tourist visit a particular place? This includes not only the day of the week and the hours of the day, but also the atmospheric conditions of the weather. For example, some activities cannot be undertaken if it is raining.

Figure 10. What, where, and when

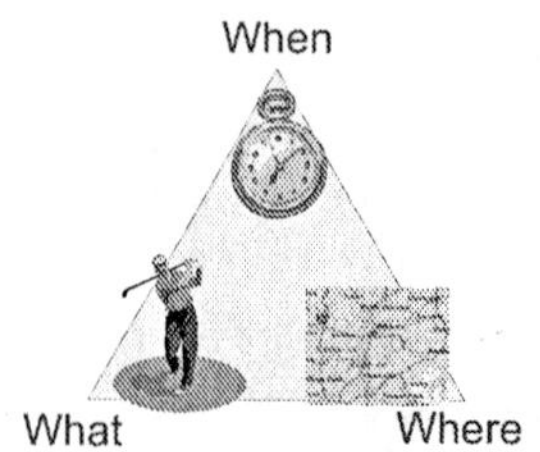

There are several ways of building ontologies (Fernández López, 1999; Jones, Bench-Capon, & Visser, 1998; Uschold & Gruninger, 1996). Our approach has involved the following steps:

- We have devised a unique and explicit definition for concepts from the tourism domain. Examples of concepts include *nightlife, sightseeing, relaxation,* and *shopping.* These definitions were precise enough to discriminate the various concepts in the ontologies.
- A root node concept has then been selected to embrace the variety of tourism domain-relevant concepts.
- Concepts were arranged and structured using classes and subclasses. The resulting ontology was transformed into a hierarchical tree. For example, *nightlife, sightseeing, relaxation,* and *shopping* are subclasses of the concept *activity.*
- Information concerning the disjointedness of classes was made explicit. Relations, such as inverse and transitivity, were also identified. For example, the *sightseeing* concept is disjoint from the *shopping* concept.
- Background knowledge for each concept was added to express domain-relevant properties. For example, a tourism organization has a telephone number, a fax number, an address, and an e-mail.

Ontology Creation

In an early stage of our project, the ontologies were implemented using Protégé (n.d.) editor. This was a very time-consuming task since it was necessary to find out information about real tourism activities and infrastructures on the Web and feed them into the knowledge base.

The main components of the tourism ontologies are concepts, relations, instances, and axioms. A concept represents a set or class of entities within the tourism domain. Activity, Organization, Weather, and Time are examples of concepts used. These concepts were represented in OWL in the following way:

```
...
<owl:Class rdf:ID="Activity"/>
<owl:Class rdf:ID="Organization"/>
<owl:Class rdf:ID="Weather"/>
<owl:Class rdf:ID="Time"/>
<owl:Class rdf:ID="Directions"/>
<owl:Class rdf:ID="Transportation"/>
...
```

The class **Activity** (which answers to the question "What") refers to sports, such as skiing, sightseeing or any other activity, such as shopping or visiting a theatre. The class **Organization** (which answers to the question "Where") refers to the places where the tourist can carry out an activity. Examples of infrastructure that provide the means for exerting an activity include restaurants, cinemas, or museums. The classes **Time** and **Weather** (which answers to the question "When") refers to the time and weather conditions which allow a tourist to carry out an activity at a certain place. The ontologies also include relations which describe the interactions between concepts or the concept's properties. For example, the concepts Fishing and Hiking are subconcepts of the concept Sport.

```
...
<owl:Class rdf:ID="Fishing">
   <rdfs:subClassOf>
     <owl:Class rdf:about="#Sport"/>
   </rdfs:subClassOf>
  </owl:Class>
  <owl:Class rdf:ID="Hiking">
   <rdfs:subClassOf>
     <owl:Class rdf:about="#Sport"/>
   </rdfs:subClassOf>
</owl:Class>
...
```

The ontologies also include associative relationships. Relationships relate concepts across a taxonomy of concepts. For example, the relationship hasActivity related the class **Organization** with the class **Activity**. This means that an organization in the tourism industry may supply a kind of activity to its customer, such as Hiking and Surfing.

```
...
  <owl:ObjectProperty rdf:ID="hasActivity">
   <rdfs:range rdf:resource="#Activity"/>
   <rdfs:domain rdf:resource="#Organization"/>
</owl:ObjectProperty>
...
```

While classes describe concepts in the domain, specific elements of a class are instances. For example, a class of **WeatherConditon** represents all the weather conditions that can be verified. Specific weather conditions are instances of this class, such as Cloudy, Showers, and Scattered Showers. However, deciding whether something is a concept of an instance is difficult and often depends on the application (Brachman, McGuinness, Patel-Schneider, Resnick, & Borgida, 1991).

Finally, axioms are used to constrain the values for classes and instances. Axioms are used to associate classes and properties with either partial or complete specifications of their characteristics and to give other logical information about classes and properties (W3C, 2004). For example:

```
...
 <owl:Class rdf:about="#Surfing">
  <rdfs:subClassOf rdf:resource="#Sport"/>
  <owl:disjointWith rdf:resource="#Hiking"/>
</owl:Class>
...
```

This example expresses that instances belonging to one subclass, for example, Surfing, cannot belong to another subclass, for example, Hiking. A partial view of one of the e-tourism ontologies developed using Protégé (n.d.) is illustrated in Figure 11.

Creating Dynamic Packages

Dynamic packages are automatically created by the dynamic packaging engine. Our architecture includes not only the dynamic packaging engine, but also the rule editor, rule repository, and the rule engine (Figure 12).

The configuration of the dynamic packaging engine involves the following activities. During the rule development phase, the rule designer defines packaging rules using the rule editor application. The rule editor, a component that provides an interface to the rule repository, supports the creation and modification of packaging rules through a graphical user interface. Packaging rules are codified and stored in an integrated repository, providing a central point for definition and change, which can later drive dynamic package construction.

Packaging rules are logic statements that describe the policies and procedures to create dynamic packages for travel consumers. When traditional rule programming approaches are used, packaging rules are hard coded into the applications themselves, making rules difficult to develop and expensive to modify. By contrast, using a rule repository, packaging rules are stored externally and are separated from the dynamic packaging application, making the creation and modification of rules easier.

Figure 11. Using Protégé to develop e-tourism ontologies

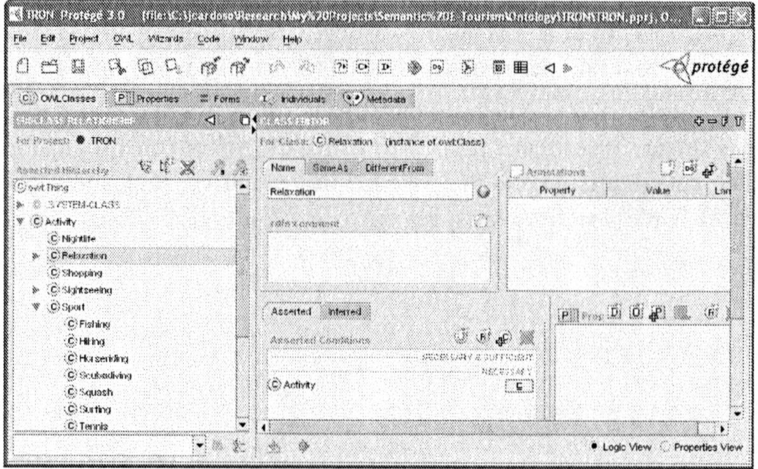

Figure 12. Dynamic packaging engine architecture

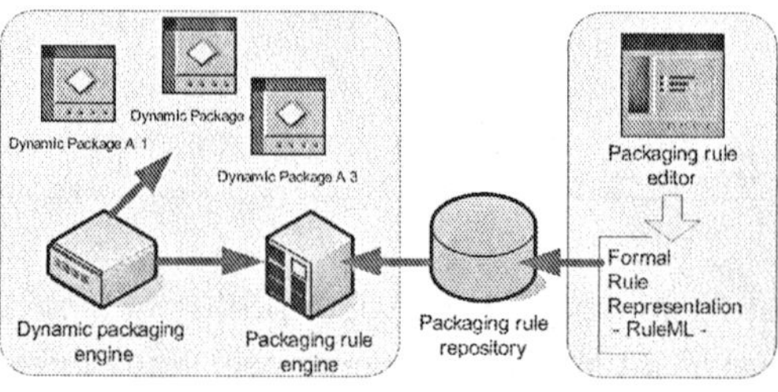

The packaging rules engine and repository architecture provide a structure for separating dynamic packaging logic from dynamic packaging applications. This separation is one of the main advantages of using a rule engine to implement packaging rules since it allows changes to be made to the created packages to reflect new business policies. Packaging rules can be used to define new travel products and services, offer new promotions, or define high and low travel seasons.

Packaging Rules

A packaging rule is a statement that influences which tourism products will be part of a dynamic package. Dynamic packages are constructed in real time based on a set of constraints that are specified using packaging rules. For example, a travel agency may define that a dynamic package, which includes a trip and 5-day stay in New York, should cost less $3,000. In this example, three packaging rules define dynamic packages to create: Rule1 (duration, 5 days), Rule2 (local, New York), and Rule3 (less than, $3,000).

Since these rules are business oriented, they are defined and managed by business people. This makes the packaging rule approach attractive to dynamic packaging applications since users become an integral part of any package construction. The use and management of explicit packaging rules has several benefits for dynamic packaging applications:

- shorter time needed for changing packaging rules and making this change effective in dynamic package construction decreases;
- increased profit on travel products by a faster reaction to changing market demands and taking into account current market conditions; and
- improved customer satisfaction due to a better customization of travel products and services according to customer preferences.

In the travel industry, most organizations do not formally identify or store rules. Instead, although travel managers and travel agents use rules periodically, they exist only in the software code that runs packaging applications. Rules are "lost" in application code. As a result, the people that are directly in contact with the rules that dictate what sort of travel packages should be created, at a given time of year under specific market conditions, are not travel managers or travel agents but rather the information systems (IS) staff who convert packaging requirements into lines of code. Moreover, when rules are embedded in application code it becomes difficult to locate and change business logic and each alteration requires recompiling application code. Separating packaging rules from application code allows packaging policies to be easily communicated and understood by all employees, and rules can be managed in isolation from application code.

Formal Specification of Packaging Rules

Packaging rules can be expressed using formal languages. Examples of languages include UML[4], the ILOG rules language,[5] the Business Rules Markup Language (BRML[6]), and RuleML[7]. RuleML is an XML markup language for rules based on declarative logic and allows rules to be expressed as modular components using standard XML tags. Facilities are offered to specify different types of rules such as derivation, transformation, and reaction rules. One very attractive capability is the ability to specify queries and inferences on ontologies and mappings between ontologies. This last feature was the main reason why we have selected RuleML to model packaging rules. Since our shared global data model is expressed using an ontology, it makes sense to use a rule modeling language that can express packaging rules using the concepts present in our e-tourism ontologies. For example, the sentence, "renting an AVIS car, class **B**, costs thirty euros per day," is a packaging rule which is modeled using RuleML in the following way,

```
<Atom>
  <Rel>renting</Rel>
  <Ind>AVIS</Ind>
  <Ind>car</Ind>
  <Ind>class B</Ind>
  <Ind>per day</Ind>
  <Ind>30 euros</Ind>
</Atom>
```

A more complex example would be to model the sentence, "a customer is premium if he has spent a minimum of 5,000 euros on a travel package."

```
<Implies>
  <head>
    <Atom>
      <Rel>premium</Rel>
      <Var>customer</Var>
    </Atom>
  </head>
  <body>
    <Atom>
      <Rel>spending</Rel>
      <Var>customer</Var>
      <Ind>minimum of 5000 euro</Ind>
    </Atom>
  </body>
</Implies>
```

Packaging rules expressed in RuleML and semantics go hand in hand since they are independent of the inference engine used to implement an application. This allows exchange of rules between different engines. Before executing packaging rules, the rules are translated to an inference engine language, such as Java Expert System Shell (Jess)[8], LISP, or Prolog.

Types of Packaging Rules

We can identify several categories of rules for packaging applications. Namely, fact rules, computation rules, inferred knowledge rules, action enabling rules, and constraint rules (Von Halle, 2001). The following examples describe the several categories of rules used in dynamic package applications.

Fact rules. A simple fact rule is "renting an AVIS car, class **B**, costs thirty euros per day." This example of a rule has already been given previously with the illustration of the corresponding modeling in RuleML.

Computation rules. Calculate the price of a dynamic package for a customer by subtracting any discounts (hotel, car, and flight discounts) from the base fee:

PackagePrice =
BasePrice – HotelDiscount – CarDiscount – FlightDiscount

Inferred knowledge rules. The following rules state than if a customer buys a travel package which costs more than 5,000 euros, then he/she will have a discount of 15% on the price of the package minus 3,000 euros.

If PackagePrice > 5000
THEN Discount = 0.15*(PackagePrice–3000)
ELSE Discount = 0.

Action enabling rules. These rules, also called triggers, force dynamic packaging applications to take some predefined actions on the occurrence of an event. For example, a customer should be notified if his/her credit card is rejected.

IF rejection of credit card payment
THEN notify customer

Constraint rules. An example of this type of rule designates that the final price of a dynamic package should always be inferior to the sum of its individual products.

(PackagePrice – Discount) <= sum(Individual travel products)

Dynamic Packaging Engine

The dynamic packaging engine is responsible for reading the rules specifications and generating valid packages, that is, travel packages that comply with the packaging rules. The engine relies on linear programming (LP) to generate packages dynamically. LP is a subset of mathematical programming that allows packaging rules to be represented as linear equations. The LP module makes constrained decisions to maximize (or minimize) a linear objective function associated with package requirements. An example of the decisions the LP module could make is how many days a traveler can spend in a five star hotel in Lisbon, Portugal, near the ocean, with a rented car, for 1,500 euros.

Once packaging rules are represented using linear equations, as either the objective or constraint, an LP can be used to solve very large problems generating an optimum dynamic package. This means that given an objective function used in the LP, one can be certain that the best possible dynamic package will be constructed. The speed and quality of the dynamic package configurations produced by the LP module allows planners to explore different scenarios with different packaging prices, number of days a customer wishes to stay at a location, or levels of comfort provided by a hotel.

Future Trends

Travel agents are faced with changes in the tourism industry that have led to reduced commission revenues. For example, in 1997, the major United States airlines reduced the commission rate payable to traditional travel agencies and online travel agencies from 10% to 8%, and from 8% to 5%, respectively. In addition, as of 1998, many airlines have implemented a zero commission (Joystar, 2005). Additionally, vacation providers are expected to follow the airlines and eventually apply zero commissions (Forrester, 2005). As a result, travel agents have to look for new ways to increase their profit margins. One way is to acquire tools to offer their own services to dynamically package their client's holiday requirements. This added value will allow travel agents to earn their margins through a combination of reduced commission and booking fees. Therefore, dynamic packaging is critical to today's travel industry; airlines, hotels, tour operators, and travel agencies need to create custom packages for consumers. The development and implementation of modern dynamic packaging application is therefore a major concern for the travel industry.

The Semantic Web promises to provide applications for Internet users through the use of metadata (e.g., RDF and OWL) attached to various information resources on the Web. In the future, these new technologies associated with the Semantic Web will be the foundation of "killer apps" providing a higher level of service to overcome the serious limitations of current Web technology in finding, integrating, understanding, interpreting, and processing information. This Semantic Web is based on machine processable semantics of data, enabling information processing via a computer improving the mechanization for many information processing tasks. Ontologies are necessary to link formal semantics with real world semantics and applications are needed to demonstrate how the Semantic Web can become a reality. Due to the requirements of dynamic packaging applications (e.g., interoperability, integration, knowledge inferring, and rule management), this type of application represents a good subject to develop a new breed of systems based on the Semantic Web.

Conclusion

With the growth of the demand for customized tourism itineraries, (online) agencies seek technology that provides their personnel and clients with the flexibility to put together unique dynamic packages from a range of alternatives, without having to be aware of the intricacy of contract rules and pricing issues. The concept of dynamic packaging is to bundle all the components selected by a traveler to produce one reservation. Despite where the inventory originates, the package that is created is treated as one operation and entails only one payment from the customer.

Even though the idea of dynamic packing has to some extent already been implemented by major online travel agencies (for example, Expedia, Travelocity, and Orbitz), we believe that current dynamic packing applications need to be enhanced with emerging technologies to facilitate the interoperability and integration of tourism data sources to speed up the time to market response. Previous studies have shown that the strategic potential of dynamic packaging technologies is currently limited due to interoperability and integration problems of existing travel information systems. In this chapter, we have described a systematic approach to deal with the lack of travel standards and to enable the data integration of travel data sources using the latest development on the Semantic Web: semantics and ontologies. We conclude that for the travel industry the Semantic Web can considerably improve dynamic packing applications.

Another limitation of current dynamic packing applications is the lack of solution to adequately manage the rules that govern the dynamic creation of travel packages. Traditional approaches hard code rules into dynamic packing applications. This solution does not permit the separation of packaging rules from application code. As a result, rules cannot be easily changed, managed, shared, or reused to reflect new business policies since they are hidden in the code. With the use of packaging rules, business users (i.e., nonprogrammers) can add and modify rules in an implementation-independent, business rule language. The use of packaging rules defined using semantic standards, such a RuleML, allows rules to be executed by different rule engines and therefore shared across the travel industry.

References

Arpírez, J. C., Corcho, O., Fernández-López, M., & Gómez-Pérez, A. (2003). WebODE in a nutshell. *AI Magazine, 24,* 37-47.

Barnett, M., & Standing, C. (2001). Repositioning travel agencies on the Internet. *Journal of Vacation Marketing, 7*(2), 143-152.

Bass, L., Clements, P., & Kazman, R. (1998). *Software architecture in practice.* Addison Wesley.

Bechhofer, S., Horrocks, I., Goble, C., & Stevens, R. (2001). *OilEd: A reason-able ontology editor for the Semantic Web.* Paper presented at the Joint German/Austrian conference on Artificial Intelligence (KI2001), Vienna.

Business Process Execution Language for Web Services (BPEL4WS). (2003). *Specification: Business process execution language for Web services version 1.1.* IBM. Retrieved February from http://www-106.ibm.com/developerworks/webservices/

Brachman, R. J., McGuinness, D. L., Patel-Schneider, P. F., Resnick, L. A., & Borgida, A. (1991). Living with classic: When and how to use a KL-ONE-like language. In J. Sowa (Ed.), *Principles of semantic networks: Explorations in the representation of knowledge* (pp. 401-456). Morgan Kaufmann.

Buhalis, D. (2002). *E-tourism: Information technology for strategic tourism management.* Longman.

CBS NEWS. (2003, July 28). *Online travel sites' new take off.* Retrieved from http://www.cbsnews.com/stories/2003/07/28/tech/main565494.shtml

Chinnici, R., Gudgin, M., Moreau, J., & Weerawarana, S. (Eds.). (2003, January 24). *Web services description language (WSDL) Version 1.2, W3C Working Draft 24.* Retrieved from http://www.w3.org/TR/2003/WD-wsdl12-20030124/

Christensen, E., Curbera, F., Meredith, G., & Weerawarana, S. (Eds.). (2001, March 15). *W3C Web services description language (WSDL).* Retrieved from http://www.w3c.org/TR/wsdl

Compaq Web Language (CWL). (2005). Retrieved 2005 from http://research.compaq.com/SRC/WebL/

Darpa Agent Markup Language (DAML). (2005).

DERI International. (2005). *E-tourism working group.*. Retrieved 2005 from http://www.deri.org/research/groups/

Dombey, A. (1998). *Separating the emotion from the fact—The effects of new intermediaries on electronic travel distribution.* Paper presented at the ENTER Information and Communications Technologies in Tourism Conference, Istanbul, Turkey.

European Travel Agent's and Tour Operators' Association (ECTAA). (2004). Retrieved from http://www.ectaa.org/ECTAA%20English/Areas_dealt_with/Air_transport.htm#crs

Fernández López, M. (1999). *Overview of methodologies for building ontologies.* Paper presented at the Proceedings of the IJCAI-99 workshop on Ontologies and Problem-Solving Methods (KRR5), Stockholm.

Forrester. (2005). Forrester Research. Retrieved from http://www.forrester.com/

Gorton, I., Almquist, J., Dorow, K., Gong, P., & Thurman, D. (2005). *An architecture for dynamic data source integration.* Paper presented at the 38th Hawaii International Conference on System Sciences (HICSS-38).

Hospitality. (2005). *Trends in the online intermediary market: Travel agency/intermediary market. Hospitality eBusiness strategies.* Retrieved from http://www.hospitalityebusiness.com/hr081903142951.html

HotelOnline. (2002, October). *Global distribution systems in present times.* Retrieved from http://www.hotel-online.com/News/PR2002_4th/Oct02_GDS.html)

Inkpen, G. (1998). *Information technology for travel and tourism* (2nd ed.). Essex, UK: Addison Wesley Longman Ltd.

Jones, D. M., Bench-Capon, T. J. M., & Visser, P. R. S. (1998). *Methodologies for ontology development.* Paper presented at the Proceedings IT&KNOWS Conference of the 15th IFIP World Computer Congress, Budapest.

Joystar. (2005). *JYSR annual report.* Joystar Inc. Retrieved from the World Wide Web.

Lake, D. (2001). *American go online for travel information.*

Lawrence, R., & Barker, K. (2001). Integrating data sources using a standardized global dictionary. In W. Abramowicz & J. M. Zurada (Eds.), *Knowledge discovery for business information systems* (pp. 153-172). Kluwer Academic Publishers.

Lenzerini, M. (2002). *Data integration: A theoretical perspective.* Paper presented at the Twenty-First ACM SIGMOD-SIGACT-SIGART Symposium on Principles of Database Systems (PODS 2002), Madison, Wisconsin.

Mullaney, T. J. (2004). Design your own discount getaway. *Business Week*. Retrieved from http://www.adinfo.businessweek.com/magazine/content/04_10/b3873101_mz070.htm

National Information Standards Organization (NISO). (2005). *Guidelines for the construction, format, and management of monolingual thesauri*. Retrieved from http://www.niso.org/standards/resources/z39-19a.pdf

O'Connor, P. (2003). Online pricing—An analysis of hotel company practices. *Cornell Hotel & Restaurant Administration Quarterly, 44*(1), 10-19.

OntoEdit. (n.d.). (Version 0.6) [Computer Software]. AIFB, University of Karlsruhe. Retrieved 2005, from http://www.ontoknowledge.org/tools/ontoedit.shtml

Open Travel Alliance. (2004). Retrieved from www.opentravel.org

PRNewswire. (2002, April 9). *Travelocity.com ranks as top travel planning site for business travelers*. Retrieved from http://www.corporate-ir.net/ireye/ir_site.zhtml?ticker=TVLY&script=413&layout=-6&item_id=277266

Protégé. (n.d.). (Version 3.1.1) [Computer software]. Stanford Medical Informatics. Retrieved 2005, from http://protege.stanford.edu/

Rayport, J. F., & Jaworski, B. J. (2001). *E-commerce*. Boston: McGraw-Hill.

Riebeek, H. (2003). The ticket chase. *IEEE Spectrum*. Retrieved from http://www.spectrum.ieee.org/WEBONLY/publicfeature/jan03/tair.html

Robbins, R. J. (1996). Bioinformatics: Essential infrastructure for global biology. *Journal of Computational Biology, 3*(3), 465-478.

Universal Description Discovery, and Integration (UDDI). (2002). Retrieved from http://www.uddi.org/

Uschold, M., & Gruninger, M. (1996). Ontologies: Principles, methods and applications. *Knowledge Engineering Review, 11*(2), 93-155.

Von Halle, B. (2001, April). Building a business rules system, part 4. *DM Review Magazine*. Retrieved from http://www.dmreview.com/article_sub.cfm?articleId=3201

Werthner, H., & Ricci, F. (2004). E-commerce and tourism. *Communications of the ACM, 47,* 101-105.

Wiederhold, G. (1994). *Interoperation, mediation and ontologies*. Paper presented at the International Symposium on the Fifth Generation Computer Systems, Workshop on Heterogeneous Cooperative Knowledge-Bases, Tokyo.

World Tourism Organization. (2006). *Tourism 2020 vision*. Retrieved 2006, from http://www.unwto.org/facts/menu.html

World Wide Web Consortium. (2005a). *Resource description framework*. Retrieved from http://www.w3.org/RDF/

World Wide Web Consortium (W3C). (2005b). *XML schema.* Retrieved from http://www.w3.org/XML/Schema

World Wide Web Consortium (W3C). (2002). *Simple object access protocol 1.1.* Retrieved from http://www.w3.org/TR/SOAP/

World Wide Web Consortium (W3C). (2004). *Web ontology language (OWL).* Retrieved 2004, from http://www.w3.org/2004/OWL/

XML. (2005). *Extensible Markup Language (XML) 1.0 (Third Edition), W3C Recommendation 04 February 2004.* Retrieved from http://www.w3.org/TR/REC-xml/

Endnotes

[1] http://www.tiscover.com/

[2] http://www.gulliver.ie/

[3] http://www.opentravel.org/

[4] http://www.uml.org/

[5] http://www.ilog.com/products/jrules/lifecycle/language.cfm

[6] IBM Business Rules for E-Commerce: http://www.research.ibm.com/rules/home.html

[7] The Rule Markup Initiative: http://www.ruleml.org/

[8] http://herzberg.ca.sandia.gov/jess/

Chapter II

A Semantic Service-Oriented Architecture for Business Process Fusion

Athanasios Bouras, National Technical University of Athens, Greece
Panagiotis Gouvas, National Technical University of Athens, Greece
Gregoris Mentzas, National Technical University of Athens, Greece

Abstract

Most enterprises contain several heterogeneous systems, creating a fuzzy network of interconnected applications, services, and data sources. In this emerging business context, a clear need appears to link these former incompatible systems by using enterprise application integration (EAI) solutions. We propose a semantically enriched service-oriented business applications (SE-SOBA) framework that will provide a dynamically reconfigurable architecture enabling enterprises to respond quickly and flexibly to market changes. We also propose the development of a pure semantic-based implementation of the universal description, discovery, and integration (UDDI) specification, called pure semantic registry (PSR), which provides a flexible, extendable core architectural component allowing the deployment and business exploitation of Semantic Web services. The implementation of PSR involves the development of a semantic-based repository and an embedded resource definition framework (RDF)-based reasoning engine, providing strong query and inference capabilities to support effective service discovery and composition. We claim that when SE-SOBAs are combined with PSR and rule-based formalizations of business scenarios and processes, they constitute a holistic business-driven semantic integration framework, called FUSION, applied to intra- and inter- organizational EAI scenarios.

Introduction

In today's fiercely competitive global economy, companies are realizing that new initiatives such as e-business, customer relationship management, and business intelligence go hand-in-hand with the proven organization-wide EAI strategy. The goal of EAI is to integrate and streamline heterogeneous business processes across different applications and business units while allowing employees, decision makers, and business partners to readily access corporate and customer data no matter where it resides. More and more, EAI involves integrating information and processes not only across the enterprise but also beyond organizational walls to encompass business-to-business (B2B) integration supporting large scale value-added supply chains across the enlarged worldwide economy.

Business process fusion is the transformation of business activities that is achieved by integrating the interfaces of previously autonomous business processes by pipelining different middleware technologies and enabling the effective (semi-) automated exchange of information between various systems within a company or between enterprises. The development of SOBAs (which constitutes a set of independently running services communicating with each other in a loosely coupled message-based manner) and the publishing of Web services may implement the vision of business process fusion, by providing an abstraction layer for the involved interfaces through the Web service description language (WSDL). While SOBA and Web services have already made headway within large organizations, the technology will start filtering down to small- and medium-sized enterprises (SMEs) and will expand into supply chains. This architecture will also play a significant role in streamlining mergers and acquisitions, by linking previously incompatible systems.

Despite the aforementioned trends, users and professionals have high expectations towards software applications and enterprise application integration. They want to access the content they need, while this content must be accurate and free of redundancy. So, the enterprise applications must be intuitive and easy to use; reusable and extendable; implemented in a short and inexpensive way; and within the current information technology (IT) legacy environment. Enterprise applications and information systems also need to support a more general notion that involves relating the content and representation of information resources to entities and concepts in the real world.

This need imposes the use and interpretation of semantics in EAI. Semantic interoperability will support high-level, context-sensitive, information requests over heterogeneous information resources, heterogeneous enterprise applications, hiding systems, syntax, and structural heterogeneity. This semantically enriched approach eliminates the problem of knowing the contents and structure of information resources and the structure and architecture of heterogeneous enterprise applications.

Semantics and ontologies are important to application integration solutions because they provide a shared and common understanding of data, services, and processes that exist within an application integration problem domain, and how to facilitate communication between people and information systems. By leveraging this concept we can organize and share enterprise information, as well as manage content and knowledge, which allows better interoperability and integration of inter- and intra-enterprise information systems.

We claim that recent innovations in the development of SE-SOBA—which enlarge the notion of service-oriented architecture (SOA) by applying Semantic Web service technology and using ontologies and Semantic Web markup languages to describe data structures and messages passed through Web service interfaces—combined with the rule-based formalization of business scenarios and processes will provide a dynamically reconfigurable architecture that will enable enterprises to respond quickly and flexibly to market changes, thereby supporting innovation and business growth, increasing the potential for an improved return on IT investments, and a more robust bottom line.

The structure of this chapter is as follows: in the following section, we define the concept of EAI and present the traditional and current trends of EAI from the technology perspective. In the section called *The Road to Enterprise Application Integration,* we present the way that the emerging Semantic Web technologies apply to EAI scenarios and analyze the state-of-the-art technologies and techniques. The conceptual framework, called FUSION, which we propose referring to the innovative business-driven, semantic-enriched, service-oriented architecture, as well as the proposed business-oriented ontologies that extends OWL-S (World Wide Web Consortium, 2004) Service Profile are defined in the next section, called *FUSION Conceptual Framework,* while the technical implementation of our approach is presented in *FUSION Technical Implementation.* Moreover, the section *FUSION Adoption: Integration Scenario and Applying Methodology* specifies a light FUSION adoption methodology and a typical application scenario of the proposed solution. Finally, we present further work; future trends and technologies; and concluding remarks.

The Road to Enterprise Application Integration

Traditional Enterprise Application Integration

Most enterprises contain a systemic infrastructure of several heterogeneous systems, creating a complex, fuzzy network of interconnected applications, services, and data sources, which is not well documented and expensive to maintain (Samtani & Sadhwani, 2001). Moreover, the introduction of multi-oriented, separate legacy systems concerning enterprise resource planning (ERP), customer relationship management (CRM), supply chain management (SCM), e-business portals and B2B transactions, increases the complexity of systems integration, making the support of the interoperability among these systems a challenging task.

In this emerging business context, a clear need appears to link these former incompatible systems to improve productivity and efficiency. The solution to this need is what is called *EAI, which can be defined as the use of software and architectural principles to bring together (integrate) a set of enterprise computer applications* (see Figure 1). The goal of EAI is to integrate and streamline heterogeneous business processes across different applications and business units. We distinguish between intra- and inter-organizational enterprise application integration. Intra-organizational EAI, commonly referred as application to application integration (A2A) (Bussler, 2003a), specifies the automated and event-driven exchange of information between heterogeneous enterprise applications and systems operating within an organization or enterprise. On the other hand, inter-organizational EAI, or else B2B integration

Figure 1. The enterprise system environment: With and without an EAI system

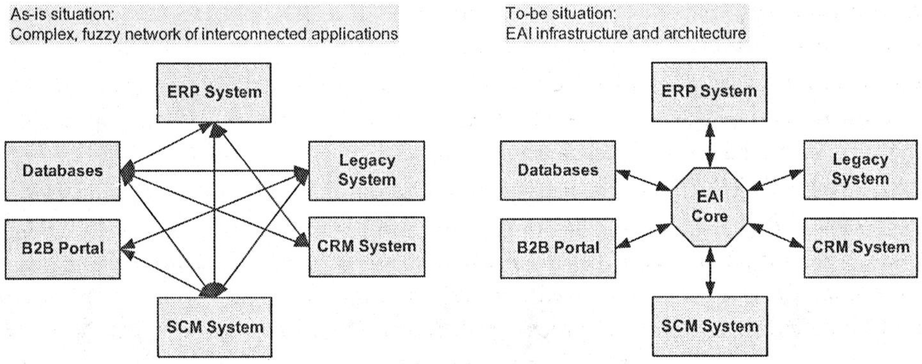

(Bussler, 2003a), specifies the automated and event-driven information exchange between various systems of several collaborating organizations and enterprises. Moreover, Apshankar et al. (2002) identify different types of EAI levels/layers, explaining the various dimensions of the integration task, namely:

- data-oriented integration, occurring at the database and data source level, either real time or non-real time, constituting the most widespread form of EAI today;
- function or method integration, involving the direct and rigid application-to-application integration of cross-platform applications over a network—it can be achieved using custom code, application program interface (APIs), remote procedure calls (RPCs) or distributed middleware and distributed objects (CORBA, RMI, DCOM);
- user interface integration, consisting on using a standardized user interface for accessing a group of legacy systems and applications. The new presentation layer is integrated with the existing business logic of the legacy systems or packaged applications; and
- business process integration, occurring at the business process level.

In recent years, most enterprises and organizations have made extensive investments in several EAI systems and solutions that promise to solve the major integration problem among their existing systems and resources. The business driver behind all these traditional EAI projects is to integrate processes across third-party applications as well as legacy systems to decrease the number of adapters one has to develop if connecting two systems (Laroia & Sayavedra, 2003). Therefore, the traditional EAI focuses (Haller, Gomez, & Bussler, 2005) on the message-based communication of software applications interfaces, by pipelining different middleware technologies and developing various adapters, connectors, and plug-ins to provide efficient messaging support among heterogeneous systems, allowing their effective interconnection. As traditional EAI efforts lack of an upper abstraction layer and standardized architectures and implementations, a new integration challenge is emerging: the interoperability among various vendor-dependent EAI systems and solutions. The growth of the EAI market and the involvement of new EAI vendors have intensified the integration problems identified, considering the standardization of integration frameworks and architectures a necessity. The development and introduction of Web service enabled service-oriented architecture solutions, completely based on widely known and accepted standards, overcomes the aforementioned EAI obstacles.

Web Services-Enabled Service-Oriented Architecture

The SOA is an architectural style for building software applications that use services available in a network such as the Web (Mahmoud, 2005). It promotes loose coupling between software components so that they can be reused. Applications in SOA are built based on services, which constitute implementations of well-defined business functionalities and can then be consumed by clients in different applications or business processes, enabling enterprises to leverage existing investments by allowing them to reuse existing applications and promise interoperability between heterogeneous applications and technologies. SOA-based applications are distributed multi-tier applications that have presentation, business logic, and persistence layers. Services are the building blocks of SOA applications. While any functionality can be made into a service, the challenge is to define a service interface that is at the right level of abstraction. Services should provide coarse-grained functionality. SOA is emerging as the premier integration and architecture framework in today's complex and heterogeneous computing environment. Previous attempts did not enable open interoperable solutions, but relied on proprietary APIs and required a high degree of coordination between groups. SOA can help organizations streamline processes so that they can do business more efficiently and adapt to changing needs and competition, enabling the software as a service concept.

Web services, the preferred standards-based way to realize SOA, are designed to support interoperable machine-to-machine interaction over a network.[1] This interoperability is gained through a set of Extensible Markup Language (XML)-based open standards. In specific, the Web services architecture (WSA)[2] and the Web Services Interoperability Model (WS-I)[3] comprising three emerging key technologies: such as Web Services Description Language (WSDL),[4] Simple Object Access Protocol (SOAP),[5] and UDDI.[6] These standards provide a common approach for defining, publishing, and using Web services. The Web services interface is described in a machine-processable format (specifically WSDL). Other systems and Web services interact with the Web service in a manner prescribed by its description using SOAP-messages, typically conveyed using Hyper Text Transfer Protocol (HTTP) with an XML serialization in conjunction with other Web-related standards.

In the literature, the Web services are defined as:

1. "loosely coupled, reusable software components that semantically encapsulate discrete functionality and are distributed and programmatically accessible over standard Internet protocols,"[7]
2. "a new breed of application, which are self-contained, self-describing, modular applications that can be published, located, and invoked across the Web. Web Services perform functions, which can be anything from simple request to complicated business processes."[8]

The typical business scenario (Kreger, 2001), invoking and benefiting from the Web services-oriented solutions, identifies as core element of the implementation of the Web service architecture the UDDI services registry that acts as an intermediary between Web services providers and requesters, storing and categorizing services in taxonomies (directory services) (see Figure 2). The service provider deploys Web services and defines their service description, representing its available services, applications, and system features and publishes them in the service registry. The service requester takes advantage of the search capabilities of the registry's directory service, searches the registry trying to find the composed service required and uses it, binding with the service provider. The main entities identified in a Web services-based business scenario, the service registry, the supplier (service provider), and the client (service) requester, interact in three ways: (1) the service provider publishes (publish activity) the WSDL service description in the service registry in order to allow the requester to find it, (2) the service requester retrieves (discover activity) a service description directly or queries the service registry for the type of service required, and (3) the service requester invokes or initiates an interaction (invoke activity) with the service at run time using the binding details in the service description to locate, contact, and invoke the service.

Web services, in their current form of loosely bound collections of services, are more of an ad hoc solution that can be developed quickly and easily, published, discovered, and bound dynamically (Samtani & Sadhwani, 2001). Web service-enabled SOA encourages and supports the reuse of existing enterprise assets, for example, already developed services and applications and allows the creation and deployment of new services from the existing infrastructure of systems. In other words, the Web service-enabled SOA facilitates businesses to leverage existing investments by al-

Figure 2. Web services architecture, models and standards

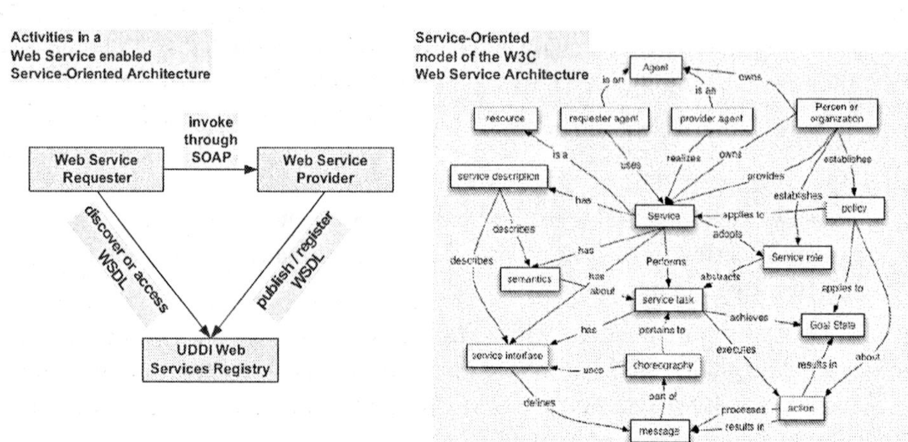

lowing them to reuse existing applications and promises interoperability between heterogeneous applications and technologies. SOA provides a level of flexibility that was not possible before (Mahmoud, 2005) in the sense that:

- The Web services are software components with well-defined interfaces that are implementation independent, separating completely the service interface from its implementation. The deployed Web services are used and consumed by clients (services requesters) that are not concerned with how these services will execute their requests.
- The Web services are self-contained (perform predetermined tasks) and loosely coupled (for independence).
- The Web services can be dynamically discovered.
- Composed services can be built from aggregates of preexisting Web services.

A few essential differences between traditional EAI solutions and Web services (Samtani & Sadhwani, 2001) are presented in Table 1.

Although, the Web services applied to specific EAI scenarios provide an abstraction and flexibility layer supporting SOA and simplifying the application integration, they are based on exclusively syntactical-oriented technologies, not defining formally the semantics of services interfaces and of the data structures of the messages Web services exchanges. The main reason resulting in the failure of the majority of EAI implementations (some articles even account for 70% of EAI projects as failure)[9] is that the semantics of different systems have to be formally defined and integrated at one point. The lack of formal semantics regarding the applications and services to be integrated makes it difficult for software engineers and developers to manually interconnect heterogeneous applications, impeding the automation regarding application integration, data exchange, and complex services composition. Engineers integrating the enterprise application systems have to know the meaning of the low-level data structures in order to implement a semantically correct integration. No formal definition of the interface data exist (Bussler, 2003b), which implies that the knowledge of every developer of applications involved in the integration project is assumed to be consistent.

Therefore, the problem that still exists, which the traditional Web services technologies are weak to solve, refers to the formalization and the documentation of the semantics related to the interfaces and the data structures of the deployed Web services. By applying Semantic Web technologies to SOAs and deploying Semantic Web services so as to integrate various systems, the notion of Semantic Web services enables SOA is emerging, paving the way to the semi-automated semantic-based enterprise application integration.

Table 1. Traditional EAI and Web services: Identified differences

Aspect	Traditional EAI vs. Web Service Enabled EAI
Simplicity	Web Services are much simpler to design, develop, deploy, maintain, and use as compared to a typical, traditional EAI solution which may involve distributed technology such as DCOM and CORBA.
Reusability	Once the framework of deploying and using Web Services is ready, it is relatively easy to compose new, aggregated services, reuse the existing IT systems infrastructure and automate new business processes spanning across multiple applications.
Open Standards	Unlike proprietary, traditional EAI solutions, Web Services are based on open XML-based standards such as WSDL, UDDI, SOAP and this is probably the single most important factor that leads to the wide adoption of Web Services technologies. Web Services are built on existing and ubiquitous protocols eliminating the need for companies to invest in supporting new network protocols.
Flexibility	Traditional EAI solutions require endpoint-to-endpoint integration. Changes made at one end have to be propagated to the other end, making them very rigid and time consuming in nature. Web Services based integration is quite flexible, as it is built on loose coupling between the application publishing the services and the application using those services.
Cheap	Traditional EAI solutions, such as message brokers, are very expensive to implement. Web Services, in the future, may accomplish many of the same goals - cheaper and faster.
Scope	Traditional EAI solutions consider and treat applications as single entities, whereas Web Services allow companies to break down complex services into small independent logical units and build wrappers around them.
Efficiency	Web Services allow applications and services to be broken down into smaller logical components, which make the integration of applications easier as it is done on a granular basis.
Dynamic	Web Services provide a dynamic approach to integration by offering dynamic interfaces, whereas traditional EAI solutions are pretty much static in nature.

Semantic Web Services in EAI Scenarios

The Emerging Semantic Web Services

The long-term goal of the Web services effort is seamless interoperation among networked programs and devices. Once this is achieved, Web services can be seen as providing the infrastructure for universal plug-and-play and ubiquitous computing (Weiser, 1993). However, the main obstacle of achieving interoperability among deployed Web services is that the technical and functional description (profile) of the services is based on semi-formal natural language descriptions, which are not formally defined, not allowing computers to understand and interpret the data to be exchanged among Web services. The Semantic Web initiative's purpose is similar to that of the Web services (Preece & Decker, 2002): to make the Web machine processable rather than merely *human processable*. Thus, Web services are considered as an essential ingredient of the Semantic Web and benefit from the Semantic Web technologies. Key components of the Semantic Web technology are:

- a unified data model such as RDF,
- languages with well defined, formal semantics, built on RDF, such as the Web ontology language (OWL) DARPA agent markup language and ontology inference layer (DAML+OIL), and
- ontologies of standardized terminology for marking up Web resources, used by semantically enriched service level descriptions, such as OWL-S (former DAML-S, DAML-based Web service ontology).

Enriching Web services descriptions with formal defined semantics by introducing the notion of semantic markup, leading towards the Semantic Web services (see Figure 3), enables machine-interpretable profiles of services and applications, realizing the vision of dynamic and seamless integration. As this semantic markup is machine—processable and—interpretable, the developed semantic profiles of Web services can be exploited to automate the tasks of discovering Web services, executing them, composing them, and interoperating with them (McIlraith et al., 2001b), moving a step forward towards the implementation of intelligent, Semantic Web services.

The combination of Web services and Semantic Web technologies, resulting in the deployment of machine processable and, therefore, usable for automation Semantic Web services, supports and allows a set of essential automated services regarding the use of deployed Web services (McIlraith et al., 2001a; McIlraith et al., 2001b):

- automatic Web service discovery, involving automatic location Web services that provide a particular functionality and that adhere to requested properties expressed as a user goal,
- automatic Web service composition, involving dynamic combination and aggregation of several Web services to provide a given functionality,
- automatic Web service invocation, involving automatic execution of an identified Web service by an agent, and
- automatic Web service interoperation within and across organizational boundaries.

Figure 3. Towards intelligent, Semantic Web services (Bussler, Fensel, & Maedche, 2002)

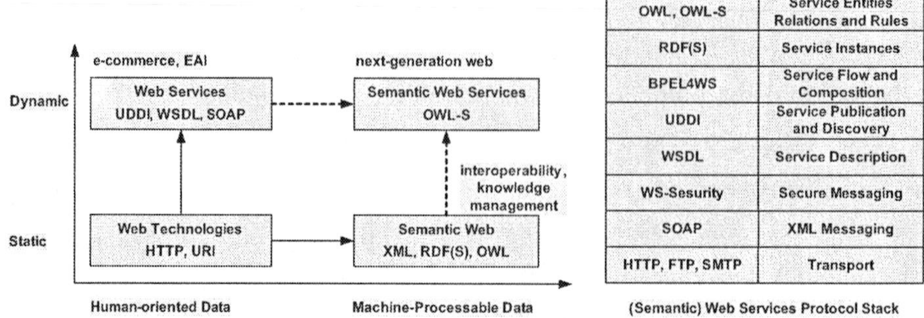

These semantically enriched Web services-oriented features can constitute the ideal solution to integration problems, as they enable dynamic, scalable, and reusable cooperation between different systems and organizations. Table 2 summarizes the main improvements that the semantic markup resulted in Web services:

Semantic Web Services Registries

As presented in the first section, the Web services architecture involves three core entities: (1) the service provider (supplier), (2) the service requester (client), and (3) the business services registry serving as a business mediator. The Semantic Web services deploy a similar architectural schema, with the crucial difference that the service technical and functional descriptions are semantically enriched with concepts defined in reference ontologies. However, current widely—known and—used service registries (i.e., UDDI and ebXML registry) specifications and implementations do no support the effective handling of semantic profiles of Web services, and a number of research activities have taken place, recently, trying to semantically enrich the standardized service registries. Their common goal has focused on the capability of registries to store and publish semantic data, so as to facilitate the semantic-based description of Web services, the ontology-based categorization and discovery of Web services, and, therefore, the semantic integration of business services and applications.

In specific, Moreau, Miles, Papay, Decker, and Payne (2003) present an approach and implementation for service registration and discovery that uses an RDF triple store to express semantic service descriptions and other task/user-specific metadata, using a mechanism for attaching structured and unstructured metadata. The result is an extremely flexible service registry that can be the basis of a sophisticated

Table 2. Web services vs. Semantic Web services

Dimension	Existing Web Services	Semantic Web Services
Services	Simple	Composable
Requestor	Human (developer)	Agent
Provider	Registration	No registration
Mediator	Key Player	Facilitator
Description	Taxonomy	Ontology
Descriptiveness	Closed world	Open world
Representation	Syntax-based	Semantics-based

semantically enhanced service discovery engine. This solution extends service descriptions using RDF and changes UDDI APIs for support of semantic search. Moreover, Pokraev, Koolwaaij, and Wibbels (2003) present the design and implementation of an enhanced UDDI server, capable of storage, matching, and retrieval of semantically rich service profiles that contain contextual information, mapping DAML-S to UDDI publish message and introducing, with their approach, additional elements such as a matchmaker, an ontology repository, and a proxy API to invoke UDDI APIs. The approach of Pokraev et al. (2003) does not change the publish and inquiry interfaces of the UDDI. In addition, Paolucci, Kawamura, Payne, and Sycara (2002) show how DAML-S service profiles, which describe service capabilities within DAML-S, can be mapped into UDDI records and how the encoded information can be mapped within the UDDI registry to perform semantic matching. This work proposes semantic search based on an externally created and operated matchmaker, as the semantic data are stored outside of the UDDI registry, while the mapping is implemented with links from the UDDI tModel to the semantic profile of the Web service. Finally, Srinivasan, Paolucci, and Sycara (2005) base the discovery mechanism on OWL-S. OWL-S allows to semantically describe Web services in terms of capabilities offered and to perform logic inference to match the capabilities requested with the capabilities offered. Srinivasan et al. (2005) propose OWL-S/UDDI matchmaker that combines the better of two technologies.

As shown previously, current technologies and research efforts, towards the realization of semantic-enriched services registry, use current UDDI implementation and try to extend their functionalities with semantic-based capabilities, introducing external matchmakers and mapping techniques. We claim that a pure semantic-based implementation of the UDDI specification, called *pure semantic registry,* provides a flexible, extendable core architectural component to allow the deployment and business exploitation of Semantic Web services. The implementation of the PSR involves the design and development of a semantic-based repository and an embedded RDF-based reasoning engine. The PSR enables and supports the storage, administration, and handling of the deployed Semantic Web services and their profiles in a unique semantic repository. The semantic service profiles are annotated by using internally store domain ontologies facilitating, thus, the ontology-based categorization of services. Finally, the semantic registry benefits from its powerful RDF-based query and inference engine to support effective service discovery and composition.

FUSION Conceptual Framework

FUSION: Towards the Business Intelligent Semantic SOA

The FUSION solution is an integration framework that facilitates the integration of heterogeneous enterprise applications that exist in the same organization or in different organizations. The design of the FUSION approach has been based on a layer-oriented architecture (see Figure 4), using several structural components and preexisting technologies (Web services, semantics, services registry, etc.) benefiting from the typical advantages of each technology. This innovative, structured compilation of technologies and EAI techniques reduces the integration obstacles, which each technology when applied to EAI scenarios could face, enabling the intelligent integration of business services.

Figure 4. Layer-oriented EAI architecture

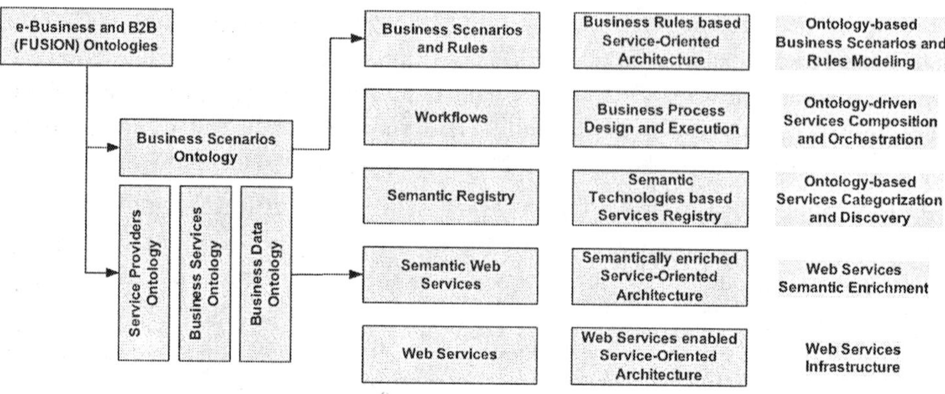

In specific, FUSION framework involves:

- A Web services infrastructure, which provides an initial interoperable capability based on Web services interface and communication integration, serving as a common deployment basis for all the enterprise applications and business services. As the Web services infrastructure applies the notion of SOA to the proposed framework, FUSION basis constitutes a pragmatic, applied SOA architecture.
- A *semantic enrichment layer,* which adds semantics to the technical and functional descriptions of the Web services, making the ontology-annotated Web services understandable and profiles machine interpretable. The semantic enrichment layer extends the notion of SOA with formal, well-defined semantics, moving towards a semantically enriched SOA.
- A semantic registry that constitutes an implementation of the latest UDDI specification based on Semantic Web technologies, supporting and semantically extending the main functionalities of service registries (i.e., UDDI and ebXML registries): the storage, categorization and discovery of the deployed business Web services. The FUSION semantic registry does not proposes a new registry architecture and specification, but it constitutes an alternative of the implementation that benefits from the intelligent ontology-based categorization, the strong RDF-based query language and inference engine.
- A *business process layer* facilitating the design and execution of Web services processes and workflows. The designed workflows invoke the business services stored in the semantic registry, retrieving them by using the semantic-based services of the registry. The interaction of the process design and execution environment with the service registry facilitates the automatic service discovery, composition, and invocation, supporting the interoperability among previous incompatible enterprise applications.
- A *business scenarios and rules layer* that defines and models, using formal ontologies that conceptualize e-business and B2B transactions, typical business scenarios occurring within companies and/or across collaborating enterprises. The formal business rules are transformed into parameterized workflow models, and are executed within the business process layer.

The upper two business-oriented layers, the business process layer and the business scenarios and rules layer adds business intelligence in the applied SOA, allowing the automated composition and orchestration of the deployed Web services, and supporting the automatic integration of business services. Apart from the aforementioned layers, the FUSION framework involves an ontology-based layer, which interacts with most of the rest of the integration layers. FUSION ontologies, which formalize the concepts, the relations, and the events existing in an e-business environment, are separated in three main ontologies:

- The *business data ontology* defines the basic business data types and relations used in business services and transactions. The business data ontology is taken into consideration in the semantic enrichment of the deployed Web services, so as to define formally the data structure of the SOAP messages exchanged during a business transaction.
- The *business service ontology* conceptualizes the functionality of a given application that is used to annotate the functional profiles of Web services (during the semantic enrichment phase).
- The *business scenarios ontology* models the business rules identified, by business analysts and consultants during the business scenarios phase, in typical inter- and intra-organizational business scenarios. The ontology-based business rules defined are used in the business processes design to enable the composition of complex, aggregated Web services.

The next sections present in detail the FUSION conceptual framework, specify the several integration layers required for realizing business intelligent semantic SOA applied to inter- and intra-organizational and/or enterprise EAI scenarios, analyze how FUSION ontologies extends the OWL-S upper ontology concepts, and define the OWL-S representation of services.

FUSION Integration Layers

Web Services Infrastructure and Semantic Enrichment Layer

The conceptual architecture of the FUSION integration approach is based on a Web services infrastructure (see Figure 5). The, so-called, *Web service-enabled SOA infrastructure* allows the deployment of Web service software instances of each business applications and services, respectively, so as to *provide a first integration layer, regarding the interfacing (WSDL) and communication (SOAP) of initially incompatible business applications.*

Although, this first layer of abstraction, involving WSDL interfaces, provides a universal standards-based, highly flexible and adaptable implementation of business applications integration (Haller et al., 2005), the problem of documenting and understanding the semantics of these interfaces not only still exists, but it becomes a crucial issue to deal with. The significance of interpreting semantics in a machine understandable way arises from the continuously increasing average amount of

Web services that are stored in typical UDDI registries used in the Web service-enabled SOA approach, which makes it difficult for the developer and/or software engineer to manually integrate and put together the suitable Web services. That is why FUSION framework contains a second integration layer (see Figure 5) that *adds formal and well-defined business data and services functionality semantics in the Web services descriptions and interfaces*, enlarging the notion of SOA and Web services applying common reference business ontologies.

This second integration layer supports the semantic enrichment of the Web services descriptions (WSDL files) taking into account two basic facets. Firstly, we should provide a formal description of the functionality of the Web service in order to facilitate efficient categorization and discovery of Web services. Therefore, the business service ontology is needed to identify the events that could occur in an e-business and/or B2B environment and to organize the business logic of this domain, creating an ontology-based dictionary conceptualizing functionality aspects of potential services of the e-business domain.

As real-life business services contain several and quite complex parameters and structures, we have recognized the need of developing the business data ontology formalizing the types of data contained in WSDL interfaces as well as the structure of the information that Web services exchange through SOAP messages. So, the FUSION second integration layer provides the mechanism, the graphical interface,

Figure 5. FUSION (Semantic) Web services-enabled SOA infrastructure

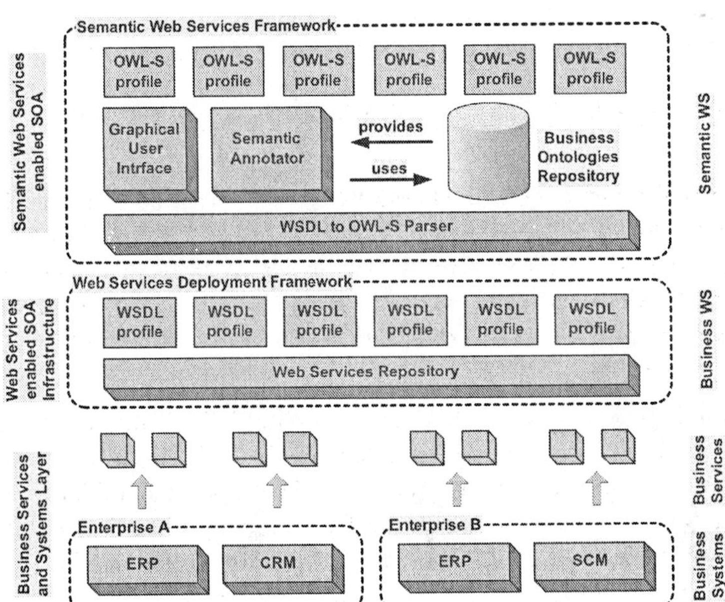

and the common-reference business ontologies, to semantically annotate the Web services profiles using the appropriate functionality and data concepts, and to create semantically enriched OWL-S descriptions of the Web services software instances, applying and leveraging the use of the *Semantic Web services in service-oriented architecture* deployed to business environments.

Semantic Business Services Registry

Once the Web services instances are deployed and their OWL-S semantic profiles are created, they should be categorized and published in business service registries in order to allow users (i.e., agents and humans) to discover, compose, and use, on demand, the services published there. As the most common service registries (i.e., UDDI and ebXML registries) do not support the storage and maintenance of ontologies and/or semantic profiles—Internally to the registry, methods have been developed to associate the set of semantics that characterizes a Web service with the service advertised through the business registry. A common drawback identified to all the existing techniques, trying to add semantics or semantically enrich predefined service registries, is that the reference ontologies and the semantic profiles of the Web service instances are stored externally to the registry, using informal, complex mapping tables and association rules to support the basic UDDI and ebXML registries services, they fail to embed effectively the dynamic and flexible Semantic Web technologies in the main services powered by such registries: categorization and discovery of Web services.

The FUSION approach has studied the methodologies and the lessons learned by research efforts focusing on the semantic enrichment of formal service registries and tries a different and innovative orientation. As the FUSION approach seeks to benefit more from the emerging Semantic Web technologies and standards, it moves towards the implementation of a "pure" *FUSION semantic registry*, based on a full functional RDF semantic repository (see Figure 6). FUSION approach develops a "thin-UDDI" API, internally to the semantic registry, to realize the basic set of functions of the traditional registries. In order for the proposed approach to be fully compliant with the dominant standards of the e-business domain (i.e., UDDI), FUSION transforms the XSD Schema of the latest UDDI specification in a RDF-Schema stored in the developed RDF repository, so as to preserve the widely known informational and relational infrastructure of the UDDI registry and to take advantage of its well-defined internal structure. This implementation benefits from the new possibilities provided by the RDQL query language when combined with the reasoning and inference engine of the RDF repository facilitates. Therefore, the FUSION semantic registry supports the storage and lifecycle management of RDF files and reference ontologies, internally, while it uses the query language and the inference engine provided to enable categorization and discovery services based on well-defined (formal) common semantics.

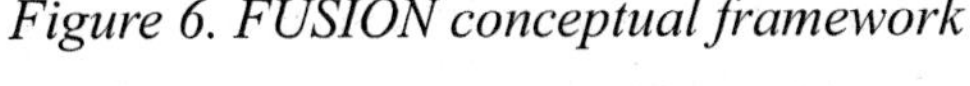
Figure 6. FUSION conceptual framework

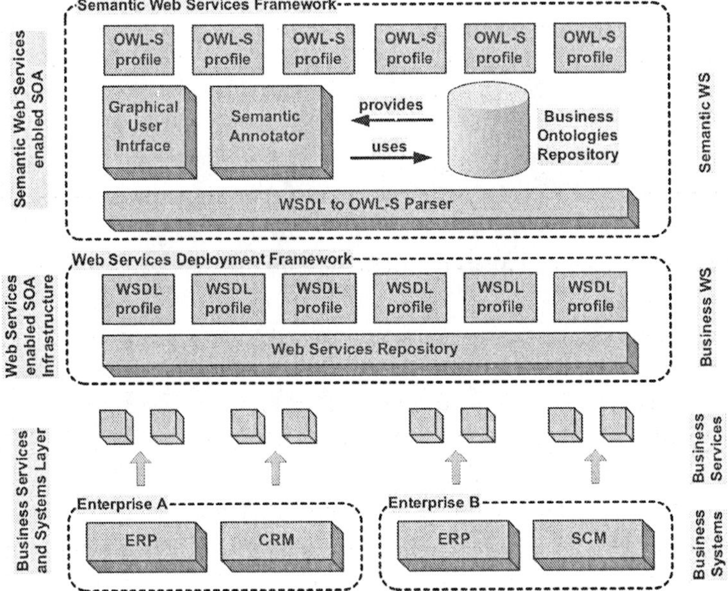

Business-Oriented Layers

Furthermore, an upper layer of abstraction is needed in FUSION approach to move the EAI efforts, which follows the SOA and Web services architectures, a step forward towards the vision of the intelligent Web services and the *business intelligent semantic SOA*. This "ultimate" integration layer invokes the use of business process-driven workflows and modeling, taking into account and analyzing the most typical e-business and/or B2B scenarios, so as to design workflows that model the behavior of the selected business services in a business process interaction.

The intelligent SOA allows the experience and knowledge of business consultants and experts to be conceptualized and embedded to typical business scenarios, facilitating the formal modeling and execution of business processes using the Business Process Execution Language for Web Services (BPEL4WS) workflow modeling language. While the business consultants develop and model the desirable business scenarios, they define the Web services required by referring to the functionality aspects of services and using the common reference business services ontology. As this service functionality-oriented ontology is also used to annotate, characterize, and categorize the deployed Web service in the common semantic registry, the execution defined workflow models realizes the automated composition of intelligent Web services and the orchestration of flexible, complex business services.

FUSION Ontologies and OWL-S Web Services

OWL-S: Semantic Markup for Web Services

There have been a number of efforts to add semantics to the discovery process of Web services. An upper ontology for services has already been developed and presented to the Semantic Web services project of the DAML program, called OWL-S (formerly DAML-S). OWL-S upper service ontology provides three essential types of knowledge about a service, each characterized by the question it answers:

- What does the service provide for prospective clients? The answer to this question is given in the "profile," which is used to advertise the service. To capture this perspective, each instance of the class Service presents a ServiceProfile (see Figure 7).
- How is it used? The answer to this question is given in the "process model." This perspective is captured by the ServiceModel class. Instances of the class Service use the property describedBy to refer to the service's ServiceModel.
- How does one interact with it? The answer to this question is given in the "grounding." Grounding provides the needed details about transport protocols. Instances of the class Service have a supports property referring to a Service-Grounding.

Figure 7. OWL-S service profile classes and properties

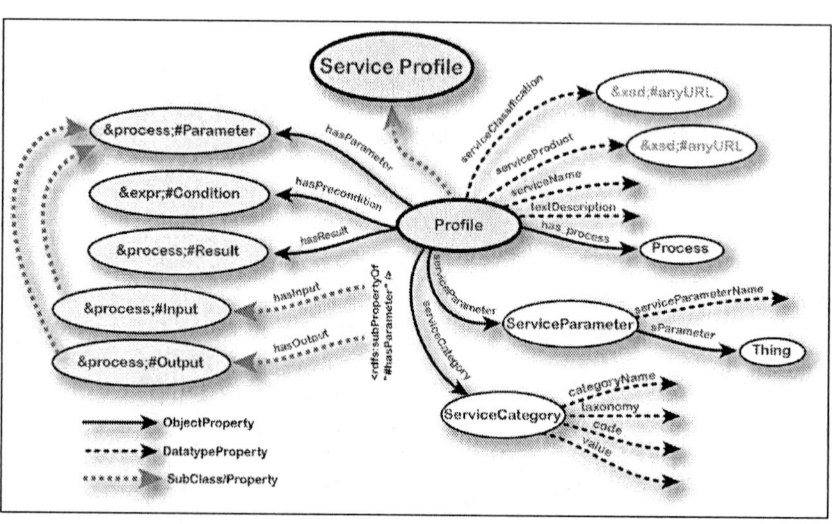

Figure 8. OWL-S and WSDL mapping

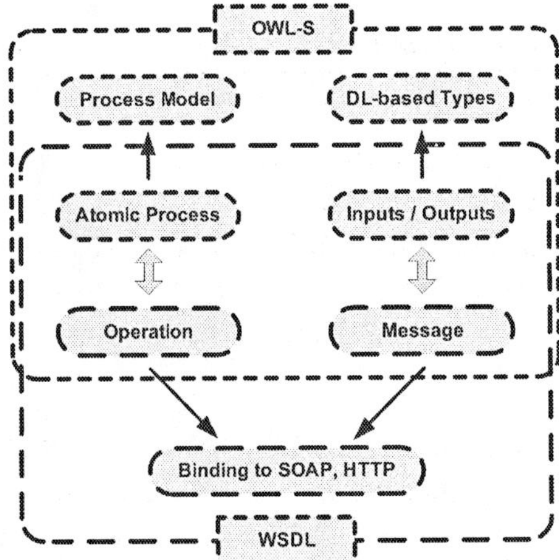

Generally speaking, the service profile provides the information needed for an agent to discover a service, while the service model and service grounding, taken together, provide enough information for an agent to make use of a service, once found.

The grounding concept in the OWL-S ontology provides information about how to access (invoke) the service, that is, details on the protocol, message formats, serialization, transport, and so forth. It is viewed as a mapping from an abstract to a concrete specification of those service description elements that are required for interacting with the service. OWL-S only defines such grounding for WSDL and SOAP (see Figure 8), although additional groundings can be defined. A summary of the automation support each upper level concept (or its subconcepts) of the OWL-S ontology is intended to cover is given in Table 3.

Table 3. Purpose of OWL-S upper level concepts

Upper level concept	Automation support
Profile	• Discovery
Model	• Planning • Composition • Interoperation • Execution monitoring
Grounding	• Invocation

Figure 9. OWL-S ontology and business-oriented extensions

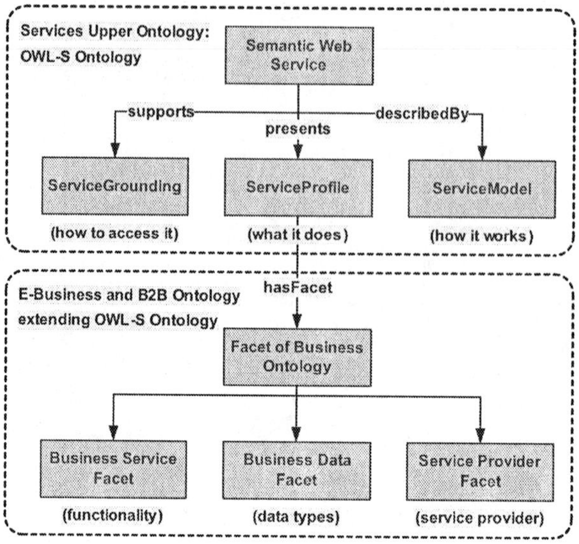

Business-Oriented OWL-S Extension for Describing Web Services

In the complicated business services, the service profile should provide a clear description of the functionality of the service to be used, while the service model involves retrieving the suitable Web service and the service grounding the way the object is exchanged. As the OWL-S ontology provides a high abstraction layer for semantic description of Web services, a business-oriented extension of OWL-S service profile is needed (see Figure 9) to provide the ontology-based infrastructure enabling the semantic description of business services concerning three main aspects: (1) the business service provider entity, (2) the functionality of the Web service, and (3) the data types that the Web service exchanges.

This business-oriented OWL-S extension, called e-business and B2B ontology, provides the necessary semantics, concepts, classes, and interrelations, to characterize the Web services deployed by annotating the OWL-S profiles of services with formal, well-defined semantics.

FUSION Ontologies

For the realization of the business services ontology-based infrastructure that is presented in the paragraph, we have developed three interconnected ontologies, called the FUSION ontologies, that describe the various entities and components that participate in business transactions. The FUSION ontologies serve the objective of making the technical realization as declarative as possible.

The FUSION ontologies constitute the *cornerstone for the semantic description and modeling of business-oriented web services*. The core objective of these business ontologies is to facilitate efficient business collaboration and interconnection between heterogeneous, incompatible services supporting the semantic fusion of service-oriented business applications that exist within an enterprise or in several collaborating companies.

The FUSION ontologies conceptualize the identified attributes, concepts, and their relationships of the service-oriented businesses applications and will be developed in three layers, each of them referring to a significant business entity—aspect: the service provider, the service functionality, and the services data types. This multi-layer architecture of FUSION ontologies provides a rich representation of service-oriented business applications, captures the significant requirements of both services functionality and data, supports efficient representation of services in intra- and inter-organizational level, and provides a flexible structure that could be easily refined and updated. The ontologies define:

- the basic description of the functionality that the business services provides to the end user (functional semantics) in order to capture the (semi-) formal representation of the functional capabilities of Web services in order to support the semantic-based discovery and automated composition of Web services, annotating the operations of services software instances as well as providing preconditions and effects—the business service ontology provides this type of information;
- the data types and relevant semantics required for representing the message structures and information that the Web services exchange (data/information semantics), capturing the (semi-) formal definition of data in input and output messages of a Web service, supporting discovery and interoperability by annotating input and output data of Web services using data-oriented ontologies—this information is specified in the business data ontology;
- the processes and scenarios identified in typical intra- and inter-organizational business transactions using a rule-based modeling approach (process and execution semantics), facilitating the automated composition and orchestration of complex Web services and workflows—this information is formally defined by the business scenarios ontology; and
- the categorization of the business entities that provide the deployed Web service software instances—this information is provided by the *service provider ontology*.

During the development of the FUSION ontologies, we have taken into consideration and examined already available ontologies and e-business standards. As a result, we have reused and built on already established and widely used domain knowledge, eliminating the danger of "reinventing the wheel." So, we have based on two dominants XML-based business standards: ebXML (the Core Components Technical Specification and the Catalog of Common Business Processes) and RosettaNet (the Technical Dictionary and the Business Dictionary) defining a list of terms which can be used in business documents, as well as in other formal business vocabularies and taxonomies.

FUSION Technical Implementation

FUSION architecture is in line with the applied SOA architecture targeting smooth integration and dynamic service creation of services related with an ERP and a CRM system. Consequently the basis of the architecture is the ERP and the CRM software components. *FUSION adoption guideline* requires the existence of:

- a standard set of *exported Web services* that facilitate the software's functionality. These Web services will be used for dynamic service creation during a complex service composition;

Figure 10. FUSION technical architecture overview

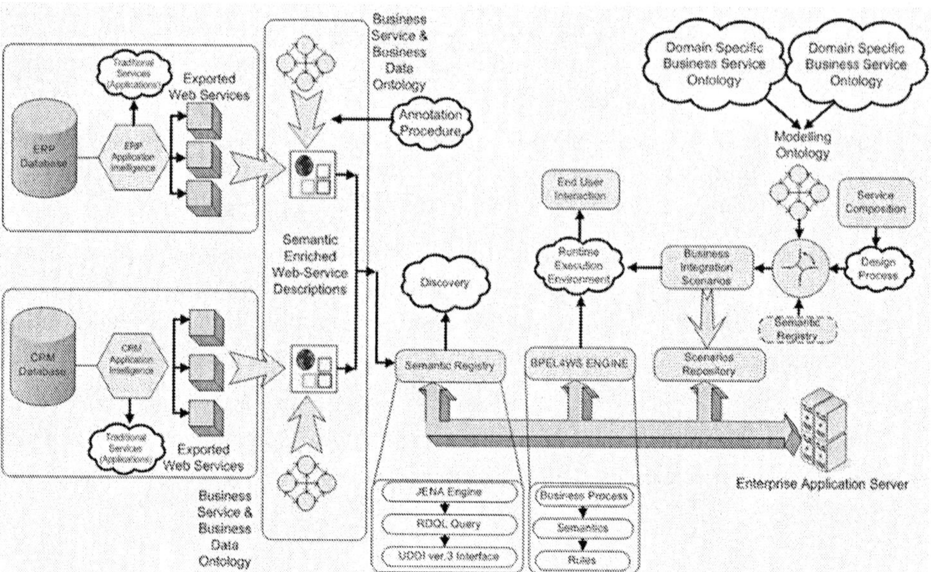

- a functional ontology, which is a domain specific ontology used for the semantic annotation of exported Web services; and
- An annotation procedure that aims at the semantically enrichment of Web services' description.

FUSION Architecture

An overview of FUSION architecture is presented in Figure 10.

As mentioned previously, the elementary component in a SOA approach is Web services, since Web services provide a standard means of interoperating between different software applications running on a variety of platforms and/or frameworks. Web services are characterized by their interoperability and extensibility as well as their machine-processable descriptions thanks to the use of XML, and they can then be combined in a loosely coupled way in order to achieve complex operations. Consequently the first step of the FUSION adoption guideline is the provision of simple services derived from ERP and CRM functionality (domain specific functionality). This is an extremely crucial task since simple services can interact with each other in order to deliver sophisticated added-value services. However it is not a trivial task because *SOA is a complete overhaul* impacting how systems are analyzed, designed, built, integrated, and managed.

The next step is the semantic annotation of exported Web services and more specifically the semantic annotation of their WSDL file. As mentioned previously, WSDL is an XML format for describing network services as a set of endpoints operating on messages containing either document-oriented or procedure-oriented information. The operations and messages are described abstractly, and then bound to a concrete network protocol and message format to define an endpoint. Related concrete endpoints are combined into abstract endpoints (services). WSDL is extensible to allow description of endpoints and their messages regardless of what message formats or network protocols are used to communicate, however, the only bindings described in this document describe how to use WSDL in conjunction with SOAP 1.1, HTTP GET/POST, and MIME.

The cornerstone of FUSION architecture is, as expected, the *enterprise application server* which encapsulates the following modules:

- *semantic registry,* which is a variation of a classic Web services registry used for service discovery, and
- a *business process execution engine,* which executes Business Process Execution Language (BPEL) scenarios.

Semantic Registry

The extension of traditional Web services to Semantic Web services raises the necessity of semantic support in current Web services registries. A lot of effort has been put into this field. Research that has been conducted with the aim of extending registries so they could support semantic discovery can be classified into two groups:

- those who extend legacy Web services standards by adding semantic annotation to reinforce the discovery function in registries, and
- those who preserve semantic advertisements into legacy registries by mapping semantic information into the *registry information model.*

FUSION approach aims to tackle this issue in a more unified way through the implementation of a PSR. PSR is a variation of a classic registry (UDDI, ebXML) that can store additional semantic metadata that accompany the Web service description model. PSR handles ebXML v.2.5 and UDDI v.3. At first all the entries of each registry are converted into OWL-S ontologies with additional classes. The persistence model of PSR is not based in a database but in an integrated ontology. Service discovery within the ontology is made using RDQL queries. The semantic registry utilizes Jena[10] for storage and discovery. Jena is a Java framework for writing Semantic Web applications developed under HP Labs Semantic Web Programme. It features:

- statement-centric methods for manipulating an RDF model as a set of RDF triples,
- resource-centric methods for manipulating an RDF model as a set of resources with properties,
- cascading method calls for more convenient programming,
- built in support for RDF containers—bag, alt, and seq,
- enhanced resources—the application can extend the behavior of resources,
- integrated parsers and writers for RDF/XML (ARP), N3, and N-TRIPLES, and
- support for typed literals.

BPEL Engine

Since many organizations are moving from an object-oriented paradigm for managing business processes toward a service-oriented approach, services are becoming the fundamental elements of application development. At the same time, BPEL has become the de facto standard for orchestrating these services and managing flawless execution of business process. The confluence of these trends is presenting some interesting opportunities for more flexible, cost-effective management of business processes.

ERP and CRM business processes contain multiple decision points. At these decision points, certain criteria are evaluated. Based on these criteria or business rules, business processes change their behavior. In essence, these business rules drive the business process. Frequently, these rules are embedded within the business process itself or inside custom Java code, which can cause several problems such as:

- Business rules change more often than the processes themselves, but changing and managing embedded business rules is a complex task beyond the abilities of most business analysts. Thus, as business rules change, programmers often have to commit expensive time to this task.
- Most organizations lack a central rules repository. Consequently, any organization-wide change in policy cannot be applied across all business processes.
- Business processes cannot reuse rules. Hence, IT personnel end up designing rules for each and every process, often leading to inconsistency or redundancy.

The best way to avoid these problems is to use a rules engine to separate business processes from business rules. In this approach, rules are exposed as services and BPEL processes leverage these services by querying the engine when they reach decision points. This approach is much more flexible—Instead of coding rules in programming languages or inside a process, rules can be manipulated graphically. Business users with tools can write rules themselves and make post-deployment rule changes without IT assistance. With business users doing most of the updates and enhancements, maintenance costs can be reduced substantially. Consequently, rule engines and BPEL are complementary technologies.

It is rather important to delineate rules from processes. Hence, a major decision in FUSION architecture is how to implement business policies, business processes, and supporting business logic. Business logic is spread across three different layers of the IT infrastructure: (1) business process, (2) Web services, and (3) rules (see Figure 11).

Figure 11. FUSION IT infrastructure

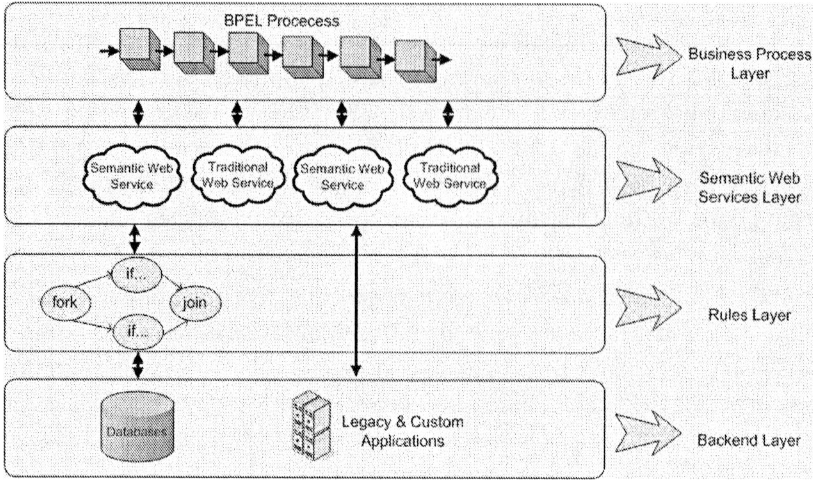

Business Process Layer

This layer is responsible for managing the overall execution of the business process. These business processes, implemented using BPEL, can be long running, transactional, and persistent. The BPEL engine supports audit and instrumentation of workflow and thus is well suited for:

- separating less volatile workflow steps from more volatile business rules,
- implementing line-of-business processes,
- implementing process flows requiring compensation,
- supporting large-scale instantiation of process flows,
- designing process flows that need auditing, and
- orchestrating heterogeneous technologies such as connectors, Web services, and Web Services Invocation Framework (WSIF)-enabled logic.

Semantic Web Services Layer

The Web services layer exposes the existing application layer functionality as services. Multiple business processes can then reuse these services, thereby fulfilling the promise of a SOA.

Web services implement functional and domain logic. Functional methods are typically stateless and medium grained. Web services may, for example, contain utility methods, entity operations, and inquiry methods for system data. Web services can be implemented using multiple technologies and hide differences among implementation platforms. Thus, this layer is well suited for:

- implementing medium-grained methods for a particular entity/domain area,
- integrating legacy code/third-party tools, and
- encapsulating logic, custom code, and implementation from the application layer.

Rules Layer

The rule engine is typically the home for complex logic that involves a number of interdependencies between entities and order-dependent logic calculation. Extracting business rules as a separate entity from business process leads to better decoupling of the system, which, in consequence, increases maintainability.

Rules engines allow for evaluation of rules sets in parallel and in a sequential order. In addition, rules have the ability to evaluate the values of input and intermediate data and determine if a rule should be fired. This modular design provides a simpler and more maintainable solution than traditional Java procedural code.

Furthermore, rules are declarative and allow high-level graphical user interface (GUI) editing by business analysts. Modern rule engines execute extremely quickly and provide built-in audit logging. The typical traits of a rules layer are as follows:

- contains coupled and complex logic,
- supports efficient business logic evaluation using parallel execution,
- contains complex return structure built from multiple business rule evaluations,
- allows for translation of domain logic into simple rules, and
- implements highly volatile business policy.

Because rules are exposed as services in the Web services layer, they can be reused across all inter-enterprise applications, making the development of new applications and integrations easier.

In the scope of FUSION approach BPEL4WS has been used. BPEL4WS provides a language for the formal specification of business processes and business interaction protocols. By doing so, it extends the Web services interaction model and enables it to support business transactions. BPEL4WS defines an interoperable integration model that should facilitate the expansion of automated process integration in both the intra-corporate and the B2B spaces. IBM BPWS4J[11] has been utilized in the scope of FUSION solution. BPWS4J includes a platform upon which can be executed business processes written using the BPEL4WS and a tool that validates BPEL4WS documents. Additionally, the enterprise application server includes a scenario *repository* that stores already existing BPEL scenarios for future use.

FUSION Adoption: Integration Scenario and Applying Methodology

Typical Integration Scenario: Multinational, Franchising Firms

A typical use case scenario, applying FUSION framework to solve EAI problems, refers to multi-national, franchising firms and is presented in the following section. Multi-national, franchising firms constitute a typical integration case, because of the fact that they involve several, geographically distributed legacy systems that need to be integrated at one point so as to facilitate the exchange of crucial business information among the networked franchising companies. As national systems work in isolation, any business interaction between headquarters is done currently, by mail, phone, or fax. Today, most of the steps in international workflows require human participation and batch data exchange to complete. For example, phone calls and human conversations are instantiated to carry out simple product availability requests and mails containing financial reports are exchanged for the purpose of financial auditing.

Humans, by making implicit interpretations of exchanged information, can reach a common understanding about things. Machines, on the contrary, require explicit and formal information interpretations in order to communicate. But, the company has concluded that manual execution of activities is expensive, while it does not allow jobs to repeat as often as needed. Human conversations and batch data exchanges are point-to-point interactions restricted to proprietary information structures. Even a fully automated point-to-point connection requires specific meanings and tightly bounded ends, which implies large volumes of implementation effort.

Franchising Firms Application Scenario

Product, inventory, demand, and financial concepts must have consistent meanings throughout the national headquarters network. For example, product classifications will keep a unique identity and a set of well-defined properties for each product across the enterprise. Once a common repository of semantics has been established, Web services can be formally described by using common meanings from that pool. Services can then be published in registries public to all national headquarters, thereby becoming available for process composition. Semantic description and publishing of Web services deliver interoperable business services, which mean that services will exhibit consistent accessibility to any business process composite that wish to use it. Both stock management and purchase management processes may use a service that returns product stock levels in sibling headquarters and discovering and binding to that service will execute identically. Business operations planned for reengineering should be modeled from scratch and services recognized as parts should be described and published. Product availability and product stock level requests are business services that already exist in current stock management and purchase management processes.

By enabling national headquarters to publish loose-coupled, commonly accessed Web services the company becomes capable to compose highly automated business activities, avoiding thus human intervention. Services participating in a composite process of stock, purchase, or financial control are now selected from common pools (service registries). Therefore, no point-to-point connections are necessary, and the internals of the headquarters systems remain intact. Business processes are composed and executed at a higher semantic (abstract) level.

Expected Results and Added Value: The Business Perspective

The deployment of a business intelligent semantic service-oriented architecture to a multi-national, franchising firm, which requires several business transactions and information exchange, provides significant benefits to the firm, including:

- common access to all relevant information and functionality (interoperability), due to semantic networks and the common service registry (in place of "hard-wired" point-to-point connections),
- better quality of business services, due to standardization in service descriptions and publishing,
- business process reengineering (BPR) and analysis opportunities, due to changes that FUSION will bring in the very nature of business,

- faster responds to market changes, due to BPR flexibility,
- savings in resources, time, and money, as processes will be modeled and run automatically, and
- centralized management capabilities.

The FUSION solution intends to provide the national headquarters with a semantic service infrastructure, which will enable semantic service-oriented integration and interoperability, towards a vision of gradually incorporating all headquarters of a multi-national franchising firm into a virtual enterprise environment. The franchising firm should follow the adoption framework described next, in order to apply the FUSION integration solution to its enterprise system environment.

A Methodology for Applying the FUSION Solution

As described in the previous sections, FUSION solution allows the integration of heterogeneous enterprise applications that exist in the same organization or in different organizations. The FUSION solution involves the creation, administration,

Figure 12. FUSION typical application scenario

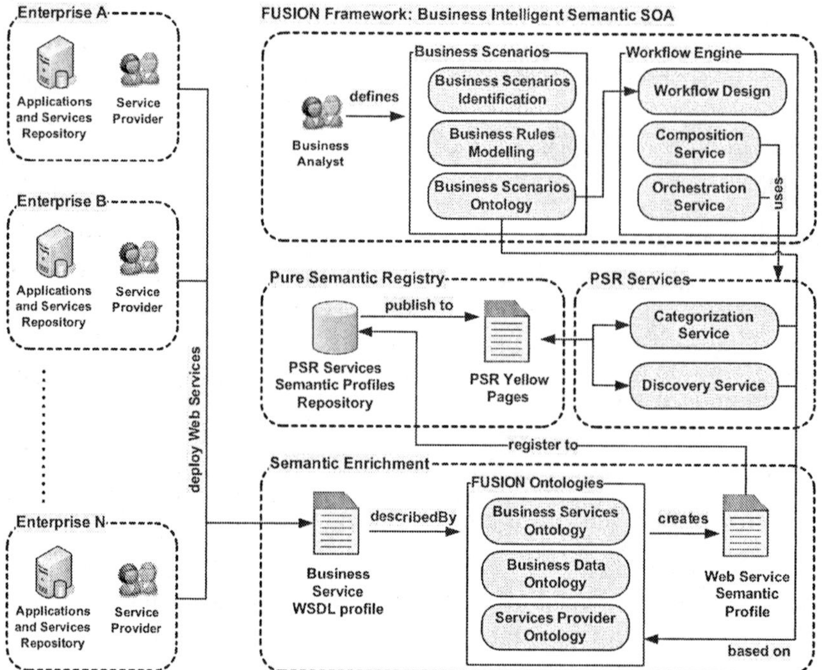

and deployment of Web services software instances of preselected features of the enterprise applications and the development of their semantic description (profile) based on the annotation of the technical descriptions of Web services with functionality concepts and semantics defined in the FUSION ontologies that serve as a common reference allowing the semantic integration of the business applications. The deployed Web services instances and their developed profiles will be stored and published at the business services registry (pure semantic registry [PSR]) that constitutes a semantic-based implementation of the UDDI specification and supports the categorization and discovery services of the PSR.

The step-oriented way we envision software engineers and business analysts of cooperating enterprises and organizations (service providers) to work with the FUSION solution (see Figure 12), in order to allow the semantic interoperability based on business intelligence among former incompatible business services and applications, is presented as follows:

- **Step 1. "As is analysis" of the pilot experiments.** This constitutes an in-depth analysis of the current situation of the service providers. The business analysts identifies the business systems and applications (e.g., legacy systems, ERP, CRM, SCM, etc.) existing within the environment of the service providers and selects the specific features and services of the existing business systems to be semantically integrated. The business analysts specifies both technically and functionally the selected business services.
- **Step 2. Deployment of Web service software instances.** The software engineers of the service provider company create and administrate Web services instances that realize the preselected features of the business applications.
- **Step 3. Web service semantic profile creation.** The business analysts identifies the concepts (e.g., product, contact, order) that are related to the deployed Web services and use well-defined concept models (business data and services ontologies) to enrich the technical description of the Web services instances.
- **Step 4. Semantic profiles publishing.** The software engineers register the semantically enriched functional and technical profiles of the provided business services on the PSR. The registered Web services are published at the, so-called, "yellow pages" of the registry, which support fully functional ontology-based categorization and discovery services.
- **Step 5. Business concepts analysis.** The business analysts identify the typical business scenarios involving the preselected enterprise applications. The business analyst defines formally the concepts and relations that exist within the identified scenarios and models these integration scenarios using a rule-based approach formalized in the developed business scenarios ontology.

- **Step 6. Services orchestration.** The software engineers design workflows that materialize the aforementioned identified business scenarios so as to support the semantic-driven orchestration of aggregated, complex compositions of Web services instances.

A service provider or a group of collaborating service providers should precede in the implementation of the activities described in these six phases in order to realize selected integration scenarios.

Conclusion and Future Work

In this chapter, we have proposed a semantic integration framework, called FUSION, based on Web services and Semantic Web technologies. Our proposed approach introduces the deployment of SE-SOBAs that enlarge the notion of SOA by using ontologies to describe data structures and messages passed through Web service interfaces. We have also proposed the development of a pure semantic-based implementation of the UDDI specification, called Pure Semantic Registry.

The combination of SE-SOBAs with the pure semantic-based registry and the rule-based formalization of business scenarios and processes constitute a business-driven semantic integration framework applied to intra- and inter-organizational integration scenarios. Moreover, we have specified the FUSION adoption framework that constitutes a light, concrete methodology that supports enterprises and organizations to apply the FUSION integration solution to their enterprise system environment, as well as a typical integration scenario that uses the case of multinational, franchising firms.

The combination of Web services, Semantic Web technologies, and SOA results in the deployment of semantic SOA architectural framework, which is based on machine processable and, therefore, usable for automation semantic Web services, supporting a set of essential automated services regarding the use of the deployed SE-SOBAs: (1) automatic SE-SOBAs discovery, automatic complex, (2) aggregated SE-SOBAs composition, (3) automatic SE-SOBAs invocation (execution), and (4) automatic SE-SOBAs interoperation within and across organizational boundaries. The proposed semantic SOA framework, FUSION, enables the formalization and the documentation of the semantics related to the interfaces and the data structures of the deployed Web services, a capability that could not be supported by the current Web services-enabled SOA and technologies.

As the functional and technical FUSION architecture is already well specified and defined, the basic technical, structural components are being developed. However, a lot of work is still to be done towards the finalization of the integrated FUSION technical solution, its deployment in real enterprise scenarios, and the evaluation of the proposed semantic service-oriented architecture.

Acknowledgments

The work presented in this chapter constitutes the core conceptual and technical architecture and framework of a European Commission so-funded project, entitled FUSION. FUSION project is a specific targeted research project that focuses on semantic interoperability, enterprise application integration, and B2B process fusion. Led by SAP AG, the FUSION consortium consists of 14 partners from five European countries (Germany, Poland, Greece, Hungary, Bulgaria), including research institutes, technology providers, innovation transfer bodies, as well as end users.

References

Apshankar, K., Chang, H., Clark, M., Fernandez, E., Fletcher, P., Hankison, et al. (2002). *Web services business strategies and architectures.* UK: Expert Press.

Bussler, C. (Ed.). (2003a). *B2B integration: Concepts and architecture.* Berlin Heidelberg: Springer-Verlag.

Bussler, C. (2003b). The role of Semantic Web technology in enterprise application integration. *IEEE Computer Society, Bulletin of the Technical Committee on Data Engineering, 26*(4), 62-68.

Bussler, C., Fensel, D., & Maedche, A. (2002). A conceptual architecture for Semantic Web enabled Web services. *ACM Special Interest Group on Management of Data, 31*(4), 2429.

Haller, A., Gomez, J., & Bussler, C. (2005). Exposing Semantic Web service principles in SOA to solve EAI scenarios. In *Proceedings of the Workshop on Web Service Semantics: Towards Dynamic Business Integration, International Conference on the World Wide Web.*

IBM. (2000, November). Web services—the Web's next revolution. *The IBM Web services tutorial.*

Kreger, H. (2001). *Web services conceptual architecture (WSCA 1.0).* IBM, Retrieved October 11, 2005, from http://www.ibm.com/software/solutions/webservices/pdf/WSCA.pdf

Laroia, A., & Sayavedra, L. (2003). EAI business drivers. *EAI Journal, 2,* 27-29.

Mahmoud, Q. (2005). *Service-oriented architecture (SOA) and Web services: The road to enterprise application integration (EAI).* Technical Articles, Sun Development Network. Retrieved October 19, 2005, from http://java.sun.com/developer/technicalArticles/WebServices/soa/

McIlraith, S., Son, T., & Zeng H. (2001a). Mobilizing the Web with DAML-enabled Web service. In *Proceedings of the 2nd International Workshop on the Semantic Web,* Hong Kong, China (pp. 82-93).

McIlraith, S., Son, T., & Zeng, H. (2001b). Semantic Web services. *IEEE Intelligent Systems, 16*(2), 46-53.

Moreau, L., Miles, S., Papay, J., Decker, K., & Payne, T. (2003). *Publishing semantic descriptions of Web services.* Technical report presented at Semantic Grid Workshop at The Ninth Global Grid Forum (GGF9), Chicago.

Paolucci, M., Kawamura, T., Payne, T. R., & Sycara, K. (2002, May 27-28). Importing the Semantic Web in UDDI. In C. Bussler, R. Hull, R., S. A. McIlraith, M. E. Orlowska, B. Pernici, & J. Yang, J. (Eds.), *Revised papers, lecture notes in computer science 2512* (pp. 225-236). Berlin Heidelberg: Springer-Verlag.

Pokraev, S., Koolwaaij, J., & Wibbels, W. (2003). Extending UDDI with context-aware features based on semantic service descriptions. In *Proceedings of the International Conference on Web Services, ICWS '03* (pp. 184-190). CSREA Press.

Preece, A., & Decker, S. (2002). Intelligent Web services. *IEEE Intelligent Systems Journal, 17*(1), 15-17.

Samtani, G., & Sadhwani, D. (2001). EAI and Web services, easier enterprise application integration? Web services business strategies and architectures. In P. Fletcher & M. Waterhouse (Eds.), *Web Services business strategies and architectures* (pp. 39-54). Expert Press.

Srinivasan, N., Paolucci, M., & Sycara, K. (2005). An efficient algorithm for OWL-S based semantic search in UDDI. In J. Cardoso & A. Sheth (Eds.), *Revised selected papers, lecture notes in computer science* (Vol. 3387, pp. 96-110). Berlin Heidelberg: Springer-Verlag.

Stencil Group. (2001, June). *Defining Web services: The stencil scope* (Analysis memo).

Weiser, M. (1993). Some computer science problems in ubiquitous computing. *Communications of the ACM, 36*(7), 74-84.

World Wide Web Consortium (W3C). (2004, November 22). *OWL-S: Semantic markup for Web services* (W3C member submission). Retrieved from http://www.w3.org/Submission/OWL-S/

Endnotes

1 W3C Web Services Glossary. Retrieved from http://www.w3.org/TR/ws-gloss/

2 http://www.w3.org/TR/ws-arch/

3 http://www.ws-i.org/Profiles/Basic/2003-05/BasicProfile-1.0-WGAD.htm

4 http://www.w3.org/TR/wsdl/

5 http://www.w3.org/TR/SOAP/

6 http://www.uddi.org/

7 The Stencil Group (2001) (www.stencilgroup.com/ideas_scope_200106 wsdefined.html)

8 The IBM Web Services tutorial (IBM, 2000) (http://www-106.ibm.com/developerworks/edu/ws-dw-wsbasicsi.html)

9 Integration Consortium. (2004). Thoughts from the EAI Consortium Leaders: Avoiding EAI Disasters. Retrieved from http://www.dmreview.com/article_sub.cfm?articleId=8086.

10 http://jena.sourceforge.net/

11 IBM Corporation. (2002). BPWS4J: A platform for creating and executing BPEL4WS processes. Retrieved from http://www.alphaworks.ibm.com/tech/bpws4j

Appendix

Term	Explanation
Business Process	A collection of related structural activities that produce something of value to the organization, its stake holders or its customers. The recipe for achieving a commercial result.
Business Process Fusion	Business process fusion is the transformation of business activities that is achieved by integrating the interfaces of previously autonomous business processes by pipelining different middleware technologies and enabling the effective (semi-)automated exchange of information between various systems within a company or between enterprises
CRM	Customer Relationship Management (CRM) enables organizations to better serve their customers through the introduction of reliable processes and procedures for interacting with those customers.
EAI	Enterprise Application Integration is the use of software and architectural principles to bring together (integrate) a set of enterprise computer applications. The goal of EAI is to integrate and streamline heterogeneous business processes across different applications and business units.
ERP	Enterprise resource planning system is a management information system that integrates and automates many of the business practices associated with the operations or production aspects of a company.
Service	Service is the non-material equivalent of a good provided to customers.
Se-SOBA	Semantically-enriched Service-Oriented Business Applications (SE-SOBA) - a set of independently running services communicating with each other in a loosely coupled message-based manner using ontologies and semantic web mark-up languages to describe data structures and messages passed through their web service interfaces
SOA	Service Oriented Architecture - a software architectural concept that defines the use of services, which communicate with each other involving simple data passing, to support the requirements of software users.
SOBA	Service Oriented Business Applications - a set of independently running services communicating with each other in a loosely coupled message-based manner
Web Service	Web service is a software system designed to support interoperable machine-to-machine interaction over a network

Chapter III

A Design Tool for Business Process Design and Representation

Roberto Paiano, Università di Lecce, Italy
Anna Lisa Guido, Università di Lecce, Italy

Abstract

In this chapter the focus is on business process design as middle point between requirement elicitation and implementation of a Web information system. We face both the problem of the notation to adopt in order to represent in a simple way the business process and the problem of a formal representation, in a machine-readable format, of the design. We adopt Semantic Web technology to represent process and we explain how this technology has been used to reach our goals.

Introduction

Today, the impact of business processes within companies gains more and more importance and provides tools to the managers, and methodologies useful to understand and manage them are a must. It is important to integrate business processes in the overall information system (IS) architecture with the goal to provide, to the managers, the right flexibility, to avoid the reimplementation of the applications in order to follow the business process changes, and to adapt the existing applications to a different management of the existing business logic. As a consequence the process-oriented management requires both the ability to define processes and the ability to map them in the underlying system taking into consideration the existence of heterogeneous systems.

It is clear that business and information technology (IT) experts must work together to provide the right flexibility to the IS and thus to improve the overall management. The semantic gap between business and IT experts is a problem in the development of an overall system oriented to the improvement of the business process. The first thing to do to solve this problem is to study a common language between these two classes of users with very different requirements:

- Business experts will focus on the processes and on the direct management of them in order to modify the company work without giving many technical details: A change to the process must be immediately translated in a change to the applications that implement it.
- IT experts require more details about processes and require simplicity in order to understand the process flow and thus application requirements.

Business process design is the middle point between requirement elicitation and Web IS implementation that is between business and IT experts. The tool that supports business process design must be the same for both business and IT users and must answer to two different key aspects:

- easy to use with a notation easy to understand and allows to gives all technical details but, at the same time, hiding the complexity to the final user, and
- supports the export of the process design in a formal way in order to give to the IT experts all the process detail that they need. The process description must be machine readable.

In our research work we consider these two aspects by two approaches:

- the use of a standard notation for business process representation, and
- the use of an ontological language that, thanks to its flexibility and machine-readable feature, is able to express all process complexity in a formal way.

In the next section of this chapter we explain the background about the concept of business process management (BPM) and the analysis of several BPM suites, and then we explain the open issue and the possible solutions related to the BPM suites. Next, we present our approach to the business process representation and we provide an overview about business process management notation (BPMN), Semantic Web languages, and about the concept of the metamodel. In the next section we explain what metamodel means and what the main problems are in the meta object facility (MOF) approach. In the section: *BPMN Ontological Metamodel: Our Approach to Solve MOF Problems* we explain how to solve problems about the classical metamodel approach with the use of the Web Ontology Language (OWL) and then, in the next section, we explain the steps followed to develop the ontological metamodel. Finally, we highlight the future trends about our research work and the conclusions.

Background

Since the 1990s, process management has gained more and more importance in companies. Process management began to affirm with the *business process re-engineering (BPR) theory* (Hammer, 1990) that allows us to improve company management thanks to the analysis and redefinition of the company's processes. BPR theory does not give a structured approach to the introduction of the process in the overall IS architecture but the process logic was in the mind of IT experts that were free to implement them.

Starting from BPR, the evolution was workflow idea (proposed and supported by Workflow Management Coalition [http://www.wfmc.org]), which is the automation of some companies' processes where only people performed process steps. BPR theory and workflow idea allow to take into consideration vertical processes involving a single company department, but process, usually, covers several departments (a process may involve also several companies), so BPR and workflow do not cover the overall company complexity.

The traditional vertical vision of the company that locates business logic in functional areas is not the best way to provide the overall vision of the company and to improve process management, so this vision is today abandoned: Managers need a horizontal vision with the goal to manage the overall flow and to understand and correct—in the most rapid way possible—managements errors. Obviously, we speak about administrative business processes extended throughout the entire organization where they take place.

Actually, the attention is turned to the BPM with an innovative idea that allows us to have a horizontal (rather than vertical) vision of the company and to consider processes where steps are performed both from people and systems. The goal of BPM is to make explicit the process management in the IS architecture. Process logic is, today, hidden in the application level and, often, the way with which this is made is in the mind of the IT experts of the company, and it is not well documented. The IS obtained is difficult to maintain. A change to the process logic needs a revision to the business logic, and this requires a lot of time and incurs high costs. The processes are not explicit and thus it is very difficult to monitor and manage them.

There are a lot of BPM suites on the market that try to make explicit the definition and management of the processes. A recent study (Miers, Harmon, & Hall 2005) compares different BPM suites (http://www.Fuego.com; http://www.ilog.com; http://www.popkin.com; http://www.w4global.com; http://www.filenet.com) from different points of view such as cost, platform, user interface, and so forth. These BPM suites allow us to represent processes and to manage their execution; and they provide administration tools that allow us to manage processes and users involved in the system. Several suites focus on document management and thus on the possibility to manage, with a high degree of security, documents that are involved in the process, versioning, and so forth. BPM suites also provide a Web application that allows different actors in the process to load their task and to work with it. In the Web application a single user can view and work with the process and, despite this being visible in the Web, each user has access to only one page and thus information, navigation, and transactional aspects of Web application are not taken into consideration. An important aspect of the BPM suites is the application program interface (API) that allows us to develop a custom application but does not supply any information about design.

BPM Suites: Open Issue and Possible Solutions

The main problems highlighted in the study of these suites are:

- the high cost of suites are difficult to apply in small- to medium-sized companies, and they require high investments both to purchase hardware and to train people in the company that will use these frameworks;

- ad hoc notation to represent processes that are often hard to read and to understand both from business experts and from IT experts and thus the semantic gap problem is not solved; and
- there is a lack of methodology that helps in the transition from process design to the final Web application.

In this study we focus on two of these main problems: high costs and process representation.

Small- to medium-sized companies may have several advantages from BPM suite because it helps to control all the company activities in a simple and easy way. Small- to medium-sized companies have several economic problems in acquiring these suites, a part from hardware and software costs there is the necessity to reach skilled people able to work with these complex suites. The difficulty to acquire hardware, software, and people make it impossible for these companies to adopt the BPM suite and, of consequence, to improve their overall management.

In regards to a low-cost BPM suite, there is another important problem: BPM suite may be used both from IT and from business people but business people have a technical experience about management and they do not understand IT technical aspects; IT experts do not know management aspects. The semantic gap is very large and hard to cover, so it is important to take into consideration only notations that are easy to learn both by IT and business experts. The business process notation must be, of consequence, simple, easy to use, and easy to understand both by business experts and by IT experts, in a few words, the notation to represent processes must cover the semantic gap between business and IT experts.

There is a different way to represent business process. Unified modeling language (UML) activity diagram, for example, allows a defining process but it is not simple to understand: As an example, the actor of the processes is not immediately visible. The same problem is true for the traditional workflow representation, that is, it is not intuitive and allows defining only the process flow without taking into consideration human and/or system interaction. UML, standard de facto in the software analysis, may be useful for IT experts but hard to learn, to use, and to understand for business experts; workflow may be, instead, useful for business experts but hard to understand for IT experts.

Exploring several notations, we study a recent notation (White, 2004) proposed by the business process management initiative (BPMI) that, thanks to its simplicity and completeness, seems the best way to represent a process.

BPMN, today, is not a standard but it is supported by several companies, and it does not allow designing information, strategies, or business rules.

The design obtained through BPMN is clear and it is easy to understand which actors (human or system) are involved in the process and what the relationships are between them.

To complete a BPM suite the graphical process representation is not enough to automate the business process so we need a formal representation of the process.

Starting from BPMN notation (and from its complexity) we observe that there is not a well-defined, machine-readable standard to represent a process (business process execution language [BPEL]; business process execution language for Web services [BPEL4WS], and so forth). From these considerations, the final goal of our study is to develop a light framework to manage processes. This framework will be efficient, easy to use, and low cost. In this phase of our study we focus on the design and implementation of a business process editor and we face two main problems: (1) the choice of the notation to adopt in the business process design, and (2) the choice of the formal language to adopt in order to make the design machine readable.

Business Process Representation: Our Approach

The first and most important problem to solve to reach the goal to define a low cost framework that supports process definition and management is to select the notation to adopt. The notation must cover the semantic gap between business and IT experts and must answer to two main requirements: completeness and simplicity. These aspects may be found in the BPMN notation: Its main goal is to cover the gap between IT and business experts, which is the gap between process design and process implementation. BPMN notation is, also, very easy to learn and to understand, so we select it as the notation to represent processes.

As we saw in the previous section, BPMN notation is not tied to a specific machine-readable format but there are several machine-readable formats not yet standard. In our research work, we explored several alternatives before choosing a language to represent processes; finally, we chose to use ontology *in an innovative way*: Our use of ontology is different from the traditional Semantic Web where ontology describes, in general, a domain of knowledge. We adopt both the ontology and the concept of metamodel: Ontology is, in our research work, the language to represent both the BPMN metamodel (that we develop) and the process model starting from the metamodel. The ontological language used in our research work is OWL (World Wide Web Consortium, 2004a): a text language without graphical notation.

To understand the following part of our study we introduce an overview about BPMN notation, next a brief definition of ontology and of the semantic languages, and finally, we present the concept of metamodel.

BPMN Notation Overview

In daily BPM, business experts start their analysis with the design in the large of the process: Details are given to the design in the following steps. Implementation details, that are details needed in the implementation phase, are given in the last step of the analysis and are obviously given by IT experts and not by business experts. To follow this natural evolution from design in the large to design in the small, BPMN notation is made up of two different levels of details:

- a core object (business process diagram modeling objects) made up of base elements that allow us to define a process in the large; and
- an extension mechanism that allows us to extend core objects and to add properties to obtain a detail level near to the detail needed in the implementation phase.

These different detail levels make the final design easy to understand not only by experts of the notation but also by nonexperts of the notation and thus by IT experts that may operate directly in the design by adding their details. So, in the design phase both IT and business experts may provide all the details needed.

Business process diagram modeling objects are made up of four different groups of primitives: Flow Object, Connecting Object, Swimlanes, and Artifact (Figure 1).

Figure 1. Main primitives of BPMN notation

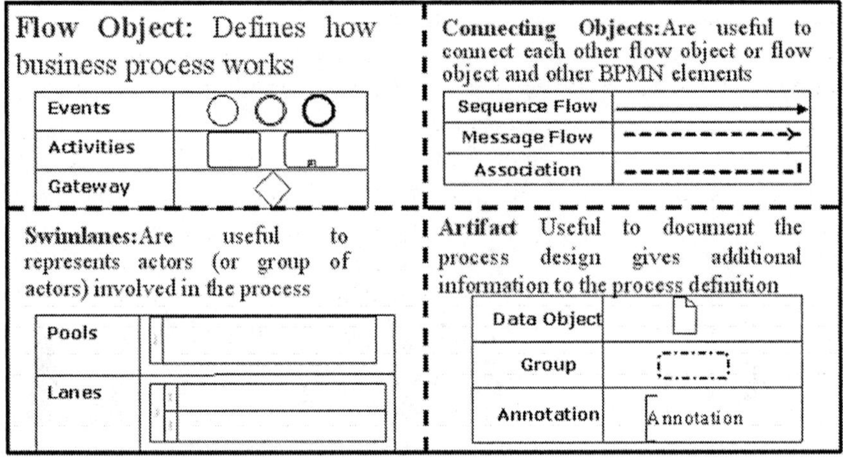

Flow objects have three types: *Events* that represent something that occurs during the normal process execution; events have a cause (trigger) or an impact (result). Different icons allow us to define start, intermediate, or end an event. Internal market (and this is another detail level) represents triggers that define the cause of the events. For example, start event may be a circle without any icon or may have an envelope icon to represent that the process starts when a message is arriving. A complete set of events and icons are shown in Figure 2.

Another type of Flow Object is *activities,* which is generic work that a company performs. Activities may be of two different types: *task* and *sub-process*. Task is an atomic activity, that is, the work not broken down to a finer level of process model detail; sub-process is an activity made up of several subactivities.

The third type of Flow Object is the *gateway* used to control the divergence and convergence of multiple sequence flow. Gateway represented with a diamond has, as events, different icons to represents different possible flow control behavior.

Flow objects may be connected to each other or may be connected to Artifact by three different types of connecting objects: *sequence flow* is used to connect a Flow Object with the next Flow Object that will be performed in the process. The second Connecting Object is the *message flow* used to show the flow of messages between two participants (participants are represented by Swimlanes); finally *associations* are used to connect information (Artifact) with Flow Object.

Swimlanes are used to group Flow Object, Connecting Object, and Artifact. Swimlanes are made up of Pools that represents a participant in a process. A Pool may be sub-partitioned by lanes used to organize and categorize activities. For example if the designer wants to represent the activity in an office and to highlight the role of each person in the process, it is possible to use a Pool to represent the office and, within the Pool, lanes will be used to represent each person.

Figure 2. Events icon defined in BPMN notation

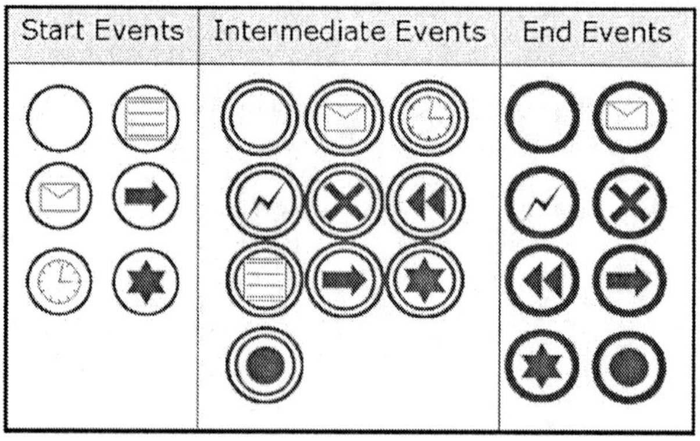

Start Events | Intermediate Events | End Events

Artifact may be used for documentation purposes and does not have direct effect on the normal process flow. Artifact may be of three different types: (1) *data object* that is often used to represent a document required and/or produced by an activity; (2) *group* is often used to identify activities in different Pools, and finally (3) *text annotation* helps designers to give additional (textual) information to the reader of the design.

In order to have a final diagram easy to understand, BPMN notation defines connection rules for both sequence flow and for message flow. Connection rules are useful to understand how Flow Object, Swimlane, and Artifact may be connected to each other, and what condition is required to connect them together. As an example, message flow cannot connect objects in the same Lane but only objects in two different Lanes; similarly sequence flow cannot connect an object in two different Lanes but only objects in the same Lane.

At this point we can observe that with four different types of objects (and relative subtypes) and following simple connecting rules, business users are able to design the process in all its complexity, but implementation details are needed.

BPMN defines another detail level: each BPMN elements has its own properties. Suppose, for example, that the designer defines a start event of type "message." In the implementation phase IT experts need to know what message is required and what technology is used to send/receive the message. Start event has among its property the attribute message that allows us to supply the message to send/receive and the attribute implementation to define the technology used to receive the message (Web services or other technology).

Other details about property are out of the scope of this work but will be found in the BPMN specification. Here we want to underline all the BPMN complexity and the different level of detail that composes this notation; thanks to this different details level it is possible to use the same notation both for business and for IT people.

What is Ontology?

The traditional philosophic concept of ontology, that is, "a systematic explanation of being," has been inherited in the artificial intelligence (AI) with several definitions. In the AI idea, ontology is the study of something that exists or may exist in some domain; ontology may be defined as terms linked together to define a structure in a well-defined application domain.

The definition of ontology near to the IT aspect is given by Gruber (1993, pp. 199-220): "ontology is a formal, explicit specification of a shared conceptualization." The concept of conceptualization is the abstraction of some concept through the definition of some peculiar characteristic; the term *explicit* is related to the fact that constraints about the concept must be defined in an explicit way; finally, *formal* means that ontology must be defined in a machine-readable format.

Ontology is a collection of terms and related definitions or a map of concepts where we can forward or backward from one concept to another in a well-defined domain.

The application of the ontology in the Semantic Web was defined by Berners-Lee, Hendler, and Lassila (2001) as "the semantic web is not a separate web but an extension of the current one in which information is given well-defined meaning, better enabling computers and people to work in cooperation." The necessity to go over traditional Web and to go into the Semantic Web is due to the fact that the Web contains a tremendous amount of data, information, and knowledge freely available but poorly organized: A large amount of information is in textual format, thus it is difficult to filter and to extract content.

Traditional Web works on information retrieval are based on keyword search and on manual classification of the content: To reach information on the Web we need to write a keyword on a search engine and thus to manually filter between all results to reach the right result nearest to our goal. Semantic Web is oriented to the semantic information retrieval, and on a machine-machine cooperation aimed to select the right information based on the concept behind the keyword. The goal of the Semantic Web is to make explicit the knowledge and to integrate different sources of knowledge with the goal to extract knowledge from knowledge.

Semantic Web Languages

Behind the idea of Semantic Web, the World Wide Consortium (W3C) works around languages for knowledge representation. One of the main goals of the ontology is the interoperability of both syntactic and semantic. Semantic interoperability means that ontology must be machine readable, that is, it must be interpreted by a machine in a well-defined format. Syntactic interoperability is the ability to provide support to a reason that is to learn from the data. Languages born to support ontology are different: The first ontology language is resource description language (RDF) (W3C, 2004c) and RDF schema (RDFS) (W3C, 2004b).

RDF has a model similar to the entity-relationship model which allows us to give interoperability through applications that interact with each other in order to exchange information on the Web in a machine-readable format. RDF does not give reasoning support but has the basis to achieve this. The three main concepts of RDF are:

- **Resource.** Anything that will be defined in RDF is named Resource. Resource is named by a uniform resource identifier (URI) and can be a Web page or part of it; a resource can be an object in the real word not directly accessible on the Web.

- **Property.** Property allows us to define a characteristic of a resource through a binary relationship between two resources or between a resource and a well-defined data type.
- **Statement.** It is a sentence with a fixed structure: subject, predicate, and object. Subject and predicate must be a resource while an object may be a literal. Statement allows us to represent complex situations if the object is used as a subject on a new statement.

Successors of RDF (and RDF schema) are Darpa Agent Markup Language (DAML) and Ontology Interchange Language (OIL); these two languages are antecedent to the Ontology Web Language (OWL) used today.

OWL allows us to provide more machine readability than extensible markup language (XML), RDF, and RDF schema. In the Semantic Web, OWL is used when information must be processed from application (and not only presented to human). OWL allows us to provide a detailed description of any domain.

OWL added new vocabulary (compared to RDF and DAML+OIL) to describe classes and relationships; it supports a useful mechanism to integrate different ontologies. OWL is made up of three different languages each of them is the extension of its ancestor:

- OWL lite allows us to give simply a taxonomy without complex constraint.
- OWL description logic (OWL DL) gives high complexity, completeness, and decidability.
- OWL full gives expressiveness but does not give decidability.

The OWL main primitives are:

- **Classes.** Classes allow the abstraction of some concepts. Each class has a set of properties (each one for specific concept characteristics). A class would be composed by subclasses.
- **Properties.** There are two types of properties: DataType specific to each class and ObjectProperty used to create a link between classes. ObjectProperty has both domains: class (to which the property is connected) and range (the possible values of the property). In each class we can indicate "restrictions" that define constraints.
- **Individuals.** Individuals are objects with the characteristics defined by classes and properties. Both classes and properties may have individuals.

What is Metamodel?

The metamodel idea was born about 10 years ago and the interest around it is increasing. A metamodel can be defined as a language to describe a model, so, to create a metamodel it is important to work in an abstract level. Metamodel allows us to describe a well-defined methodology, so, starting from the metamodel, it will be possible to define a model: metamodel provide, in a few words, guidelines for model definition.

The introduction of the metamodel idea has brought forth the introduction of metacase tools. Standard case tools support a fixed notation hard coded in tools: A change in the methodology requires a change in the code of the tool and this fact requires high costs and a lot of time. Metacase tools, based on the metamodel, allow us to separate notation from the methodology definition, so a change in the methodology will reflect in the tool with a few changes (or without change) in the code. To be included in the metacase tool a metamodel must be well defined so it must answer to three important requirements: a metamodel must be:

- **Complete.** It must cover all the primitives of the methodology that represent.
- **Extensible.** Metamodel must follow the methodology evolution so it will be possible to adapt the metamodel in a simple way without redefining it from scratch.
- **Semantic.** Metamodel must express all the semantics of the methodology primitives in order to give the right meaning to each element.

To avoid confusion between metamodel and model, we explain the meta-object facility (MOF) approach to meta-model proposed by the Object Management Group (OMG) (http://www.omg.org). MOF architecture is very helpful because it allows us to separate, in a simple way, the concept of the meta-model from the concept of the model: A model will be an instantiation of the meta-model.

MOF approach is based on a 4-level architecture. It allows us to define a language for the methodology representation and to use this language for model definition. The 4-level architecture proposed by OMG is very helpful to separate different levels of abstraction.

As show in Figure 3 in the M3 level (the meta-meta model level) the MOF language, that is, the abstract language used to describe MOF metamodel, is defined. In the M2 level MOF approach allows us to define the metamodel. MOF is object oriented and strictly connected to UML: UML notation is used to express MOF metamodel. The main MOF elements are classes, associations, and packages; moreover, to express

Figure 3. MOF and ontological approaches compared

Level \ Approach	MOF	Ontological
Meta-meta model (M3)	MOF-language	OWL-language
Meta-model (M2)	Classes, associations, packages	Ontological classes and properties
Model (M1)	Derived classes, associations, packages	Instances of classes and properties
Data (M0)	Data	Data

model rules it is necessary to define constraints. MOF does not force the use of a particular language but suggests the object constraint language (OCL) (OMG, 1997). Starting from the metamodel defined in the M2 level, the designer of a particular methodology using metamodel (guidelines for methodology) designs its model. Finally M0 level represents data of a specific model.

MOF Metamodel: Open Issue

The architecture proposed by OMG is very helpful to obtain a meta-model of BPMN notation, but in our study we highlight some problems related to the language in the M3 level strictly related to UML that impose some limits when used to define metamodel.

The first problem is about the *metamodel semantics*: It is very important to assign a meaning to every metamodel concept in order to have the meaning of each methodology primitive. In MOF approach the use of stereotypes to define primitives which are not directly supported by UML is intensive: A lot of primitives are not directly supported by UML and, thus, all primitives are represented by stereotypes. Metamodel semantics, consequently, coincide with stereotype semantics. Furthermore, the *lack of semantics* creates confusion to the unskilled designer during the practical applications of modeling concepts. The explicit presence of semantics helps the designer to understand how the modeling concepts should be used.

Another problem strictly connected to semantics concerns *semantic relationships among classes*: MOF allows us to use only two relationships: aggregation and association. In the definition of a metamodel methodology it is necessary to define specific methodology relationships (different from association and aggregation) with its relative semantics.

Another problem is that *relationships among classes* are lost in the transition from metamodel to model. Supposing that in the metamodel we have a relationship among classes: When we define the model, relationships among classes must be redefined because relationships are not inherited by the model. This problem could be solved creating intermediate classes to represent the relationships; the disadvantage of this solution is that it will make the model unreadable for the large number of intermediate classes.

Finally, in the MOF approach, each class has specific primitive attributes. If an attribute is the same for two different concepts, in MOF approach it is defined once for each class because each attribute is strictly connected to each class. This MOF limit creates confusion letting designers think that semantics are different for each attribute, while semantics are the same.

Another problem is the metamodel *flexibility,* that is, the possibility to enrich the model with new primitives defined in methodology or to add new characteristics to the primitives already defined. The solution proposed by UML (both 1.x and 2.0 [OMG, 2001; OMG, 2003]) is to enrich the UML metamodel with the extension mechanism. The *extension mechanism approach* is based on a good knowledge of UML. Another problem related to the language evolution concerns the unique name assumption principle: In the UML approach different words must refer to different objects. In order to meet methodology evolution, it is often necessary to define new versions of concepts (defined before) and to use the same name. The unique name assumption makes it impossible. The UML and MOF do not support the *dynamic classification of classes*. It is possible that, when metamodel is extended to include the methodology evolution, two classes must be replaced by their intersection: The instance of the new class contains both previous classes. This is not possible in UML, since every instance can be only the instance of a class and not the instance of two classes at the same time.

It is important to have a machine-readable description of the model. In MOF approach we use XML metadata interchange (XMI) as a model representation language (but we are free to use any XML description). XMI is an OMG standard and there are different formats according to the graphic editors that produce it. A model description must be understandable in an easy and univocal way by the software agent and preferably should be a W3C standard.

Finally, classes, attributes, and relationships are insufficient to express all the methodology primitives and so, in the MOF approach there is an external language, OCL, to describe the methodology constraints.

The Ontology Layer: Ontology Representation of BPMN Notation

It is clear that to define all business process design details it is a hard task and cooperation between business and IT experts is a must. These two types of users must work on the same project and each of them must add the right detail to the design based on their point of view. To insert the process design in the overall IS architecture, that is, to make explicit and tangible the knowledge embedded in the mind of IT and business experts, it is important to represent in a machine-readable format the overall business process design with all details.

The project of BPMI is to define standards in order to cover the overall chain starting from the business process design (through BPMN notation) to a business process execution language, and finally, the efforts will be focused on a business process query language that allows us to reach, through the right questions, information about processes. The choice of BPMN notation to design business process does not tie to a particular machine-readable format because, although there are big efforts in this direction, there is not a standard machine-readable format to represent business processes. Starting from these problems in our research work, our idea (Figure 4) is to add an ontology layer. The choice of ontology (in our approach we adopt Semantic Web technologies different from the Semantic Web idea) helps us to provide, immediately, a process representation in a machine-readable format and, thanks to its flexibility, ontology will help, when necessary, to translate in any formal language the model obtained when this formal language will be defined and will be standard.

Figure 4. The ontology layer

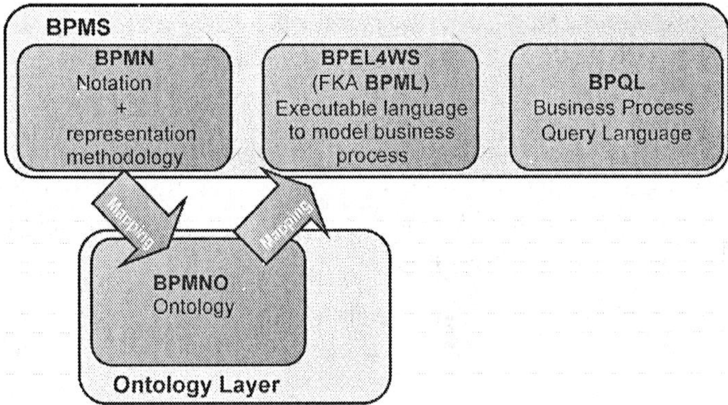

BPMN Ontological Metamodel: Our Approach to Solve MOF Problems

In order to solve the MOF problems highlighted, we look to other languages different from MOF. In our research work we adopt an innovative language more expressive than MOF: we choose OWL.

The architecture that we adopt in our work is the MOF 4-level architecture but the language in the M3 level is OWL, instead of MOF language thus, the metamodel in M2 level is made up of ontological classes and ontological properties linked together. Finally in the M1 level we obtain the model through instantiation of classes and property previously defined. The M0 level represents, also in our approach, the data of a specific model.

Ontology and OWL as metamodel definition languages help us to obtain several advantages such as:

- **Metamodel semantic:** OWL allows us to define a semantic to what we represent through classes and properties that allow us to express characteristics of classes.
- **Semantic relationship:** OWL and ontology allow us to define ad hoc relationships different from UML where there are only two types of relationships: aggregation and association.
- **Standard description of the model:** By using OWL it is possible to obtain a machine-readable description of the model that a software agent may read in univocal way. OWL is supported by W3C differently from other formats such as XMI (XMI is the export format starting from UML model). XMI is an OMG standard (and not W3C) but there are different formats based on the graphical editor that allow us to define the model.
- **Graphical representation:** Ontological languages are based on text and not on a specific notation so it is possible to provide to the metamodel and to the model a specific graphical representation based on a methodology and not on a general representation.

Our research contribution is oriented to use ontology in a different way from the Semantic Web technologies, which is the traditional one. Following the 4-layer architecture proposed by MOF, we focus on the M3 and M2 levels. In the M3 level (metamodel level) we define all BPMN primitives through classes and properties. Classes and properties are, in some cases, not sufficient to express all BPMN primitives so we also adopt instances of some classes and properties to define the metamodel. The M2 level is made up only by instances of classes and properties that have already been defined. Classes and properties (the metamodel) are the guidelines for the design in order to define the model, that is, to insert the instance of the model.

We develop an ontological metamodel where classes and properties are defined in order to express all BPMN primitives. In our ontological BPMN metamodel we define not only the main primitives but also properties of each of them.

In our approach we develop BPMN metamodel following different steps:

- Analysis of BPMN specification in order to extract the main concept: each concept is defined as ontological class.
- Analysis of BPMN in order to extract details of each concept defined in the previous step: each concept is modeled as ontological subclasses tied to the main classes.
- Analysis of BPMN in order to extract concepts that support the concept defined in the previous steps. Each concept is defined as ontological class.
- Analysis of BPMN in order to extract properties that allow us to provide a semantic to concepts previously defined. It is important to define both Object properties that allow us to link together concept and Data Type properties, that is, simple type.
- Analysis of BPMN in order to reach some concept that is not modeled by classes and properties but as an instance of classes and properties.

In the following section we explain in detail the BPMN ontological metamodel.

Development of BPMN Ontological Metamodel

In the development of the BPMN ontological metamodel we follow the BPMN specification and we try to translate in ontological classes the main concepts defined in BPMN specification.

In the BPMN ontological metamodel we define two main types of classes: Concrete and Abstract classes. Concrete classes are classes that may contain instances when we define a specific model starting from the metamodel. Abstract classes are used only to define BPMN concepts but these classes cannot contain instances of a specific model. Each Abstract class has at least one Concrete class where it is possible to define instances.

In the BPMN metamodel we define both the four different groups of primitives defined in BPMN specification and two other concepts: the concept of the business process diagram and the concept of process.

- **Business process diagram.** It is a Concrete class; it contains general information about design such as author, creation date, and so on. Following the BPMN specification a business process diagram is made up of several Pools.
- **Process.** This concept has been defined to contain the process design that is all the BPMN elements that allow us to define different steps in the process execution design. Process is a Concrete ontological class and has three ontological subclasses of type "Specialization."[1] **AbstractProcess,PrivateProcess, and CollaborativeProcess**. in order to meet the BPMN definition of Process.
- **Swimlane:** This concept has been defined in order to make a generalization of Pool and Lane. *Pool* and *Lane* are concrete subclasses (of type "specialization") of the abstract class Swimlane. The concept of Pool, following the BPMN definition, allows us to define an actor (a person or/and a machine) of the process. A Pool may contain a Lane, Flow Object (defined below) or nothing. The ontological class Lane meets the concept of Lane defined by BPMN and is defined in order to allow the definition of a Lane within a Pool.
- **FlowObject.** With regards to following the BPMN specification, the ontological Abstract class FlowObject is defined as a superclass that contains three subclasses: Activity, Events, and Gateway. The abstract class FlowObject is linked to the concrete classes Activity, Events and Gateway with a "Specialization" relationship. Both Activity, Task, and Event have a subclass that allows us to define the specific characteristics defined in BPMN specification. As an example to define three different type of Event (Start, Intermediate, End) we define three different subclasses of the class Event.
- **Artifact.** With regards to following the BPMN specification, the ontological class Artifact allows us to define information not tied to the process flow. Ontological class Artifact (an Abstract class) contains three Concrete subclasses Annotation, Data Object, and Group.
- **ConnectingObject.** With regards to following BPMN notation, Connecting Object is defined as a superclass that contains three different subclasses SequenceFlow, MessageFlow, and Association Flow.

The abstract class GenericBusinessProcessObject is the generalization of the last four concrete classes in the bullet item (SwimLane, FlowObject, Artifact and ConncetingObject). In the GenericBusinessProcessObject class we define the datatype property shared by these four classes. The datatype property are:

- **Categories.** In BPMN specification it has documentation purpose; in the metamodel it is a datatype property of type "text."
- **Documentation.** As categories, it is a datatype property of type "text."
- **Name.** It is a text data type property that allows us to define a unique name in the business process diagram for each Generic Business Process Object.

Properties defined in the Abstract classes cannot contain instances but, thanks to the class-subclass the relationship property will be inherited by subclasses until the subclasses will be concrete.

At this point the main concepts of BPMN are represented as ontological classes. In order to link together the main concepts we define the Object Property in the proper classes.

The use of Object Property in the BPMN ontology is a little different from the traditional Semantic Web. An example is useful in understanding this interesting aspect. Each process may be composed by different GenericBusinessProcessObject, and it is not a must to define in each process all the GenericBusinessProcessObject defined in the BPMN specification. If each GenericBusinessProcessObject is defined only by its name a solution may be to define in the class Process several properties (datatype properties) each of one of the generic business process. The generic business process is a more complicated concept: It has several subclasses and each of them has its own properties. To solve this problem in the metamodel that we developed, we adopt an Object Property "hasGenericBusinessProcessObject," which has the class Process as domain and the class GenericBusinessProcessObject as range. The OWL code is in Figure 5.

In this way it is possible, when defining the model starting from the metamodel, to define several instances of the property "hasGenericBusinessProcessObject" each of them define a specific business process object with its own properties. Starting from this example, we define, in the same way, the property "hasSwimlane." This property has the ontological class BusinessProcessDiagram as domain and the on-

Figure 5. OWL code of hasGenericBusinessProcessDiagramGraphical Object

```
<owl:InverseFunctionalProperty
rdf: ID="hasGenericBusinessProcessObject">
    <rdfs:range rdf:resource="#BusinessProcessObject">
    <rdfs:domain rdf:resource="#Process"/>
    <rdf:type
   rdf:resource="http://www.w3.org/2002/07/owl#ObjectProperty"/>
     </owl:InverseFunctionalProperty>
```

Figure 6. Core classes and relationship

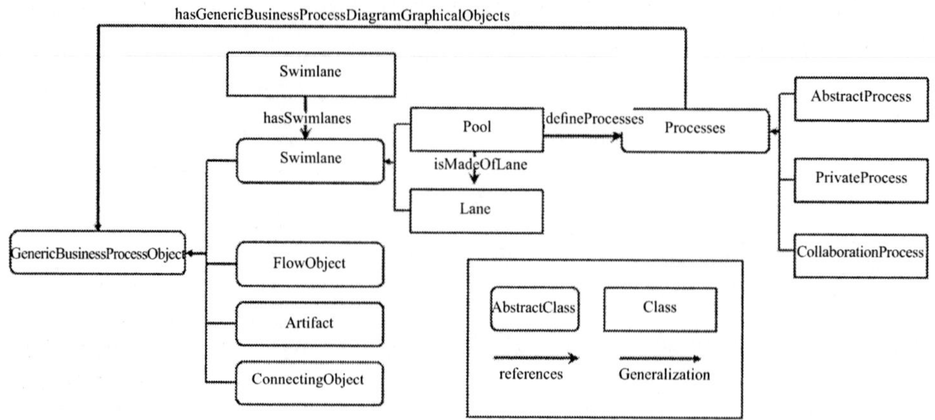

Figure 7. Ontological property belongsToLane and belongsToPool

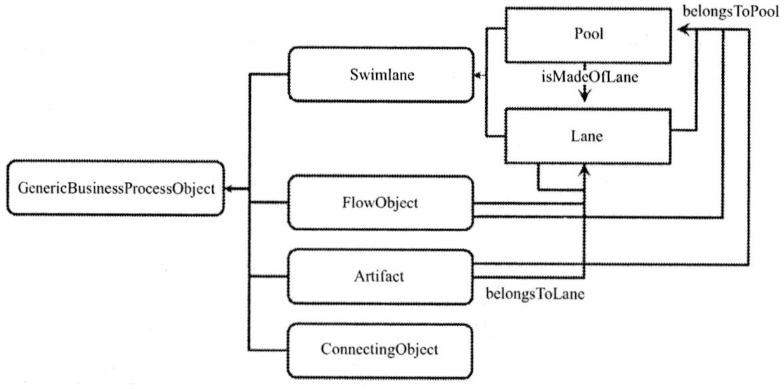

Figure 8. OWL code of the "belongsToPool" properties

```
<owl: ObjectProperty rdf:ID="belongsToLane">
   <rdfs:range rdf:resource="#Lane"/>
   <rdfs:domain>
     <owl:Class>
       <owl:unionOf rdf:parseType="Collection">
          <owl:Class rdf:about="#FlowObject"/>
          <owl:Class rdf:about="#Lane"/>
          <owl:Class rdf:about="#Artifact"/>
       </owl:unionOf>
     </owl:Class>
   </rdfs:domain>
```

tological class Swimlane as range. Finally, we define the property "isMadeOfLane" to state that each Pool (class Pool is the domain of this property) may contain one or more Lane (range of property).

Starting from previous consideration the core classes and main relationship of the ontology metamodel are represented in Figure 6.

Some special cases have been faced during the development of the BPMN ontology metamodel.

A Pool, following BPMN specification, may contain both a Lane and a GenericBusinessProcessObject (different from Swimlane) (Figure7). The problem is how to model this concept: make two different Object Properties or the same? The best solution, following the ontology idea, is to provide the same Object Property because the semantics of the relationship are the same. We define the Object Property "belongsToPool" with only one class as range (the ontological class Pool) and the domain as the union of the other classes: Flow Object, Artifact, and Connecting Object. In this way the same property, depending on the context, is used to express both the fact that a Lane belongs to Pool and to lay Flow Object, Artifact, and Connecting Object to the specific Pool.

In the same way, the Object Property "belongsToLane" (Figure 8) is used both to model the fact that one Lane can contain another Lane and to define which Flow Object and/or Artifact are defined in the same Lane.

Additional Classes

In order to cover all the BPMN complexity, during the BPMN metamodel development, we define concepts modeled as ontological classes, not clearly defined in the BPMN specification. As an example we consider the class Trigger. We observe that a trigger is the mechanism that allows an event to start, so a trigger is what allows the events to start. BPMN specification defines some properties for a trigger; for example, if a trigger is of type Timer, it has the property timeCycle that defines the duration of the event and timeDate that define when the event starts. We link the Ontological class Trigger with the Event by the property "hasTrigger." The class Trigger is made up of several subclasses each of them, following BPMN specification, expressing a special type of trigger (Figure 9).

Finally, to define all the BPMN properties of each BPMN primitives we define, where appropriate, ontological properties to meet the BPMN specification.

Figure 9. Ontological class trigger

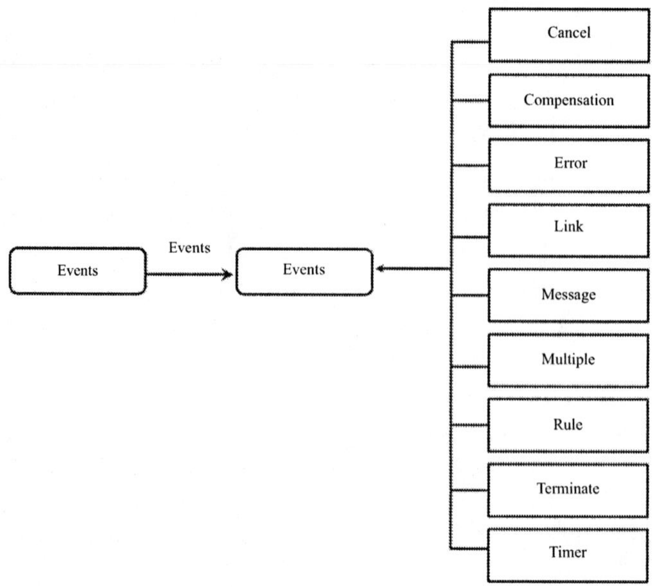

From the BPMN Metamodel to the Ontological Business Process Model

Starting from the metamodel, previously defined, it is possible to define a business process model defining instances of ontological classes and properties (we talk about concrete ontological classes). Suppose that we want to define a simple business process made up of one Pool and of a star event, one task and the end event. The task is linked to the start and end event with sequence flow.

We define an instance of the class Process and we define the instances of all (of some of them) properties defined by BPMN specification and in the metamodel. Following the property "isDefinedInPool" we define a Pool (and all its properties). Following the property "hasGenericBusinessProcessDiagramObject" (starting from the class process) we define the Start Event, the task, the End Event and two sequence flow: one has the start event as source and the task as target and another has the task as source and the end event as target.

Obviously, the BPMN ontological metamodel development is supported by our editor where it is hidden the BPMN complexity and the final design (with or without all details) may be saved in OWL format. The process representation so obtained follows the metamodel and it is an instance of it.

Future Trends

Starting from an ontological definition of the BPMN metamodel and thus from an ontological definition of the model, our next step is oriented to two different directions.

One way is to understand the possible key performance indicator and thus to design and implement a tool able to make the *simulation* of the process in order to provide to the manager the possibility to understand possible management and/or design errors and to correct them immediately. The ontology representation of the process may help in this work thanks to the possibility to associate rules to the ontology and thus to think on a reasoning tool.

Starting from the idea to define a light framework to manage processes and to help in the design and implementation of Web application based on a process design, we look to the *guidelines* that support the steps from process design to Web application design. Guidelines will be, as soon as possible, a *Web application design methodology* that supports the process definition: This design methodology will cover the gap in the traditional Web application design methodology based on a "user experience" paradigm but not focused on a process.

Conclusion

Starting from the necessity to introduce the process management in the overall IS architecture, our work focuses on the description of business process in a formal way aimed to automate the business process management. The focus is first on the notation to adopt: We think that the notation must be complete and expressive with the goal to cover the traditional semantic gap between business and IT experts. Our choice is the BPMN notation because BPMN goal is nearer to our goal. We focus also on the formal description of the business process in a machine–readable language. Observing that to represent the process we need a metamodel that is a guideline in the model definition, the focus on the 4-layer MOF metamodel is very helpful for our purpose but we highlight that the UML language used is poor for several reasons. So we introduce an innovative way to think on ontology different from the traditional Semantic Web use. OWL provides us several advantages both in the description of the metamodel and in the description of the model. OWL and Semantic Web technologies will help us in our future works.

References

Berners-Lee, T., Hendler, J., & Lassila, O. (2001, May). The Semantic Web. *Scientific American, 284*(5), 34-43.

Gruber, T. R. (1993). A translation approach to portable ontology specifications. *Knowledge Acquisition, 5*, 199-220.

Hammer, M. (1990). *Reengineering work: Don't automate, obliterate. Harward Business Review, 68,* 104-112.

Miers, D., Harmon, P., & Hall, C. (2006). *The 2006 BPM suites report Realise 2.0.* Retrieved September 30, 2006, from http://www.bptrends.com/reports_toc_01.cfm

Retrieved March 15, 2005, from http://www.bptrends.com

Object Management Group (OMG). (1997, September). *Object constraint language specification* (Version 1.1).

Object Management Group (OMG). (2001, September). *Unified modeling language specification* (Version 1.4).

Object Management Group (OMG). (2003, September 8). *UML 2.0 superstructure specification* (Version 2.0).

White, S. A. (2004, May 3). *Business process modeling notation (BPMN)* (Version 1.0). Retrieved May, 2004, from http://www.bpmn.org

World Wide Web Consortium (W3C). (2004a, February 10). OWL *Web ontology language reference.*

World Wide Web Consortium (W3C) (2004b, February 10). *RDF vocabulary description language 1.0: RDF Schema.*

World Wide Web Consortium (W3C) (2004c, February 10). *RDF/XML syntax specification.*

Endnote

[1] Specialization subclass is also called IS-A, and it allows us to connect a general concept with a more specific concept. In our example an AbstractProcess IS-A Process.

Chapter IV

Automatically Extracting and Tagging Business Information for E-Business Systems Using Linguistic Analysis

Sumali J. Conlon, University of Mississippi, USA
Susan Lukose, University of Mississippi, USA
Jason G. Hale, University of Mississippi, USA
Anil Vinjamur, University of Mississippi, USA

Abstract

The Semantic Web will require semantic representations of information that computers can understand when they process business applications. Most Web content is currently represented in formats such as text, that facilitate human understanding, rather than in the more structured formats, that allow automated processing and computer understanding. This chapter explores how natural language processing (NLP) principles, using linguistic analysis, can be employed to extract information from unstructured Web documents and translate it into extensible markup language (XML)—the enabling currency of today's e-business applications, and the founda-

tion for the emerging Semantic Web languages of tomorrow. Our prototype system is built and tested with online financial documents.

Introduction

Business decision makers demand relevant, accurate, and complete information about the marketplaces in which they compete. The World Wide Web is a rich but unmanageably huge source of human-readable business information—some novel, accurate, and relevant—some repetitive, wrong, or out of date. As the flood of Web document tops 11.5 billion pages and continues to rise (Gulli & Signorini, 2005), the human task of grasping the business information it bears seems more and more hopeless. Today's Really Simple Syndication (RSS) news syndication and aggregation tools provide only marginal relief to information-hungry, document-weary managers and investors. In the envisioned Semantic Web, business information will come with handles (semantic tags) that computers can intelligently grab onto, to perform tasks in the business-to-business (B2B), business-to-consumer (B2C), and consumer-to-consumer (C2C) environments.

Semantic encoding and decoding is a difficult problem for computers, however, as any very expressive language, for example, English provides a large number of equally valid ways to represent a given concept. Further, phrases in most natural (i.e., human) languages tend to have a number of different possible meanings (semantics), with the correct meaning determined by context. This is especially challenging for computers. As a standard artificial language emerges, computers will become semantically enabled, but humans will face a monumental encoding task. For e-business applications, it will no longer be sufficient to publish accurate business information on the Web in, say, English or Spanish. Rather, that information will have to be encoded into the artificial language of the Semantic Web—another time-consuming, tedious, and error-prone process. Pre-standard Semantic Web creation and editing tools are already emerging to assist early adopters with Semantic Web publishing, but even as the tools and technologies stabilize, many businesses will be slow to follow. Furthermore, a great deal of textual data in the pre-Semantic Web contains valuable business information, floating there along with the out-dated debris. However, the new Web vessels—automated agents—cannot navigate this old-style information. If the rising sea of human-readable knowledge on the Web is to be tapped, and streams of it purified for computer consumption, e-business systems must be developed to process this information, package it, and distribute it to decision makers in time for competitive action. Tools that can automatically extract and semantically tag business information from natural language texts will thus comprise an important component of both the e-business systems of tomorrow, and the Semantic Web of the day after.

In this chapter, we give some background on the Semantic Web, ontologies, and the valuable sources of Web information available for e-business applications. We then describe how textual information can be extracted to produce XML files automatically. Finally, we discuss future trends for this research and conclude.

Background

The World Wide Web Consortium (W3C) is leading efforts to standardize languages for knowledge representation on the Semantic Web and is developing tools that can verify that a given document is grammatically correct according to those standards. The XML standard, already widely adopted commercially as a data interchange format, forms the syntactic base for this layered framework. XML is semantically neutral, so the resource description framework (RDF) adds a protocol for defining semantic relationships between XML-encoded data components. The Web ontology language (OWL) adds to RDF tools for defining more sophisticated semantic constructs (classes, relationships, constraints) still using the RDF-constrained XML syntax. Computers can be programmed to parse the XML syntax, find RDF-encoded semantic relationships, and resolve meanings by looking for equivalence relationships as defined by OWL-based vocabularies or ontologies.

Ontologies are virtual dictionaries that formally define the meanings of relevant concepts. Ontologies may be foundational (general), or domain-specific and are often specified hierarchically, relating concepts to one another via their attributes. As ontologies emerge across the Semantic Web, many will overlap, and different terms will come to define any given concept. Semantic maps will be built to relate the same concepts defined differently from one ontology to another (Doan, Madhavan, Domingos, & Halevy, 2002). Software programs called intelligent agents will be built to navigate the Semantic Web, searching not only for keywords or phrases, but also for concepts semantically encoded into Web documents (Berners-Lee, Hendler, & Lassila, 2001). They may also find semantic content by negotiating with semantically enhanced Web services, which Medjahed, Bouguettaya, and Elmagarmid (2003) define as sets "of functionalities that can be programmatically accessed through the Web" (p. 333). Web services may process information from domain-specific knowledge bases, and the facts in these knowledge bases may, in turn, be represented in terms of an ontology from the same domain. An important tool for constructing domain models and knowledge-based applications with ontologies is Protégé (n.d.). Protégé is a free, open-source platform.

Ontologies are somewhat static, and should be created carefully by domain experts. Knowledge bases, while structurally static, should have dynamic content. That is, to be useful, especially in the competitive realm of business, they should be continually updated with the latest, best-known information in the domain and regularly purged of knowledge that has become stale or been proven wrong. In business domains, the world evolves quickly, and processing the torrents of information describing that evolution is a daunting task. Much of the emerging information about the business world is published online daily in government reports, financial reports such as those in the electronic data gathering, analysis, and retrieval (EDGAR) system database, and Web articles by such sources as the *Wall Street Journal (WSJ)*, *Reuters*, and the *Associated Press*. Such sources contain a great deal of information, but in forms that computers cannot use directly. They therefore need to be processed by people before the facts can be put into a database. It is desirable, but impossible for a person, and expensive for a company, to retrieve, read, and synthesize all of the day's Web news from a given domain and enter the resulting knowledge into a knowledge base to support the company's decision making for that day. While the protocols and information retrieval technologies of the Web make these articles reachable by computer, they are written for human consumption and still lack the semantic tags that would allow computers to process their content easily. It is a difficult proposition to teach a computer to correctly read (syntactically parse) natural language texts and correctly interpret (semantically parse) all that is encoded there. However, automatically learning even some of the daily emerging facts underlying Web news articles could provide enough competitive advantage to justify the effort. We envision the emergence of e-business services, based on knowledge bases fed from a variety of Web news sources, which serve this knowledge to subscribing customers in a variety of ways, including both semantic and nonsemantic Web services.

One domain of great interest to investors is that dealing with the earnings performance and forecasts of companies. Many firms provide market analyses on a variety of publicly traded corporations. However, profit margins drive their choices of which companies to analyze, leaving over half of the 10,000 or so publicly traded U.S. companies unanalyzed (Berkeley, 2002). Building tools, which automatically parse the earnings statements of these thousands of unanalyzed smaller companies, and which convert these statements into XML for Web distribution, would benefit investors and those companies themselves, whose public exposure would increase, and whose disclosures to regulatory agencies would be eased. A number of XML-based languages and ontologies have been developed and proposed as standards for representing such semantic information in the financial services industry, but most have struggled to achieve wide adoption. Examples include News Markup Language (NewsML) (news), Financial products Markup Language (FpML) (derivatives), Investment Research Markup Language (IRML) (investment research), and the Financial Exchange Framework (FEF) Ontology (*FEF: Financial Ontology,* 2003; *Market Data Markup Language,* 2000). However, the Extensible Business Markup Language (XBRL), an XML-derivative, has been emerging over the last several years as an e-business standard format for electronic financial reporting, having enjoyed early endorsement by such industry giants as NASDAQ, Microsoft, and PricewaterhouseCoopers (Berkeley, 2002). By 2005, the U.S. Securities and Exchange Commission (SEC) had begun accepting voluntary financial filings in XBRL, the Federal Deposit Insurance Corporation (FDIC) was requiring XBRL reporting, and a growing number of publicly traded corporations were producing financial statements in XBRL (XBRL, 2006).

We present a prototype system that uses natural language processing techniques to perform information extraction of specific types of facts from corporate earnings articles of the *Wall Street Journal*. These facts are represented in template form to demonstrate their structured nature and converted into XBRL for Web portability.

Extracting Information from Online Articles

This section discusses the process of generating XML-formatted files from online documents. Our system, Flexible Information extRaction SysTem (FIRST), analyzes online documents from the *WSJ* using syntactic and simple semantic analysis (Hale, Conlon, McCready, Lukose, & Vinjamur, 2005; Lukose, Mathew, Conlon, & Lawhead, 2004; Vinjamur, Conlon, Lukose, McCready, & Hale, 2005). Syntactic analysis helps FIRST to detect sentence structure, while semantic analysis helps FIRST to identify the concepts that are represented by different terms. The overall process is shown in Figure 1. This section starts with a discussion of the information extraction literature. Later, we discuss how FIRST extracts information from online documents to produce XML-formatted files.

Information Extraction

The explosion of textual information on the Web requires new technologies that can recognize information originally structured for human consumption rather than for data processing. Research in artificial intelligence (AI) has been trying to find ways to help computers process tasks which would otherwise require human judgment. NLP, a sub-area of AI, is a research area that deals with spoken and written human languages. NLP subareas include machine translation, natural language interfaces, language understanding, and text generation. Since NLP tasks are very difficult, few NLP application areas have been developed commercially. Currently, the most successful applications are grammar checking and machine translation programs.

To deal with textual data, information systems need to be able to understand the documents they read. Information extraction (IE) research has sought automated ways to recognize and convert information from textual data into more structured,

Figure 1. Information extraction and XML tagging process

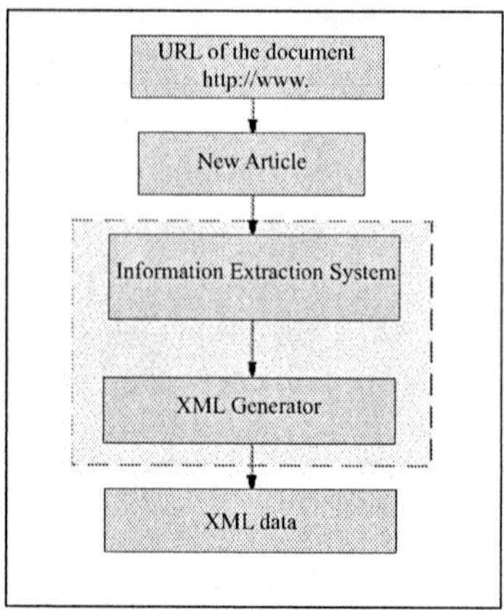

computer-friendly formats, such as display templates or database relations (Cardie, 1997; Cowie & Lehnert, 1996).

Many business areas can benefit from IE research, such as underwriting, clustering, and extracting information from financial documents. Some previous IE research prototypes include System for Conceptual Information Symmarization, Organzia-tion, and Retrieval (SCISOR) (Jacobs & Rau, 1990), EDGAR-Analyzer (Gerdes, 2003), Edgar2xml (Leinnemann, Schlottmann, Seese, & Stuempert, 2001). Moens, Uyttendaele, and Dumortier (2000) researched the extraction of information from databases of court decisions. The major research organization promoting information extraction technology is the Message Understanding Conference (MUC). MUC's original goals were to evaluate and support research on the automation and analysis of military messages containing textual information.

IE systems' input documents are normally domain specific (Cardie, 1997; Cowie & Lehnert, 1996). Generally, documents from the same publisher, reporting stories in the same domain, have similar formats and use common vocabularies for expressing certain types of facts—styles that people can detect as patterns. If knowledge engineers who build computer systems team up with subject-matter experts who are fluent in the information types and expression patterns of the domain, computer systems can be built to look for the concepts represented by these familiar patterns. Humans do this now, but computers will be able to do it much faster.

Unfortunately, the extraction process presents many difficulties. One involves the syntactic structure of sentences, and another involves inferring sentence meanings. For example, it is quite easy for a human to recognize that the sentences "The Dow Jones industrial average is down 2.7%" and "The Dow Jones industrial average dipped 2.7%" are semantically synonymous, though slightly different. For a computer to extract the same meaning from the two different representations, it must first be taught to parse the sentences, and then taught which words or phrases are synonyms. Also, just as children learn to recognize which sentences in a paragraph are the topic or key sentences, computers must also be taught how to recognize which sentences in a text are paramount versus which are simply expository. Once these key sentences are found, the computer programs will extract the vital information from them for inclusion in templates or databases.

There are two major approaches to building information extraction systems: the *knowledge engineering approach* and the *automatic training approach* (Appelt & Israel, 1999). In the knowledge engineering approach, knowledge engineers employ their own understanding of natural language, along with the domain expertise they extract from subject matter experts, to build rules which allow computer programs to extract information from text documents. With this approach, the grammars are generated manually, and written patterns are discovered by a human expert, analyzing a corpus of text documents from the domain. This becomes quite labor-intensive as the size, number, and stylistic variety of these training texts grows (Appelt & Israel, 1999).

Unlike the knowledge engineering approach, the automatic training approach does not require computer experts who know how IE systems work or how to write rules. A subject matter expert annotates the training corpus. Corpus statistics or rules are then derived automatically from the training data and used to process novel data. Since this technique requires large volumes of training data, finding enough training data can be difficult (Appelt & Israel, 1999; Manning & Schutze, 2002). Research using this approach includes Neus, Castell, and Martín (2003).

Advanced research in information extraction appears in journals and conferences run by several AI and NLP organizations, such as the MUC, the Association for Computational Linguistics (ACL) (www.aclweb.org/), the International Joint Conference on Artificial Intelligence (IJCAI) (http://ijcai.org/), and the American Association for Artificial Intelligence (AAAI) (http://www.aaai.org/).

FIRST: Flexible Information extRaction SysTem

This section discusses our experimental system FIRST. FIRST extracts information from financial documents to produce XML files for other e-business applications.

According to Appelt and Israel (1999), the knowledge engineering approach performs best when linguistic resources such as *lexicons* are available, when knowledge engineers who can write rules are available, and when training data is sparse and expensive to find. Based on these constraints, our system, FIRST, employs the knowledge engineering approach. FIRST is an experimental system for extracting semantic facts from online documents. Currently, FIRST works in the domain of finance, extracting primarily from the *WSJ*. The inputs to FIRST are news articles while the output is the information in an explicit form contained in a template. After the extraction process is completed, this information can be put into a database or converted into an XML-formatted file. Figure 2 shows FIRST's system architecture.

FIRST is built in two phases: the build phase and the functional phase. The build phase uses resources such as the training documents and some tools, such as a KeyWord In Context (KWIC) index builder (Luhn, 1960), the CMU-SLM toolkit (Clarkson & Rosendfeld, 1997; Clarkson & Rosendfeld, 1999), and a part-of-speech tagger, to analyze patterns in the documents from our area of interest. Through the knowledge engineering process, we learn how the authors of the articles write the stories—how they tend to phrase recurring facts of the same type. We employ these recurring patterns to create rules which FIRST uses to extract information from new Web articles.

In addition to detecting recurring patterns, we use lexical semantic relation information from WordNet (Fellbaum, 1998; Miller, Beckwith, Fellbaum, Gross, & Miller, 1990; Miller, 1995) to expand the set of keywords to include additional relevant terms that share semantic relationships with the original keywords. The following subsection describes our corpus, the KWIC index generator, the CMU-SLM toolkit, and the part of speech tagger. WordNet, which contains information on lexical semantic relations, is discussed after that.

Figure 2. System architecture of FIRST

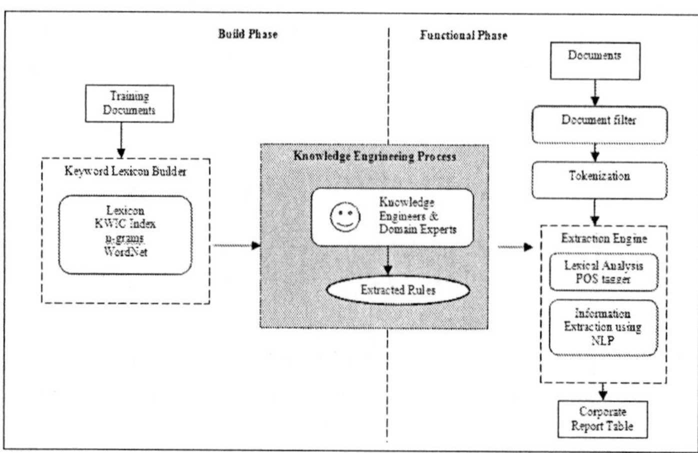

The Corpus and Rule Extraction Process

To generate rules that enable FIRST to extract information from online documents, we look for written patterns in a number of articles in the same domain. FIRST's current goal is to extract information from the *WSJ* in the domain of corporate finance. Figure 3 shows a sample *WSJ* document published in 1987.

We use articles from the *WSJ* written in 1987 as a training data set to help us find patterns in the articles. Each article is tagged using Standard Generalized Markup Language (SGML). SGML is an international standard for the definition of device-independent, system-independent methods of representing texts in electronic form. These tags include information about, for example, the document number, the headline, the date, the document source, and the text.

Since there are many ways to express the same sentence meaning, we have to look at as many patterns as possible. We generate a KWIC index to see the relationships between potential keywords and other words in the corpus sentences.

A KWIC index file is created by putting each word into a field in the database. After that, the first word is removed and each remaining word is shifted one field to the left in the row. The process continues until the last word in the sentence is put

Figure 3. A sample WSJ document published in 1987

```
<DOC>
<DOCNO> WSJ870323-0171 </DOCNO>
<HL> Patten Corp. Negotiating
A Possible Joint Venture</HL>
<DD> 03/23/87</DD>
<SO> WALL STREET JOURNAL (J)</SO>
<IN> PAT </IN>
<DATELINE> STAMFORD, Vt. </DATELINE>
<TEXT>

Patten Corp. said it is negotiating a possible joint venture with Hearst Corp. of New York and
Anglo-French investor Sir James Goldsmith to sell land on the East Coast.

Patten, which buys and sells parcels of undeveloped land in the Northeast, said it would help
Hearst and Mr. Goldsmith sell land holdings along the Eastern Seaboard. But the company
wouldn't elaborate. "Nothing has been agreed to," said Donald Dion, executive vice president
and treasurer.

Hearst Corp. wouldn't comment, and Mr. Goldsmith couldn't be reached.

In New York Stock Exchange composite trading Friday, Patten's shares rose $2.375, to
$25.375.
Mr. Dion, explaining the recent increase in the stock price, said, "Obviously, it would be very
attractive to our company to work with these people."

</TEXT>
</DOC>
```

into the first position. Figure 4 shows part of the KWIC index (the first 10 words) for the sentence "Patten Corp. said it is negotiating a possible joint venture with Hearst Corp. of New York and Anglo-French investor Sir James Goldsmith to sell land on the East Coast."

We have generated more than 5 million rows of data. When many sentences are generated in the file, we look at the key terms that we believe may be used to express important information—the specific types of information we aim to extract. For example, suppose we believe that the word *sale* will lead to important information about stock prices, but we are not sure how other words relate to the word *sale.* We therefore select all the rows in the database that contain the word *sale,* using the following structured query language (SQL) statement:

```
Select W1, W2, W3, W4, W5
From WSJ_1987
Where W1 like 'sale%'
Order by W1, W2;
```

Many rows are returned from this SQL statement. Some rows are useful and show interesting patterns but some are not. Figure 5 shows some sample rows that have the word *sales* appearing in column 1. Using this technique, we are able to find several patterns within which the word *sales* appears.

We also look for patterns using *n-gram* data produced by the Carnegie Mellon Statistical Language Modeling (CMU-SLM) Toolkit (http://www.speech.cs.cmu.edu/SLM_info.html). The CMU-SLM toolkit provides several functions, including word frequency lists and vocabularies, word bigram and trigram counts, bigram- and trigram-related statistics, and various back off bigram and trigram language models. Table 1 shows some 3-gram and 4-gram data.

Figure 4. Sample rows from a KWIC index file

W1	W2	W3	W4	W5	W6	W7	W8	W9	W10
Patten	Corp.	said	it	is	negotiating	a	possible	joint	venture
Corp.	said	it	is	negotiating	a	possible	joint	venture	
said	it	is	negotiating	a	possible	joint	venture		
it	is	negotiating	a	possible	joint	venture			
is	negotiating	a	possible	joint	venture				
negotiating	a	possible	joint	venture					
....									
venture									

Figure 5. Sample rows from KWIC index file where "sales" appears in column 1

W1	W2	W3	W4	W5
sales	declined	42%,	to	$53.4
sales	declined	between	1%	and
sales	declined	by	1%,	
sales	declined	slightly,	because	of
sales	declined	to	$475.6	million,
sales	declined	to	9.14	billion
sales	fell	3.7%	to	3.02
sales	fell	31%	during	the
sales	fell	33%	to	about
sales	fell	7.5%	to	99,107
sales	increased	3%	to	$477
sales	increased	3.1%	from	December,

Table 1. Sample 3-grams and 4-grams

3-grams	4-grams
reiterated its range 1	searching. In the meantime, 1
results come only 1	second-quarter growth of 40,000 1
retail stores, fell 1	sees second-quarter growth of 1
revenue of $38.4 1	service and technology revenues 1
revenue, including hardware 1	service lets users pause 1
revenue. "They were 1	share in the year 1
revenues for the 1	share, compared with a 1
revenues to $155.0 1	share, on revenue of 1
rises Fri May 1	shares climbed to $8.00 1
rose 19 percent. 1	signed a key distribution 1
rose by 72,000. 1	significantly narrower quarterly loss 1
rosy results come 1	so they are getting 1
said Hudson Square 1	software system, which the 1
said TiVo is 1	solid growth in subscribers, 1

There are two types of n-gram patterns we are interested in, for example, a word such as *sales*

- Patterns where ***sales*** is the ***first*** term and with n-1 words after it:

sales	declined	42%,	to	$53.4
sales	declined	to	$475.6	million,

- Patterns where ***sales*** is the ***last*** word, with n-1 words before it:

increase	of	50%	in	***sales***
10%	increase	in	the	***sales***

These patterns help us to generate rules for information extraction. The following shows a simple rule that FIRST uses to extract information about financial items such as sales, and their relation to financial *status* words such as *increase* or *decrease*.

Extraction Rule to Identify Financial Status (increase, decrease…)

- Example of a proximity rule for financial status:

 Let ***n1*** be the optimal proximity within which a financial item appears ***before*** financial status

 Let ***n2*** be the optimal proximity within which a financial item appears ***after*** financial status

for each financial item status keyword

  if

   a financial item is present within *n1* words before the keyword

   or

   financial item is present within *n2* words after the keyword

  then

   consider the keyword as a possible candidate for financial status

  end if

end for

Thus, for the sentence "***sales*** declined 42%, to $53.4," FIRST fills the slots in the templte as:

Financial Item: sales
Financial Status: decline
Percentage Change: 42%
Change Description: to $53.4

Exhibit A.

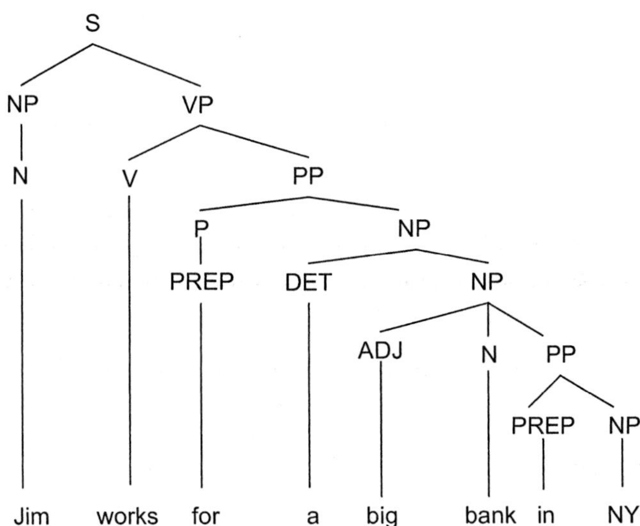

Syntactic Analysis

Syntactic analysis helps FIRST to identify the role of each word and phrase in a sentence. It tells whether a word or phrase functions as subject, verb, object, or modifier. The sentence: "Jim works for a big bank in NY," for example, has the following sentence structure, or *pars tree.* (See Exhibit A.)

This parse tree shows that the subject of the sentence is "Jim," the verb is the present tense of "work," and the modifier is the prepositional phrase "for a big bank in NY."

In general, most natural language processing systems require a sophisticated knowledge base, the lexicon (a list of words or lexical entries), and a set of grammar rules. While it would be possible to use a full-fledged parser to incorporate grammar rules into a system like ours, we felt that a part-of-speech tagger would be more robust. Specifically, we use the Lingua-EN-Tagger (n.d.) as a tool for part-of-speech tagging. Lingua-EN-Tagger is a probability-based, corpus-trained tagger. It assigns part-of-speech tags based on a lookup dictionary and a set of probability values (http://search.cpan.org/dist/Lingua-EN-Tagger/Tagger.pm).

The sentence "Campbell shares were down $1.04, or 3.5 percent, at $28.45 on the New York Stock Exchange on Friday morning," for example, is tagged by Lingua-EN-Tagger (n.d.) as:

<nnp>Campbell</nnp> <nns>shares</nns> <vbd>were</vbd> <rb>down</rb> <ppd>$</ppd> <cd>1.04</cd> <ppc>,</ppc> <cc>or</cc> <cd>3.5</cd> <nn>percent</nn> <ppc>,</ppc> <in>at</in> <ppd>$</ppd> <cd>28.45</cd> <in>on</in> <det>the</det> <nnp>New</nnp> <nnp>York</nnp> <nnp>Stock</nnp> <nnp>Exchange</nnp> <in>on</in> <nnp>Friday</nnp> <nn>morning</nn> <pp>.</pp>

Here, nnp, for example, indicates a proper noun. The tagged output and knowledge of English grammar help us to identify sentence structure. This helps us to learn "who does what to whom?" from a sentence, which in turn helps us to extract information more accurately.

FIRST uses information from the part-of-speech tagger to identify the sentence structure. This structure is then used in its extraction rules. Some sample FIRST rules using syntactic information, analyzing sentences that contain key terms used in the proximity rule (earlier), are shown next:

Case 1: Examples where financial status appears after financial item—financial item and status words bolded

<nns>Sales</nns> <vbd>rose</vbd> <cd>5.7</cd> <nn>%</nn> <to>to</to> <ppd>$</ppd> <cd>2.22</cd> <cd>billion</cd> <in>from</in> <ppd>$</ppd> <cd>2.1</cd> <cd>billion</cd> <det>a</det> <nn>year</nn> <in>ago</in> <pp>.</pp>

<nnp>Campbell</nnp> <nnp>Soup</nnp> <nnp>Co.</nnp> <vbd>said</vbd> <nnp>Friday</nnp> <jj>quarterly</jj> **<nns>profits</nns> <vbd>were</vbd> <jj>flat</jj>** <pp>.</pp>

The following is an example of a rule to identify financial status for this case:

for each keyword that is a candidate for denoting a *financial item* (e.g., *sales*)

  if the tagger has identified that keyword as a noun or plural noun in the sentence
  then a form of a corresponding *financial status* keyword (e.g., "increase") should be present in the immediately *following* verb phrase
  end if
end for

We maintain a lexicon of candidate keywords for denoting financial items (e.g., *sales, revenue,* and *profits*), as well as a lexicon of candidate keywords for denoting financial status (e.g., *rise, increase,* and *decrease*). In the previous examples:

<vbd>rose</vbd>

and

<vbd>were</vbd> <jj>flat</jj>

form the respective verb phrases. Thus for the first sentence, FIRST fills the lots as:

Financial Item: sales Financial Status: rose

For the second sentence, FIRST fills the lots as:

Financial Item: profits Financial Status: were flat

Case 2: Examples where status appears before financial item—financial item and status words bolded

<det>The</det> <nnp>Camden</nnp> <ppc>,</ppc> <nnp>N.J.</nnp> <ppc>,</ppc> <nn>company</nn> <vbd>saw</vbd> **<jj>strong</jj> <nns>sales</nns>** <pp>.</pp>

<det>The</det><nn>company</nn> <vbd>saw</vbd> <det>a</det> <cd>6</cd> <nn>%</nn> <to>to</to> <cd>9</cd> <nn>%</nn> <nn>sequential</nn> **<nn>increase</nn>** <in>in</in> **<nns>sales</nns>** <in>from</in> <jj>last</jj> <nn>quarter</nn> <pp>.

The following is an example of a rule to identify financial status for this case:

for each keyword that is a candidate for denoting a *financial item* (e.g., *sales*)

if the tagger has identified that keyword as a noun or plural noun in the sentence
then a form of a corresponding *financial status* keyword (e.g., *increase*) should be present in the immediately *preceding* verb phrase
end if
end for

In the previous examples:

<vbd>saw</vbd> <jj>strong</jj>
and
<nn>increase</nn>

respectively precede the financial item **sales**. Thus for the first statement, FIRST fills the lots as:

Financial Item: sales
Financial Status: strong

For the second sentence, FIRST fills the lots as:

Financial Item: sales
Financial Status: increase

Semantic Analysis

FIRST does *not* do full semantic analysis, but it is able to recognize that certain words have similar meanings. FIRST relies heavily on WordNet as a source of such semantic information. WordNet is an online lexical database developed by the Cognitive Science Laboratory at Princeton University, under the direction of Professor George A. Miller (Fellbaum, 1998; Miller et al., 1990; Miller 1995). WordNet is organized around a lexical concept called a synonym set, or *synset*—a set of words that can be interchanged in some context without changing the truth value of the proposition in which they are embedded. WordNet contains information about nouns, verbs, adjectives, and adverbs. Each synset consists of a list of words (or phrases) and the pointers that describe the relation between that synset and other synsets. These semantic relations between words include: hypernymy/hyponymy (or superordinate/subordinate relationships) (e.g., a "car door" is-a-kind-of "door"); antonymy (or opposites) (e.g., "hate" is an antonym of "love"); entailment; and meronymy/holonymy (or part-of relationships) (e.g., "lock" is-a-part-of-a "door.") (http://wordnet.princeton.edu/man/wngloss.7WN).

The following shows WordNet's hypernyms for the word *finance.*

1. commercial_enterprise 2. business 3. business_enterprise 4. management 5. direction 6. economics	7. economic_science 8. political_economy 9. committee 10. commission 11. nondepository_financial_institution	12. minister 13. government_minister 14. assets 15. pay 16. credit

When many concepts are interconnected, semantic networks can be formed (Miller & Fellbaum, 1991). A semantic network, or net, represents knowledge using graphs, where arcs interconnect the nodes. The nodes represent objects or concepts and the

Figure 6. A sample input file for extraction

http://online.wsj.com/article/0,,BT_CO_20050217_002896,00.html
Nextel Commun 4Q EPS 41c Vs 55c
DOW JONES NEWSWIRES
February 17, 2005 4:27 p.m.

Analysts surveyed: 24

First Call EPS estimates can reflect either net income, operating income, or funds from operations. The company's earnings figure is on a diluted basis. First Call assumes earnings estimates from analysts are on a diluted basis.

RESTON, Va. -- Nextel Communications Inc.'s (NXTL) fourth-quarter earnings fell 26% as a 19% revenue gain from the addition of 955,000 subscribers wasn't enough to offset the effects of a higher tax bill and a gain in the year-ago quarter.

Nextel, which plans to merge with Sprint Corp. (FON), issued 2005 adjusted per-share earnings guidance of $1.75, well below 2004's reported adjusted earnings of $1.87 a share.

In a press release Thursday, the wireless telecommunications company said net income fell to $471 million, or 41 cents a share, from $634 million, or 55 cents a share, in the year-earlier quarter.

The latest quarter included a charge of $20 million, or 2 cents a share, to retire debt. The year-ago quarter included a charge of $106 million, or 10 cents a share, for debt retirement and a gain of $213 million, or 19 cents a share, from the sale of investments.

A Thomson First Call survey of 24 analysts projected earnings of 39 cents a share. Quarterly revenue rose 19% to $3.58 billion from $3.01 billion a year ago.

......

Figure 7. Output of the extraction process

```
Org Name: NEXTEL COMMUNICATIONS INC.

Financial Item: earnings
Financial Quarter: fourth-quarter
Financial Status: fell
Financial Fact: fact
Percentage Change: 26%
Financial Item: income
Financial Quarter: year-earlier quarter
Financial Status: lower
Financial Fact: fact
Change Description: from $634 million to $471 million
Financial Item: revenue
Financial Status: rose
Financial Fact: fact
Percentage Change: 19%
Change Description: from $3,01 billion to $3.58 billion
```

links represent relations between nodes. The network defines a set of binary relations on the set of nodes (Sowa, 2000, n.d.).

The Output

We tested FIRST with some online financial articles appearing in the online edition of the *WSJ,* such as the Web article shown in Figure 6.

FIRST produces output in a template, as shown in Figure 7.

System Performance

FIRST was evaluated using the standard evaluation criteria: recall, precision, and the F-measure. Recall measures, as a percentage, how many of the embedded facts FIRST is able to find and extract from a target document or collection of documents. Precision measures how accurately FIRST extract these facts. Both measures are found by comparing FIRST's extraction results with manual extractions of the same documents by domain experts. For example, suppose the template has 20 slots, and the domain experts are able to find answers to fill all 20 slots, but the system is only able to find 15 correct answers. Then the recall is 15/20 = 75%. If the system finds 20 answers for the 20 slots, but only 12 are accurately filled, then the precision rate is 12/20 = 60%.

The F-measure combines recall and precision into a single measure. It uses the harmonic mean of precision and recall, which is:

F-measure = 2 *(recall * precision) / (recall + precision)

(Van Rijsbergen, 1979)

We evaluated FIRST by comparing the output of the system and the answers that people found from the same articles. We ran FIRST using *WSJ* documents in the domain of finance. We measured the system using recall, precision, and F-measure values as follows:

$$\text{Recall} = \frac{\text{The number of items correctly tagged by the system}}{\text{The number of possible items that experts would tag}}$$

FIRST's Recall = 85%

$$\text{Precision} = \frac{\text{The number of items correctly tagged by the system}}{\text{The number of items tagged by the system}}$$

FIRST's Precision = 90%

$$\text{F-measure} = \frac{2(R*P)}{R + P}$$

FIRST's F-measure = 87.43%

Figure 8. A document used by FIRST for extraction

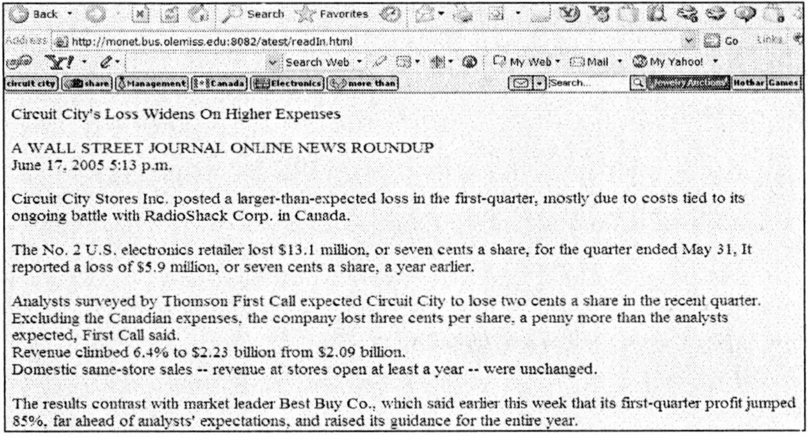
Circuit City's Loss Widens On Higher Expenses

A WALL STREET JOURNAL ONLINE NEWS ROUNDUP
June 17, 2005 5:13 p.m.

Circuit City Stores Inc. posted a larger-than-expected loss in the first-quarter, mostly due to costs tied to its ongoing battle with RadioShack Corp. in Canada.

The No. 2 U.S. electronics retailer lost $13.1 million, or seven cents a share, for the quarter ended May 31. It reported a loss of $5.9 million, or seven cents a share, a year earlier.

Analysts surveyed by Thomson First Call expected Circuit City to lose two cents a share in the recent quarter. Excluding the Canadian expenses, the company lost three cents per share, a penny more than the analysts expected, First Call said.
Revenue climbed 6.4% to $2.23 billion from $2.09 billion.
Domestic same-store sales -- revenue at stores open at least a year -- were unchanged.

The results contrast with market leader Best Buy Co., which said earlier this week that its first-quarter profit jumped 85%, far ahead of analysts' expectations, and raised its guidance for the entire year.

Figure 9. User interface page

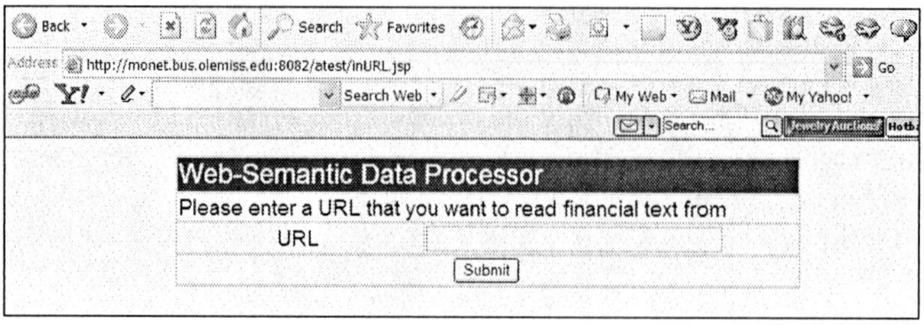

http://monet.bus.olemiss.edu:8082/atest/inURL.jsp

Web-Semantic Data Processor

Please enter a URL that you want to read financial text from

URL

Submit

Figure 10. The XML formatted output file

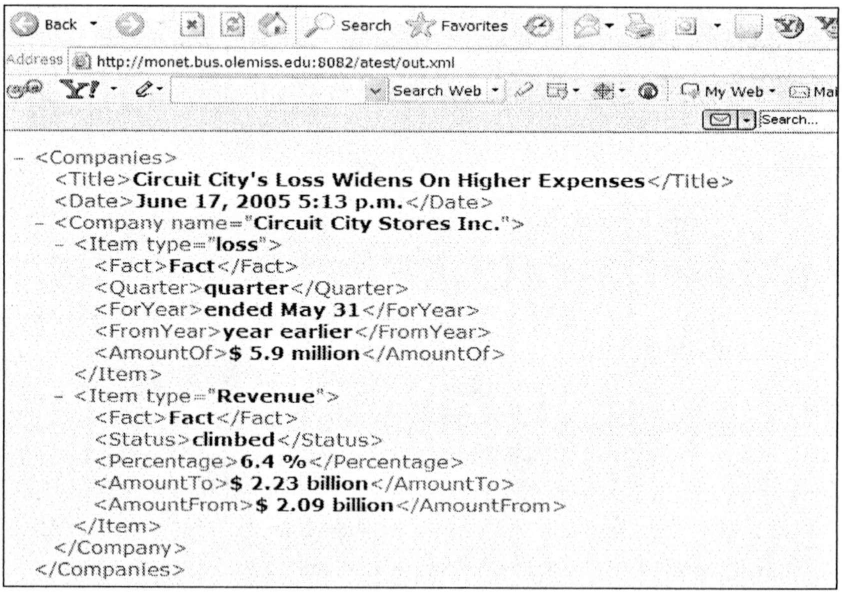

http://monet.bus.olemiss.edu:8082/atest/out.xml


```
- <Companies>
    <Title>Circuit City's Loss Widens On Higher Expenses</Title>
    <Date>June 17, 2005 5:13 p.m.</Date>
  - <Company name="Circuit City Stores Inc.">
    - <Item type="loss">
        <Fact>Fact</Fact>
        <Quarter>quarter</Quarter>
        <ForYear>ended May 31</ForYear>
        <FromYear>year earlier</FromYear>
        <AmountOf>$ 5.9 million</AmountOf>
      </Item>
    - <Item type="Revenue">
        <Fact>Fact</Fact>
        <Status>climbed</Status>
        <Percentage>6.4 %</Percentage>
        <AmountTo>$ 2.23 billion</AmountTo>
        <AmountFrom>$ 2.09 billion</AmountFrom>
      </Item>
    </Company>
  </Companies>
```


XML Formatting

To maximize the usefulness of a system like FIRST, it should extract facts and record them in a format that will travel well from one e-business application to another. XML is such a format. Thus, FIRST has been enhanced with an XML converter. To convert an online *WSJ* corporate earnings article to into XML, the article's URL is entered into a browser by the user. This triggers the FIRST system to semantically process the article. The facts extracted from FIRST are fed as input to the XML processor, which is implemented in Java. Data items are tagged as a set of companies or organizations, along with generic header information, like the title and date, followed by each company's financial details, such as company name, earnings, revenue information, and so forth. A sample input file is shown in Figure 8. Figure 9 shows the user interface page while Figure 10 shows results that the XML processor sent back to the browser in XML format.

Future Trends

Information extraction from natural language will become increasingly important as the number of documents on the Web continues to explode. This makes timely manual processing ever less feasible as a means of seeking competitive advantage in business. Such processing will continue to be a difficult task, and in fact, one that cannot be perfectly achieved.

In addition to the manual pattern-based, rule creation techniques discussed in this article, machine learning algorithms are also being used by some researchers to teach computers to recognize the meanings of new texts based on known meanings of previously human-deciphered texts. We plan to hybridize our own technique to include machine learning algorithms, to see if they incrementally enhance the recall and precision of FIRST.

The explosion of Web documents, many of which are different descriptions of the same facts, will also bring about the need to recognize which facts are conceptually equivalent. Craven et al. (2002) refer to this as the *multiple Elvis problem.* In our current work, we extract from and filter out, duplicate facts from multiple Web sources, including not only the *WSJ* but also *Reuters,* and use this information to create a knowledge base that contains only novel facts. Semantically conflicting facts are identified and quarantined until new information validates or disavows one or the other, and the conflict can be resolved. In this approach, the multiple sources of a given fact are remembered (via URL references to the source articles) for verification purposes, but each fact is stored only once.

Since Web information providers may be slow to convert their existing content into a rich XML format, much of the semantic encoding may have to be done by third party e-business service providers, or by end users themselves, using browser-side extracting and encoding tools, such as the Thresher tool proposed by Hogue and Karger (2005).

If the Web evolves as expected, online information will be encoded in the XML-based semantic language layers of RDF, RDF Schema, and OWL. Ontologies will emerge in various domains, including those of financial services and reporting. To adapt FIRST to the Semantic Web, we will teach it to convert extracted facts into semantic facts that, unlike XBRL, reference terms in some RDF-based financial ontology. These semantic facts can then be automatically discovered by automated agents on the Web. We will also build our own Web service on top of the FIRST knowledge base, to provide explicit informational functions based on FIRST knowledge.

Conclusion

For e-business systems to maximally empower those seeking informational advantage in the fast-moving world of business, these systems must present accurate, timely, and relevant information. Much of this information becomes available quarterly, monthly, weekly, daily, or hourly, in the form of corporate reports or online news articles which are prepared for the human reader. Humans are creative thinkers, but slow and inefficient processors of information. Businesses that can leverage computing technology to process this information more quickly and efficiently should reap a competitive advantage in the marketplace. Manually converting existing textual data into the relations and data structures of today's e-business applications or into the knowledge networks of tomorrow's Semantic Web is, again, a costly enterprise for humans. Thus, artificial intelligence, machine learning, and other unconventional approaches must be employed to automatically extract facts from existing Web texts and convert them to portable formats that conventional software tools can process. We show that, from documents in a specific domain, where specific types of facts appear in somewhat regular textual forms, natural language processing techniques can be effectively used to extract relevant facts and convert them into XML. Our work adds to a growing body of research establishing the increasing role information extraction can play in developing competitive e-business services.

References

Appelt, D., & Israel, D. (1999, August). *Introduction to information extraction technology*. Retrieved February 19, 2006, from http://www.ai.sri.com/~appelt/ie-tutorial/

Berkeley, A. (2002). *The road to better business information: Making a case for XBRL*. Retrieved February 19, 2006, from http://xml.coverpages.org/MS-FinancialXBRLwp.pdf

Berners-Lee, T., Hendler, J., & Lassila, O. (2001, May). The Semantic Web. *Scientific American*, 34-43.

Cardie, C. (1997). Empirical methods in information extraction. *AI Magazine, 18*(4), 65-80.

Clarkson, P., & Rosendfeld, R. (1997). Statistical language modeling using the CMU-Cambridge toolkit. *Proceedings of the 7th European Conference on Speech Communication and Technology* (pp. 2707-2710). Rhodes, Greece.

Clarkson, P., & Rosenfeld, R. (1999). Carnegie Mellon statistical language modeling (CMU-SLM) toolkit (Version 2) [Computer software]. Retrieved February 19, 2006, from http://www.speech.cs.cmu.edu/SLM_info.html

Copestake, A. (2004). *8 lectures on natural language processing*. Retrieved February 19, 2006, from the University of Cambridge, Computer Laboratory Web site: http://www.cl.cam.ac.uk/Teaching/2002/NatLangProc/revised.pdf

Cowie, J., & Lehnert, W. (1996). Information extraction. *Communications of the ACM, 39*(1), 80-91.

Craven, M., DiPasquo, D., Freitag, D., McCallum, A., Mitchell, T., Nigam, K., et al. (2000). Learning to construct knowledge bases from the World Wide Web. *Artificial Intelligence, 118*(1-2), 66-113.

Doan, A., Madhavan, J., Domingos, P., & Halevy, A. (2002). Learning to map between ontologies on the Semantic Web. *Proceedings of the Eleventh International Conference on the World Wide Web* (pp. 662-673). ACM Press.

Fellbaum, C. (1998). *WordNet: An electronic lexical database*. Cambridge, MA: MIT Press.

Financial Exchange Framework (FEF): Financial Ontology. (2003). Retrieved February 19, 2006, from http://www.financial-format.com/fef.htm

Gerdes, J., Jr. (2003). Edgar-Analyzer: Automating the analysis of corporate data contained in the SEC's Edgar Database. *Decision Support Systems, 35*, 7-9.

Greenwood, M., Wroe, C., Stevens, R., Goble, C., & Addis, M. (2002). Are bio-informaticians doing e-business? *Proceedings of the EuroWeb 2002 Conference*. Retrieved February 19, 2006, from http://www.cs.man.ac.uk/~marg.mygrid/eWIC_greenwood2.htm

Gulli, A., & Signorini, A. (2005). The indexable Web is more than 11.5 billion pages. *Special interest tracks and posters of the 14th International Conference on the World Wide Web* (pp. 902-903). Retrieved February 19, 2006, from http://www2005.org/cdrom/docs/p902.pdf

Hale, J., Conlon, S., McCready, T., Lukose, S., & Vinjamur, A. (2005). Building discerning knowledge bases from multiple source documents, with novel fact filtering. *Proceedings of the Eleventh Americas Conference on Information Systems* (pp. 1552-1558). Omaha, NE.

Hogue, A., & Karger, D. (2005). Thresher: Automating the unwrapping of semantic content from the World Wide Web. *Proceedings of the 14th International Conference on the World Wide Web* (pp. 86-95). Chiba, Japan.

Jacobs, P. S., & Rau, L. (1990). SCISOR: Extracting information from on-line news. *Communications of the ACM, 33*(11), 88-97.

Leinnemann, C., Schlottmann, F., Seese, D., & Stuempert, T. (2001). Automatic extraction and analysis of financial data from the EDGAR database. *South African Journal of Information Management, 3*(2). Retrieved February 19, 2006, from http://generalupdate.rau.ac.za/infosci/conf/thursday/Leinnemann.htm

Lingua-EN-Tagger. (n.d.). (Version 0.13)[Computer software]. Retrieved February 19, 2006, from http://search.cpan.org/dist/Lingua-EN-Tagger/Tagger.pm

Luhn, H. P. (1960). Keyword-in-context index for technical literature (KWIC index). *American Documentation 11*, 288-295.

Lukose, S., Mathew, F., Conlon, S., & Lawhead, P. (2004). Extracting financial information from text documents. *Proceedings of the Tenth Americas Conference on Information Systems* (pp. 1933-1939). New York.

Manning, C., & Schutze, H. (1999). *Foundations of statistical natural language processing* (5th ed.). Cambridge, MA: MIT Press.

Market Data Markup Language (MDML). (2000, December 28). Retrieved February 19, 2006, from http://xml.coverpages.org/mdml.html

Medjahed, B., Bouguettaya, A., & Elmagarmid, A. (2003). Composing Web services on the Semantic Web. *VLDB Journal, 12*(4), 331-351.

Miller, G. A. (1995). WordNet: A lexical database for English. *Communications of the ACM, 38*(11), 39-41.

Miller, G. A., Beckwith, R., Fellbaum, C., Gross, D., & Miller, K. J. (1990). Introduction to WordNet: An on-line lexical database. *International Journal of Lexicography, 3*(4), 235-244.

Miller, G. A., & Fellbaum, C. (1991). Semantic networks of English. In B. Levin & S. Pinker (Eds.), *Lexical and conceptual semantics* (pp.197-229). Amsterdam: Elsevier Science Publishers, B.V.

Moens, M., Uyttendaele, C., & Dumortier, J. (2000). Intelligent information extraction from legal texts. *Information and Communications Technology Law, 9*(1), 17-26.

Neus, C., Castell, N., & Martín, M. (2003). A portable method for acquiring information extraction patterns without annotated corpora. *Natural Language Engineering, 9*(2), 151-179.

Protégé. (n.d.). (Version 3.1.1) [Computer software]. Retrieved February 19, 2006, from http://protege.stanford.edu/index.html

Sharples, M., Hogg, D., Hutchinson, C., Torrance, S., & Young, D. (n.d.). *Computers and thought: A practical introduction to artificial intelligence*. Retrieved February 19, 2006, from http://www.informatics.susx.ac.uk/books/computers-and-thought/gloss/node1.html

Sowa, J. F. (2000). *Knowledge representation: Logical, philosophical, and computational foundations*. Pacific Grove, CA: Brooks/Cole.

Sowa, J. F. (n.d.). *Semantic networks*. Retrieved February 19, 2006, from http://www.jfsowa.com/pubs/semnet.htm

Van Rijsbergen, C. J. (1979). *Information retrieval* (2nd ed.). London: Butterworths.

Vinjamur, A., Conlon, S., Lukose, S., McCready, T., & Hale, J. (2005). Automatic extraction and generation of XML documents from financial reports. *Proceedings of the Eleventh Americas Conference on Information Systems* (pp. 3398-3405). Omaha, NE.

Williams, D. (2005). Combining data integration and information extraction techniques. Paper presented at the *22nd British National Conference on Databases*. Retrieved February 19, 2006, from http://www.dcs.bbk.ac.uk/~dean/dmbncod2005_deanw.pdf

Terms and Definitions

E-business. E-business is the use of Internet technologies to improve key intra-business, business-to-business, or business-to-consumer processes. (Greenwood, Wroe, Stevens, Goble, & Addis, 2002)

Extensible business markup language (XBRL). XBRL is a subset of XML that is emerging as an e-business standard format for representing financial information on the Web. (Berkeley, 2002)

Information extraction (IE). "Finding pre-defined entities from text and using the extracted data to fill slots in a template using shallow NLP techniques." (Williams, 2005, p. 1)

Knowledge representation. Knowledge representation is the study of formalisms with which human knowledge can be modeled (Sharples, Hogg, Hutchinson, Torrance, & Young, n.d.), or the specific encoding of semantic information in some language.

Lexicon. Lexicon is the dictionary of all the words in the language, which may contain many types of information about each word, for example, what part of speech it is (its lexical category), and what its distributional properties are. (Sharples et al., n.d.).

n-gram. An n-gram is a word listed along with a sequence of words that either precede or follow it in a given text, where **n** is the total number of words in the sequence.

Natural language processing (NLP). NLP is a subfield of artificial intelligence and linguistics, concerned with "the automatic (or semi-automatic) processing of human language." (Copestake, 2004, p. 4)

Part-of-speech tagging. "Part-of-speech tagging is the task of labeling (or tagging) each word in a sentence with its appropriate part of speech." (Manning & Schutze, 1999, p. 341)

Semantic parsing. Semantic parsing is a natural language processing approach that "attempts to build a meaning representation of a sentence from its syntactic parse in a process that integrates syntactic and semantic processing." (Manning & Schutze, 1999, p. 457)

Chapter V

Semantic Web Services and BPEL: Semantic Service-Oriented Architecture Economical and Philosophical Issues

Marc Rabaey, Belgian Defence and Vrije Universiteit Brussel, Belgium
Herman Tromp, Ghent University, Belgium
Koenraad Vandenborre, Hogeschool Gent and Ghent University, Belgium
Eddy Vandijck, Vrije Universiteit Brussel, Belgium
Martin Timmerman, Royal Military Academy, Belgium

Abstract

An emerging technology like business process execution language (BPEL) and its implementation in BPEL for Web services (BPEL4WS) gives extra possibilities in describing business processes. It further adheres, as a technology, in a consistent way to the underlying Web service-based implementation technology and is a perfect fit for service-oriented architectures (SOA) as they are currently implemented throughout organizations as a successor to enterprise application integration (EAI). However, BPEL4WS, in its current implementation, will only serve in a static way for production workflows. In this chapter we discuss how Semantic Web services through a semantic service-oriented architecture (SSOA) can be used to extend BPEL4WS to create ad hoc and collaborative workflows.

Introduction

New (business) applications based upon Web services are very promising. An example is enterprise resource planning (ERP) with Web services. Today, more and more vendors agree upon Web services standards. One of them is BPEL4WS. However, at this moment only static workflows can be created with BPEL4WS.

Since SOA has made a breakthrough in EAI and e-business and since SOA uses Web services, we will look at the possibilities of SOA in this context.

Today, programmers still need to make the link between a Web service and the application that supports a particular step in a business process. Semantic Web services may add a dynamic dimension to workflow systems. In this way it becomes possible to automate ad hoc and collaboration workflows. The BPEL workflow manager can decide, based on the results returned by Semantic Web services, which Semantic Web services will perform the next step in the workflow.

This and the other services of SOA need to be adapted to the semantic technology. This is our contribution to the SSOA.

In the remainder of this chapter, the following topics will be treated in more detail:

- business context of an organisation;
- business processes and workflow where BPEL4WS could be used with Semantic Web services;
- BPEL4WS and dynamic workflows;
- issues about information management;
- decision-making process, since software has to make autonomously itself some decisions;
- the roadmap of SSOA; and
- finally, further research concerning SSOA and the conclusions.

Business Context

Business Environment

In this ever faster changing world organisations have to be very flexible in organising their resources and processes. As a consequence the speed of decision making has to increase, otherwise opportunities may be lost. However, the problem is not only the speed but also the selection of relevant and correct intelligence in the wealth of information to support the decision making

Information and communication technology (ICT) could be an answer to these issues, but then the human factor will always reduce the speed of treating information. Therefore ICT applications must receive more autonomy to collect and interpret information into intelligence and to make the decisions themselves.

This implies that an ICT application must be capable of interacting with its environment to acquire and use resources in a coherent way to attain its goals. An example is the use of *intelligent agents.* An intelligent agent is software that can define its own strategy to attain its objectives. Strategy implies the appropriate use of the right choice of resources. If the resources are not known in advance then the intelligent agent has to know the characteristics of the resources to make the right choice of resources. Consequently, it has to treat semantics.

Because, nowadays, the Internet is the virtual space where everything is happening, we will look at Semantic Web technologies. But first we will discuss the functioning of an organisation (processes) and the use of its information, so that the context of Semantic Web technologies is defined.

Capability Approach

The board of directors of an enterprise would like the enterprise to have some effects on the society (outcomes) by using its *capabilities,* which will then perform actions (output) to obtain these effects. The sum of these effects is the vision of the enterprise. The wanted effects will be described in a number of scenarios. Therefore, the chief executive officer (CEO) will configure capabilities, as the product of capacity and competence, to perform actions for all relevant scenarios. In the ever faster changing world, these capabilities have to be flexible and easy to reconfigure.

Modules deliver the necessary capabilities, where one module can serve multiple capabilities. An example is the Belgian Defence. The Belgian political leaders wanted to have some effects on the society (outcomes) by using the military power, which have to perform actions (output) to obtain these effects. The wanted effects are described in a number of scenarios (such as peace keeping operations, humanitarian actions). Therefore, the Military Command had configured capabilities to perform actions for all scenarios. However, due to budgetary and operational reasons, not all scenarios can be covered at the same moment. So the political leaders have expressed which has to be the maximum deployment of forces (capabilities) at the same time. Then Military Command has defined modules which can be used for minimum one capability, but also for the maximum asked capabilities (at the same time).

The modules are composed of resources. In the process area of capabilities generation, modules and/or resources are acquired following investment and recruiting plans (acquisition function). So we have a schema of outcomes – outputs – capabilities – modules – resources.

Each capability produces one or more outputs to its (internal and/or external) clients. The client expects a level of quality and service related to this output. In a business-process-to-business-process context the output (quantity and quality), time frame, and services are described in a service level agreement (SLA) (Rabaey, Vandenborre, Tromp, & Hoffman, 2005).

In Figure 1 a capability is composed of modules, but each module can be seen as a capability itself composed of other modules. By drilling down we reach, at a certain point, modules that cannot be decomposed anymore into other modules. This is the atomic module, and it has only resources such as material and human resources to manage.

Figure 1.

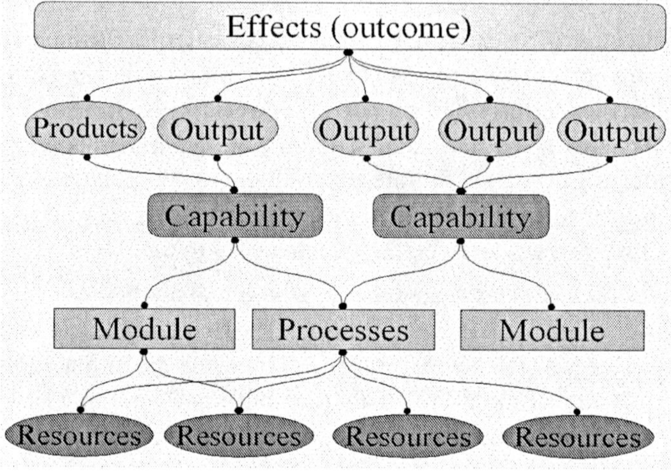

Figure 2.

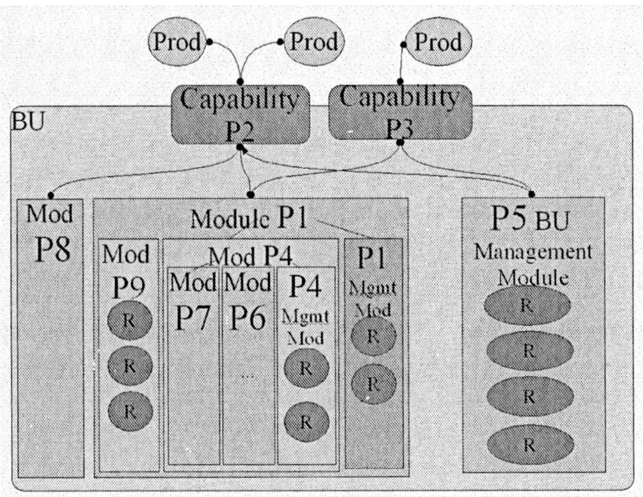

In Figure 2 we see that a business unit has two capabilities P2 and P3. P2 has three modules: P5 which is the management module of P2 (and P3) and is atomic, P8 from an external partner, and P1. P1 itself has as capability two modules: P4, P9, and P1-M (the management module of P1). P4 has three modules: its management module, P7 and P6. So each capability can be decomposed until it reaches atomic modules or modules serviced by partners, this is why we call this the *Matryoshka* representation.

For example, a Chinese business unit XYZ has two capabilities (P2 and P3) to produce goods, but not simultaneously. Module P1 (production) and P5 (management) form the capability P3 to produce a good for the domestic market.

If XYZ wants to export a similar type of good to the U.S. market then XYZ needs module P8 from a partner to adapt the product to the U.S. regulations. However in this case, XYZ is capable of producing an additional product.

Module P1 is the main production process, which besides the management module, is composed of P9 (assembling) and P4 (delivering parts). The latter is managed by the P4 management module. P7 and P6 are the modules of the suppliers of parts.

Each capability has always its own management module to manage the modules and/or resources in the capability container.

The modules (processes) are described in a business process management (BPM) tool of the enterprise. Probably all the supporting processes will be put in a catalogue called *service* (processes) *catalogue.* However not only business processes but also ICT programs may be part of the service catalogue. Especially programs which are (hidden) workflows can, besides providing information, also provide services or products: car assurance, travel tickets, ordering and receiving goods in a production line (see next paragraph).

Virtual Organisation

As seen previously, services can be delivered by external partners. These services may be the deployment of resources in a module or one or more modules (processes) in the capabilities (outsourcing). If all modules are outsourced then a capability is a virtual organisation of modules.

A step further is the creation of virtual capabilities: the holonic enterprise. One of the results of the interpretation of the work by Hammer and Champy (1993) was the Holonic Enterprise by McHugh, Merli, and Wheeler (1995). Companies work together in a virtual space called the Holonic Enterprise (Figure 3). It is a networked organisation where (ideally) every company does outsource its noncore business to the other nodes (called holons). The huge obstacle at that time was the heterogeneity of applications and computer systems. Easy integration of the processes through ICT was quite impossible.

Fortunately, the Internet hype moved people and companies to more open standards. Technologies such as GRID computing (Zimmerman, Tomlinson, & Peuser, 2003) can even make the ICT infrastructure transparent to the ICT applications. GRID is

Figure 3.

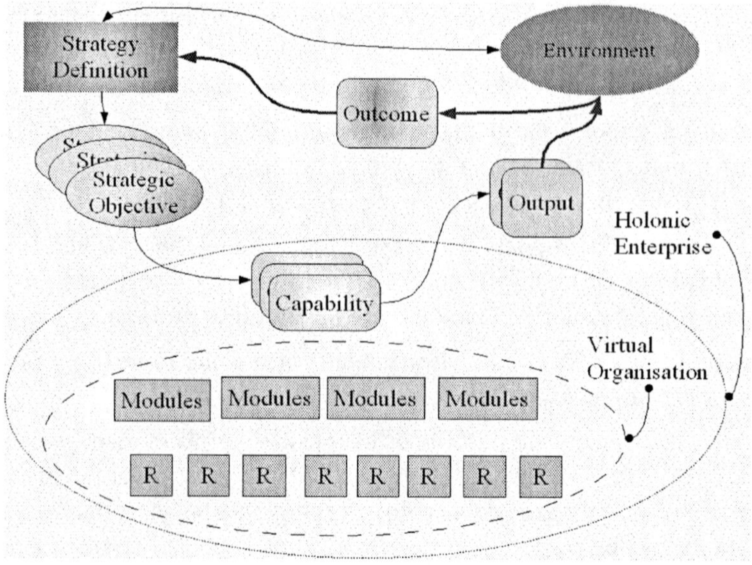

a resource-sharing technology without a central control instance, spanning multiple institutions across the network. GRID technology covers any type of computing resource (storage, CPU, etc.) as well as applications supporting business processes and their individual activities. It promotes flexible configuration of business processes running on a GRID infrastructure and therefore enables short response times and on-demand adaptations to business requirements.

So a GRID refers to an infrastructure providing the applications ofbusiness processes the transparent use of ICT services, like storage, data repositories, wherever they are provided. Like the Holonic Enterprise, a GRID creates a virtual organisation and implements a sort of meta-operating system (meta-OS) providing applications with functions and services that shields the underlying system resources and their specific implementation technology.

Regarding the ICT applications themselves, we may introduce SOA. SOA suits well to support the capability approach. The main purpose of SOA is to detect discrete functions contained in enterprise applications and to organise them along with new functions (building blocks) into services that will be used by the business processes, discussed in the next point. A service may be information or a decision providing function or a workflow. The latter is also presented as an automated business process, therefore an application and as already mentioned, ICT programs can also be modules (services catalogue).

Business Processes

Strategy

Regarding the military (Bernard, 1976; Liddell Hart, 1991), *grand strategy* is the art to combine resources of an organisation to attain its objectives. This is determined by the first principle of the Art of War, being the balance between objectives and resources. If a company uses too many resources to attain the objectives, then it is not efficient. If too few resources are used, then the company will not be effective and it will not attain its objectives.

As a result of the balance between goals and means, two types of strategy will be derived from the grand strategy: the *business strategy* and the *resources strategy*. Examples of resources are human resources, financial resources, and ICT.

The business strategy will define strategic objectives that have to be attained by the (core) business units through their processes. Linked to these strategic objectives are the key performance indicators (KPI). The balanced scorecard (BSC) created by Kaplan and Norton (1996) is an efficient management tool to communicate the strategy in the organisation and to collect the feedback of that strategy by exploiting the KPI (Rabaey, 2005).

The strategy itself is realised by business processes. These processes may belong to one or more organisations.

Processes

Rabaey, Hoffman, and Vandenborre (2004) define a business process as a logical set of activities that consumes resources to attain its objectives. In the organisation of the business processes, we have the second alignment of goals and means. The resource managers and the business unit managers will discuss the operational use of resources (organisation) in an interdisciplinary forum; interdisciplinary because of the multitude of functional domains (Rabaey, 2004a). The result is the providing of the resources and their service levels (SLA).

From a business perspective, a resource or service provider will be evaluated on the delivery of the service (SLA) and the quality of service (QoS). Thus the BSC of the resource or service provider (strategy) will hold strategic objectives focused on the SLA (Rabaey, 2004b).

Anyhow, the deployment of resources in a business process is the result of a decision process (of the interdisciplinary forum). If software must be able to choose and to deploy itself the resources and the modules of its capability (see the *Capability Approach* section), then it must be capable to understand the characteristics and the purposes to attain its imposed objectives.

Rabaey, Leclercq, Vandijck, Hoffman, and Timmerman (2005b) give an example when they conceptually describes a system to simulate the capabilities generation and operational use of these capabilities based on intelligent agents. The characteristics of the resources modules are defined in a *knowledge base,* which the intelligent agents can query. These agents interact with each other until a certain number of scenarios are defined (optimisation of the capabilities generation within budget restrictions).

Workflow

Automating partly or totally a business process was first done by a workflow system. Before discussing BPEL4WS or BPEL in the context of SOA, workflow is looked at in more detail.

Kobielus (1997) defines a *workflow* as "the flow of information and control in a business process" (p. 32). Plesums (2002) adds explicitly the ICT aspects to the workflow definition: "In the last 15 years or so we finally have developed tools to not only do the work, but to manage the workflow. More than just procedural documents, that workflow process is defined formally in the workflow computer system. The process is managed by a computer program that assigns the work, passes it on, and tracks its progress" (p. 19).

The Workflow Management Council (WfMC, 1995) states: "Workflow is concerned with the automation of procedures where documents, information or tasks are passed between participants according to a defined set of rules to achieve, or contribute to, an overall business goal. Whilst workflow may be manually organised, in practice most workflow is normally organised within the context of an IT system to provide computerised support for the procedural automation" (p. 6), and therefore WfMC defines workflow as "The computerised facilitation or automation of a business process, in whole or part" (p. 6), and a workflow system as "A system that completely defines, manages and executes workflow through the execution of software whose order of execution is driven by a computer representation of the workflow logic" (p. 6).

Workflow systems are often related to business process reengineering (BPR) because of the fundamental rethinking of business processes with ICT. Riempp (1998) starts from these optimised processes to the execution of the workflows (pp. 47-52). (See Figure 4.)

The optimised business processes are often represented through a graphical business process model. However the BPM tools do not only "draw" the business processes but add management attributes to the business processes and their business process steps, such as the needed competence to execute an activity, or the used ICT applications.

Figure 4. (Source: Riempp, 1998, pp. 47-52)

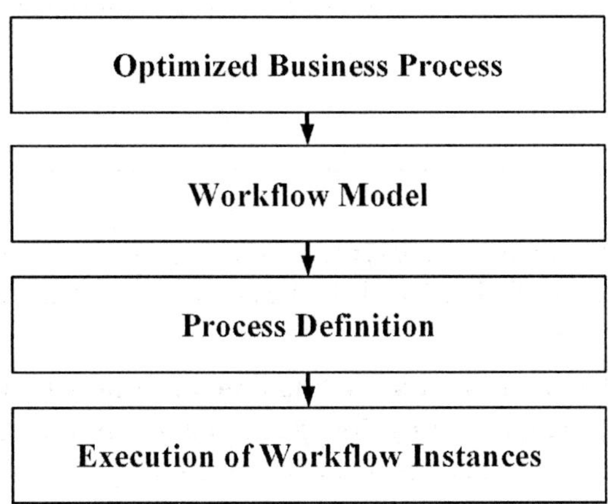

Figure 5. (Source: Riempp, 1998, p. 52)

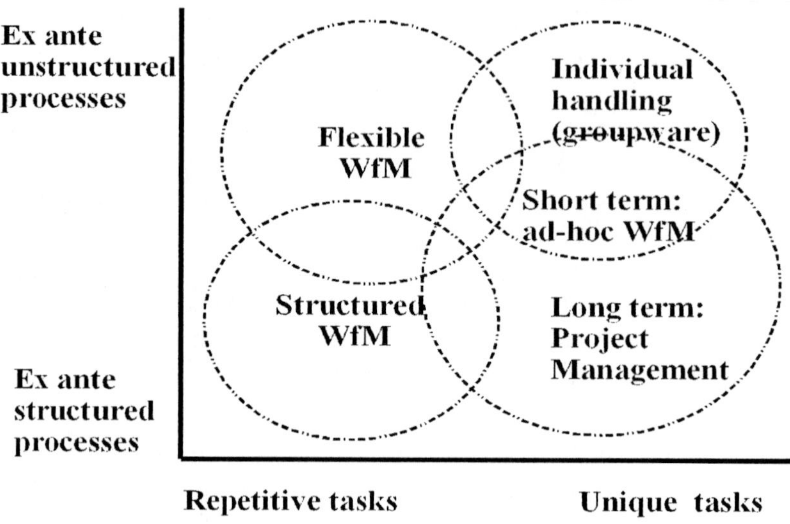

The workflow model is derived from the business process model. Mostly it is described in a formal (graphical) language. In this way the business process is defined in the workflow system and is ready to be executed if it is instantiated.

Different types of workflows exist (Plesums, 2002; Rabaey, Vandijck, & Tromp, 2003; Riempp, 1998). The first type is the ad hoc or collaborative workflow and is characterised by negotiation, and a new workflow is defined for each use.

The second type is the production workflow. A production workflow is predefined (ex ante structured) and prioritised. It is mostly linked to customised ICT applications. Thus it supports high volumes and there are no negotiations about who will do the work or how it will be handled.

The third type is the administrative workflow, and it is a cross between the ad hoc and the productive workflow with lower transaction rates and form-based, recurrent processes.

So we have unstructured and structured workflows to do unique or repetitive tasks. Riempp (1998) depicts (see Figure 5) the management categories of unstructured versus structured processes (workflows) on one axis and repetitive versus unique tasks on another (p. 52).

Regarding the unique tasks, for the ex ante structured processes Riempp (1998) defines project management. The less structured is the individual handling, where groupware can be used. The ad hoc workflow management (WfM) is in between.

For repetitive tasks, the production and administrative workflows are designated concerning the ex ante structured processes (structured WfM). Flexible workflow management has no type. In this case usually an ad hoc WfM is used to quickly build workflows, which are later transformed into structured workflow types.

Organising the resources and modules in a capability is at the tactical level, as is the designing of the workflows. The steering and the executing of the workflows are at the operative level. In the situation of ex ante structured processes no collaboration issues exist, nor do decisions have to be made.

The opposite case is the situation of ex ante unstructured processes. Although the WfMC (1995) writes that "documents, information or tasks are passed between participants according to a defined set of rules" (p. 6) in a workflow, decisions need to be made to choose the next step in the workflow.

The mentioned rules concern "the execution of software whose order of execution is driven by a computer representation of the workflow logic" (WfMC, 1995, p. 6). The rules are applied to the metadata and some attributes of the workflow objects.

In an ex ante unstructured process the next step is decided by the performer of the current step. When the performer is a human being then he has to know the (business) rules which have to be applied in that particular case. If we would like to automate the workflow (process) then we need to substitute the human for a software program. Therefore, it must have the knowledge to analyse the context to decide which will be the next step. Without semantics, the software can only decide at a syntactical level, not at the knowledge level.

So no semantic issues can be treated in the higher defined framework of the WfMC, however if software has to resolve the problems related to the ex ante unstructured processes, then semantics have to be taken into account.

Business Process Execution Language

From a business perspective, Web services can be viewed as the latest, dynamic stage in the e-business evolution, but also as a simple low-cost enterprise application vehicle supporting the cross platform sharing of functions and data (Zimmerman et al., 2003). The greatest advantage in the business and technical domains is that either party can continue to use his/her own technology without being influenced by the technology of the other parties. Existing skills and assets can be fully leveraged; implying that the investments in the organisation of processes and the used are safe (Rabaey et al., 2003). This is the case for operative collaboration, but business integration on the strategic and tactical level implies, nevertheless, considerable changes in the business and resources strategy (Rabaey, Vandenborre, et al., 2005).

By using a universal communication medium (Internet, extranet) and an integration system, a company can attract additional partners (customers, suppliers, government, etc.) and improve its organisational effectiveness and efficiency (Barry, 2003) in a SOA environment (see also http://www.service-architecture.com). As a matter of fact, Web services make it possible to exchange data and to participate in business processes between companies as well as different business units within the same company.

A Web service can also be the interface between an application and the so-called executable workflows. BPEL4WS is the main effort in this domain.

The BPEL4WS or BPEL is an extensible markup language (XML)-based language for the formal specification of business processes, where each step in the business process is executed by a Web service (Barry, 2003; Rabaey et al., 2003). But the BPEL itself is also a Web service, meaning that a Web service can not only be a procedure or activity, but also a real business process with long cycle transactions. So, in the services catalogue not only business processes are registered, but also Web services (see the *Capability Approach* section).

Rabaey et al. (2003) state that the vision behind high-level description languages such as BPEL4WS, is the paradigm shift from distributed computing to distributed business process execution. BPEL4WS is an XML-based standard, which enables users to specify processes as an aggregation of Web services. The service flows define the order of activities, where a flow is a directed graph representing activities as nodes and interactions as links connecting the nodes. The activity implementations are described via Web services description language (WSDL) port types.

With BPEL4WS, generic (abstract) processes can be defined that contain empty activities. The work on the business process definition can therefore be separated from its implementation (in analogy with the object-oriented paradigm).

So if we look at the higher mentioned definition of a business process as a set of logically connected activities to attain a certain objective, then Web services can represent these activities or can be this executable business process, which can be internal to one organisation or can span several organisations.

Cross Border Business Collaboration

Doshi, Goodwin, Akkiraju, and Verma (2005) state that since SOAs are more widely deployed, it will become more common to use Web services to link both intra-enterprise and inter-enterprise to attain the common business objectives (business process integration and management [BPIM]).

Rabaey, Vandenborre, et al. (2005) goes into more detail on the consequences of business integration on the business and resources strategy. Since the capability approach is used, it becomes more and more difficult to determine to which enterprise a capability belongs. The borders are those of the capability. Moreover, with the holonic enterprise collaboration is preferred above integration. Therefore, we propose the term cross border business collaboration (XBC).

Dynamic Workflows

Semantic Web

With the increasing introduction of SOA in enterprises and government organisations, there will be a lot of BPEL available on the Internet. As a consequence, the number of Web services will exponentially grow. Similar to Web pages, it will become more and more difficult to discover the right Web service (BPEL); so some intelligence will be needed to help the applications or the people to find the Web services that are required.

The solution for the problems with the Web pages is the Semantic Web. It is the representation of data on the World Wide Web. It is based on the resource description framework (RDF), which integrates a variety of applications using XML for syntax and uniform resource identifier (URI)s for naming (see http://www.w3.org/2001/sw).

The idea behind the Semantic Web is to make the Web as intelligent as possible. Therefore, the Semantic Web uses technologies such as RDF, agents, and databases. Rabaey et al. (2003) introduces business intelligent agents (BIA) to aid users or applications to choose the best Web service, so these Web services are classic Web services, not Semantic Web services.

Intelligent Agents

Knapik and Johnson (1998) quote Atkinson: "Intelligent Agents are software entities that carry out some set of operations on behalf of a user or another program with some degree of independence or autonomy, and in so doing, employ some knowledge or representation of the user's goals or desires." Another quote of them is about a generic operation definition (of Majewski). An intelligent agent (IA) should have:

- **Autonomy:** Agents operate without the direct interaction of humans or others, and have some kind of control of their internal state.
- **Social ability:** Agents interact with other agents (and possibly humans) via some kind of agent communication language.

- **Reactivity:** Agents perceive their environment and respond in a timely fashion to changes that occur in it.
- **Proactivity:** Agents do not simply act in response to their environment; they are able to exhibit goal-directed behaviour by taking the initiative (For ethical reasons, some authors as Murch and Johnson [1998] do not accept that intelligent agents are self-motivating.).

Business Intelligent Agents

Related to business processes, intelligent agents act and react to their environment, which in this case is the *business context*, which Rabaey et al. (2003) calls BIAs. A program (or another intelligent agent) or a human (through a Web application) can activate the BIA. In the first situation, the BIA can work autonomously; in the other situation, it will assist a human in the selection and handling of the Web services.

BIA can be used to perform a business process or a part of a process, but business processes imply business transactions. The BIA should not only be able to build up *transactions* but also resolve the problems of stopping an ongoing, not fully terminated transaction just like BPEL4WS.

The business context can be described in an enterprise knowledge management system (Rabaey et al., 2005b). Agents can be used to manage internally the gained knowledge. Yoon, Broome, Sing, and Guimaraes (2005) propose a system of intelligent agents where one is a supervisor who controls the information flow between the sensors and the agents responsible for the knowledge management.

Regarding Web services, Maamar, Sheng, and Benatalah (2003) propose a system of interleaving Web services, meaning that the composition and execution of Web services may be done in parallel. As a consequence, this allows handling the execution of context of the Web service (dynamic information). They use intelligent agent software to implement this capability, and by doing this, Web services can delegate their work to each other. Recently Mateos, Zunino, and Campo (2005) discussed the use of MoviLog for developing intelligent agents that interact with Web services (see next point).

Research has also been done to *dynamically* bind Web services, so that Web services provide clients with run time information that is pertinent to its execution and business logic. When faced with multiple service providers who can provide the same functional service, the client can dynamically select the current best service provider for its required service, according to the client's constraints and information gathered about the service providers at run time (Padovitz, Krishnaswmy, & Loke, 2003).

Besides working with Web services, the BIA must work with nonWeb services programs. This implies that the BIA must be capable of generating another type of agent, which interfaces with those systems. In the other way, the BIA is also a service for other programs, so it can publish its services just as Web services. In that case the BIA has to generate another agent that will be responsible for the publishing and handling of Web services requests.

BIA and Semantics

The BIA may not only be able to choose the best Web service but it can also chain up different Web services to a workflow. Opposite to BPEL4WS, BIA can design *dynamic workflows*.

But Doshi et al. (2005) discuss the problems of working with Web services in the case of dynamic workflow composition. Doshi et al. state that the advent of Web services has made automated workflow composition relevant to Web-based applications. One technique is the artificial intelligence (AI)-based classical planning. However, workflows generated in this way suffer from the paradoxical assumption of deterministic behaviour of Web services, then requiring the additional overhead of operative monitoring to recover from unexpected behaviour of services due to service failures, and the dynamic nature of real-world environments. Doshi et al. propose a solution based on Markov decision processes (demonstrated with a supply chain scenario).

Indeed with the classic Web services, BIA will be confronted with semantic issues. It is preferable that the detected Web services are provided with semantic capabilities. Hausmann, Heckel, and Lohmann (2005) propose a model-based development of Web service descriptions wherein *ontologies* are combined with a unified modelling language (UML)-based description of the service. This should enable a precise matching concept, so that the formation of ad hoc collaborations on a global scale is rendered possible.

Recently Mateos et al. (2005) discussed the use of MoviLog for developing intelligent agents that interact with Web services. Mateos et al. are extending MoviLog to handle ontologies written in DARPA Agent Markup Language + Ontology Inference Layer (DAML+OIL) a Web resource description language that extends RDF.

Regarding the use of intelligent agents and Semantic Web services, a lot of research has to be done. Hopefully, the results of this research will be generally accepted, so that people can focus on the business context and not on useless Babel-like confusion.

Until now the focus has been on processes, workflows, and the possible use of Web services or intelligent agents to render the processes more dynamic and flexible. However, ICT treats also another aspect of the organisation: information.

Figure 6.

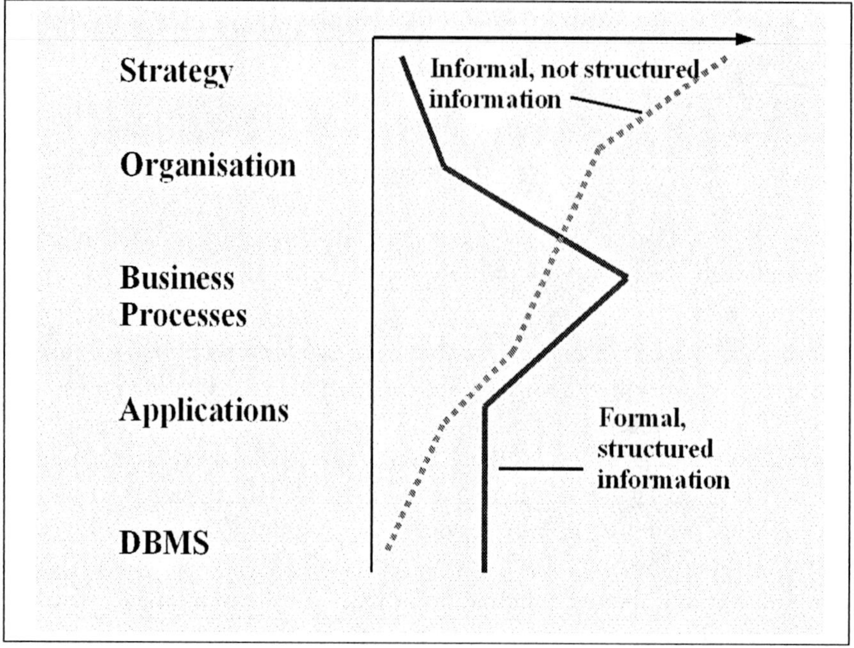

Embedded Information System

Information

Organisations and their processes cannot function without information. To determine the strategy, an organisation will bring its means and its goals in balance (Bernard, 1976; Liddell Hart, 1991). Therefore it will seek a permanent way for information that can be transformed to intelligence (analysed and integrated information needed for a decision process (Rabaey, 2005). This strategy is then deployed throughout the organisation to the processes. As already treated, processes are the modules which form the capabilities to produce the output (see Figure 6).

An information system supports the information housekeeping of the organisation and its processes. "The term 'information system' means a discrete set of information resources organized for the collection, processing, maintenance, transmission, and dissemination of information, in accordance with defined procedures, whether automated or manual" (U.S. Office of Management & Budget [OMB], 1996).

Instead of exchanging information between processes and managing these processes, the automation of an information system into applications tend to facilitate the

Coventry University

Lanchester Library

Tel 02476 887575

Borrowed Items 28/02/2013 12:49

XXXX1234

Item Title	Due Date
38001003979584	
* E-business	21/03/2013
38001005075852	
* The real business of web de	21/03/2013
38001004335059	
* Doing eBusiness	21/03/2013
38001005456979	
* Semantic web technologies	21/03/2013

Amount Outstanding : £1.20

* Indicates items borrowed today

Thankyou

www.coventry.ac.uk

Figure 7.

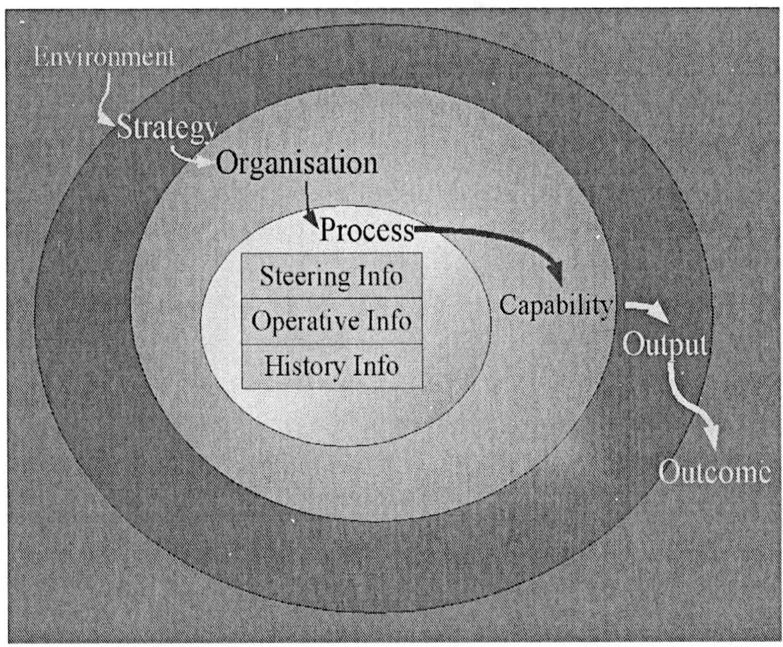

information exchange between applications, meaning that applications start to live their own lives and that processes have to adapt to the applications (e.g., ERP).

However, the information in the *processes* should be used on different levels: steering information, operative information, and historical information. These types of information will be found in BPM tools. In the last few years we can see an effort to merge BPM aspects and ICT aspects into one tool. However, a mental gap exists between both worlds. BPM people think process wise, while ICT people think application wise, meaning only some parts of the processes are automated and relevant information is stored in databases. Reporting on transactions is based on the information kept in these databases. As a matter of fact, only historical information is kept in these databases. Information about steering and executing the processes are not stored in databases.

Some of the information (steering and operative) can implicitly be registered in the models of automated workflows. But a data query cannot be performed on these models.

Figure 7 shows the volume of informal and formal information in an organisation. As we may see regarding the formal information, the business processes hold the most information due to the fact that they contain the business context, the steering and operative information.

Research by Rever SA (a spin-off of the Belgian University Notre Dame de la Paix) shows that 40-60% of the data structure and flow in ICT are in the applications and are thus not in databases. The University Notre Dame de la Paix is developing the software DB-Main to do a reversed engineering by analysing the databases and the programs. The result is a *conceptual model* from which a logical model for any type of database system can be derived down to the operative schemes (Hainaut & Henrard, 2003; Hick & Hainaut, 2003; Henrard, Hick, & Thiran, 2003).

Since the environment of the organisation is permanently changing and thus the organisation also, the information system of the organisation has to be adapted to the new situation. As a consequence, part of the databases will change, so that after a while a new reengineering has to be performed.

So, if a business process could be fully automated and it holds itself the information, then a consistent part of the producible and needed information will be embedded in the business process. This is even possible for processes in XBC. Referring to the capability approach, the housekeeping of the information of a capability is done by the management module (see also Vandenborre, Heinckiens, Hoffman, & Tromp, 2003). This can be done with SOA and Web services by providing the organisation with a flexible architecture of easy customisable applications.

Virtual Data Federation

The consequence is that if somebody needs to collect information then that person will have to query each process management module. This resembles to Virtual Data Federation or Enterprise Information Integration (EII) issues.

Friedman (2004a) writes:

Gartner positions EII as a goal, not a technology. The goal is to achieve a state where the various data assets of the enterprise are integrated to best meet the needs of the business:

- *Delivering a timely and complete view of critical entities and events*
- *Providing connectivity and accessibility to data across multiple platforms and databases*
- *Ensuring the consistency of data underpinning related applications*

As such, the goal of EII differs little from the general goals of data integration, which has been a focus of enterprises for the last three decades. (p. 1)

At its core, EII technology performs virtual data federation based on distributed database queries (Friedman, 2004b, 2005).

However, the biggest problem is to know if the semantic of one item is the same in all the databases. This is the added value of software like DB-Main (Hick & Hainaut, 2003), which produces a conceptual or semantic model of the organisational information. From there on through logical and physical models the operative models are defined. Again, this will only be a snapshot if the maintenance of all models is not done. In this era of globalisation and merges, the chance is great that information re-engineering will frequently be performed.

Two kinds of capabilities with embedded information systems can be determined. Self-supporting capabilities have their own embedded information system, self-ordained capabilities also, but they can determine their own strategy related to their environment.

Decision Making

Intelligence

If software has to choose itself other resources, then it may have to seek for information to prepare its decision making. The needed information to reduce the uncertainty of the decision maker at a level that is acceptable is called intelligence.

As mentioned previously, collecting intelligence is the only rule of the first principle of the Art of War (balance between resources and objectives). To the military "Intelligence is the product resulting from the collection, evaluation, analysis, integration, and interpretation of all available information, that concerns one or more aspects of foreign nations or of areas of foreign operations, and that is immediately or potentially significant to military planning and operations" (*Defense Security Service Definitions,* 2005).

This definition says that not all information is intelligence and that only after a process of collecting, evaluating, analysing, integrating, and interpreting of information, intelligence can be created. Once the intelligence is created, then it can be used for two purposes (Figure 8):

Figure 8.

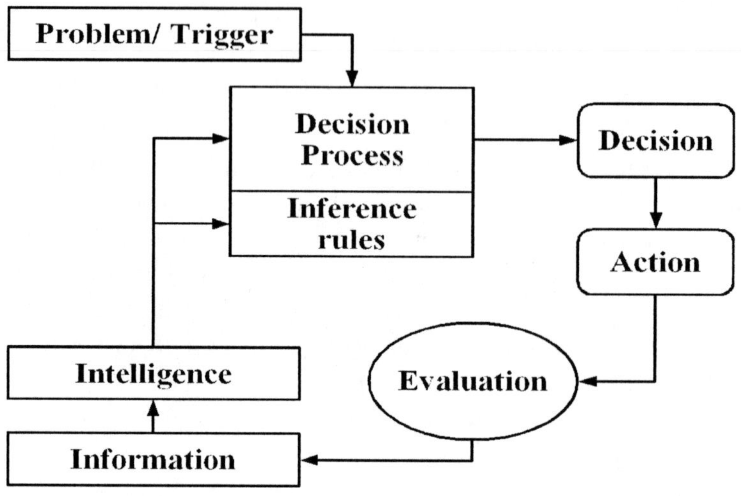

Figure 9.

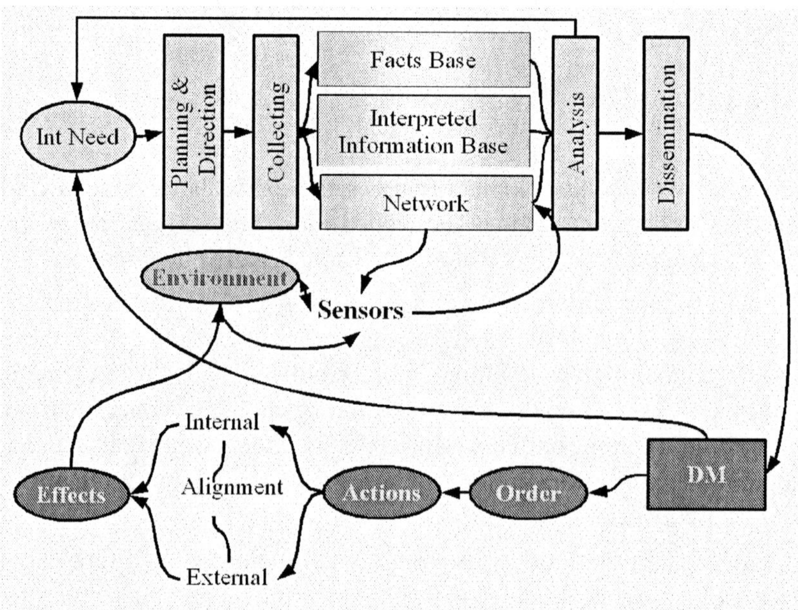

Figure 10.

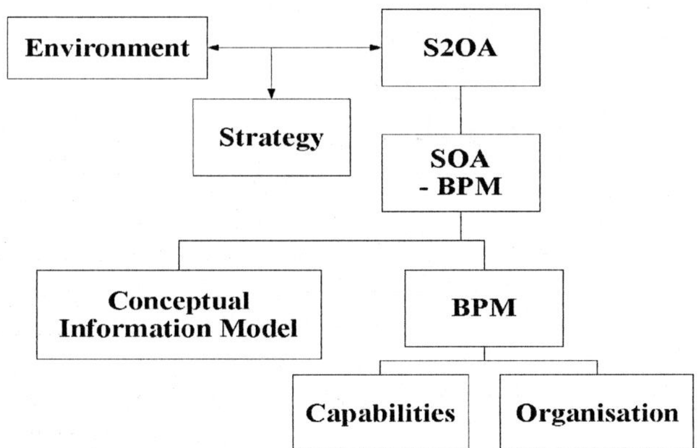

- reduction of the *uncertainty* around the solution for the problem and
- improvement of the *inference rules* of the decision process.

The reduction of the uncertainty can be linked to the context of the decision maker (awareness) and the needed information to make decisions, while inference rules are related to the knowledge domain of the decision maker.

If the decision has been taken that caused an action then the effect of this action has to be evaluated to learn from this action (feedback). Otherwise the decision maker cannot learn from his/her success or failure. So if the software has to make a choice to use a resource (Web service), then it must be able to execute this decision process.

If we combine the decision process with the intelligence process, then a two-way communication is needed: One way to express the information need from the decision-making process to the intelligence process and another in the opposite direction with the asked information (pull) or with spontaneously generated intelligence.

The intelligence process will check if the need can be covered with information in its intelligence base (see Rabaey, Leclercq, Vandijck, Hoffman, & Timmerman, 2005a for more details), if not then it will give its network (sensors) the order to seek for the relevant information. If it is found then the assessment process leading eventually to intelligence will be started.

Rabaey et al. (2005a) proposes a SOA-based solution because of the fact that the intelligence capability can be formed of modules, which correspond with business steps in the intelligence process. An intelligent agent-based solution can be found in Yoon et al. (2005).

Regarding the intelligence process, a conclusion is that no commercial software is yet capable to design (tactical level) processes, nor defines objectives at strategic level, like humans can do. However at operative level it is possible.

Semantic Service-Oriented Architecture (SSOA)

Now that we have discussed the capability approach, business processes, the information issues, and the intelligence process, regarding Semantic Web services and business intelligent agents, we may conclude that SSOA will not be there tomorrow. Certainly, in the domain of information management there are a lot of problems, which are necessary, not all technical problems, on the contrary. Nevertheless, Semantic Web technology is the way to go and it proves already its utility.

Regarding the SSOA, the information issues have first to be resolved. Figure 10 depicts the roadmap.

The *conceptual information* has (urgently) to be defined, simultaneously the organisation has to be defined, and the business processes have to be modelled in the BPM tool following the capability approach.

Once BPM and the conceptual information model are defined, then they have to be merged into SOA-BPM, where the capabilities should manage their own (embedded) information system. The next step is the introduction of *semantics in the capabilities* (SSOA), so that they manage their own modules and resources and interact with their environment (self-supporting capabilities), or even define their own objectives (strategy) in a relationship with the environment (self-ordained capabilities).

But, as already mentioned, it has to start with the conceptual information model to solve the problems of information management.

Further Research

Service-Oriented Investment

Rabaey, Vandijck, and Hoffman (2005) propose a method to *evaluate* EAI, which has been extended to SOA and XBC. It maps the interactions between processes and applications and assesses different aspects (business coverage, technical stability, costs) in a global view, which is then presented to the interdisciplinary forum.

At first glance, this is typically an investment method for ICT projects. However, with the SOA fitting the capability approach, the question can be asked, if this method can be adapted to fit capability investments.

Instead of applications (rendering information services), all services are then evaluated. The service-and-effect diagram is then the map on which the interdisciplinary forum can decide. Due to the complexity of this map and therefore a high degree of uncertainty, classical investments are inadequate. Since uncertainty is an important factor, options could be used.

An option can be defined as "a right but not an obligation, to buy or sell something at a predefined price on or before a certain date (Miranda, 2003, p. 167). Options were originally meant for financial markets (financial options) where the underlying asset is of financial nature (such as a stock or an exchange rate). Real options have tangible assets or projects as underlying asset.

The different options are sequentially put in a tree structure. In a branch, an option can only be realised if its predecessors exist. However with the capability approach, services (capabilities) can be used anywhere, they are independent from most of the other services (in the realisation).

The service-oriented investment will be tested in real cases.

Accounting System

"There ain't such a thing as a free lunch." So, the use of Web services must be paid. Sometimes the customer cannot know how many Web services will be implicated, because if Web services have the same intelligence as BIA, then Web services can invoke other Web services or even BIA. In this situation we have a cascade of Web services and/or intelligent agents. However, it would be more preferable that the business process itself—through its intelligent agents—could determine which Web service is the best suited to fulfil its need, regarding some criteria as objective coverage, reliability, availability, and price. The cascading of Web services with the control of the business process or at least the logging by the business process must be considered to evaluate the QoS of the different Web services. Research has to be done to find a system of evaluation of QoS (e.g., estimated response time, reliability, expected output), combined with the financial evaluation.

Security System

Related to the accounting system and its QoS, is the security system. Is the called agent or Web service, really what it is supposed to be? In the static way of finding and using Web services, the programmer checks the credentials of the called Web service. In the case of, for example, dynamic workflows, the calling Web service has to figure itself out if the called Web service is the right one. Therefore authentication and authorisation should be managed by approved independent "certifying" agencies, so that the calling Web service can be sure that it will be using the right (called) Web service.

Conclusion

The question was, by adding semantics to Web services, are dynamic executable workflows possible? Can BPEL4WS be made dynamic, so that ad hoc, productive, and administrative workflows can be designed and executed with the same technology?

First the capability approach was discussed, and SOA is well suited to adopt this approach. At first glance, BPEL4WS with Semantic Web services could be used, but at this early stage only for operative tasks (not at the strategic or tactical level).

The discussion on information showed us that the related problems are important enough that by not first solving these problems the good use of semantics in Web technology is jeopardised. Certainly, this is true when this "information" is used to create intelligence to reduce the uncertainty of the decision maker (thus software) and to improve its inference rules.

Finally, we have proposed a roadmap to reach SSOA.

References

Barry, D. K. (2003). *Web services and service-oriented architecture*. Amsterdam: Morgan Kaufmann.

Bernard, H. (1976). *Totale Oorlog en revolutionaire oorlog, Band I*. Brussels: Royal Military Academy (in Dutch).

Defense Security Service (DSS) Definitions. (2005). Retrieved October 24, 2006, from http://www.dss.mil/isec/appendixc.htm

Doshi, P., Goodwin, R., Akkiraju, R., & Verma, K. (2005). Dynamic workflow composition using markov decision processes. *International Journal of Web Services Research, 2*(1), 1-17.

Friedman, T. (2004a). *Clarifying the meaning of enterprise information integration*. Gartner.

Friedman, T. (2004b). *'EII' vendors offer virtual data federation technology*. Gartner.

Friedman, T. (2005). *Acquisitions expand Sybase's data integration offerings*. Gartner.

Hainaut, J.-L., & Henrard, J. (2003). *The nature of data reverse engineering*. Université De Notre Dame à Namur, FUNDP, Namur.

Hammer, M., & Champy, J. A. (1993). *Reengineering the corporation: A manifesto for business revolution*. New York: Harper Collins.

Hausmann, J. H., Heckel, R., & Lohmann, M. (2005). Model-based development of Web service descriptions enabling a precise matching concept. *International Journal of Web Services Research, 2*(2), 67-84.

Henrard, J., Hick, J.-M., & Thiran, P. (2003, May 22). Strategies for data reengineering. In *Proceedings of FNRS contact day on Software (re-)engineering*, Louvain-la-Neuve, Belgium.

Hick, J.-M., & Hainaut, J.-L. (2003). Strategy for database application evolution: The DB-MAIN approach. In G. Goos, J. Hartmanis, & J. van Leeuwen (Eds.), *Proceedings of 22th International. Conference on Conceptual Modelling (ER 2003)* (LNCS 2813, pp. 291-306). Springer Verlag.

Kaplan, R. S., & Norton, D. P. (1996). *The balanced scorecard: Translating strategy into action*. Boston. Harvard Business School.

Knapik, M., & Johnson, J. (1998). *Developing intelligent agents for distributed systems*. McGraw-Hill.

Kobielus, J. G. (1997). *Workflow strategies*. Foster City, CA: IDG Books Worldwide.

Liddell Hart, B. H. (1991). *Strategy*. London: Meridian.

Maamar, Z., Sheng, Q. Z., & Benatalah, B. (2003, July 14-15). *Interleaving Web services composition and execution using software agents and delegation*. Paper presented at Web Services and Agent-Based Engineering (WSABE2003), Melbourne, Australia.

Mateos, C., Zunino, A., & Campo, M. (2005). Integrating intelligent mobile agents with Web services. *International Journal of Web Services Research, 2*(2), 85-103.

McHugh, P., Merli, G., & Wheeler III, W. A. (1995). *Beyond business process reengineering*. West Sussex: Wiley.

Miranda, E. (2003). *Running the successful hi-tech project office*. Boston: Artech House.

Murch, R., & Johnson, T. (1998). *Intelligent software agents*. Prentice Hall PTR.

Padovitz, A., & Krishnaswmy, S., & Loke, S. W. (2003, July 14-15). *Towards efficient selection of Web services*. Paper presented at Web Services and Agent-Based Engineering (WSABE2003), Melbourne, Australia.

Plesums, C. (2002). Introduction to workflow. In *Workflow Handbook 2002 of Workflow Management Council.* Retrieved October 24, 2006, from http://www.wfmc.org/

Rabaey, M. (2004a, May 23-26). *Investment in ICT: A holistic business approach.* Paper presented at the 15th Information Resource Management Association (IRMA) International Conference, New Orleans, LA.

Rabaey, M. (2004b). *Strategic decision-making regarding EAI.* Ghent University, Institute of Permanent Education.

Rabaey, M. (2005, June 1-2). *CAF and e-cost.* Paper presented at the 2nd CAF Event, Luxembourg.

Rabaey, M., Hoffman, G., & Vandenborre, K. (2004, April 3-7). *Aligning business and resource strategy: An interdisciplinary forum for investments.* Paper presented at the 13th International Conference on Management of Technology (IAMOT2004), Washington, DC.

Rabaey, M., Leclercq, J.-M., Vandijck, E., Hoffman, G., & Timmerman, M. (2005a). Intelligence base: Strategic instrument of an organisation (NATO IST-055 Specialist Meeting). The Hague, Netherlands.

Rabaey, M., Leclercq, J.-M., Vandijck, E., Hoffman, G., & Timmerman, M. (2005b). Resources and capabilities planning with an intelligent agents dynamic system. *Division Concept of the Assistant Chief of Staff Evaluation.* Belgian Ministry of Defence.

Rabaey, M., Vandenborre, K., Tromp, H., & Hoffman, G. (2005, September 26-29). *Classification of IT-integration based on business collaboration.* Paper presented at IPSI 2005 Montenegro.

Rabaey, M., Vandijck, E., & Hoffman, G. (2005). *An evaluation framework for enterprise application integration.* Paper presented at the 16th IRMA International Conference on Software & Systems Engineering and Their Applications (ICSSEA), San Diego, CA.

Rabaey, M., Vandijck, E., & Tromp, H. (2003, December 2-4). *Business intelligent agents for enterprise application integration.* Paper presented at the 16th International Conference on Software & Systems Engineering and their Applications (ICSSEA 2003), Paris.

Riempp, G. (1998). *Wide area workflow management: Creating partnership for the 21st century.* London: Springer-Verlag.

U.S. Office of Management & Budget. (1996). Memorandum for heads of executive departments and establishments: Management of federal information resources (OMB A-130). Retrieved October 24, 2006, from http://www.whitehouse.gov/omb/circulars/a130/a130trans4.html

Vandenborre, K., Heinckiens, P., Hoffman, G., & Tromp, H. (2003, June 3-6). *Coherent enterprise information modelling in practice.* Paper presented at the 13th European Japanese Conference on Information Modelling and Knowledge bases, Kitakyushu, Japan.

Workflow Management Council (WfMC). (1995, January 19). Reference model—The workflow reference Model (WFMC-TC-1003, 1.1).

Yoon, V., Broome, B., Sing, R., & Guimaraes, T. (2005). Using agent technology for company knowledge management. *Information Resources Management Journal, 18*(2), 94-113.

Zimmerman, O., Tomlinson, M., & Peuser, S. (2003). *Perspectives on Web services.* Berlin: Springer.

Glossary of Terms

Business intelligent agent (BIA): BIA is an intelligent agent that dynamically executes business processes or part of it, to attain its imposed business objectives.

Business process execution language for Web services (BPEL4WS or BPEL): BPEL4WS (or BPEL) is an XML-based language for the formal specification of business processes, where each step in the business process is executed by a Web service.

Cross business border collaboration (XBC): XBC is a framework where EAI, EII, and the capability approach are merged in a SOA.

Capability: Capability is a logical set of modules (processes) to produce one or more outputs with a certain service level.

Information: Information is any communication or representation of knowledge such as facts, data, or opinions in any medium or form, including textual, numerical, graphic, cartographic, narrative, or audiovisual forms (OMB A-130).

Intelligence: Intelligence is the product of the intelligence process, which collects, analyses, integrates, and interprets information. It disseminates the intelligence to the customer, with the purpose to reduce the uncertainty on a problem (decision) and/or to improve the inference rules.

Semantic service-oriented architecture (SSOA): SSOA is the addition of Semantic Web technology to service-oriented architecture, so that SOA-related service can be made dynamic.

Workflow: Workflow is the computerised facilitation or automation of a business process, in whole or part.

Chapter VI

Enhancing E-Business on the Semantic Web through Automatic Multimedia Representation

Manjeet Rege, Wayne State University, USA
Ming Dong, Wayne State University, USA
Farshad Fotouhi, Wayne State University, USA

Abstract

With the evolution of the next generation Web—the Semantic Web—e-business can be expected to grow into a more collaborative effort in which businesses compete with each other by collaborating to provide the best product to a customer. Electronic collaboration involves data interchange with multimedia data being one of them. Digital multimedia data in various formats have increased tremendously in recent years on the Internet. An automated process that can represent multimedia data in a meaningful way for the Semantic Web is highly desired. In this chapter, we propose an automatic multimedia representation system for the Semantic Web.

The proposed system learns a statistical model based on the domain specific training data and performs automatic semantic annotation of multimedia data using eXtensible Markup Language (XML) techniques. We demonstrate the advantage of annotating multimedia data using XML over the traditional keyword based approaches and discuss how it can help e-business.

Introduction

An Internet user typically conducts separate individual e-business transactions to accomplish a certain task. A tourist visiting New York might purchase airfare tickets and tickets to a concert in New York separately. With the evolution of the Semantic Web, as shown in Figure 1, the user can conduct one collaborative e-business transaction for the two purchases. Moreover, he/she can also take a virtual tour of New York city online, which actually might be a collection of all videos, images, and songs on New York appearing anywhere on the World Wide Web. With the continuing growth and reach of the Web, the multimedia data available on it continue to grow on a daily basis. For a successful collaborative e-business, in addition to other kinds of data, it is important to be able to organize and search the multimedia data for the Semantic Web.

With the Semantic Web being the future of the World Wide Web of today, there has to be an efficient way to represent the multimedia data automatically for it. Multimedia data impose a great challenge to document indexing and retrieval as it is highly unstructured and the semantics are implicit in the content of it. Moreover, most of the multimedia contents appearing on the Web have no description available with it in terms of keywords or captions. From the Semantic Web point of view, this

Figure 1. Collaborative e-business scenario on the Semantic Web

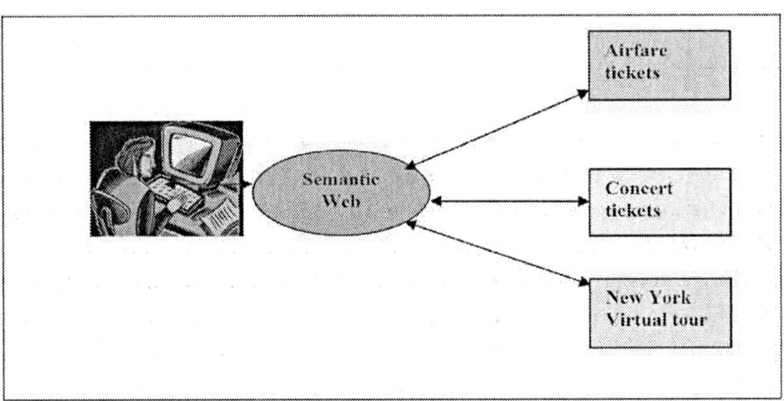

information is crucial because it describes the content of multimedia data and would help represent it in a semantically meaningful way. Manual annotation is feasible on a small set of multimedia documents but is not scalable as the number of multimedia documents increases. Hence, performing manual annotation of all Web multimedia data while "moving" them to the Semantic Web domain is an impossible task. This we believe is a major challenge in transforming today's Web multimedia data into tomorrow's Semantic Web data.

In this chapter, we propose a generic automatic multimedia representation solution for the Semantic Web—an XML-based (Bray, Paoli, & Sperberg-McQueen, 1998) automatic multimedia representation system. The proposed system is implemented using images as an example and performs domain-specific annotation using XML. Specifically, our system "learns" from a set of domain-specific training images made available to it a priori. Upon receiving a new image from the Web that belongs to one of the semantic categories the system has learned, the system generates appropriate XML-based annotation for the new image, making it "ready" for the Semantic Web. Although the proposed system has been described from the perspective of images, in general it is applicable to many kinds of multimedia data available on the Web today. To our best knowledge, there has been no work done on automatic multimedia representation for the Semantic Web using the semantics of XML. The proposed system is the first work in this direction.

Background

The term *e-business* in general refers to online transactions conducted on the Internet. These are mainly classified into two categories: business-to-consumer (B2C) and business-to-business (B2B). One of the main differences between these two kinds of e-businesses is that B2C, as the name suggests, applies to companies that sell their products or offer services to consumers over the Internet. B2B on the other hand are online transactions conducted between two companies. From its initial introduction in late 1990s, e-business has grown to include services such as car rentals, health services, movie rentals, and online banking. The Web site CIO.com (2006) reports that North American consumers have spent \$172 billion shopping online in 2005, up from \$38.8 billion in 2000. Moreover, e-business is expected to grow even more in the coming years. By 2010, consumers are expected to spend \$329 billion each year online. We expect the evolving Semantic Web to play a significant role in enhancing the way e-business is done today. However, as mentioned in the earlier section, there is a need to represent the multimedia data on the Semantic Web in an efficient way. In the following section, we review some of the related work done on the topic.

Ontology/Schema-Based Approaches

Ontology-based approaches have been frequently used for multimedia annotation and retrieval. Hyvonen, Styrman, and Saarela (2002) proposed ontology-based image retrieval and annotation of graduation ceremony images by creating hierarchical annotation. They used Protégé (n.d.) as the ontology editor for defining the ontology and annotating images. Schreiber, Dubbeldam, Wielemaker, and Wielinga (2001) also performed ontology-based annotation of ape photographs, in which they use the same ontology defining and annotation tool and use Resource Definition Framework (RDF) Schema as the output language. Nagao, Shirai, and Squire (2001) have developed a method for associating external annotations to multimedia data appearing over the Web. Particularly, they discuss video annotation by performing automatic segmentation of video, semiautomatic linking of video segments, and interactive naming of people and objects in video frames. More recently, Rege, Dong, Fotouhi, Siadat, and Zamorano (2005) proposed to annotate human brain images using XML by following the MPEG-7 (Manjunath, 2002) multimedia standard. The advantages of using XML to store meta-information (such as patient name, surgery location, etc.), as well as brain anatomical information, has been demonstrated in a neurosurgical domain. The major drawback of the approaches, mentioned previously, is that the image annotation is performed manually. There is an extra effort needed from the user's side in creating the ontology and performing the detailed annotation. It is highly desirable to have a system that performs automatic semantic annotation of multimedia data on the Internet.

Keyword-Based Annotations

Automatic image annotation using keywords has recently received extensive attention in the research community. Mori, Takahashi, and Oka (1999) developed a co-occurrence model, in which they looked at the co-occurrence of keywords with image regions. Duygulu, Barnard, Freitas, and Forsyth (2002) proposed a method to describe images using a vocabulary of blobs. First, regions are created using a segmentation algorithm. For each region, features are computed and then blobs are generated by clustering the image features for these regions across images. Finally, a translation model translates the set of blobs of an image to a set of keywords. Jeon, Lavrenko, and Manmatha (2003) introduced a cross-media relevance model that learns the joint distribution of a set of regions and a set of keywords rather than the correspondence between a single region and a single keyword. Feng, Manmatha, and Lavrenko (2004) proposed a method of automatic annotation by partitioning each image into a set of rectangular regions. The joint distribution of the keyword annotations and low-level features is computed from the training set and used to annotate testing images. High annotation accuracy has been reported. The readers are referred to Barnard, Duygulu, Freitas, and Forsyth (2003) for a comprehensive review on this topic. As we point out in the section, "XML-Based Annotation," keyword annotations do not fully express the semantic meaning embedded in the multimedia data. In this paper, we propose an Automatic Multimedia Representation System for the Semantic Web using the semantics of XML, which enables efficient multimedia annotation and retrieval based on the domain knowledge. The proposed work is the first attempt in this direction.

Proposed Framework

In order to represent multimedia data for the Semantic Web, we propose to perform automatic multimedia annotation using XML techniques. Though the proposed framework is applicable to multimedia data in general, we provide details about the framework using image annotations as a case study.

XML-Based Annotation

Annotations are domain-specific semantic information assigned with the help of a domain expert to semantically enrich the data. The traditional approach practiced by image repository librarians is to annotate each image manually with keywords or captions and then search on those captions or keywords using a conventional text search engine. The rationale here is that the keywords capture the semantic content of the image and help in retrieving the images. This technique is also used by television news organizations to retrieve file footage from their videos. Such techniques allow text queries and are successful in finding the relevant pictures. The main disadvantage with manual annotations is the cost and difficulty of scaling it to large numbers of images.

MPEG-7 (Manjunath, 2002, p. 8) describes the content—"the bits about the bits"—of a multimedia file such as an image or a video clip. The MPEG-7 standard has been developed after many rounds of careful discussion. It is expected that this standard would be used in searching and retrieving for all types of media objects. It proposes to store low-level image features, annotations, and other meta-information in one XML file that contains a reference to the location of the corresponding image file. XML has brought great features and promising prospects to the future of the Semantic Web and will continue to play an important role in its development. XML keeps content, structure, and representation apart and is a much more adequate means for knowledge representation. It can represent semantic properties through its syntactic structure, that is, by the nesting or sequentially ordering relationship among elements (XML tags). The advantage of annotating multimedia using XML can best be explained with the help of an example. Suppose we have a New York image (shown in Figure 2) with keywords annotation of Statue of Liberty, Sea, Clouds, Sky. Instead of simply using keywords as annotation for this image, consider now that the same image is represented in an XML format.

Note that the XML representation of the image can conform to any domain-specific XML schema. For the sake of illustration, consider the XML schema and the corresponding XML representation of the image shown in Figure 3. This XML schema stores foreground and background object information along with other meta-information with keywords along various paths of the XML file. Compared with keyword-based approaches, the XML paths from the root node to the keywords are able to fully express the semantic meaning of the multimedia data. In the case of the New York image, semantically meaningful XML annotations would be "image/semantic/foreground/object=Statue of Liberty, image/semantic/foreground/ object = Sea, image/semantic/ background/ object = Sky, image/semantic/background /object =Clouds". The semantics in XML paths provides us with an added advantage by differentiating the objects in the foreground and background and giving more meaningful annotation.

We emphasize that the annotation performed using our approach is domain-specific knowledge. The same image can have different annotation under a different XML schema that highlights certain semantic characteristics of importance pertaining to that domain knowledge. We simply use the schema of Figure 3 that presents image foreground and background object information as a running example.

Overview of System Architecture

The goal of the proposed system is to represent multimedia data obtained from the Web in a meaningful XML format. Consequently, this data can be "moved" to the Semantic Web in an automatic and efficient way. For example, as shown in Figure

Figure 2. Comparison of keyword annotation and XML-path-based annotation

Image	Original Annotation	XML annotation
	Statue of Liberty Sea Sky Clouds	image/semantic/foreground/object = Statue of Liberty image/semantic/foreground/object = Sea image/semantic/background/object= Sky image/semantic/background/object= Clouds

Figure 3. An example of an XML schema and the corresponding XML representation of an image

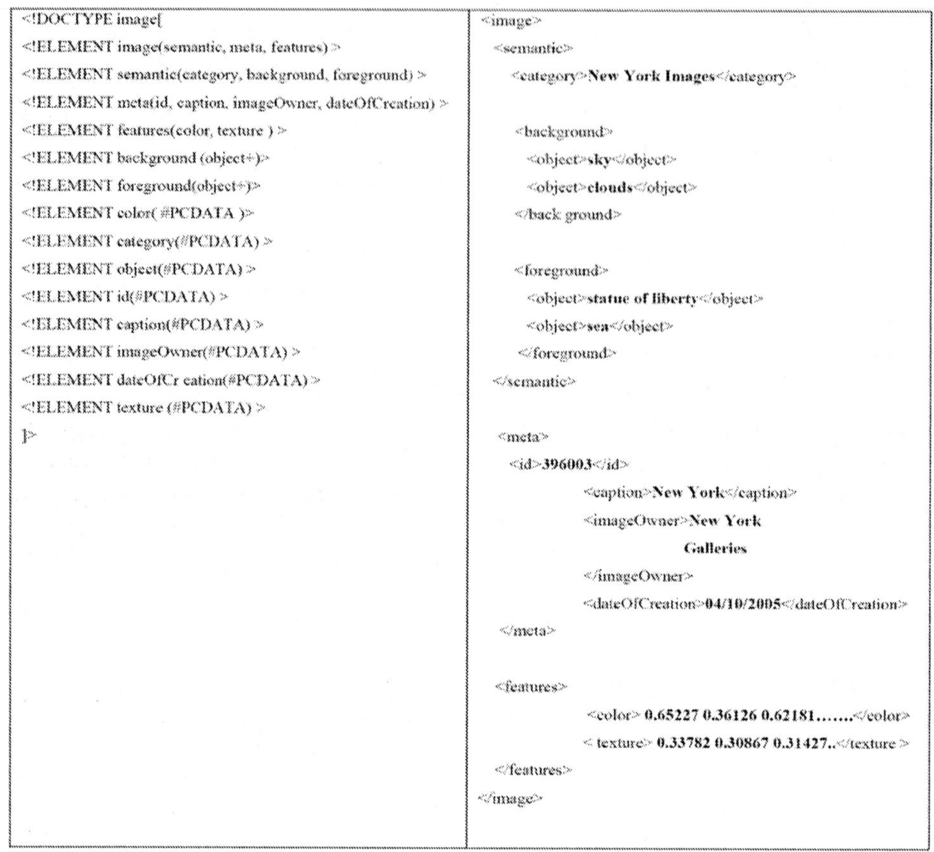

```
<!DOCTYPE image[
<!ELEMENT image(semantic, meta, features) >
<!ELEMENT semantic(category, background, foreground) >
<!ELEMENT meta(id, caption, imageOwner, dateOfCreation) >
<!ELEMENT features(color, texture ) >
<!ELEMENT background (object+)>
<!ELEMENT foreground(object+)>
<!ELEMENT color( #PCDATA )>
<!ELEMENT category(#PCDATA) >
<!ELEMENT object(#PCDATA) >
<!ELEMENT id(#PCDATA) >
<!ELEMENT caption(#PCDATA) >
<!ELEMENT imageOwner(#PCDATA) >
<!ELEMENT dateOfCr eation(#PCDATA) >
<!ELEMENT texture (#PCDATA) >
]>
```

```
<image>
  <semantic>
    <category>New York Images</category>

    <background>
      <object>sky</object>
      <object>clouds</object>
    </back ground>

    <foreground>
      <object>statue of liberty</object>
      <object>sea</object>
    </foreground>
  </semantic>

  <meta>
    <id>396003</id>
              <caption>New York</caption>
              <imageOwner>New York
                          Galleries
              </imageOwner>
              <dateOfCreation>04/10/2005</dateOfCreation>
  </meta>

  <features>
              <color> 0.65227 0.36126 0.62181.......</color>
              < texture> 0.33782 0.30867 0.31427..</texture >
  </features>
</image>
```

4, the system first receives an image from the Web. The image could be received by a *Web image provider* which is an independent module outside of the system that simply fetches domain-specific images from the Web and passes them onto our system. The Web image provider could also be a "Web spider" that "crawls" among domain-specific Web data sources and procures relevant images. The image is then preprocessed by two other modules, namely, *image divider* and *feature extractor*. An image usually contains several regions. Extracting low-level features from different image regions is typically the first step of automatic image annotation since regions may have different contents and represent different semantic meaning. The image regions could be determined through either image segmentation (Shi & Malik, 1997) or image cutting in the image divider. For low-level feature extraction, we used some of the features standardized by MPEG-7.

Figure 4. System architecture

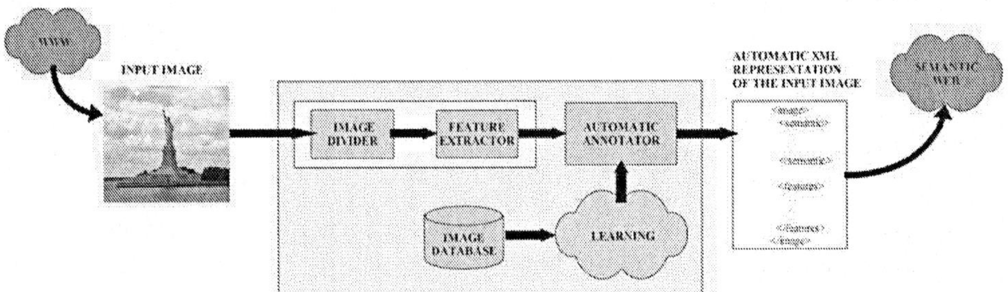

The low-level features extracted from all the regions are passed on to the *automatic annotator*. This module learns a statistical model that links image regions and XML annotation paths from a set of domain-specific training images. The training image database can contain images belonging to various semantic categories represented and annotated in XML format. The annotator learns to annotate new images that belong to at least one of the many semantic categories that the annotator has been trained on. The output of the automatic annotator is an XML representation of the image.

Statistical Model for Automatic Annotation

In general, image segmentation is a computationally expensive as well as an erroneous task (Feng et al., 2004). As an alternative simple solution, we have the image divider partition each image into a set of rectangular regions of equal sizes. The feature extractor extracts low-level features from each rectangular region of every image and constructs a feature vector. By learning the joint probability distribution of XML annotation paths and low-level image features, we perform the automatic annotation of a new image.

Let X denote the set of XML annotation paths, T denote the domain-specific training images in XML format, and let t be an image belonging to T. Let x_t be a subset of X containing the annotation paths for t. Also, assume that each image is divided into n rectangular regions of equal size.

Consider a new image q not in the training set. Let $f_q = \{f_{q1}, f_{q2}, \ldots f_{qn}\}$ denote the feature vector for q. In order to perform automatic annotation of q, we model the joint probability of f_q and any arbitrary annotation path subset x of X as follows,

$$P(x, f_q) = P(x, f_{q1}, f_{q2}, \ldots, f_{qn}) \quad (1)$$

We use the training set T of annotated images to estimate the joint probability of observing *x* and $\{f_{q1}, f_{q2}, \ldots, f_{qn}\}$ by computing the expectation over all the images in the training set.

$$P(x, f_{q1}, f_{q2}, \ldots, f_{qn}) = \sum_{t \in T} P(t)\, P(x, f_{q1}, f_{q2}, \ldots, f_{qn} \mid t) \qquad (2)$$

We assume that the events of observing x and f_{q1}, f_{q2}, f_{qn} are mutually independent of each other and express the joint probability in terms of P_A, P_B and P_C as follows:

$$P(x, f_{q1}, f_{q2}, \ldots f_{qn}) = \sum_{t \in T} \{ P_A(t) \prod_{a} P_B(f_a|t) \prod_{path \in x} P_C(path|t) \prod_{path \notin x} (1 - P_C(path|t)) \}$$

(3)

where P_A is the prior probability of selecting each training image, P_B is the density function responsible for modeling the feature vectors, and P_C is a multiple Bernoulli distribution for modeling the XML annotation paths.

In the absence of any prior knowledge of the training set, we assume that P_A follows a uniform prior and can be expressed as:

$$P_A = \frac{1}{\|T\|} \qquad (4)$$

where ||T|| is the size of the training set. For the distribution P_B, we use a nonparametric, kernel-based density estimate:

$$P_B(f\,|t) = \frac{1}{n}\sum_i \frac{\exp\{-(f - f_i)^T \Sigma^{-1} (f - f_i)\}}{\sqrt{2^k \Pi^k |\Sigma|}} \qquad (5)$$

where f_i belongs to $\{f_1, f_2, \ldots, f_n\}$ the set of all low-level features computed for each rectangular region of Σ image t. is the diagonal covariance matrix which is constructed empirically for best annotation performance.

In the XML representation of images, every annotation path can either occur or might not occur at all for an image. Moreover, as we annotate images based on object presence and not on prominence in an image, an annotation path if it occurs can occur—at most—once in the XML representation of the image. As a result, it is reasonable to assume that the density function P_C follows a multiple Bernoulli distribution as follows:

$$P_C(\text{path}|\text{t}) = \frac{(\gamma\alpha_{path,t} + N_{path})}{(\gamma + \|T\|)} \quad (6)$$

where γ is a smoothing $\alpha_{path,t} = 1$ parameter, if the path occurs in the annotation of image *t*, else it is zero. N_{path} is the total number of training images that contain this *path* in their annotation.

Experimental Results

Our image database contains 1,500 images obtained from the Corel data set, comprising 15 image categories with 100 images in each category. The Corel image data set contains images from different semantic categories with keyword annotations performed by Corel employees. In order to conduct our experiments, we require a training image database representing images in XML format. Each XML file should contain annotation, low-level features, and other meta-information stored along different XML paths. In the absence of such a publicly available data, we had to manually convert each image in the database to an XML format conforming to the schema shown in Figure 3. We performed our experiments on five randomly selected image categories. Each image category represents a distinct semantic concept. In the experiments, 70% of the data are randomly selected as the training set while the remaining were used for testing.

Automatic Annotation Results

Given a test image, we calculate the joint probability of the low-level feature vector and the XML annotation paths in the training set. We select the top four paths with the highest joint probability as the annotation for the image. Compared with other approaches in image annotation (Duygulu et al., 2002; Feng et al., 2004), our annotation results provide more meaningful description of a given image.

Figure 5 shows some examples of our annotation results. We can clearly see that the XML-path-based annotation contains richer semantic meaning than the original keyword provided by Corel. We evaluate the image annotation performance in terms of recall and precision. The recall and precision for every annotation path in the test set is computed as follows:

Figure 5. Examples of top annotation in comparison with Corel keyword annotation

Image		
Corel keyword Annotation	plane, jet, wheels, sky	sky, clouds, train, tracks
Automatic XML based Annotation	image/semantic/background/object=sky, image/semantic/foreground/object=plane, image/semantic/foreground/object=jet, image/semantic/foreground/object=wheels	image/semantic/background/object=sky, image/semantic/background/object=clouds, image/semantic/forgeround/object=train, image/semantic/forgeround/object=tracks,

$$\text{recall} = \frac{q}{r}$$

$$\text{precision} = \frac{q}{s}$$

where q is the number of images correctly annotated by an annotation path, r is the number of images having that annotation path in the test set, and s is the number of images annotated by the same path. In Table 1 we report the results for all the 148 paths in the test set as well as the 23 best paths as in Duygulu et al. (2002) and Feng et al. (2004).

Table 1. Annotation results

Number of Paths with recall > 0 is 50		
Annotation Results	**Results on all 148 paths**	**Results on top 23 paths**
Mean per-path recall	0.22	0.83
Mean per-path precision	0.21	0.73

Retrieval Results

Given specific query criteria, XML representation helps in efficient retrieval of images over the Semantic Web. Suppose a user wants to find images that have an *airplane* in the background and *people* in the foreground. State-of-the-art search engines require the user to supply individual keywords such as "airplane," "people," and so forth or any combination of keywords as a query. The union of the retrieved images of all possible combinations of the aforementioned query keywords is sure to have images satisfying the user specified criteria.

However, a typical search engine user searching for images is unlikely to view beyond the first 15-20 retrievals, which may be irrelevant in this case. As a result, the user query in this scenario is unanswered in spite of images satisfying the specified criteria being present on the Web. With the proposed framework, the query could be answered in an efficient way. Since all the images on the Semantic Web are represented in an XML format, we can use XML querying technologies such as XQuery (Chamberlin, Florescu, Robie, Simeon, & Stefanascu, 2001) and XPath (Clark & DeRose, 1999) to retrieve images for the query "image/semantic/background/object = plane & image/semantic/foreground/object = people". This is unachievable with keyword-based queries and hence is a major contribution of the proposed work.

Figure 6 shows some examples of the retrieval results. In Table 2, we also report the mean average precision obtained for ranked retrieval as in Feng et al. (2004).

Figure 6. Ranked retrieval for the query image/semantic/background/object = "sky"

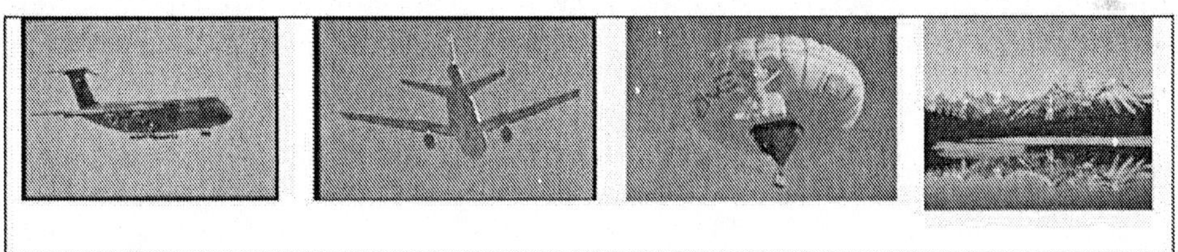

Table 2. Mean average precision results

All 148 paths	Paths with recall > 0
0.34	0.38

Since the proposed work is the first one of its kind to automatically annotate images using XML paths, we were unable to make a direct comparison with any other annotation model. However, our annotation and retrieval results are comparable to the ones obtained by Duygulu et al. (2002) and Feng et al. (2004).

Conclusion and Discussion

With the rapid development of digital photography, more and more people are able to share their personal photographs and home videos on the Internet. Many organizations have large image and video collections in digital format available for online access. For example, film producers advertise movies through interactive preview clips. News broadcasting corporations post photographs and video clips of current events on their respective Web sites. Music companies have audio files of their music albums made available to the public online. Companies concerning the travel and tourism industry have extensive digital archives of popular tourist attractions on their Web sites. As this multimedia data is available—although scattered across the Web—an efficient use of the data resource is not being made. With the evolution of the Semantic Web, there is an immediate need for a semantic representation of these multimedia resources. Since the Web is an infinite source of multimedia data, a manual representation of the data for the Semantic Web is virtually impossible. We present the Automatic Multimedia Representation System that annotates multimedia data on the Web using state-of-the art XML technologies, thus making it "ready" for the Semantic Web.

We show that the proposed XML annotation has a more semantic meaning over the traditional keyword-based annotation. We explain the proposed work by performing a case study of images, which in general is applicable to multimedia data available on the Web.

The major contributions of the proposed work from the perspective of multimedia data sources representation can be stated as follows:

- **Multimedia annotation:** Most of the multimedia data appearing on the World Wide Web are unannotated. With the proposed system, it would be possible to annotate this data and represent it in a meaningful XML format. This we believe would enormously help in "moving" multimedia data from World Wide Web to the Semantic Web.
- **Multimedia retrieval:** Due to representation of multimedia data in XML format, the user has an advantage to perform a complex semantic query instead of the traditional keyword based.

- **Multimedia knowledge discovery:** By having multimedia data appear in an XML format, it will greatly help intelligent Web agents to perform Semantic Web mining for multimedia knowledge discovery.

From an e-business point of view, semantically represented and well-organized Web data sources can significantly help the future of a *collaborative* e-business by the aid of intelligent Web agents. For example, an agent can perform autonomous tasks such as interact with travel Web sites and obtain attractive vacation packages where the users can bid for a particular vacation package or receive the best price for a book across all the booksellers. It is important to note that in addition to multimedia data, once other data sources are also represented in accordance with the spirit of the Semantic Web, the opportunities for collaborative e-business tasks are endless.

References

Barnard, K., Duygulu, P., Fretias, N., Forsyth, D., Blei, D., & Jordan, M. I. (2003). Matching words and pictures. *Journal of Machine Learning Research, 3,* 1107-1135.

Bray, T., Paoli, J., & Sperberg-McQueen, C. M. (1998, February 10). *Extensible markup language (XML) 1.0.* Retrieved October 15, 2006, from http://www.w3.org/TR/1998/REC-xml-19980210

Chamberlin, D., Florescu, D., Robie, J., Simeon, J., & Stefanascu, M. (2001). *XQuery: A query language for XML.* Retrieved from http://www.w3.org/TR/xquery

CIO.com. (2006). *The ABCs of e-commerce.* Retrieved October 15, 2006, from http://www.cio.com/ec/edit/b2cabc.html

Clark, J., & DeRose, S. (1999, November 16). *XML path language (XPath) Version 1.0.* Retrieved August 31, 2006, from http://www.w3.org/TR/xpath

Duygulu, P., Barnard, K., Freitas, N., & Forsyth, D. (2002). Object recognition as machine translation: Learning a lexicon for a fixed image vocabulary. In *Proceedings of European Conference on Computer Vision, 2002* (LNCS 2353, pp. 97-112). Berlin; Heidelberg: Springer.

Feng, S. L., Manmatha, R., & Lavrenko, V. (2004). Multiple Bernoulli relevance models for image and video annotation. In *Proceedings of IEEE Conference on Computer Vision Pattern Recognition, 2004* (Vol. 2, pp. 1002-1009).

Hyvonen, E., Styrman, A., & Saarela, S. (2002). Ontology-based image retrieval. In *Towards the Semantic Web and Web services, Proceedings of XML Finland Conference*, Helsinki, Finland (pp. 15-27).

Jeon, J., Lavrenko, V., & Manmatha, R. (2003). Automatic image annotation and retrieval using cross-media relevance models. In *Proceedings of the 26th Annual International ACM SIGIR Conference on Research and Development in Information Retrieval*, Toronto, Canada (pp. 119-126). New York: ACM Press.

Manjunath, B. S. (2002). *Introduction to MPEG-7: Multimedia content description interface.* John Wiley and Sons.

Mori, Y., Takahashi, H., & Oka, R. (1999). Image-to-word transformation based on dividing and vector quantizing images with words. In *Proceedings of First International Workshop on Multimedia Intelligent Storage and Retrieval Management.*

Nagao, K., Shirai, Y., & Squire, K. (2001). Semantic annotation and transcoding: Making Web content more accessible. *IEEE Multimedia Magazine, 8*(2), 69-81.

Protégé. (n.d.). (Version 3.1.1) [Computer software]. Retrieved February 19, 2006, from http://protege.stanford.edu/index.html

Rege, M., Dong, M., Fotouhi, F., Siadat, M., & Zamorano, L. (2005). Using Mpeg-7 to build a human brain image database for image-guided neurosurgery. In *Proceedings of SPIE International Symposium on Medical Imaging*, San Diego, CA (Vol. 5744, pp. 512-519).

Schreiber, A. T., Dubbeldam, B., Wielemaker, J., & Wielinga, B. (2001). Ontology based photo annotation. *IEEE Intelligent Systems, 16*(3), 66-74.

Shi, J., & Malik, J. (1997). Normalized cuts and image segmentation. In *Proceedings of 1997 IEEE Conference on Computer Vision Pattern Recognition*, San Juan (pp. 731-737).

Chapter VII

Ontology Exchange and Integration via Product-Brokering Agents

Sheng-Uei Guan, Brunel University, UK
Fangming Zhu, National University of Singapore, Singapore

Abstract

Agent-based e-commerce has been booming with the development of the Internet and agent technologies. However, little effort has been devoted to exploring the learning and evolving capabilities of software agents. This chapter addresses the issues of evolving software agents in e-commerce applications. An agent structure with evolutionary features is proposed with a focus on internal hierarchical knowledge. We argue that the knowledge base of an intelligent agent should be the cornerstone for its evolution capabilities, and the agent can enhance its knowledge base by exchanging knowledge with other agents. In this chapter, product ontology is chosen as an instance of knowledge base. We propose a new approach to facilitate ontology exchange among e-commerce agents. The ontology exchange model and its formalities are elaborated. Product-brokering agents have been designed and implemented, which accomplish the ontology exchange process from request to integration.

Introduction

Intelligent agents are already on the Web, freeing us from some drudgework of searching and keeping us up to date automatically. For example, software agents may help users sift through the mass of data and make intelligent decisions. However, applications of software agents in e-commerce are just burgeoning. In the recent decade, agent-based e-commerce (Dignum & Cortés, 2001; Glushko, Tenenbaum, & Meltzer, 1999) has emerged and attracted many efforts in academic and industrial fields. The motivation of introducing software agents into e-commerce is to overcome the arising barricades such as overload of information, difficulty in searching, lack of negotiation infrastructure, and so forth. Software agents have demonstrated tremendous potential in conducting various e-commerce activities such as comparison shopping, negotiation, payment, and auction (Guttman & Maes, 1999; Krishna & Ramesh, 1998). However, these novel e-commerce applications also bring up some new technical challenges to the agent technology such as security, authentication, and privacy. Much research work has concentrated on these issues (Corradi, Montanari, & Stefanelli, 1999; Greenberg, Byington, & Harper, 1998), as they are essential in e-commerce applications.

The academia has not reached a generally accepted definition for software agents. In general, software agents are software entities that carry out some set of operations on behalf of a user or another program with some degree of independence or autonomy. Agents differ from traditional software in that they are personalized and autonomous. They can be personalized to the end users' preferences. Furthermore, they are adaptive and can learn from past experiences. In addition, in a scenario of multi-agent environments, agents can interact with each other. Therefore, coordination, cooperation, and communication have become the most important external properties for agents. In this chapter, we explore the evolutionary features of software agents based on these basic properties.

Mobility is another exciting feature for agents, especially with the development of the Internet (Yang & Guan, 2000). Mobile agents can move from one machine to another, across different platforms or architectures. Adding mobility to software agents will improve the potential of their applications in e-commerce. With mobility, agents can now move from one e-commerce service provider (ESP) to another and carry on their execution from where they left off in the previous ESP. In this way, mobile agents can not only retrieve information or negotiate prices from one ESP but also they can compare the prices from the other ESPs before deciding for the end user. However, to take advantage of this feature, interoperability of agents across different platforms must be ensured.

When agents are initially created, they have little knowledge and experience. Although agent owners may give some basic knowledge or functionality to these agents, it is advantageous if they have the ability to learn and evolve. Furthermore, the Web environment also changes rapidly and agents should strive to adapt themselves in order to complete their tasks successfully.

Many issues are essential in agent evolution. First, evolution of agents depends on agents' knowledge and structure. Thus, a suitable agent structure for knowledge acquisition is the basic concern in agent evolution. Second, agents should have their own mechanisms to advance evolution. How to design strong and adaptive evolution mechanisms is another issue to be pursued. Third, in multi-agent systems, evolution of agents is also related to many issues, such as coordination, relationship, topology, and communication. Finally, agent owners should closely interact with the evolutionary process of their agents (Zhu & Guan, 2001).

Agents are both self-interested and social. They have their own goals, but they also seek for collaboration. The interaction with other agents should in some way or another help each individual agent to fulfill one or more of its goals. The motivation for collaboration can arise for the purpose of one temporary task, for example, information retrieval, or for a long-term objective—co-evolution.

We exploit agent evolution in the knowledge level in this chapter, as we deem that knowledge base is the cornerstone of all emergent behaviors of agents. Although agents may gain new knowledge from self-reasoning, we concentrate on knowledge exchange among agents as we argue that this is the most applicable and efficient way to acquire knowledge in a trustworthy multi-agent environment. We use product ontology as a typical instance of knowledge to test our design on evolutionary agents and employ product-brokering agents with ontological process.

A Semantic Web is therefore developed where data is shared under a common framework. The evolutionary agents share information and knowledge among themselves and conduct ontology exchange. Although the chapter is focused on product-brokering agents, the concept of evolutionary agent-based ontology exchange can be extended for other applications.

Background

Although software agents have already been under development since the last decade, only with recent advances in agent technologies, their potential and capabilities have been greatly enhanced. A number of intelligent agent-based systems have been developed for purposes of electronic commerce. MIT Media Lab's Kasbah (Chavez & Maes, 1998) is an online marketplace for buying and selling goods. A user can create a buyer agent, provide it with a set of criteria, and dispatch it into the marketplace. The Minnesota AGent Marketplace Architecture (MAGMA) (Wurman, Wellman, & Walsh, 1998) is a prototype for a virtual marketplace targeted toward items that can be transferred over the Internet. Agents can register with a server that maintains unique identifiers for the agents. AuctionBot (Wurman et al.) is a flexible, scalable, and robust auction server which supports software agents.

In our previous work, we have proposed a secure agent fabrication, evolution & roaming (SAFER) architecture, which aims to construct an open, dynamic, and evolutionary agent system for e-commerce (Zhu, Guan, & Yang, 2000). It provides a framework for agents in e-commerce and establishes a rich set of mechanisms to manage and secure them. We have already elaborated agent fabrication and roaming in Guan and Yang (1999) and Guan, Zhu, and Ko (2000) respectively. Agent evolution is an integrated part of the SAFER architecture. We have proposed a model for agent life cycle and some evolutionary computation methods to evolve agents (Zhu & Guan, 2001).

Literature in distributed artificial intelligence (DAI) and multi-agent system (MAS) has addressed agent evolution extensively. Haynes and Wainwright (1995) aim to evolve programs to control an autonomous agent capable of learning how to survive in a hostile environment. Namatame and Sasaki (1998) provide a model for investigating collective behaviors that emerge from local interaction among self-interested agents. Most of the existing research work on e-commerce agents focuses on evolving strategies for agents, extending the MAS approaches. Gimenez-Funes, Lgodo, Rodriquez-Aguilar, and Garcia-Calves (1998) use possibility-based and case-based decision models to design the bidding strategies for agents in electronic auctions. Richter, Sheble, and Ashlock (1999) develop bidding strategies which are used for electric utilities in the scenario of double auctions.

Sheth and Maes (1993) design a population of personalized information filtering agents. These agents will recommend news articles to the user based on the user's interest. Users will give each recommended article a certain score. A relevant article will receive a higher score than an irrelevant one. After a certain number of iterations, the more successful agent will be retained and be allowed to reproduce while the unfit ones are killed. In Yu, Koo, and Liddy (2000), the authors describe a neuro-genetic approach to develop an MAS which forages as well as meta-searches for multi-media information in online information sources.

There are few research efforts dedicated to agent evolution in e-commerce applications from the perspective of agent interaction, especially from the viewpoints of ontology exchange. However, it is quite usual that agents are interacting with other agents, regardless of whether they have the same or different objectives and structures. Our research considers the evolutionary process in an agent group with a focus on ontology exchange.

In order to coordinate heterogeneous agents effectively across distributed network and facilitate communication between agents, some agent communication language (ACL) and knowledge representation language have been developed, such as the Foundation of Intelligent Physical Agents (FIPA, 2003) ACL and Knowledge Query and Manipulation Language (KQML) (Finin, Fritzson, McKay, & McEntire, 1994).

KQML has become the de facto standard and is widely used in various agent-based systems. KQML provides an extensible set of primitives which defines the permissible operations that agents may attempt on each other's knowledge. It also allows agents to communicate views regarding the content and find agents relevant to process their requests.

An ontology is an explicit specification of a conceptualization. The term *ontology* is borrowed from philosophy, where an ontology is a systematic account of existence. In the context of artificial intelligence, ontology is referred to as a special kind of knowledge. Much research work has been dedicated to explore ontology-based knowledge management, which includes (1) ontological engineering to build an ontology of the subject matter, (2) characterizing knowledge in terms of ontology, and (3) providing intelligent access to knowledge. Huhns and Singh (1997) and Huhns and Stephens (1999) discuss the requirements of ontologies for software agents. Luke, Spector, Rager, and Hendler (1997) describe a set of Hyper Text Markup Language (HTML) ontology extensions for Web agents to annotate Web pages with semantic knowledge. And the paper (Mahalingam & Huhns, 1997) describes how query formation can be made simple and less complicated by using ontologies. Our chapter focuses on the product ontology for product-brokering agents, and we try to demonstrate that agents can build efficient product ontologies via collaboration and exchange with other fellow agents.

Structure of Evolutionary Agents

As mentioned earlier, agent structure is a basic concern in agent evolution. Figure 1 shows an agent structure with evolutionary features which include some hierarchical knowledge structure and the evolutionary modules.

The communication interface is responsible for communication with the owner, hosts, and other agents. Each agent is also equipped with a *receptor* and an *actor*. The receptor receives inputs from the outside world and passes information to the functionality modules or saves it in the result/data modules, while the actor enforces decisions made by the agent. The identity module contains basic elements regarding the identity of an agent, such as agent ID, certificate, and agent-digest. The functionality modules provide standard functions for agent actions and specific functions for individual purposes.

The hierarchical knowledge base stores the agent knowledge base for actions of reasoning, analysis, and decision making. It is divided into three layers, from basic beliefs to private knowledge then social knowledge. Basic beliefs can be abstracted and integrated into private knowledge. Typical social knowledge includes agent relationship, topology of merchant hosts, and other agents.

Figure 1. An agent structure with evolutionary features

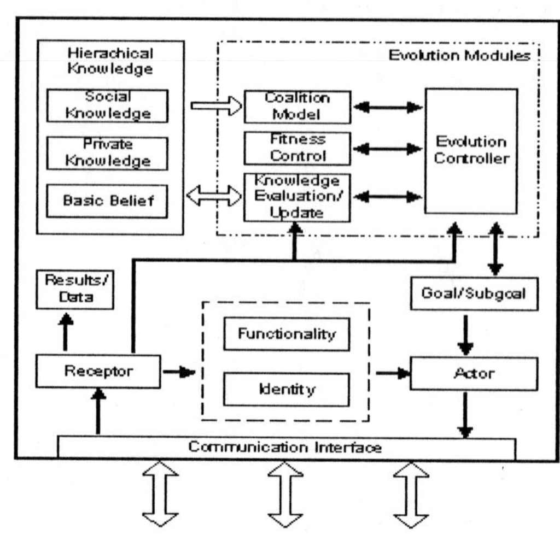

The evolutionary modules include evolution controller, coalition model, fitness control, and knowledge evaluation/update. They are responsible for evolution management. Apart from the goals which are initially set by the agent owner, evolution controller can generate new subgoals or adjust goals according to the process of evolution.

Similar with natural ecosystems, agent evolution is not an isolated process. Agents coexist in a shared environment and pursue their respective goals in the presence of other agents. A collection of agents interacting with each other can be organized as an agent group. We regard an agent group as the fundamental unit for the evolution process. Users can organize agent groups in terms of their preferences or let agents decide which groups they are willing to join. Thus, the criteria for group formation can be varied, and agents in one group can be homogeneous or heterogeneous.

Agent Ontology

According to the nomenclature of Maes' group in the MIT Media Lab (Guttman & Maes, 1999), the common commerce behavior can be described with the consumer buying behavior (CBB) model, which consists of six stages, namely, (1) need identification, (2) product brokering, (3) merchant brokering, (4) negotiation, (5) purchase and delivery, and (6) product service and evaluation. There are various types of agents existing for different stages. Therefore, the knowledge base for each type of agent is different.

The most well-known e-commerce agents are product brokering agents, also called comparison-shopping agents or shopping bots. The main function of these agents is to help users find their favorite products with certain constraints such as price, quality, and delivery time. Such agents will first assist users to construct their queries with current knowledge about product definitions, which is called ontology here. Then they will be able to locate thousands of merchants with specific products or services, and scour through millions of items. Finally, they may sort the results or offers and present them to users.

There are two main bottlenecks for deploying agents in such applications. One is that most Internet stores do not provide facilities to support or serve visiting agents. Either the Internet stores do not allow agents to access product information, or agents do not have such capability to acquire information from the stores. Another point is that agents may return with irrelevant or overwhelming information, as they cannot filter out useful information due to lack of proper knowledge of certain products. This chapter tackles the second case with a focus on product ontology.

A product ontology is a conceptualization of the real-world products. It consists of a specification of concepts to be used for expressing knowledge, including the types and classes of entities, the kinds of attributes and properties they can have, the relationships and functions they can participate in, and constraints that hold. A typical ontology for a product-brokering agent is shown in Figure 2 with a suitable tree structure for representation.

An agent aims to carry sufficient and useful ontology information within its body. There are three approaches for an agent to build its product ontology. The first choice is to approach some ontology definition provider to gain a suitable ontology definition, this may incur time and cost. The second choice is to enhance its ontology by analyzing the data collected online; but it highly relies on the agent capability and

Figure 2. A typical product ontology

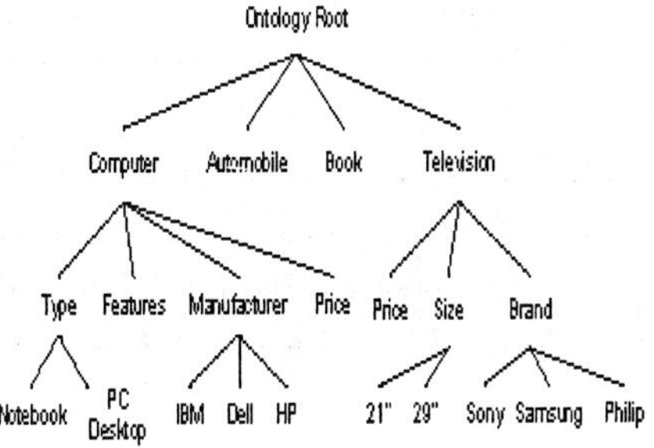

intelligence, and may also need some interaction from its owner. The last choice is to interact with other agents for ontology acquisition or exchange, and this is the focus of this chapter.

Ontology rule is a basic representation format for agent ontology and is suitable to be exchanged among agents. Actually, ontology rules can be inferred from the ontology tree. Here we give some definitions for ontology rules. Table 1 lists some examples of ontology rules.

```
<Ontology Rule>::= <Subject> <Relationship> <Object>
<Subject>::=<Entity_Grp>
<Entity_Grp>::=<Entity><Entity>...
<Entity>::=<string>
<Relationship>::=<Rlt-Element>
<Rlt-Element>::=<string>
<Object>::=<Entitity_Grp> | <Attr_Grp>
<Attr_Grp>::=<Attribute> <Attribute>...
<Attribute>::=<string>
```

Ontology is an essential knowledge base for software agents. For the aforementioned product-brokering agents, product ontology can help query reformulation with several factors:

- shape up a user request by query expansion along the downward direction of the ontology tree;
- widen a query scope context along the upward direction of the ontology tree;
- disambiguate a user request by finding the context relevant to the request; and
- reformulate a query within the same context or even by going from one context to a different context that fits better with respect to the actual wishes of the user.

Table 1. Examples of ontology rules

Rules	Entities	Relationship Element	Entities/Attributes
1	Convertible	is a type of	car
2	Car	has attributes of	engine, color
3	Color	has types of	red, white, black, blue

Ontology Exchange Model and Formalities

We assume that agents are egoistic, but they are willing to collaborate with each other to achieve their objectives. Ontology exchange is a practical way for agents to enhance their ontologies.

There are three basic ontology exchange models, namely, unilateral, bilateral, and multilateral, in terms of the number of agents involved. Here, a model of ontology exchange between an agent and several agents is shown in Figure 3. Agent S contacts agents A1 to An for certain ontology definitions. First, agent S sends a request to the other agents, encapsulating some existing ontology terms/rules in the request. Then, each corresponding agent may respond with some ontology definitions. Upon receiving responses, agent S will determine whether and how they are related with the existing ontology and which ontology pieces will be integrated at last.

Here, we only consider the terms in the ontology, as we deem that the ontologies acquired from the respondents are trustworthy. Assuming that:

Os denotes the ontology of agent S;

Oi denotes the ontology response from agent Ai;

Tr denotes the set of terms included in the request;

Ts denotes the set of terms which are currently in Os;

Ti denotes the set of terms included in Oi

Define $Sim[O_s, O_i] = Sim[T_s, T_i] = N_c / N_s$ to be the similarity between two ontologies Os and Oi, which means that the similarity of ontology is measured by the term set in

Figure 3. An agent contacting other agents for ontology definitions

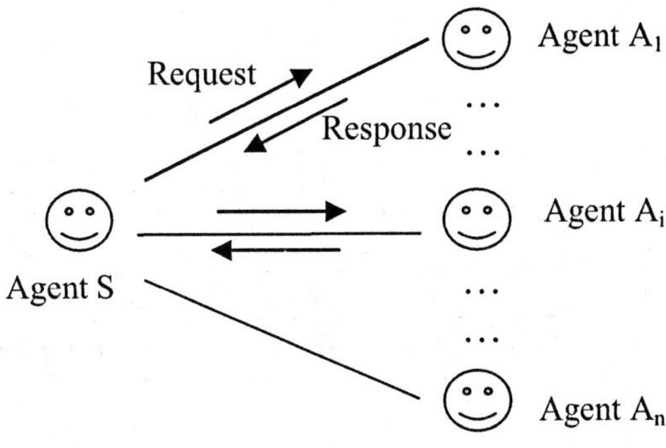

the corresponding ontologies. In this formula, Ne represents the number of terms which are the same or synonymous in both ontologies Os and Oi, and Ns represents the total number of terms in Os.

With the previous definitions, agents can determine the criteria for ontology exchange and integration. For example, when agent S is deciding which ontology piece from a respondent should be integrated, it can use a criterion such as choosing the one which has the maximum similarity with the existing ontology. If agent S decides to integrate more than one piece of ontology, then it can choose those similarity values with the top ranks.

In order to facilitate ontology exchange, communication channels should be established. There exists some standard ACLs for this purpose. KQML (Finin et al., 1994) is the most widely used ACL. KQML provides an extensible set of performatives, which defines the permissible operations between agents. The reserved performative categories include basic informative, response, query, networking, capability definition, and so forth. The following is a typical message in KQML that embeds ontology rules:

```
( tell    :sender       Agent A1
:receiver               Agent S
:language               Specified
:ontology               Product
:content          "Convertible is a type of car"
)
```

Figure 4 shows the flowchart of the ontology exchange process in an individual agent. The KQML messages coming from some other agents are received, and ontology rules in KQML messages are extracted and parsed. The resultant ontology elements will be fused into the ontology database. As for the reverse direction, some ontology rule elements are selected from the ontology database, constructed into a rule and embedded into a KQML message, and then sent to other agents. Other functional modules of agents include a representation to construct an ontology tree from the ontology database and an initiator to raise requests or enquiries.

After an agent receives ontology pieces from other agents, it will use algorithms to integrate them with its own ontology. As shown in Figure 5, an agent is integrating the incoming ontology (O_i) into its own ontology (O_s). First, the agent will check the database of synonyms and hyponyms to establish the relationship map between two ontologies. If some facts of the relationship contradict each other, the part in contradiction will be rejected or placed into a temporary set for future settlement. The compatible parts will be inserted into certain position of the old ontology. As

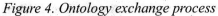

Figure 4. Ontology exchange process

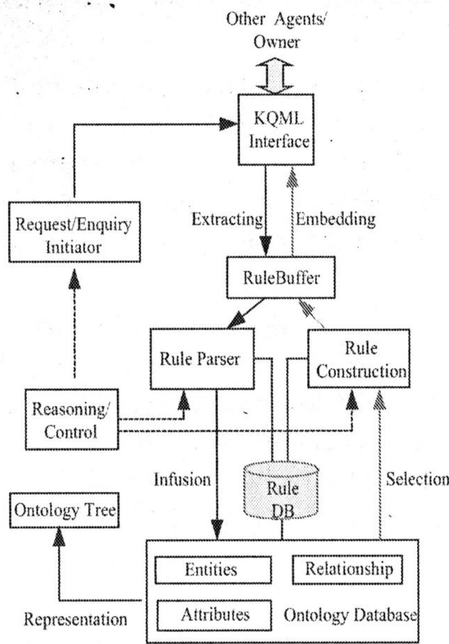

Figure 5. Ontology integration

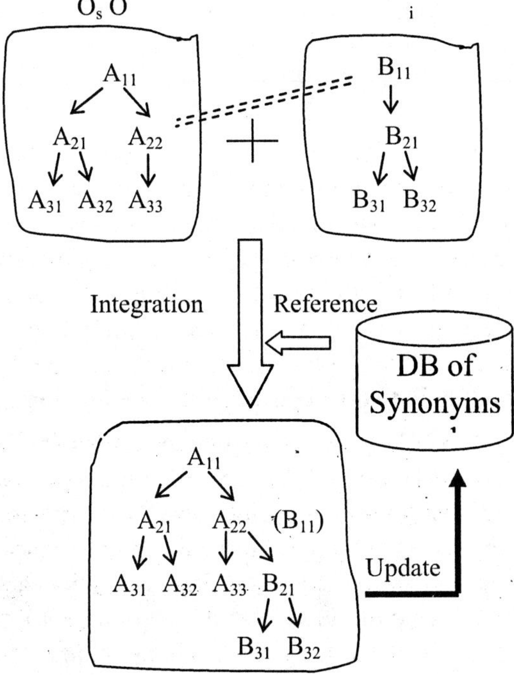

indicated in Figure 5, the agent finds that A22 and B11 are synonyms, so B11 is merged with A22 in the resultant ontology, and Oi is inserted as the child nodes under A11. The database of synonyms and hyponyms may be updated after each integration process.

Implementation

We have implemented a group of product-brokering agents, and the formalities of ontology exchange from request to integration have been successfully implemented. Users can set up their queries and dispatch agents to search for product information. Java is chosen as the language for implementation, because it has important features including robustness, security, and portability.

The implemented agent uses a tree structure to display ontology and provides an interface for a user to view and edit the ontology tree, which includes the opera-

Figure 6. A screenshot of interface for viewing and editing ontology

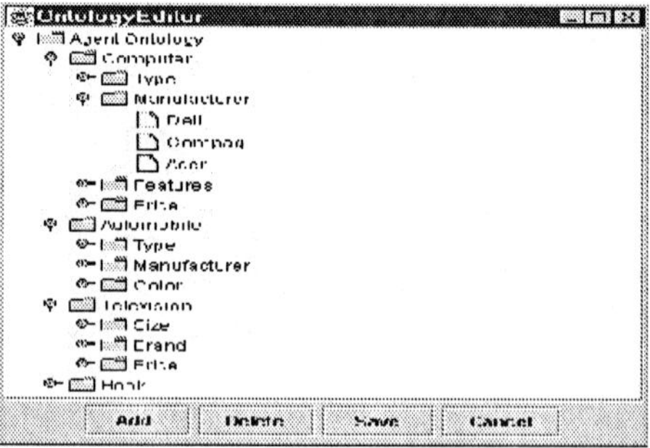

Figure 7. A screenshot of integrating ontology

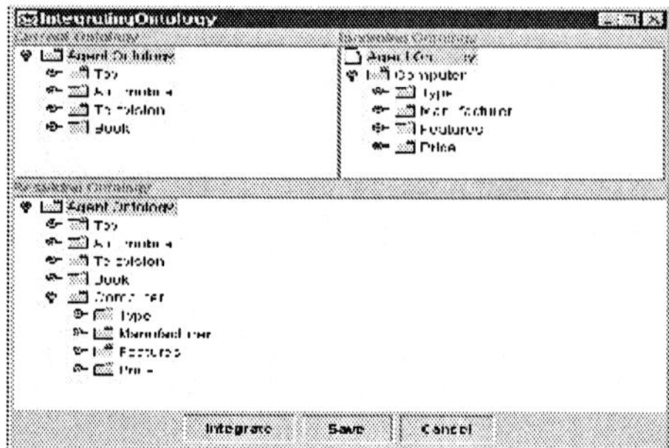

tions of adding a node, deleting a node, and saving the revised ontology, as shown in Figure 6.

Figure 7 illustrates the process of integrating ontology. The top left window shows the original ontology of the agent, and the top right window shows the ontology incoming from the other agent as the exchanged component. The resultant ontology is shown in the bottom window, which shows that the agent has merged the acquired ontology definitions about *computer.* Actually, the whole process is completed by the agent automatically.

We have also implemented the query construction process based on product ontology, as shown in Figure 8. A user specifies his queries with the aid of ontology. The interface includes three components: (1) ontology helper, (2) constraint setting, and (3) query window. The user can click the ontology tree to choose query terms, and the corresponding terms, and available selection choices will appear in the constraint setting part. Then the user can make a selection from the available set or construct new constraints. At last, these constraints can be combined to form a query, which is displayed in the query window.

Figure 8. A screenshot of query construction with the aid of ontology

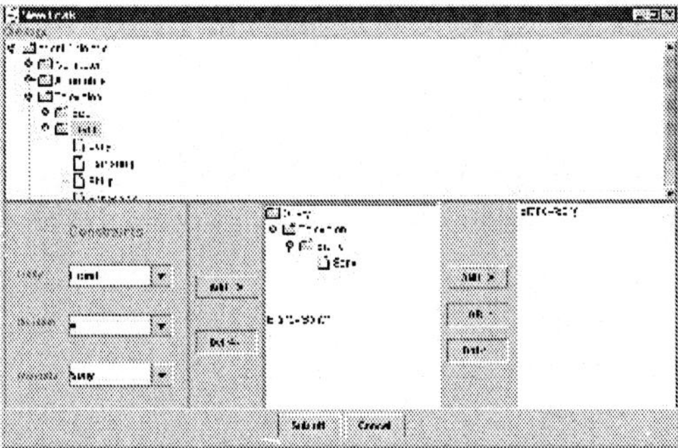

Figure 9. A screenshot showing searching results

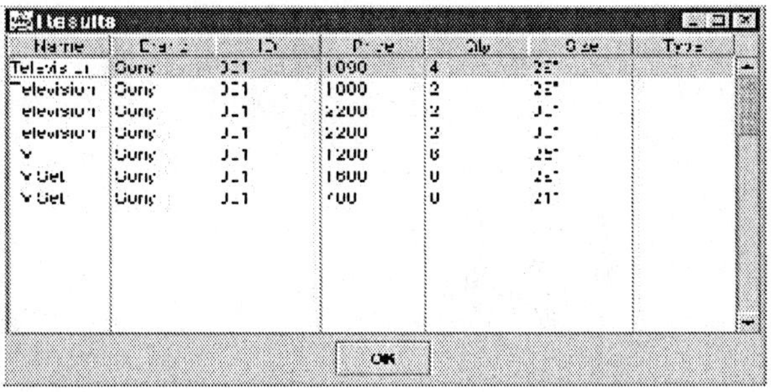

The resultant query is also visually represented as a tree like the ontology. Only terms specified with constraints will be preserved in the query tree, and the constraints will be added into the ontology tree as leaf nodes. Users can edit the query tree freely before submission. We simulate some databases for agents to search for product information. Figure 9 shows an instance of searching results with the query created in Figure 8.

Future Trends

Approaches and implementation of the ontology exchange and integration of product-brokering agents can be improved as follows. Firstly, as checking the relevance of two ontologies and identifying the integration points are much more complicated than discussed in the chapter, we are designing further approaches to outfit agents with higher intelligence and reasoning capability on these issues. Secondly, an enhanced message format embedded with Extensible Markup Language (XML) will be defined to add meaningful structure and semantics into ontology rules. Finally, the application and implementation of the Semantic Web with evolutionary agents can be extended to applications beyond product brokering.

Conclusion

This chapter addresses the issues of evolving software agents in e-commerce applications with a focus on ontology acquisition and exchange. An evolutionary agent structure with a hierarchical knowledge base is proposed to facilitate the evolutionary process. We propose a new approach for ontology exchange among e-commerce agents. The ontology exchange model and its formalities have been elaborated. Product-brokering agents have been designed and implemented. They accomplish the ontology exchange process from request to integration.

References

Chavez, A., & Maes, P. (1998). Kasbah: An agent marketplace for buying and selling goods. In *Proceedings of First International Conference on Practical Application of Intelligent Agents and Multi-Agent Technology 1998,* London (pp. 75-90).

Corradi, A., Montanari, R., & Stefanelli, C. (1999). Mobile agents integrity in e-commerce applications. In *Proceedings of the 19th IEEE International Conference on Distributed Computing Systems*, Austin, TX.

Dignum, F., & Cortés, U. (Eds.). (2001). *Agent-mediated electronic commerce III: Current issues in agent-based electronic commerce systems. Lecture notes in artificial intelligence 2003.* Berlin: Springer.

Finin, T., Fritzson, R., McKay, D., & McEntire, R. (1994). KQML as an agent communication language. In *Proceedings of the Third International Conference on Information and Knowledge Management 1994* (pp. 456-463). ACM Press.

FIPA. (2003). *Foundation of Intelligent Physical Agents*. Retrieved July 29, 2003, from http://www.fipa.org

Gimenez-Funes, E., Lgodo, L., Rodriquez-Aguilar, J. A., & Garcia-Calves, P. (1998). Designing bidding strategies for trading agents in electronic auctions. In *Proceedings of International Conference on Multi Agent Systems 1998*, Paris (pp. 136-143).

Glushko, R. J., Tenenbaum, J. M., & Meltzer, B. (1999). An XML framework for agent-based e-commerce. *Communications of the ACM, 42*(3), 106-114.

Greenberg, M. S., Byington, J. C., & Harper, D. G. (1998). Mobile agents and security. *IEEE Communications Magazine, 36*(7), 76-85.

Guan, S. U., & Yang, Y. (1999, December 15-17). SAFE: Secure roaming agent for e-commerce. In *Proceedings of the 26th International Conference on Computers & Industrial Engineering,* Melbourne, Australia (pp. 33-37).

Guan, S. U., Zhu, F. M., & Ko, C. C. (2000, December 11-13). Agent fabrication and authorization in agent-based electronic commerce. In *Proceedings of International ICSC Symposium on Multi-Agents and Mobile Agents in Virtual Organizations and E-Commerce,* Wollongong, Australia (pp. 528-534).

Guttman, R. H., & Maes, P. (1999). Agent-mediated negotiation for retail electronic commerce. In P. Noriega & C. Sierra (Eds.), *Agent-mediated electronic commerce: First international workshop on agent mediated electronic trading* (pp. 70-90). Berlin: Springer.

Haynes, T. D., & Wainwright, R. L. (1995). A simulation of adaptive agents in a hostile environment. In *Proceedings of the 1995 ACM Symposium on Applied Computing.* ACM Press.

Huhns, M. N., & Singh, M. P. (1997). Ontologies for agents. *IEEE Internet Computing, 1*(6), 81-83.

Huhns, M. N., & Stephens, L. M. (1999). Personal ontologies. *IEEE Internet Computing, 3*(5), 85-87.

Krishna, V., & Ramesh, V. C. (1998). Intelligent agents for negotiation in market games, part1: Model. *IEEE Transactions on Power Systems, 13*(3), 1103-1108.

Luke, S., Spector, L., Rager, D., & Hendler, J. (1997). Ontology-based Web agents. In *Proceedings of the 1st International Conference on Autonomous Agents 1997*, Marina Del Rey (pp. 59-66).

Mahalingam, K., & Huhns, M. N. (1997). An ontology tool for query formulation in an agent-based context. In *Proceedings of the Second IFCIS International Conference on Cooperative Information Systems* (pp. 170-178).

Namatame, A., & Sasaki, T. (1998). Competitive evolution in a society of self-interested agents. In *Proceedings of IEEE World Congress on Computational Intelligence.*

Richter, C. W., Sheble, G. B., & Ashlock, D. (1999). Comprehensive bidding strategies with genetic programming/finite state automata. *IEEE Transactions on Power Systems, 14*(4), 1207-1212.

Sheth, B., & Maes, P. (1993). Evolving agents for personalized information filtering. In *Proceedings of the Ninth Conference on Artificial Intelligence for Applications 1993*, Orlando, FL (pp. 345-352). IEEE Computer Society Press.

Wurman, P. R., Wellman, M. P., & Walsh, W. E. (1998). The Michigan Internet AuctionBot: A configurable auction server for human and software agents. In *Proceedings of the Second International Conference on Autonomous Agents 1998,* Minneapolis, MN (pp. 301-308).

Yang, Y., & Guan, S. U. (2000). Intelligent mobile agents for e-commerce: Security issues and agent transport. In S. M. Rahman & M. Raisinghani (Eds.), *Electronic commerce: Opportunities and challenges* (pp. 321-336). Hershey, PA: Idea Group.

Yu, E. S., Koo, P. C., & Liddy, E. D. (2000). Evolving intelligent text-based agents. In *Proceedings of the Fourth International Conference on Autonomous Agents 2000*, Barcelona, Spain (pp. 388-395).

Zhu, F. M., & Guan, S. U. (2001). Towards evolution of software agents in electronic commerce. In *Proceedings of the Congress on Evolutionary Computation 2001 (CEC2001), 1303-1308,* Seoul, Korea.

Zhu, F. M., Guan, S. U., & Yang, Y. (2000). SAFER e-commerce: Secure agent fabrication, evolution & roaming for e-commerce. In S. M. Rahman & R. J. Bignall (Eds.), *Internet commerce and software agents: Cases, technologies and opportunities* (pp. 190-206). Hershey, PA: Idea Group.

Chapter VIII

Web Services Discovery and QoS-Aware Extension

Chen Zhou, Nanyang Technological University, Singapore
Liang-Tien Chia, Nanyang Technological University, Singapore
Bu-Sung Lee, Nanyang Technological University, Singapore

Abstract

Web services are self-contained, self-describing modular applications. Different from traditional distributed computing, Web services are more dynamic on its service discovery and run-time binding mechanism. As big numbers of Web services appear on the Web, Web services discovery mechanism becomes essential. This chapter provides an in-depth discussion on works about Web services discovery. We first present some basis knowledge for the Web services discovery. After that we introduce some value-added services for the Web services discovery, such as the quality of service (QoS)-aware services discovery and semantics-aware service discovery. Since nonfunctional attributes, especially the QoS information, are quite important for mission critical tasks, we finally present our Semantic Web-based solution for QoS-aware service discovery and measurement. It complements Web ontology language-service (OWL-S) to achieve better services discovery, composition and measurement.

Introduction

The Web is evolving from a collection of pages to a collection of services. In both e-business and e-science, people are realizing that they can achieve significant cost savings by outsourcing and cooperation. There are increasing demands to integrate services across distributed, heterogeneous, and dynamic environments from different service providers. The emergence of Web services represents the latest development for this trend. It helps to speed up the Web's evolution from page-centric Web to service-centric Web.

The World Wide Web Consortium (W3C) defines the Web service as "a software system designed to support interoperable machine-to-machine interaction over a network. It has an interface described in a machine-processable format (specifically WSDL). Other systems interact with the Web Service in a manner prescribed by its description using SOAP messages, typically conveyed using HTTP with an XML serialization in conjunction with other Web-related standards" (Haas & Brown, 2003). Here the WSDL (Christensen, Curbera, Meredith, & Weerawarana, 2001) means Web services description language and SOAP (Box et al., 2000) means simple object access protocol. Examples of simple Web services are stock querying, current weather reporting, online dictionary, and so forth.

Web services technology is becoming the dominant choice for current distributed systems. Its adoption grows continuously in recent years and will likely keep this trend in the foreseeable future. This trend is influenced by both technical and nontechnical factors. The main technical advantage of Web services is to leverage already widely used technologies, that is, extensible markup language (XML) for representing data content and Web protocols (hypertext markup language [HTTP], file transfer protocol [FTP], and so on) for message transportation. In addition, Web services can quickly reuse the existing systems by wrapping the legacy software component into a Web service and publishing the service. As a result, small-, medium-, or large-sized businesses, with or without their existing computing and software system, can adopt the Web services system easily and cheaply. The main nontechnical advantage of Web services technology is the investment and advocation on Web service protocols and products by all major software companies (IBM, Microsoft, Sun, HP, etc.). Furthermore, the Web services protocols are controlled under several industrial standardization groups, such as W3C and Organization for the Advancement of Structured Information Standards (OASIS). Many higher level software systems have already chosen the standard Web services as building blocks. Some examples are grid services and the Semantic Web-enabled Web services.

In the Web services discovery system, the Web services architecture has three major roles: (1) a service provider, (2) a service consumer, and (3) a directory. Such an architecture enables a loose coupling of service consumer and service provider: first, the service provider publishes descriptions of its services to the directory. After that, the service consumer searches the directory to find information about an appropriate provider and its service. Finally the service consumer binds to the chosen provider and uses its service. This loose coupling is performed dynamically, that is, during the run time. This *publish-discovery-bind* model of service interaction increases the flexibility and agility of the Web services. Furthermore, this model raises the competition between service providers to force them into offering better services.

In the loosely coupled Web services architecture, the discovery process is the key for dynamic service invocation. Universal description discovery and integration (UDDI) (Von Riegen, 2002) plays the role of directory for the Web services' discovery. It consists not only of a data structure standard for all business-related descriptions of services (i.e., service publication), but also the discovery protocols that allow the service requester to gain access to the service publication and service description. After the service requester chooses the service, he/she retrieves the WSDL file to get its binding information and then invoke the target Web service using SOAP protocol. These three standards form the basis of the Web services. Most Web services' vendors support these standards to achieve the interoperability between Web services. Additional protocols are designed on top of them to offer value-added services.

As more and more Web services are published on the Web, the Web services' discovery mechanism is becoming more and more important for several reasons. First, the service requesters face a huge number of service offers. How to precisely locate the correct Web service according to the service requester's requirement is a necessary prerequisite to invoke the Web service. Second, a better Web services discovery mechanism increases the precision and efficiency for the discovery process. It is necessary for the service providers to achieve the competitive advantage. It also improves the satisfiability for the service requesters. Last, but not the least, a good service discovery mechanism improves the efficiency in the service composition process as well, especially for the automated composition of Web services. Computer-aided service composition is a planning problem, where service requester has complete information about the start and end situation. Such a planning problem has a bounded length, while on each planning step, the search space is very branchy, that is, there are many services to choose from. Therefore, reducing the search space by precise service discovery is an effective way to improve the automatic composition progress.

To provide the value-added service discovery and reduce the cost of integration, there are several requirements to be considered. In this chapter we focus on the QoS-aware service discoveries and the semantics-aware service discovery.

QoS-aware service discovery is a necessary requirement for sophisticated Web services applications. Being able to provide QoS-aware service discovery has several distinct advantages. First, it allows the discovery and execution of the service according to their QoS specifications. This forces the service provider to offer better services to achieve competitive advantage. Second, it allows the Web services to be applied in mission critical tasks. The service should provide its performance promises in critical situations. The execution of the service should be monitored during its life cycle to ensure the service conforms to the agreed service level objectives. If undesired performance is detected, the service provider can take some management activities to control the Web services' behavior. Third, the Web services adaptation can perform according to the initial requirements. The unpredictable surrounding environment definitely influences the execution of Web services. The adaptation according to the initial QoS requirement is preferable.

The Semantic Web provides a common framework that allows data to be shared and reused across application, enterprise, and community boundaries. Well-defined semantics in service discovery is important because it involves the integration problems. Web services are designed within heterogeneous environments. The integration problem is the main obstacle for people to share services. The integration problem is caused by the syntax heterogeneity and semantic heterogeneity. Syntax heterogeneity exists because the interface signatures use different data types and class hierarchies. Semantic heterogeneity originates from the different semantic meanings of the service interface parameters and its functionalities. For example, the stock inquiry service requires the name of the stock as its input. This may mean the numerical stock symbol, or company name of the stock. This will cause the ambiguous understanding of the input. To solve the integration problem, both service requester and the service provider should have the same understanding of these meanings. The semantic conflicts occur when these two partners use different interpretations for the same item.

In the following section, we will introduce some basis knowledge of Web services discovery and some works on value-added service discovery. This is followed by our work for the QoS-aware Web services discovery.

Basic Web Services Discovery and its Extensions

The following sections will describe the generic Web services architecture and its support for Web services discovery.

Web Services Architecture

An option for viewing the Web service architecture is to examine the emerging Web service protocol stack. The stack is still evolving, but currently has following five major layers (Sollazzo, Handschuh, Staab, & Frank, 2002) as shown in Figure 1.

- **Network protocols:** This layer is responsible for transporting messages between applications. Currently, this layer includes HTTP (Fielding, Gettys, Mogul, Frystyk, & Berners-Lee, 1997), simple mail transfer protocol (SMTP) (Postel, 1982), FTP (Postel & Reynolds, 1985), and newer protocols, such as blocks extensible exchange protocol (BEEP) (Rose, 2001).
- **XML-based messaging:** This layer is responsible for encoding messages in a common XML format so that messages can be understood at either end. Currently, this layer includes XML-remote procedure calls (RPC) (Winer, 1999) and SOAP (Box et al., 2000).
- **Service description:** This layer is responsible for describing the public interface to a specific Web service. Currently, service description is handled via the WSDL (Christensen et al., 2001). The service profile of OWL-S (OWL-S Coalition, 2003) is a good candidate for the semantic service description and matchmaking.
- **Service publication and discovery:** The *service publication* is regarded as a business-related description of a service; this involves some questions like: What products are associated with this service? Which organization is offering this service? UDDI (Von Riegen, 2002) not only consists of defining a data structure standard for all business-related descriptions of services (i.e., service publication) but also contains all mechanisms that allow the service requester to gain access to the service publication and service description. Thus it is also in charge of the *service discovery layer*.
- **Service flow:** This layer is responsible for prescribing an XML format for specifying service composition (also called service flow). Currently several

Figure 1. Web service protocol stack from IBM's view

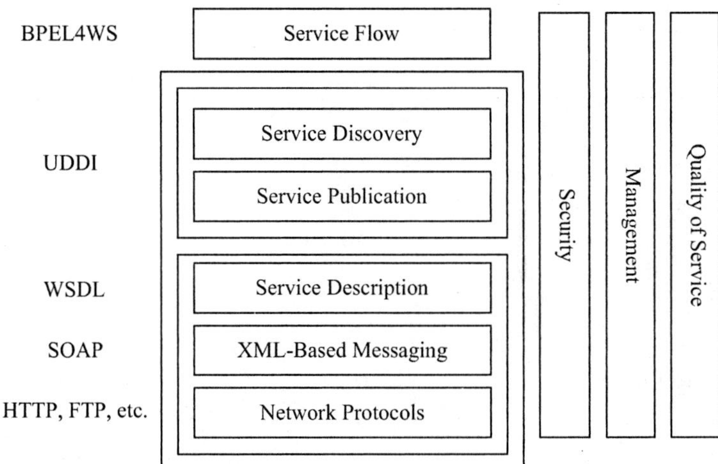

specifications are available: Web services flow language (WSFL) (Leymann, 2001), XLANG (Thatte, 2001), business process execution language for Web services (BPEL4WS) (Andrews, 2003), and OWL-S (OWL-S Coalition, 2003).

- **Orthogonal layers:** Several layers are orthogonal in Figure 1 because issues like security, management, and QoS span over all the other layers.

The basic building blocks in the Web services include SOAP, WSDL, and UDDI. SOAP provides a simple and lightweight mechanism for exchanging structured and typed information between peers in a decentralized, distributed environment using XML. This allows SOAP to be used in a large variety of systems ranging from messaging systems to RPC.

WSDL is a specification defining how Web services are described in a common XML grammar. WSDL describes four critical pieces of data: (1) interface, (2) data type, (3) binding, and (4) address information. Using WSDL, a client can locate a Web service and invoke any of its publicly available functions. WSDL therefore represents a cornerstone of the Web service architecture, because it provides a common language for describing services and a platform for automatically integrating those services.

UDDI (Von Riegen, 2002) is a specification that defines a service registry of available Web services, serving as a global electronic "yellow pages." It allows a company to publish a description of available goods and services to the registry, thus announcing itself as a service provider. Service requesters can send requests as SOAP messages to the service registry to discover a service provider for obtaining goods or services. Upon finding a potential business partner, the service requester can easily integrate with a service provider to start an e-business. Table 1 provides an overview of the main UDDI inquiry functions. Inquiry functions are further subdivided into two groups: find_xxx functions provide general search functionality, whereas get_xxx functions retrieve full records based on unique key values.

Extensions for Web Services Discovery

Although UDDI is currently the industry standard for the Web services discovery, it has certain limitations on value-added services, such as the semantic descriptions and QoS descriptions for services. Works have been done to provide value-added services for Web services discovery, or to design extension frameworks for the UDDI registry. In the following section we will present some extension works for Web services discovery.

Table 1. Main functions of the UDDI inquiry API

Function Name	Description
Find_xxx Functions	
find_binding	Searches for bindings associated with a specified service
find_business	Searches for businesses that match the specified criteria
find_service	Searches for services associated with a specified business
find_tModel	Searches for tModels that match the specified criteria
get_xxx Functions	
get_bindingDetail	Retrieves a complete bindingTemplate record
get_businessDetail	Retrieves a complete businessEntity record
get_serviceDetail	Retrieves a complete businessService record
get_tModelDetail	Retrieves a complete tModel record

Semantics-Aware Web Services Discovery

One extension for Web services discovery is to add semantics for Web services. Semantics matchmaking is not supported in UDDI. A traditional keyword matching algorithm is adopted in UDDI to discover related services. WSDL files can be retrieved from the matching services list, by which service requester binds and invokes the chosen service. However, neither UDDI nor WSDL offer precise service semantics in their description. That is, these service descriptions do not interpret the service's hierarchical position, input, output, precondition, effect, and the nonfunctional properties. Without precise semantics, service requester cannot make sure that the discovered service fully meets his/her required semantics.

Some researchers work toward the inclusion of the semantics and matchmaking ability for Web services. OWL-S is one of the most recognized works in this area. It is an OWL (Dean & Schreiber, 2004) ontology for describing Web services. With the tight connection with OWL, OWL-S aims to make Web services computer interpretable and to enable automated Web service discovery, invocation, composition, and monitoring. It defines the notions of a *service profile* (what the service does), a *service model* (how the service works) and a *service grounding* (how to use the service).

The service profile is the key component for service discovery. Its components can be divided into four sections:

- **Service profile:** Service profile provides a superclass of every type of high-level description of the service. There is a two-way relation between a service and a profile which are expressed by the properties *presents* and *presentedBy*.
- **Service name, contacts, and description:** Service name, contacts, and description provide some properties of the profile that provide human-readable information.

- **Functionality description:** Profile ontology defines the following properties of the Profile class for pointing to IOPE's (Input, Output, Precondition, and Effect): *hasParameter*, *hasInput*, *hasOutput*, *hasPrecondition*, *hasEffect.*
- **Profile attributes:** Profile attributes define additional attributes of the service, including the quality guarantees that are provided by the service, possible classification of the service, and additional parameters that the service may want to specify.

OWL-S ontology combines the explicit and implicit representation for the Web services (Sycara & Paolucci, 2004). To the explicit representation, the process model of OWL-S explicitly defines the work process ontology of the Web service. The Web service operation is defined in the process ontology directly, and the matching of the process is a straightforward task. However, this definition space is too large for different Web services with different capabilities. To the implicit representation, the service profile of OWL-S implicitly defines the state transition of the Web Service's input to its output. This definition requires only the concepts that describe the domain of the service. However the matchmaking engine needs to infer the process from its implicit representation.

OWL-S provides a representation of service's functional capability. However, some researchers have pointed out that significant improvement for the QoS model should be made for a realistic solution to OWL-S users. One current limitation of OWL-S QoS model is that it does not provide a detailed set of classes and properties to represent QoS metrics. The QoS model needs to be extended to allow a precise characterization of individual metrics.

Web service modeling ontology (WSMO) (Lausen, Polleres, & Roman, 2005) is another important work to define semantics for Web services. The WSMO provides a conceptual framework and a formal language for semantically describing all relevant aspects of Web services. There are four main elements: (1) ontologies, which provide the terminology used by other WSMO elements; (2) Web service descriptions, which describe the functional and behavioral aspects of a Web service; (3) goals that represent user desires; and (4) mediators, which aim at the automatic handling of interoperability problems between different WSMO elements. It defines a list of nonfunctional properties for Web services in its specification. The matchmaking algorithm for these nonfunctional properties needs further study. The measurement and monitoring system for service performance should be designed to make it more feasible in practice.

QoS-Aware Extension for Web Services Discovery

QoS-aware service discovery is another important value-added service for service discovery, however, it is not supported in UDDI. The QoS-related information is neither stored in UDDI's tModel nor in WSDL file. Service provider does not have a standard way to publish their service's QoS information in the UDDI registry. Service requester cannot find such information through the inquiry application program interface (API) as well. Furthermore, as described in the previous section, the semantics extensions for Web services have limited support for the QoS-aware service discovery.

The QoS issue is quite sensitive for the Web services because Web services tend to encounter performance bottlenecks. This is due to the limitations of the underlying messaging and transport protocols. Actually, the reliance on widely accepted protocols, such as HTTP and SOAP, leaves Web services with a tough burden.

HTTP is a best-effort delivery service. It is a stateless data-forwarding mechanism, which tends to create two major problems: (1) there is no guarantee of packets being delivered to the destination, and (2) there is no guarantee on the order of the arriving packets.

SOAP performance is degraded because of the following: (1) extracting the SOAP envelope from the SOAP packet is time-expensive; (2) parsing the contained XML information in the SOAP envelope using a XML parser is also time-expensive; (3) there is not much optimization possible with XML data; and (4) SOAP encoding rules make it mandatory to include typing information in all the SOAP messages sent and received. Encoding binary data in a form acceptable to XML results in overhead of additional bytes as well as processor overhead performing the encoding/decoding.

Other factors affecting Web service performance include Web server response time and availability; original application execution time in Web application server; back-end database or legacy system performance; and so forth. Since many aspects influence the Web services QoS, a good service level will require service providers to make available extra resources and efforts. Proper service discovery mechanism is necessary for selling and differentiating these services and to protect the service providers' benefits.

There are recent projects to add QoS-aware service discovery ability in UDDI. For example, the UDDI Extension (UDDIe) project, UDDI eXtension (UX) project, and so on.

UDDIe project (Shaikhali, Rana, Al-Ali, & Walker, 2003) argues that current UDDI does not provide an automatic mechanism for updating the registry when there are changes to services (and service providers). They designed UDDIe, an extension to UDDI, which supports the notion of "blue pages" to record user-defined properties associated with a service and to enable discovery of services based on these properties. UDDIe enables a registry to be more dynamic, by allowing services to hold a lease—a time period describing how long a service description should remain in the registry. UDDIe and WSDL provide an important mechanism for specifying and deploying Web services, especially when extending a WSDL document with additional attributes such as service quality and performance data. They use UDDIe to support quality of service management (QoSM) in the context of grid computing. The broker applies a weighted average (WA) selection algorithm to select the most appropriate service with respect to the client/application request and sends the result to the client/application. This framework provides a lightweight and practical solution for QoS-aware service discovery.

UX (Zhou, Chia, & Lee, 2004) is one of our previous works that facilitates requesters to discover services with good performance. This work describes the network model and design choices to be decided during implementation. Customization is provided for the service requesters to describe their preferences for discovery. In each enterprise domain, the requesters' QoS feedback is collected and summarized in a local UX server. By sharing these experiences from all requesters in the local domain, the system predicts the service's future performance according to the service's historical performance. To support the discovery between different cooperation domains, we design a general federated service and then enable the UX system's federated discovery ability based on this federated service. The system handles the federated inquiry and provides a simple view over the whole federation. This work gives a pluggable extension for UDDI to provide the QoS-aware service discovery. The problem for cross-domain service discovery is also addressed. However, this system does not have a straightforward way to extend and share new metrics definitions between service partners. This leads to our research for the formal definition of QoS metrics using ontologies.

WS-QoS (Tian, Gramm, Ritter, & Schiller, 2004) defines the XML schema for Web services to describe their services' high and low level QoS properties. The assistant framework is designed for the language specification to assist the service selection and publish. High-level, QoS requirements may be mapped to the actual QoS-enabled transport layer through its proxy. It uses ontology style to define custom metrics. Two levels of metrics, the service performance level metrics and the transport level metrics, are defined in their system. Their approach provides an efficient and QoS-aware service selection to enhance the original UDDI.

As reported in the last few examples, these QoS specifications are not based on ontology level. This creates obstacles to share domain knowledge and increases the cost of the integration. In the next section, we present our work on the QoS-aware service discovery based on the ontology level. The major purpose of this work is to simplify the integration problem and assist the QoS-aware service discovery and measurement.

QoS-Aware Service Discovery with Ontology Support

We design an ontology level service description to support QoS-aware service discovery. In practice, we can divide service discovery into two phases. In the first phase, a requester discovers the service using the functional aspect of the service—what the service does, its input and output parameters, preconditions, and effects. This phase ensures that the returned services meet the requester's basic requirements. The second phase is to identify the most appropriate service for the current task; it accounts for the nonfunctional information, such as QoS, about each service returned in the first phase. This second phase has become an important research area in process combination and resource discovery because dynamic binding and invocation are preferable.

The current service discovery process adopts keyword-matching technology to locate published Web services, a less-than-desirable situation. The returned discovery result might not satisfy the requester's intended requirements; this will likely lead to a manual process of choosing the proper service according to its semantics. From the Web services point of view, the selection criteria should at least include the service's functional and nonfunctional requirements. To fully integrate service discovery, these domain-specific criteria should be clear and processed automatically. This requires domain-specific knowledge.

In this light, Semantic Web technology is a promising innovation for service discovery. It requires that data are not only human readable, but also machine understandable. Semantic Web concepts can help provide a unifying system that minimizes misunderstandings among different partners. OWL-S aims to enable automated Web service discovery, invocation, composition, and monitoring. To cover the second phase, OWL-S has defined quality rating ontologies to describe the service's QoS information. However, as mentioned before, one current limitation of OWL-S' QoS model is that it does not provide a detailed set of classes and properties to represent QoS metrics. This motivates us to design the QoS ontology to compensate for this shortcoming of OWL-S in the second phase. In addition to defining the QoS ontology's use in the second phase of service discovery process, we further define its ability to measure QoS.

Basis for a QoS Ontology

We call our ontology OWL-QoS; it is a complementary ontology that provides detailed QoS information for OWL-S. In addition to covering a system's nonfunctional aspects, it also covers QoS measurement.

Based on the approach of using ontology, we aim to reduce the integration cost for Web services. The service integration problem inherits from syntax heterogeneity and semantic heterogeneity. We reduce the syntax heterogeneous by using the uniform ontology syntax. As to the semantic heterogeneous, we try to reduce the misunderstanding of the service's functionality by sharing OWL-S ontology, as well as the nonfunctional aspects of the service by sharing OWL-QoS ontology. Sharing the same ontology domain is required in our design for service partners to avoid the ontology mapping problem.

Nonfunctional aspects describe constraints such as service level, management statements, security policies, pricing information, and other contracts between Web services and their users. While the security of Web services is an extremely important issue, we believe that security itself is a separate research area. This work, including the QoS specification, is not about the security of Web services and the related protocols.

We include several design principles to guide our ontology design. When a Web service is designed and developed by developers before its launch, it is said to be in the design phase. On the other hand, when a service is running, or executing, it is said to be in run time. During design phase, users would normally focus on the system's functional aspects rather than nonfunctional aspects. However, the best practice is to keep QoS issues in mind during early stages of the design phase. During run time, QoS specification should provide additional information to support dynamic service discovery, composition, integration, and monitoring. These requirements need appropriate language support. As a QoS specification for Web services, our design principles include:

- **Ease of use:** Developers should find the specification easy to use and understand. A clear specification helps developers to understand the system's nonfunctional aspects and guides them toward choosing a proper system design pattern early on in development.
- **Precision and flexibility:** To allow value-added services for dynamic service discovery as well as automatic and customizable composition and integration, the QoS specification should have precision and flexibility. Precision means that it should answer the questions of when, which, where, what, and how the specification should be evaluated against the Web service (Sahai, Durante, & Machiraju, 2002). Flexibility permits the specification of customized metrics for diverse Web services.
- **Object-oriented style:** Because of the widespread acceptance of object-oriented design principles, it would help if the definitions for QoS requirements were also object oriented. When developers know the overall interface's QoS requirements, it makes sense for lower-level interfaces to inherit QoS requirements and reuse the QoS constraints from the overall interface.

- **Automatic validation:** As the project grows, automatic validation becomes important. More specifically, it is desirable to automatically check whether the specification is correct in its syntax as well as its semantics.
- **Separation of design duties:** A design should separate its measurement details for metrics from its concept definition. It is the measurement partners' task to fill in the metric measurement details according to the service execution environment. A measurement partner is the group that deploys the measurement handlers and performs the service measurement tasks. The service provider or requester can take on this role, or it can be outsourced to a third party.

Model Design

According to these design principles, we divide the ontology into a three-layer representation:

- The *profile layer* defines QoS matchmaking.
- The *property definition layer* defines properties and the domain and range constraints for such properties.
- The *metrics layer* defines QoS metrics and their measurement details.

The profile layer defines the service-level objective (SLO) for the Web service interfaces. An SLO is normally a set of parameters and their values. The profile layer declares the class QoSProfile as a shared superclass for all QoS specifications. Additional QoS constraints are added in the QoSProfile's inherited concepts. Figure 2

Figure 2. QoS profile matchmaking for service requester and service providers

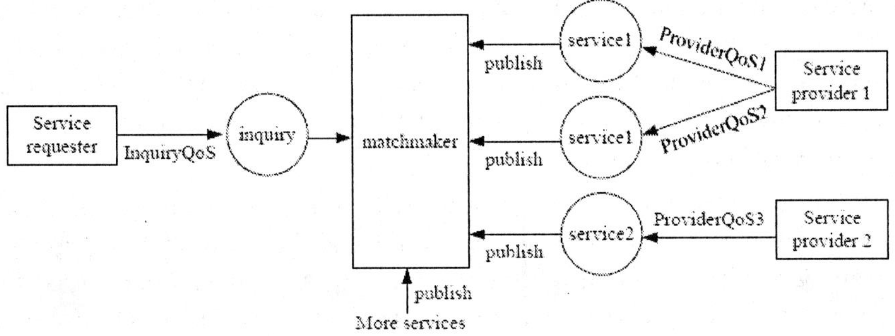

gives an example: The service requester requires a Web service that implements the service interface and satisfies the QoS constraints stated in InquiryQoS. The service provider promises to implement the service interface with the QoS constraints stated in ProviderQoS. These two descriptions are subclasses of QoSProfile but designed for different purposes.

The constraint definitions in the SLO specification cover property domain, range, and cardinality. For example, property responseTimeMS's domain is QoSProfile and its range is the metric ResponseMSMetric (the response time metric in milliseconds). Cardinality constraints govern the number of metrics values, constraining them to remain within a specified number and range of values.

Part A in Figure 3 shows an example of QoS advertisement. Suppose we want to specify the provider's advertisement for a service in which the average response time is no more than 5 seconds and the cost is no more than one dollar. According to our ontology design, this advertisement can be written in description logic's synax as:

Figure 3. Overview of OWL-QoS ontology design

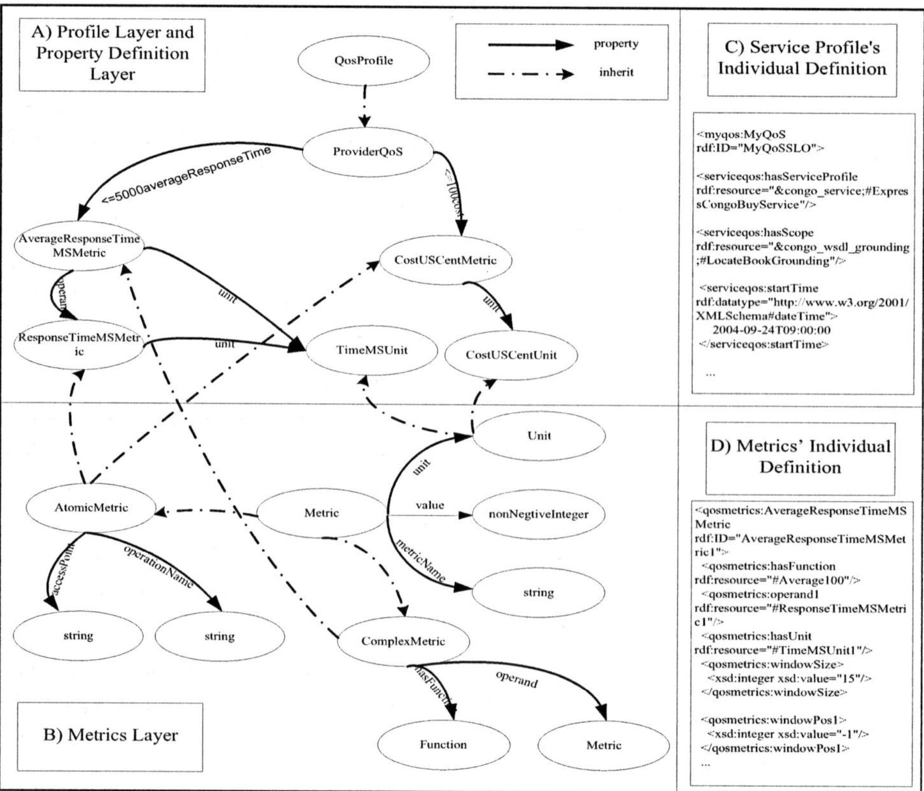

$$ProviderQoS \doteq QoSProfile \sqcap (\leq 100 cost.CostUSCentMetric) \sqcap (\leq 5000 averageResponseTimeMS) AverageResponseMSMetric$$

where $\sqcap$ indicates the conjunction of concept.

Part B of Figure 3 shows the sample of metrics layer definition. The definition of metrics layer has two purposes: Firstly, this layer defines proper QoS metrics for the QoS property's range definition. Secondly, this layer defines precise semantic meanings for a service measurement partner to measure the service and check against the guarantee. The service QoS metrics are divided into AtomicMetrics and ComplexMetrics. All metrics are subclasses of these two metrics and should inherit all the properties of these two metrics. AtomicMetric represents the metrics that collect the first hand data from managed resources using measurement handlers. The AtomicMetric's property *measureAt* answers the "where" question of the measurement. It can be set as "Server," "Client," and so forth. According to the AtomicMetric's individual definition, the measurement party generates the corresponding measurement handler and deploys the handler at the proper location. ComplexMetric defines the way to combine lower level metrics (AtomicMetric or ComplexMetric) according to its function definition. It has properties *hasFunction*, *operand*, and so on. Users can define their customized function definition or define their own function handler in Java code to process with the custom defined functions. The "what" and "how" questions of the measurement are answered by these properties.

Part C of Figure 3 defines the agreement between service requester and service provider. It answers "which" service is agreed upon and "when" the measurement evaluation is performed. Furthermore, it states some price and penalty information of the agreement. Part D of Figure 3 specifies the detailed measurement information for measurement partners.

To facilitate the speedy startup in using the QoS ontology, we design a basic AtomicMetric set according to the general requirement. A template measurement handler for each metric in this set is also developed in our system. The basic metric set contains response time, cost, invocation, and so forth. The measurement handlers for these metrics can be generated according to the corresponding template. Using these AtomicMetrics as building blocks, we also create a basic ComplexMetric set, which includes reliability, throughput, average response time, and so forth.

QoS profile's reuse is an important requirement for the service requesters and providers. The object-oriented design principle is widely used in the service component's development. Since the profile's definitions are linked directly to the service's interfaces, object-oriented style is a natural choice for the corresponding profile's definition. Corresponding to the software components' inheritance, we use conjunctive operator to refine the specific QoS requirement for the inherited interface and reuse all the inherited QoS specifications described in the super interface.

Based on this ontology definition, we divide the QoS profile's matching degree into five levels: (1) *Subsume* (if request R is super-concept of advertisement A), (2) *Exact* (if advertisement R and request A are equivalent concepts), (3) *PlugIn* (If request R is subconcept of advertisement A), (4) *Intersection* (If the intersection of advertisement A and request R is satisfiable), and (5) *Disjoint* (Otherwise it is disjoint). *Subsume* matches are considered the preferred match, since we can expect that the advertisement conforms to the request; *Exact* matches are the next best, because the advertisement is exactly the same as the request; *PlugIn* matches are considered to be the third best, as the advertisement does not fully provide the required QoS level according to the request; *Intersection* is supposed to be the fourth best, since it means that the advertisement is not incompatible with the request; and *Disjoint* is the worst case, because it shows the conflict between the advertisement and the request. This is a failed match.

Prototype System

QoS matchmaking is a process that requires a repository to take an inquiry as input and to return all of the published advertisements that conform to the inquiry's QoS requirement. A profile specification conforms to another profile specification only if it is stronger than, or equally as strong as, the other constraint. Based on this definition, we have designed a matchmaking algorithm for OWL-QoS (Zhou, Chia, & Lee, 2005), together with its prototype.

Figure 4 describes the system diagram of our matchmaker prototype. The prototype system contains an ontology repository, a converter, and an ontology reasoner. The matchmaking algorithm is defined as follows: This algorithm evaluates the relationship between the requester's and the provider's profile concepts. *Subsume*, *Exact*, *PlugIn*, *Intersection*, and *Disjoint* are the possible relationships, in ranking order from the best to the worst match. The ontology repository holds all the published Web service descriptions. The converter changes the ontology written in OWL+ ontology inference layer (OIL) and OWL to the reasoner's recognizable syntax. The reasoner is the part of the matchmaking framework that compares a QoS request specification to the service provider's published specification to determine the degree of match.

We implement four interfaces for the prototype system: (1) the inquiry interface, (2) the publish interface, (3) the browse interface, and (4) the administration interface. The inquiry interface allows the service requester to submit inquiries. If the parsing process ends successfully—that is, either reports the errors or send the parsed

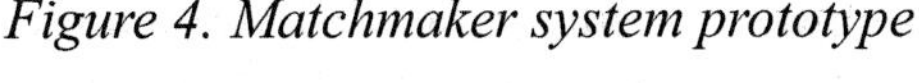

Figure 4. Matchmaker system prototype

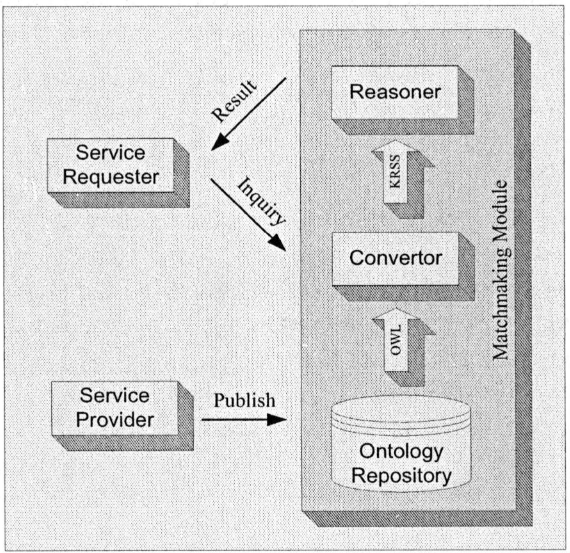

ontology to the converter—the parser stores the ontology in the server's ontology repository. Meanwhile, the converter renders the ontology into a description acceptable to the reasoner. When the requester submits the inquiry, the converter changes the inquiry and passes it to the reasoner. The reasoner then returns the matching result back to the requester. The inquiry is compared against each related QoS profile. The matchmaker generates the *Subsume* match, *Exact* match, *PlugIn* match, *Intersection* match, and *Disjoint* match list. These result lists are sorted according to their ranks and then sent back to the service requester. Figure 5 shows the ranked list of the inquiry result. The publish interface assists the service provider to publish their advertisement profiles. The browse interface enables the service requester to browse the ontologies list in the repository or view the content of a profile by the profile name or by the unique ID that represents the ontology. The administration interface provides the functionality to initialize or reload the whole knowledge base from the repository.

Figure 6 shows the inquiry time for the published knowledge base. The X axis shows the advertised profile number in the knowledge base and the Y axis shows the inquiry time for the inquiry profile. From the figure we can see that the inquiry time for the whole 500 records is less than 800 ms and the inquiry can be further processed in parallel because they do not change the knowledge base. This experiment shows the potential of using the OWL-QoS in the e-business world with Semantic Web technologies.

Figure 5. OWL QoS matchmaker's inquiry result

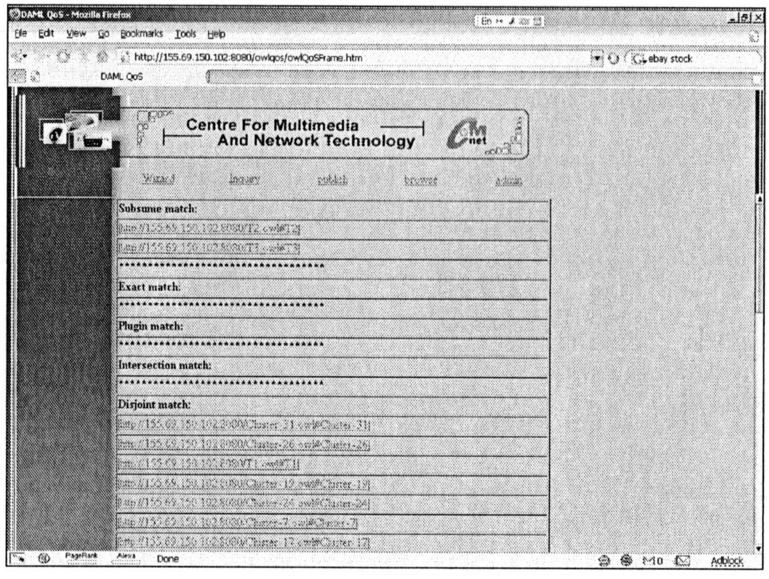

Figure 6. Advertisement's inquiry time

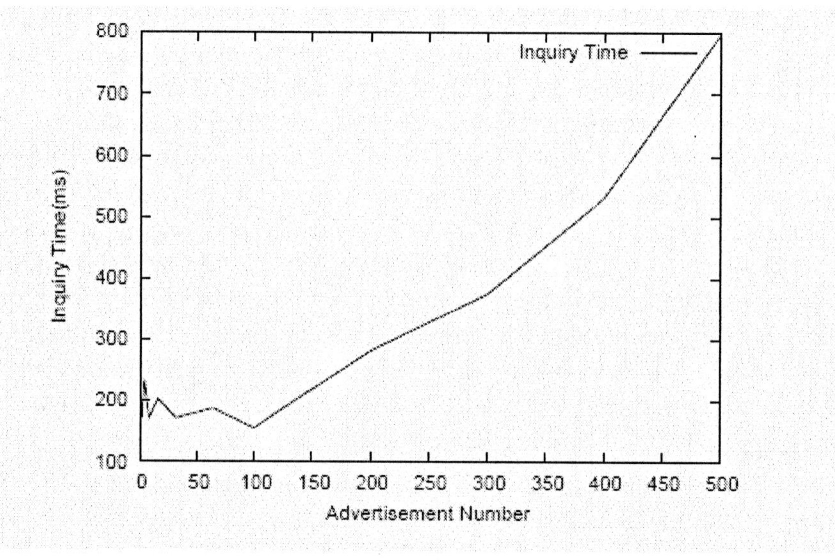

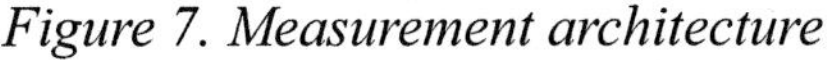

Figure 7. Measurement architecture

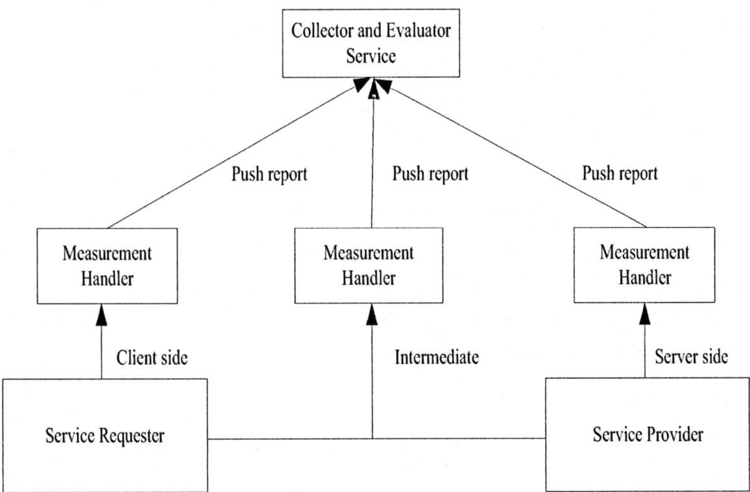

The measurement system itself should be able to plug into the measured Web service system with minimum influence. Figure 7 shows the sample architecture for the measurement system. Each measurement handler corresponds to one AtomicMetric individual, and the measurement system pushes the measured data to the collector service. Each collector corresponds to one ComplexMetric and will store the received data series for calculation. Since all the measurement components are loosely coupled, other measurement partners can participate in the measurement more conveniently. The collector receives the reports pushed from different measurement handlers and calculates the higher level metrics from low-level metrics.

The evaluator corresponds to the individual of SLO profile. It collects all related metric reports in the profile. The evaluator's main task is to generate the measurement profile concept and then compare it with the agreed SLO profile ontology. If the measurement profile concept is subsumed by the agreed SLO profile, it is deemed as compliance. Otherwise there is a violation. If any violation happens, a notification will be created and sent out to the location mentioned in the *notification* property to indicate the violation. The evaluator generates the measurement report in concept style. The benefit of this method is that different partners can share the report without misunderstanding. The meaning of the concept and related metrics are precisely defined. The outsourcing and integration can be achieved more naturally. And the run-time burden of the evaluation system is affordable. From the experiment we find that the inference time for the violation check algorithm is normally less than 1 ms.

The code generation process helps the measurement partner to speed up its measurement system development. After the parser checks the ontology and stores it, the code generator starts from the SLO for the top-level metrics. Then the code generator traverses the second-level metrics contained in the first-level ComplexMetrics, and so on. The code generation finishes when all the metric levels are completed.

In practice, measurement partners look for the ontology knowledge base to check whether the metric has been predefined. If it is not defined, they need to design this new metric concept and share this knowledge by publishing the definition to the knowledge base. The corresponding measurement handlers should be chosen or implemented by the measurement partner. Since all the metrics concept definition is shared, the service provider and service requester can reuse this knowledge base for the publishing and discovery of Web services.

Other QoS-Related Service Description Projects

There are many research works that target the description, advertising, and signing up of Web services at defined QoS levels. These are normally application layer specifications which are hardware and platform independent. They include aspect-oriented approach such as quality of service for objects (QuO) framework (Zinky, Bakken, & Schantz, 1997) and its QoS description language (QDL); object-oriented approach such as HP's QoS modeling language (QML) (Frolund & Koistinen, 1998); XML-based QoS languages such as HP's Web services management language (WSML) and its framework (Sahai et al., 2002); IBM's Web service level agreement (WSLA) language (Ludwig, Keller, Dan, King, & Franck, 2003) and its supporting framework (Dan et al. 2004), the Web services offer language (WSOL) (Tosic, Pagurek, & Patel, 2003), WS-policy (Hondo & Kaler, 2002); extensions for UDDI, such as UDDIe project (Shaikhali et al., 2003), UX system (Zhou et al., 2004), and WS-QoS framework (Tian et al., 2004); ontology level solutions like Web service modeling ontology (WSMO) (Lausen et al., 2005).

The following sections will describe these research works. We divide them into non-ontology-based works and ontology-related works.

QoS-Related Service Description without Ontology Definition

QDL is the description language for the QuO framework. Through aspect-oriented approach, an application can be decomposed into functional components and aspects, where different aspects can be programmed in different languages. QuO framework extends the CORBA functional interface definition language (IDL) with the QDL language, which consists of three sublanguages: (1) the contract description language (CDL), (2) the structure description language (SDL), and (3) the resource description language (RDL). The CDL specifies a QoS contract and it contains: *nested regions* for a possible state of QoS; *transitions* for trigger behavior when region changes; *system condition objects* for measuring QoS information; and *callbacks* for notification. SDL defines the internal structure of an object and how it consumes resources, and RDL is supposed to abstract the physical resources used by the object.

QML is a non-XML-based specification for defining multi-category QoS specifications for components in distributed object systems. Through the object-oriented approach, it provides specification refinement and simple contract types such as reliability and performance. Complex QoS specification can also be expressed, for example, using percentiles, variance, and frequency aspects. Profile refinement and conformance are defined for profile management. QML supports the specification reusability through contract and profile refinement. The well-defined semantics and reusability makes QDL and QML desirable QoS specifications; however, they are not based on XML. This leads to interoperability and integration problems with the Web services protocols.

WS-Policy is a general framework for the specification of policies for Web services. Details of the specification for particular policies will be defined in specialized languages. It is flexible because its policies are not limited in certain domain and its specification is extensible through additional specifications. However it did not provide a detailed specification for the QoS-related policies.

WSML and WSLA are developed for the XML-based specification of custom-made SLAs for Web services. They define SLAs which contain QoS constraints, prices, and management information. Appropriate management infrastructures are accompanied with these specifications since they are oriented towards management applications in enterprise scenarios. These specifications try to provide a precise and flexible solution for SLA definition. Support for templates is available in WSML and WSLA to provide the specification reusability. Compared with WSLA and WSML, our work can be viewed as a lightweight SLA. WSLA and WSML contain more sophisticated details about the QoS guarantees, price/penalty statements, and partner information. Our specification itself does not provide much detail definition for service partner's information. It depends on external ontology OWL-S to describe the provider's details and use the object-oriented approach to define the QoS profile and QoS metrics structure based on ontology level.

UDDIe allows choosing between Web services based on their QoS attributes, such as bandwidth, CPU and memory requirements. This is a lightweight and highly integrated matching framework for UDDI. However they do not support the reusable constructor for the QoS constraints yet. The adding of new attributes definition lacks a good solution for sharing between partners.

UX supports local and federated QoS-aware service discovery for UDDI. It uses the requesters' QoS feedback as the selection criteria. A basic metrics set is predefined for sharing between service requester's feedbacks. However, how to precisely define and share new metrics remains a problem. From these observations, we will proceed to investigate current work on the definition of QoS metrics using ontologies.

QoS-Related Service Description with Ontology Definition

WSOL provides formal representation of various constrains as well as management statements. Its major feature is its rich set of reusability constructs, lightweight management infrastructure, and dynamic switching protocol. Their definition of QoS metrics about how they are measured or computed is done in external ontologies. Compared with WSOL, our specification uses the uniform ontology language rather than the hybrid solution to achieve easier integration.

WS-QoS defines the XML schema for Web services to describe their services' QoS properties, which assists the service selection and publish through their service supporting system. It uses ontology style to define custom metrics. Our work uses ontology to define custom metrics as well. Our metrics are defined in terms of AtomicMetric and ComplexMetric. The metrics and QoS profiles are all defined in ontology level to reduce the integration cost.

The WSMO provides a conceptual framework and a formal language for semantically describing all relevant aspects of Web services. There are four main elements: (1) ontologies, which provide the terminology used by other WSMO elements; (2) Web service descriptions, which describe the functional and behavioral aspects of a Web service; (3) goals that represent user desires; and (4) mediators, which aim at automatically handling interoperability problems between different WSMO elements. Their nonfunctional properties define a list of general properties definitions, such as performance, financial, and so on. A semantic matchmaking algorithm is provided to match service provider's and requester's goals. Compared with our profile design, their QoS constraint details are defined in the instance level. How to reuse these individuals has not been clearly defined in their paper. We define the QoS profiles in concept level to support high reusability. Our metrics individuals contain all the necessary information for measurement partners to generate the measurement handlers, to integrate the measurement information, and to validate the service's conformance to the agreement.

The main purpose to utilize the ontology is to achieve better interoperability, automation, and extensibility. Since different Web services probably have quite different requirements, service partners often need to extend the metric sets to allow this flexibility. However, when new metrics are defined, how to share the metrics definition knowledge and how to integrate the different partner's knowledge becomes a critical problem. Our work provides an ontology design pattern for Web services to describe their QoS constraints and measurement information. The major concern of our work is the integration problem. This is also one of the major targets of Web services when integrating heterogeneous systems. The original version of our ontology is based on DARPA Agent Markup Language (DAML)+OIL and now converted to OWL version. Using the OWL ontology as its definition language provides some additional advantages over using pure XML solution:

- **Interoperability.** In a complex scenario such as an Enterprise application, there are a variety of management tools to assist the system's execution and maintenance. Semantic Web-based specification provides a way for different systems to speak the same language, hence basic integration is simplified. Uniform data also provide a better view for decision making and matchmaking. In our solution, a common ontology should be shared so that all partners in the cooperation speak and understand the same words. Previous supporting system normally uses wrappers to solve the interoperability problems, but this is a costly solution.
- **Automation.** Higher level automation is achieved through the logical view of the system's knowledge. The system aggregates knowledge from various components. Matchmaking, validation, decision making, and so forth are based on the logic in the collected knowledge rather than the hard-coded programs. Reasoner or rule engines help the system to achieve better automation.
- **Extensibility.** Different Web services have various requirements for their QoS descriptions. The new required metrics are relatively easy to be added into the knowledge base. The openness of ontology definition facilitates the sharing of experiences and speeds up the development cycle.

In addition, our profile design achieves the design principles described in the *Basis for a QoS Ontology* section. Layered design and ontology supporting tools help to make the specification *Easy of use* for general developers. Metric concept definition and metric individual details' definition help to gain *precision and flexibility* for the measurement. The QoS constraints are designed at concept level. Hence the refinement of the profile provides the *object-oriented style* feature and high reusability for the specification. The profile definition has clearly defined syntax and semantics. This allows the parser and the reasoner to do the syntax and semantics *validation* for the profile. Different portions of the specification have different purposes. The profile concept defines the QoS constraints, which is published by service provider and inquired by service requester. The profile's individual is filled in by the service requester and service provider for describing the agreement. The metrics individuals are defined and outsourced by measurement partners. This *separates the design duties* and simplifies the partial outsourcing and integration.

Conclusion

To address the metrics definition problem and specification integration problem, we present the QoS-aware services discovery using OWL-QoS ontology. This novel ontology is designed to complement OWL-S ontology in providing QoS-aware service discovery and measurement service. In our model, three concept layers (profile layer, property layer, and metrics layer), the profile individual and the metrics individuals help to separate the design duties for partners. The matchmaking algorithm for QoS property constraints with multiple matching degrees is presented. Well-defined metrics can be further utilized by measurement organizations to check whether the service provider conforms to the agreement. For different usage phases of the OWL-QoS ontology, we design the QoS matchmaking framework, the measurement framework, and the measurement code handler. Based on the ontology level, semantics in the specification helps to achieve better interoperability, automation, and extensibility. To prove the feasibility of the system in the e-business world, we test the prototype framework and find its potential usage in a real Web services environment.

In the future, Semantic Web technology will help to integrate system components and tools into a more unified system. Precisely defined semantics and unified system view will reduce the system integration cost and reuse the well-established domain knowledge. New trends in Semantic Web technology will form new solutions for system management. For example, Semantic Web rule language (SWRL), which extends the set of OWL axioms to include Horn-like rules (Horrocks et al., 2004), may help the expression of QoS adaptation rules and system management policies. QoS protocols will finally span over all layers of Web services stacks when Web services become mature.

References

Andrews, T., Curbera, F., Dholakia, H., Goland, Y., Klein, J., Leymann, F., et al. (2003). *Business process execution language for Web services version (BPEL4WS) 1.1.* Retrieved from http://www-106.ibm.com/developerworks/library/ws-bpel/

Box, D., Ehnebuske, D., Kakivaya, G., Layman, A., Mendelsohn, N., Nielsen, H. F., Thatte, S., & Winer, D. (2000, May 8). *Simple object access protocol (SOAP) 1.1.* Retrieved from http://www.w3.org/TR/2000/NOTE-SOAP-20000508/

Christensen, E., Curbera, F., Meredith, G., & Weerawarana, S. (2001). *Web services description language (WSDL) 1.1.* Retrieved from http://www.w3.org/TR/wsdl

Dan, A., Davis, D., Kearney, R., Keller, A., King, R., Kuebler, D., et al. (2004). Web services on demand: WSLA-driven automated management. *IBM Systems Journal.*

Dean, M., & Schreiber, G. (Eds.). (2004, February 10). *OWL Web ontology language reference.* Retrieved from http://www.w3.org/TR/owl-ref/

Fielding, R., Gettys, J., Mogul, J., Frystyk, H., & Berners-Lee, T. (1997). *Hypertext transfer protocol (HTTP) 1.1.* Retrieved from http://www.w3.org/Protocols/rfc2068/rfc2068

Frolund, S., & Koistinen, J. (1998). QML: Quality of service aware distributed object systems (HPL-98-10).

Hondo, M., & Kaler, C. (2002, December 18). *Web services policy framework (WS- Policy) Version 1.0.* Retrieved from http://www.verisign.com/wss/WS-Policy.pdf

Horrocks, I., Patel-Schneider, P. F., Boley, H., Tabet, S., Grosof, B., & Dean, M. (2004, May 21). *SWRL: A Semantic Web rule language combining OWL and RuleML.* Retrieved from http://www.w3.org/Submission/SWRL/

Lausen, H., Polleres, A., & Roman, D. (Eds.). (2005, June 3). *Web service modeling ontology (WSMO).* Retrieved from http://www.w3.org/Submission/WSMO/

Leymann, F. (2001). *Web services flow language (WSFL) Version 1.0.* Retrieved from http://www-3.ibm.com/software/solutions/webservices/pdf/WSFL.pdf

Ludwig, H., Keller, A., Dan, A., King, R. P., & Franck, R. (2003). *Web service level agreement (WSLA) language specification Version 1.0.* Retrieved from http://www.research.ibm.com/wsla/WSLASpecV1-20030128.pdf

OWL-S Coalition. (2003). *OWL-S: Semantic markup for Web services.* Retrieved from http://www.daml.org/services/owl-s/1.0/owl-s.html

Postel, J. B. (1982). *Simple mail transfer protocol (SMTP).* Retrieved from http://www.ietf.org/rfc/rfc821.txt

Postel, J. B., & Reynolds, J. (1985). *File transfer protocol (FTP).* Retrieved from http://www.ietf.org/rfc/rfc959.txt

Rose, M. (2001). *The blocks extensible exchange protocol core.* Retrieved from http://www.ietf.org/rfc/rfc3080.txt

Sahai, A., Durante, A., & Machiraju, V. (2002). *Towards automated SLA management for Web services.* Retrieved from http://www.hpl.hp.com/techreports/2001/HPL-2001-310R1.pdf

Shaikhali, A., Rana, O. F., Al-Ali, R. J., & Walker, D. W. (2003). *UDDIe: An extended registry for Web services.* Paper presented at the Symposium on Applications and the Internet Workshops (SAINT'03 Workshops).

Sollazzo, T., Handschuh, S., Staab, S., & Frank, M. (2002). *Semantic Web service architecture—evolving Web service standards toward the Semantic Web*. Paper presented at the 15th International FLAIRS Conference.

Sycara, K., & Paolucci, M. (2004). Ontologies in agent architectures. *Handbook on Ontologies in Information Systems, XVI*, 343-364.

Thatte, S. (2001). *XLANG Web services for business process design.* Retrieved from http://www.gotdotnet.com/team/xml_wsspecs/xlang-c/default.htm

Tian, M., Gramm, A., Ritter, H., & Schiller, J. (2004). Efficient selection and monitoring of QoS-aware Web services with the WS-QoS framework. In *Proceedings of the International Conference on Web Intelligence (WI'04)* (pp. 152-158).

Tosic, V., Pagurek, B., & Patel, K. (2003). WSOL: A language for the formal specification of classes of service for Web service. In *Proceedings of the International Conference on Web Services (ICWS2003)* (pp. 375-381).

Von Riegen, C. (Ed.). (2002). *UDDI version 2.03 data structure reference.* Retrieved from http://uddi.org/pubs/DataStructure-V2.03-Published-20020719.pdf

Winer, D. (1999). *XML-RPC specification.* Retrieved from http://www.xmlrpc.com/

World Wide Web Consortium. (2001). *Web services description language (WSDL) 1.1.* Retrieved from http://www.w3.org/TR/wsdl

XML Core Working Group. (2000). *Simple object access protocol (SOAP) 1.1.* Retrieved from http://www.w3.org/TR/SOAP/

Zhou, C., Chia, L. T., & Lee, B. S. (2004). QoS-aware and federated enhancement for UDDI. *International Journal of Web Services Research, 1*(2), 58-85.

Zhou, C., Chia, L. T., & Lee, B. S. (2005). Web services discovery with DAML-QoS ontology. *International Journal of Web Services Research, 2*(2), 44-67.

Zinky, J. A., Bakken, D. E., & Schantz, R. E. (1997). Architectural support for quality of service for CORBA objects. *Theory and Practice of Object Systems, 3*(1), 1-20.

Acronyms

BEEP	Blocks Extensible Exchange Protocol
BPEL4WS	Business Process Execution Language for Web Services
FTP	File Transfer Protocol
HTTP	Hypertext Transfer Protocol
QDL	QoS Description Language
QML	QoS Modeling Language
QoS	Quality of Service
OWL	Ontology Web Language
RPC	Remote Procedure Call
SLA	Service Level Agreement
SMTP	Simple Mail Transfer Protocol
SOAP	Simple Object Access Protocol
SWRL	Semantic Web Rule Language
UDDI	Universal Description Discovery and Integration
WSDL	Web Services Description Language
WSFL	Web Services Flow Language
WSLA	Web Service Level Agreement
WSMO	Web Service Modeling Ontology
WSOL	Web Services Offering Language

Chapter IX

A Basis for the Semantic Web and E-Business: Efficient Organization of Ontology Languages and Ontologies

Changqing Li, National University of Singapore, Singapore
Tok Wang Ling, National University of Singapore, Singapore

Abstract

This chapter introduces how to effectively organize ontology languages and ontologies and how to efficiently process semantic information based on ontologies. In this chapter we propose the hierarchies to organize ontology languages and ontologies. Based on the hierarchy of ontology languages, the ontology designers need not bear in mind which ontology language the primitives exactly come from, also we can automatically and seamlessly use the ontologies defined with different ontology languages in an integrated environment. Based on the hierarchy of ontologies, the conflicts in different ontologies are resolved, thus the semantics in different ontologies are clear without ambiguities. Also, these semantic-clear ontologies can be used to efficiently process the semantic information in Semantic Web and e-business.

Introduction

The Extensible Markup Language (XML) (Bray et al., 2004) developed by the World Wide Web Consortium (W3C) has recently emerged as a new standard for data representation and exchange on the Internet. However, the information exchange based on XML is at the syntactic level (Garshol & Moore, 2004). Nowadays, how to process and exchange semantic information becomes very important. Semantic Web and e-business are two important applications which need to process the semantic information. *Semantic Web* (Lee, 1999) means that the Web pages are annotated with the *concepts* (terms and relationships) from sharing ontologies; because Web information refers to the sharing ontologies, computers can automatically understand and process the semantic information. Similarly, when different partners (agents) of e-business refer to the sharing concepts in ontologies, they can semantically communicate with each other. This is a *semantic e-business* which is different from the traditional e-business. To process the semantic information, the traditional e-business is a person-to-person communication; now with ontologies the semantic communication of e-business partners is an agent-to-agent communication.

It can be seen that ontologies play a core role in processing semantic information. An *ontology* defines the basic terms and relationships comprising the vocabulary of a topic area, as well as the rules for combining terms and relationships to define extensions to the vocabulary (Gruber, 1993). How to organize ontologies and clearly define the semantics in ontologies are very important. Presently, the ontologies are built by different organizations for their own purposes, therefore we need to effectively organize different ontologies together with hierarchies, then the concepts of the ontologies can be efficiently used to annotate Web pages and e-business agents, and semantic information can be efficiently processed based on the well-organized ontologies.

To define ontologies, *ontology languages* are required. Ontolingua (Gruber, 1992) is an ontology interchange language which was proposed to support the design of ontologies. Loom (MacGregor, 1991), a knowledge representation system, is used to provide deductive support. We will further introduce the XML-based ontology languages in the "Background" section.

In this chapter, we propose hierarchies to effectively organize ontology languages and ontologies and discuss how to efficiently process semantic information in Semantic Web and e-business. The rest of this chapter is organized as follows. In the "Background" section, we introduce the background and the motivation of this chapter. In the "Ontology Language Organization" section, the hierarchy to organize ontology languages is proposed. We propose the hierarchy to organize ontologies and discuss how to resolve the conflicts in the ontology hierarchy in the "Building Ontology System" section. How to efficiently process the semantic information in the Semantic Web and e-business is discussed in the "Semantic Information Processing in the Semantic Web and E-Business" section. In the "Conclusion" section, we summarize this chapter.

Background

Some comparisons have been done to compare different ontology languages. Although XML(S) has no semantics, it may help bootstrap the development of content and tools for the Semantic Web (Gil & Ratnakar, 2002). Another comparison (Gomez-Perez & Corcho, 2002) about ontology languages is from three aspects, that is, (1) general issues (partitions and documentation), (2) attributes (instance attributes, class attributes, local scope, and global scope), and (3) facets (default value, type constraints, cardinality constraints, and documentation). The existing works are mainly about comparing different ontology languages, then choosing the best ontology language to use. Different from the existing works, this chapter is mainly about how to organize ontology languages and ontologies with hierarchies, therefore we mainly compare the changes of primitives in different ontology languages. From these changes, we can find the change trends of ontology languages, then it is motivated, that is, it is very important to effectively organize different ontology languages.

The Simple HTML Ontological Extensions (SHOE) (Luke & Heflin, 2000) extends HTML with machine-readable knowledge annotated, thus the implicit semantic information can be discovered by a computer. Although SHOE has the XML version, it is not based on the Resource Description Framework (RDF) (Lassila & Swick, 2004) and RDF Schema (RDFS) (Brickley & Guha, 2004).

RDF (Lassila & Swick, 2004) is a standard language of W3C for defining ontologies. RDF defines a simple model for describing relationships among resources in terms of properties and values. A resource represents anything specified by a uniform resource identifier (URI) (Lee, Fielding, & Masinter, 1998). Properties are the attributes of resources, which have either atomic entities (strings, numbers, etc.) or other resources as their values. For a person to understand the semantics of a sentence, a sentence is organized in a subject-verb-object (SVO) form. Similarly, the fundamental design pattern of RDF is to structure data as resource-property-resource triples. Here, resource can represent both subject and object in the SVO form, while property (relationship between resources) represents the verb in the SVO form. Thus, the RDF files can be processed semantically. An RDF model can be represented in three ways, namely, graph syntax, triple syntax, and RDF/XML syntax. In this chapter, we focus on the XML representation of RDF.

RDF organizes information in the SVO form, but it does not define the many standard *primitives* (see Table 1) required to construct ontologies. Thus, RDFS (Brickley & Guha, 2004) is created to provide some more basic primitives, such as "subClassOf" and "subPropertyOf" (to represent the relationships between classes or properties).

More semantic-rich primitives are added into the successors of RDFS, namely, U.S. Defense Advanced Research Projects (DARPA) DARPA Agent Markup Language (DAML) (Popp, 2000), Ontology Inference Layer (OIL) (Horrocks et al., 2001), DAML+OIL (Connolly et al., 2001a), and Web Ontology Language (OWL) (Harmelen et al., 2004).

DAML (Popp, 2000), which is funded by DARPA aims at developing a language to facilitate the semantic concepts and relationships understood by machines. The DAML language is based on RDF and RDFS.

OIL (Horrocks et al., 2001), from the On-To-Knowledge Project, is an ontology representation language that extends RDF and RDFS with additional language primitives not yet presented in RDF and RDFS.

Now the latest extension of DAML is DAML+OIL (Connolly et al., 2001b), which has some important features of OIL imported into DAML. Presently, DAML+OIL is evolving as OWL (Harmelen et al., 2004), and OWL is being promoted as the Web ontology language of W3C. OWL is almost same as DAML+OIL, but some primitives of DAML+OIL are renamed in OWL for more easily understanding.

In the "Hierarchy and Primitives of RDF and RDFS-Based Ontology Languages" section, we illustrate the hierarchies of the RDF-based ontology languages, and we compare the primitive differences among different ontology languages. Note that a primitive is a basic term in ontology languages that is used to define ontologies. In the "Motivation" section, we introduce the motivation of this chapter.

Hierarchy and Primitives of RDF and RDFS-Based Ontology Languages

RDF and RDFS are the ground of DAML, OIL, DAML+OIL, and OWL. In Table 1, we list some primitives of RDF and RDFS.

RDF and RDFS define some basic primitives, and these primitives are not capable of describing many other important concepts and relationships, for example, equivalentClass, therefore DAML, OIL, DAML+OIL, and OWL extend RDF and RDFS

Figure 1. The hierarchy of the RDF-based ontology languages

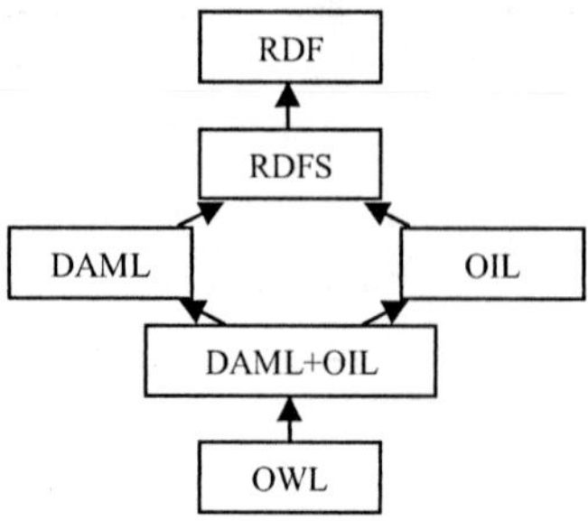

Table 1. Some primitives of RDF and RDFS

Category	Primitives	Comment
RDF	rdf:ID	Used to identify a class or property or any other resources
	rdf:resource	Used to refer to a resource; a resource represents anything specified by a URI
	rdf:Property	To define a property; the first letter of a property ID is in lower case
	rdf:Bag	An unordered collection (set) of members
	rdf:Seq	An ordered collection (set) of members
	rdf:Alt	A collection (set) of alternatives of members
RDFS	rdfs:Class	To define a Class; the first letter of a class ID is in capital
	rdfs:label	To provide a human-readable version of a resource name
	rdfs:comment	To provide a human-readable description
	rdfs:domain	To restrict the domain of a property
	rdfs:range	To restrict the range of a property
	rdfs:subClassOf	To indicate the specialization of a class
	rdfs:subPropertyOf	To indicate the specialization of a property
	rdfs:Container	Super class of rdf:Bag, rdf:Seq and rdf:Alt

by adding some new primitives. In Table 2, we compare the primitive differences among DAML, OIL, DAML+OIL, and OWL. We summarize the differences into several cases, and for each case, we only list a few primitives which satisfy this case. Cases: (1) primitives included in all the four languages; (2) primitives not included in OIL, but included in the other three languages; (3) new primitives added in DAML+OIL, used by OWL; and (4) OIL primitives not used by DAML+OIL, but used by OWL. The four different cases indicate the primitive relationships among different ontology languages.

Table 2. Primitive differences among DAML, OIL, DAML+OIL, and OWL

OIL	DAML	DAML+OIL	OWL	Comment
(1) Primitives included in all the four languages				
Class	Class	Class	Class	used to define class
inverseRelationOf	inverseOf	inverseOf	inverseOf	if P1(x,y) then P2(y,x)
FunctionalProperty	UniqueProperty	UniqueProperty	FunctionalProperty	if P(x,y) and P(x,z) then y=z
(2) Primitives not included in OIL, but included in the other three languages				
	sameClassAs	sameClassAs	equivalentClass	C1 = C2
	samePropertyAs	samePropertyAs	equivalentProperty	P1 = P2
(3) New primitives added in DAML+OIL, used by OWL				
		ObjectProperty	ObjectProperty	relates Resource to Resource
		DatatypeProperty	DatatypeProperty	relates Resource to Literal or data type
(4) OIL primitives not used by DAML+OIL, but used by OWL				
SymmetricProperty			SymmetricProperty	if P(x, y), then P(y, x)

Now we discuss how to define an ontology based on ontology languages.

Example 1. Consider a simple Person ontology shown in Figure 2. The start tag "<rdf:RDF>" at line 1 and the end tag "</rdf:RDF>" at line 16 show that this ontology complies with the RDF syntax. Lines 1-4 specify some XML namespace declarations (Bray, Hollander, & Layman, 1999), then we can use "rdf" to refer to the primitives defined in the URL "http://www.w3.org/1999/02/22-rdf-syntax-ns#" (similarly for other namespaces). The namespace "xsd" at line 4 is used to refer to XML Schema in which some data types are defined. Lines 5-8 define a class "Person" using the primitive of OWL, "owl:Class". Also we can see from lines 6 and 7 that primitives "label" and "comment" are from RDFS, therefore there is a namespace "rdfs" before "label" and "comment", that is, "rdfs:label" and "rdfs:comment". Lines 9-12 define a data type property ("owl:DatatypeProperty") "office_phone"; similarly we can define other properties for person, for example, "name", and so forth. Lines 13-15 define a property "contact_number" which is equivalent to the "home_phone".

Figure 2. A Person_Ontology represented using OWL language

```
<rdf:RDF  xmlns:rdf ="http://www.w3.org/1999/02/22-rdf-syntax-ns#"
          xmlns:rdfs="http://www.w3.org/2000/01/rdf-schema#"
          xmlns:owl="http://www.w3.org/2002/07/owl#"
             xmlns:xsd="http://www.w3.org/2000/10/XMLSchema#">
   <owl:Class rdf:ID="Person">
     <rdfs:label>Person</rdfs:label>
     <rdfs:comment>Person is a specific kind of animal.</rdfs:comment>
   </owl:Class>
   <owl:DatatypeProperty rdf:ID="office_phone">
      <rdfs:domain rdf:resource="#Person"/>
      <rdfs:range rdf:resource="xsd#string"/>
   </owl:DatatypeProperty>
   <owl:DatatypeProperty rdf:ID="contact_number">
      <owl:euqivalentProperty rdf:resource="#office_phone"/>
   </owl:DatatypeProperty>
   ...
   ...
</rdf:RDF>
```

Remark 1. The “Person” at line 5 is an original definition, while the “Person” at line 10 has a hash mark “#” before which means the “Person” at line 10 is a reference. There is no namespace (URL) before “#Person” at line 10 because “Person” is defined in the same file as “office_phone”. Because the “string” data type is defined in XML Schema (not in the same file as “Person”) and the namespace of XML Schema is “xsd”, there is an “xsd” before “#string” at line 11.

Remark 2. The first character of a class name is in uppercase, for example, the “P” in “Person” is in uppercase. The first character of a property name is in lowercase, for example, the first “o” in “office_phone” is in lowercase.

A *concept* is a term defined in ontologies which includes both the resources (entities) and the properties (relationships). For example, the “Person,” “office_phone,” and “contact_number” after the “rdf:ID” in Figure 2 are all called concepts.

Motivation

Figure 1 shows the hierarchy of different ontology languages, and from Example 1, we know that the primitives of RDF, RDFS, and OWL are used together to define an ontology. OWL is a replacement of DAML, OIL, and DAML+OIL, therefore the primitives of DAML, OIL, and DAML+OIL do not appear in the definition of an ontology which is defined with OWL. However, this is only an example which is defined now with the OWL. In practice, before OWL appears, a lot of ontologies have already been defined with ontology languages DAML, OIL, and DAML+OIL.

Can we still use those ontologies defined with DAML, OIL, and DAML+OIL in the current OWL environment? The answer is yes, in this chapter, we clearly define the hierarchy and the relationships among different ontology languages, and this hierarchy enables us to automatically use the previous ontologies defined with DAML, OIL, and DAML+OIL.

The second problem about the ontology language is that the primitives from different ontology languages should be used together to define the ontology. For example, from Example 1 and Figure 2, we can see that "rdf:ID", "rdfs:label", and "owl:Class" are used together to define the concepts in ontologies. However, it will be a burden for the ontology designer to bear in mind which ontology language the primitives are exactly from. Can we just use single namespace to refer to all the primitives, and the system can automatically translate the namespace to the proper namespaces, for example, the ontology designer can use "owl" as the namespace to refer to all the primitives, that is, "owl:ID", "owl:ID", and "owl:Class", and the system can automatically translate them back to "rdf:ID", "rdfs:label", and "owl:Class"? The answer is yes. In this chapter, we clearly define the relationships of the primitives in different ontology languages, and this will help to translate the single namespace to the proper namespaces. In this way, the efficiency of the ontology design can be improved.

Moreover, the ontologies are presently designed by different organizations for their own purposes. If we can organize all of these ontologies in an integrated environment, we can improve the usability of ontologies, and the semantic information in the Semantic Web and e-business can be processed more efficiently.

Ontology Language Organization

In this chapter, we mainly focus on the theoretical analysis of organizing ontology languages and ontologies with hierarchies, so that this method can be widely used to organize different ontology languages and ontologies, though we implement a prototype tool to organize ontology languages and ontologies in the "Architecture" section.

There already exist practical tools, for example, Daml2owl (Amin & Morbach, 2005), and so forth, that allow the translation from one language to another, but these tools are not general ones. They can only be used to translate between two specific ontology languages; however, our method is a general one, which can be used to organize all the existing ontology languages as well as the future coming ontology languages. This is the most important benefit of our approach over prior works.

In the "Operations to Organize Ontologies" section, we define some operations which can be used to describe the relationships among the primitives in different ontology languages. Based on these operations, in the "Easy Use of Ontology Languages" section, we show how to automatically use the existing ontologies defined with DAML, OIL, and DAML+OIL and show how to automatically translate the namespace to the proper namespaces.

Operations to Organize Ontologies

We use the following operations to describe the relationships among the ontology languages and the primitives in ontology languages, that is, inheritance, block, atavism, and mutation.

We use "gmoe" as the namespace before each operation. "gmoe" represents "Genetic Model for Ontology (language) Engineering", because these operations are borrowed from genetics.

1. Inheritance

The inheritance relationships of ontology languages can be seen in Figure 1. RDFS inherits RDF; DAML and OIL inherit RDFS; DAML+OIL inherits both DAML and OIL; and OWL inherits DAML+OIL. The following example shows how to use the inheritance operation to define the relationships between two ontology languages.

Example 2. As we know, DAML+OIL inherits both DAML and OIL. We use the inheritance operation shown in Figure 3 to indicate the inheritance relationship. With the inheritance operation, we need not copy the primitives in DAML and OIL into DAML+OIL. In DAML+OIL we only need to define the new primitives which can not be inherited from DAML and OIL.

2. Block

It is not enough to indicate the relationships among ontology languages with the inheritance operation only. Some primitives in previous ontology languages are not used by later ontology languages. We need to use the block operation to reflect this relationship. The following example shows how to use the block operation.

Example 3. From Figure 1, we know that DAML+OIL inherits the primitives in both DAML and OIL, but the primitive "SymmetricProperty" of OIL is not used by DAML+OIL (see Table 2). We can use the block operation to indicate that this primitive is not used by DAML+OIL.

Figure 3. Definition of DAML+OIL based on inheritance operation

```
<rdf:RDF xmlns:daml="http://www.daml.org/2000/10/daml-ont.daml#"
         xmlns:oil="http://www.ontoknowledge.org/oil/rdf-schema/2000/11/10-oil-standard#"
         gmoe:inheritance="daml, oil">
   ...
   ...
</rdf:RDF>
```

Figure 4. The use of block operation in DAML+OIL

```
<gmoe:block rdf:resource="oil#SymmetricProperty"/>
```

Figure 5. Definition of "SymmetricProperty" in OWL based on atavism

```
<gmoe:atavism rdf:resource="oil#SymmetricProperty"/>
```

3. Atavism

We found that some primitives blocked by the child ontology languages are reused by the descendant ontology languages. To process this kind of relationships we borrow the atavism mechanism in genetics. *Atavism* means that the characteristics of the grandparent do not appear at the child generation, but appear at the grandchild generation or the offspring of grandchild. We use an example to show how to use the atavism operation to process the relationships of the primitives in ontology languages.

Example 4. The "SymmetricProperty" of OIL is blocked by its child DAML+OIL, but the grandchild OWL again includes this primitive (see Table 2). Without our atavism operation, the definition of "SymmetricProperty" of OIL has to be copied into OWL, but with our atavism operation we only need to indicate in OWL that the "SymmetricProperty" in OWL is an atavism of the "SymmetricProperty" in OIL which is shown in Figure 5.

Figure 6. Definition of "Class" in OWL based on mutation operation

```
<gmoe:mutation rdf:resource="rdfs#Class"/>
```

4. Mutation or override or redefine

Furthermore, we use the mutation operation to describe the relationship that two primitives have the same name, but they have different semantics. See the following example.

Example 5. RDFS defines primitive "Class", and OWL also defines primitive "Class". Though the two "Classes" have the same name, they have different semantics; the "Class" in OWL permits greater expressiveness than the "Class" in RDFS. Thus the primitive "Class" in OWL mutates the "Class" in RDFS (see Figure 6).

Easy Use of Ontology Languages

In the "Operations to Organize Ontologies" section, we discuss how to describe the relationships among the primitives in different ontology languages based on different operations. Based on the relationship description in "Operations to Organize Ontologies," we can process the following two problems efficiently: (1) automatically use the existing ontologies defined with ontology languages DAML, OIL, and DAML+OIL; and (2) automatically translate single namespace to proper namespaces.

1. Using ontologies defined with ontology languages DAML, OIL, and DAML+OIL

Before OWL appeared many ontologies have been defined based on the ontology languages DAML, OIL, and DAML+OIL. Now DAML, OIL, and DAML+OIL are being replaced by OWL, but if we can automatically translate all the ontologies defined with DAML, OIL, and DAML+OIL to the ontologies defined with OWL, we can save a lot of time in building new ontologies based on OWL.

Because we have described the relationships among different primitives in different ontology languages, we can automatically build a mapping between different primitives, thus the ontologies defined with DAML, OIL, and DAML+OIL can be automatically translated to the ontologies defined with OWL. We use the following example for illustration.

Example 6. Suppose that there is an ontology in which a concept is defined using the primitive "daml:inverseOf" in DAML. Because OWL *inherits* DAML, and there are no changes for this primitive in DAML and OWL (see Table 2), we can directly translate "daml:inverseOf" to "owl:inverseOf". Furthermore, if a concept is defined with the primitive "oil:SymmetricProperty" in OIL, we can translate it to "owl:SymmetricProperty" because the "SymmetricProperty" in OWL is an atavism of the "SymmetricProperty" in OIL. There are no primitives in DAML, OIL, and DAML+OIL, which are blocked or overrided in OWL, therefore we need not consider these two operations in translating the ontologies defined with DAML, OIL, and DAML+OIL to ontologies defined with OWL.

With this technique, we can automatically use all the existing ontologies which are defined using the ontology languages DAML, OIL, and DAML+OIL. Therefore less effort will be paid to build new ontologies based on OWL.

2. Using single namespace to refer to all primitives in different ontologies

From Example 1 and Figure 2, we know that the primitives in RDF, RDFS, and OWL should be used together to define an ontology. It will be a burden for the ontology designer to bear in mind where each primitive exactly comes from. Based on the organization of ontology languages in the "Operations to Organize Ontologies" section, we can use single namespace to refer to all the primitives defined in different ontology languages, and we can automatically translate the single namespace to the proper namespaces.

Example 7. For the primitives "ID", "label", and "Class", the ontology designer can use them with the same namespace "owl", that is, "owl:ID", "owl:label", and "owl:Class". As we know from Figure 1, OWL inherits RDF and RDFS, thus we can search the "ID" primitive bottom up, that is, search OWL firstly, then RDFS, and then RDF. The "ID" primitive is found in RDF, therefore we change the "owl: ID" to "rdf:ID". Similarly the "owl:label" will be translated to "rdfs:label" when searching the ontology languages bottom up. For the primitive "Class", it is defined in both RDFS and OWL, and the "Class" in OWL is a mutation of the "Class" in RDFS. We will use the "owl:Class" rather than the "rdfs:Class", because the "Class" in OWL is an mutation and it is the latest one, and actually, all the ontologies are defined with "owl:Class" rather than "rdfs:Class".

The number of primitives in ontology languages is limited and their relationships are fixed, therefore based on the organization and relationship descriptions of ontology languages in the "Operations to Organize Ontologies" section, the translations in "Easy Use of Ontology Languages" section can be done without ambiguities.

Building Ontology System

In the "Ontology Language Organization" section, we describe the hierarchy of different ontology languages based on the inheritance, block, atavism, and mutation operations. These operations can also be applied to the ontology building.

As we know, the ontologies are now built by different organizations for their own purposes. It is important to organize these ontologies together in an integrated environment, then the semantic information in one domain is more complete. Only when the semantics in one domain are all defined clearly, it is true that the semantic information in Semantic Web and e-business can be processed correctly.

In this section, we firstly discuss how to organize ontologies based on the operations discussed in "Ontology Language Organization." Also we summarize the guidelines for organizing ontologies, that is, different information should be put at different hierarchies of ontologies. Furthermore, different from primitives in ontology languages, which will not change, the concepts in ontologies will change. When inserting or deleting a concept in ontologies, we should keep the ontologies consistent, otherwise it will hurt the ontologies to provide sharing information. Hence, we also discuss how to resolve the conflicts in ontology organizations.

Architecture

To make easy the use of inheritance, block, atavism, and mutation operations discussed in the "Ontology Language Organization" section, we build a graphical tool to implement these operations in ontology building. This tool can be applied to ontologies as well as ontology languages.

Example 8. Figure 7 shows that, there exists a Person_Ontology, and we need to build a Student_Ontology. Then in the "Parent Ontologies" frame, we select the "Person_Ontology", and in the "Child or grandchild Ontologies" frame, we input the ontology name "Student" and the namespace "stu" for this Student_Ontology. When clicking the "Inheritance" button, a simple Student_Ontology is automatically created which will be shown in the right "Codes" frame. In addition, as we select the "Person_Ontology" in the "Parent Ontologies" frame, all the concepts of

Figure 7. A graphical tool for ontology language and ontology organization

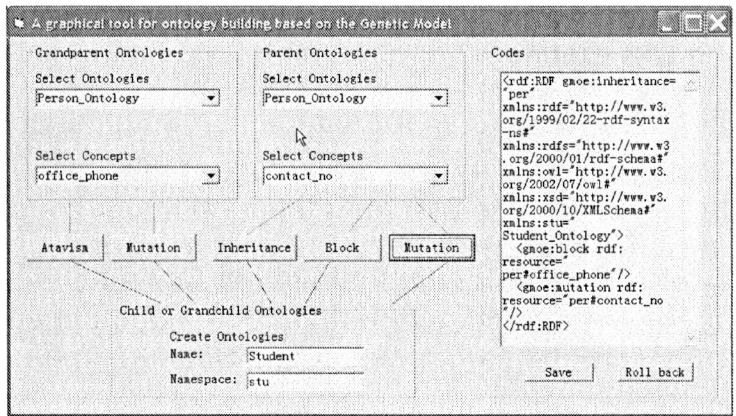

"Person_Ontology" will be listed in the "Select Concepts" combo in the "Parent Ontologies" frame (some concepts of "Person_Ontology" are defined in Figure 2), then we can select one concept, and by clicking the "Block" button, a certain concept of the parent ontology is blocked in the child ontology. Also, after selecting a concept from the parent ontology and clicking the "Mutation" button, we can indicate that certain concept of the parent ontology is mutated in the child ontology. From the right "Codes" frame of Figure 7, we can see that "office_phone" is blocked by Student_Ontology, and "contact_no" is mutated in Student_Ontology. If we click the "Save" button, the new Student_Ontology will be saved in a file; but if there are problems, we can roll back 10 steps. When a new ontology is created, it will be automatically listed in the "Select Ontologies" combos of "Grandparent Ontolo-

Figure 8. Architecture of building ontology systems

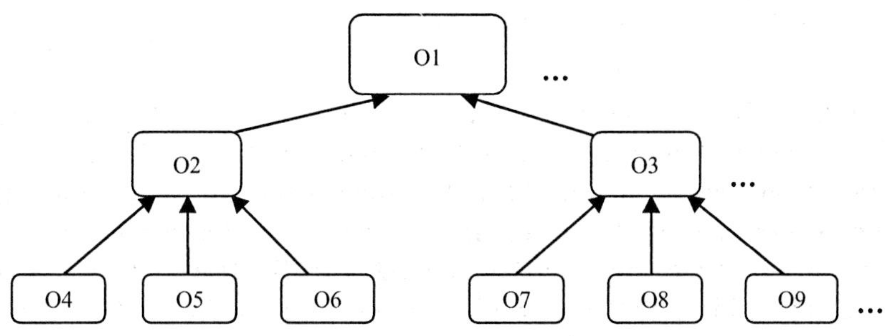

gies" and "Parent Ontologies" frames. Similarly, we can use the atavism operation to indicate that some concepts of the grandparent ontology are atavismed in the grandchild ontology or in the offspring ontologies of the grandchild ontologies. Note that the "gmoe" in Figure 7 indicates that the operations in the "Ontology Language Organization" section are a genetic model.

This tool is a prototype to indicate that the inheritance, block, atavism, and mutation operations really work in organize ontology language and ontologies. This prototype tool can be further improved for commercial use.

Next we summarize the guidelines of how to organize information in ontologies, that is, different information should be put at different hierarchies of ontologies.

The general concepts in a domain should be put in the highest level ontologies, for example, O1 in Figure 8. Here O represents Ontologies. If some concepts are specific, they should be put in the lower level ontologies, for example, O2 and O3 in Figure 8. When some concepts are more specific, they should be put in even lower ontologies, for example, O4-O9 in Figure 8. Figure 8 shows the hierarchy of ontologies. We allow multiple inheritance in ontology organizations, for example, O6 inherits both O2 and O3. In practice, the hierarchies can be more than three levels.

The hierarchy of ontologies is similar to the hierarchy of ontology languages. However, because the concepts in ontologies will change (add in, move out, and update), next we mainly discuss how to resolve the conflicts in ontology organizations.

Resolve Conflicts in Ontology Organization

Kalfoglou and Schorlemmer (2003) survey the related works on ontology mapping and indicate that most of the previous works are about finding the similarities and differences among ontologies, then the ontologies can be accessed from a common layer. There are no related works on resolving the conflicts in design ontologies. Here we discuss some techniques to resolve conflicts in designing ontologies with hierarchies.

When designing ontologies with hierarchies, it is important to keep the ontologies consistent. A concept is specified in an ontology if it is either defined or redefined for the ontology. A redefined concept overloads a similar concept in some ancestor ontologies. Figure 9 shows the hierarchies of ontologies. The O in Figure 9 represents ontologies which are displayed as rounded rectangles, and the C in Figure 9 represents concepts defined in ontologies which are displayed as parallelograms.

In this section, we discuss how to resolve the conflicts. An inherited concept is well defined if it is specified in one and only one ancestor ontology, possibly indirect. A conflict situation exists when an inherited concept is not well defined, that is, two or more ancestor ontologies specify the same concept. For example, from Figure 9,

Figure 9. Conflicts in ontology design

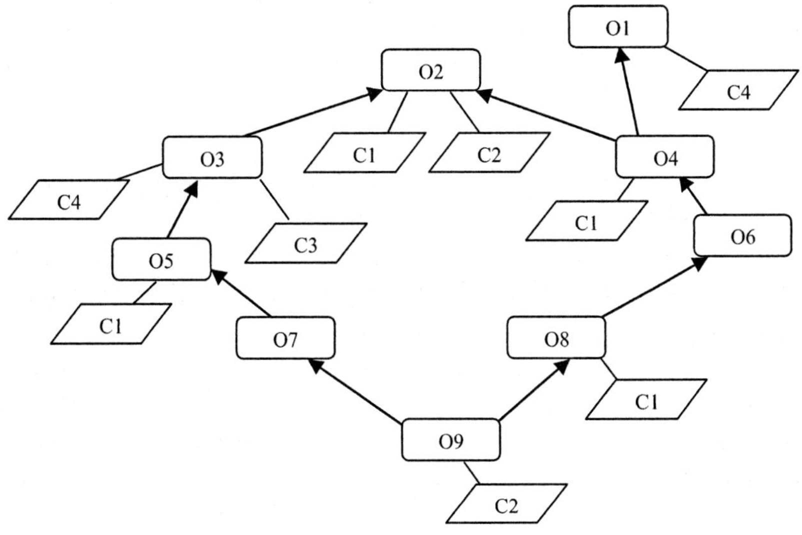

we can see that concept C1 of ontology O2 is redefined in ontologies O4, O5, and O8. C1 contributes to a conflict situation in O9, but C3 is well defined in O9.

We have the following methods to solve the conflict problem.

1. Redefining (or overriding)

The C2 in O9 and O2 in Figure 9 have the same name, thus it may be a conflict. However, if C2 in O9 is defined to override the C2 in O2, and redefined C2 with different meaning, then there are no conflicts.

2. Explicitly selecting or renaming

We use an example to show how to use explicitly selecting or renaming to solve conflicts.

Example 9. If the two C4 in O3 and O1 of Figure 9 have the different semantics, there will be a conflict in O9. To solve this conflict, we have two options. The first option has the ontology designer explicitly mention that the C4 in O9 is inherited from the C4 in O3. However, explicitly selecting has a problem, that is, some

Figure 10. Resolve conflicts by redesigning the organizations of ontologies

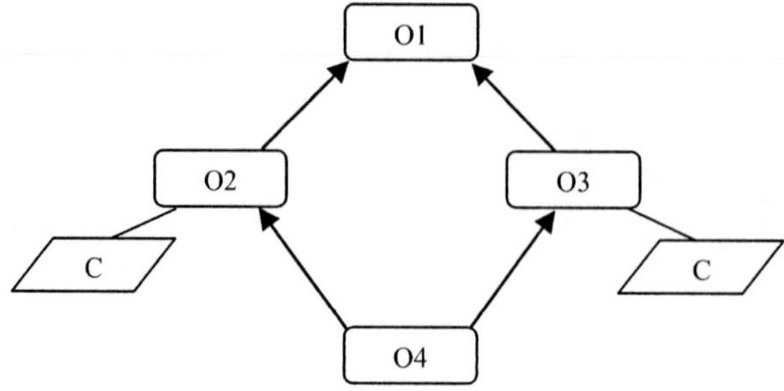

Figure 11. Factor to parent ontology

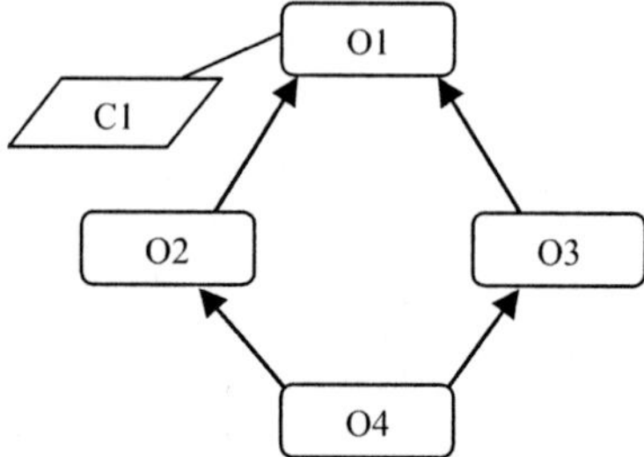

information will be lost. If O9 explicitly mentions that O9 uses the C4 in O3, the information of the C4 in O1 can not be inherited by O9, which is a loss of information. The second option to process this conflict is rename the C4 in either O3 or O9 or both; in this way, all the information can be kept without lost.

3. Redesigning the organizations of ontologies (e.g. factoring)

We use the ontology hierarchies shown in Figure 10 to introduce this conflict resolving approach. The two Cs in ontologies O2 and O3 have the same semantics, and they have the same name. Obviously, there will be confusion when O4 inherits C from O2 and O3. In ontology design, the semantics of each concept in the ontology should be clear without any ambiguities because the concepts are shared by the Semantic Web or e-business applications for semantic information processing.

Figure 12. Factor to an intermediate level of ontology

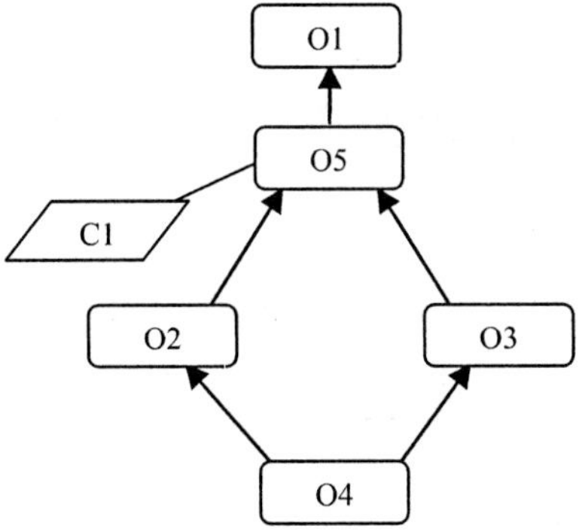

To process this conflict, there are two cases to consider.

1. If O1= O2 ∪ O3, Figure 11. shows that we can factor C to the parent ontology of Q2 and O3, that is, O1. In this way, O4 inherits concept C from a single ancestor ontology, therefore there are no conflicts.
2. If O1 ⊃ O2 ∪ O3, then we create ontology O5 such that O5 = O2 ∪ O3, and factor C to O5. Figure 12 shows this approach. In this way, the conflict can be resolved, and the C is at an appropriate level.

Algorithm to Resolve Conflicts

Figure 13 shows the algorithm to resolve conflicts, which is a formal summary of the cases in the "Resolve Conflicts in Ontology Organization" section.

With these conflict processing approaches, when inserting concepts into or deleting concepts from ontologies, we should be careful to make the ontologies consistent without conflicts (Ling & Teo, 1993).

Semantic Information Processing in the Semantic Web and E-Business

The present Web exists in the HTML and XML formats for persons to browse. Recently there is a trend towards the Semantic Web where the information can be

Figure 13. Algorithm to resolve conflicts

```
Given ontologies with hierarchies
FOR each conflict situation in the hierarchy DO
    Let the conflict situation be ontologies A, B1, ..., Bn (n > 1) where B1, ..., Bn are
    the nearest ancestor ontologies of A that specify a property p.
    /* Note that a ancestor ontology of some Bi may itself specify a property p. */
    /* Check the semantics of p in B1, ..., Bn */
    IF semantics of p is the same in B1, ..., Bn THEN
        IF intersection of B1, ..., Bn is empty THEN
          ***Design error, since ontology A (which is the intersection of B1, ..., Bn) is empty
        ELSE
          ******/* same semantics (Factoring) */
            IF there exists a more general ontology K which is UNION of B1, ..., Bn THEN
              Factor p to ontology K
            ELSE
              Resolve the conflict by either:
              (a) creating a general ontology K that is the UNION of B1, ..., Bn and
                  factoring p to K.
              OR
              (b) Explicitly choosing one parent ontology to inherit the property.
            ENDIF
        ENDIF
    ELSE
        /* different semantics */
        Let G1, G2, ..., Gm be sets of mutually exclusive ontologies from B1, ..., Bn such
        that ontologies in a group share the same semantics for p. Resolve the conflict in A
        by adopting one of the following:
        (a) redefine p in ontology A, /* not a good solution */ or
        (b) Rename p in Gj to, say, p_Gj for j = 1, ..., m to reflect their different semantics.
            To conform to the unique name assumption. Each p in the schema that has the
            same semantics as P_Gj must be renamed to p_Gj.
            FOR each group Gj (j = 1, ..., m) with 2 or more ontolgoies having property
            p_Gj DO
                /* An conflict situation exists between ontology A and the ontologies in Gj;*/
                /* p_Gj has the same semantics in the ontologies of Gj */
                Resolve the conflict in ontology A using the method described in *** and
                ******.
            ENDFOR
    ENDIF
ENDFOR
```

processed and understood by a computer. The present e-business also requires that the semantic information can be automatically exchanged among different agents of the e-business partners.

When the concepts in different ontologies are defined with *clear semantics* and *without conflicts*, the sharing concepts in ontologies can be used to annotate the Semantic Web pages or the agents of the e-business partners. If the information in two different Semantic Web pages refers to the same concept from the same ontology, the information has the same semantics, otherwise the information is different in the two Semantic Web pages. This can be automatically recognized by the computer. It is similar for the semantic information processing in e-business.

Figure 14. Semantic information processing in Semantic Web and e-business

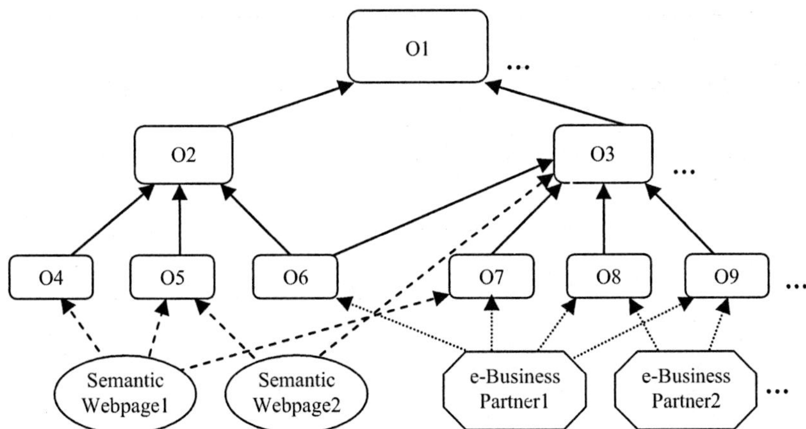

We use an example to show how to achieve the automatically and semantically exchange of information.

Example 10. Figure 14 shows how to process the semantic information in Semantic Web and e-business applications based on the ontology hierarchy introduced in the "Building Ontology System" section. We consider the Semantic Web pages firstly. Semantic Webpage1 refers to ontologies O4, O5, and O7. Semantic Webpage2 refers to ontologies O5 and O3. If some information in Semantic Webpage1 is annotated with the concepts from O4, obviously Semantic Webpage2 has no such information corresponding to Semantic Webpage1, that is, Semantic Webpage1 is semantically different from Semantic Webpage2 for such information. If some information in Semantic Webpage1 is annotated by the concepts from O5, it is possible that Semantic Webpage1 and Semantic Webpage2 have the same semantic information because Semantic Webpage2 is also annotated with concepts from O5; they can exchange the semantic information. Semantic Webpage1 is annotated with the concepts from O7, Semantic Webpage2 is annotated with the concepts from O3, and we can see that O7 inherits O3. Therefore if Semantic Webpage1 is annotated with the concepts newly defined in O7, Semantic Webpage1 and Semantic Webpage2 do not have the same semantic information about the concepts in O7. If Semantic Webpage1 is annotated with the concepts in O7 which are inherited from O3, Semantic Webpage1 and Semantic Webpage2 may have the same semantic information about the concepts in O3. It is similar for the semantic information exchange among the e-business partners.

Figure 15. Framework to organize ontology languages, ontologies and semantic applications

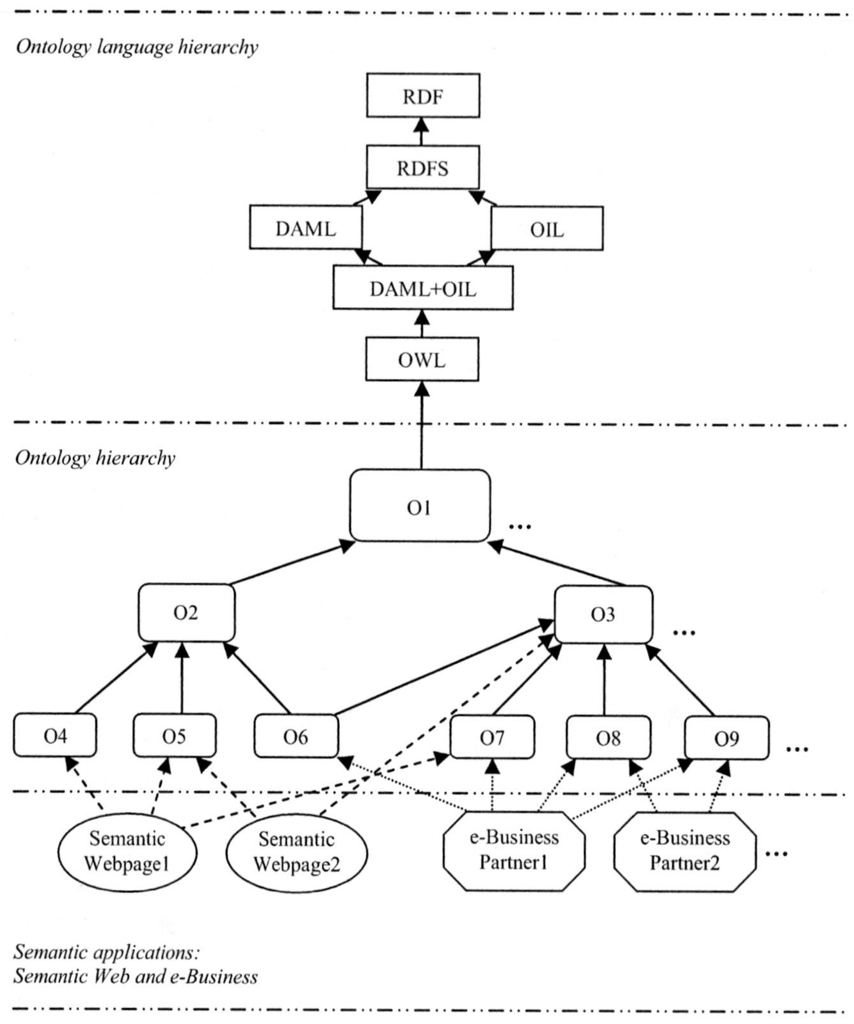

Because we organize ontologies with hierarchies, it is easy to find the appropriate concepts in ontologies (based on classifications and levels) to annotate the Semantic Web pages and the agents for e-business partners. Also, because of the hierarchy of ontologies, it is faster to process the semantic information, that is, it is faster to search and map the concepts in ontologies based on hierarchies; the search is only at several related (related to the semantic information in semantic Web or e-business) paths of the ontology hierarchy, but not all the paths.

Conclusion

In this chapter, we discuss how to effectively organize ontology languages and ontologies and discuss how to efficiently process semantic information in Semantic Web and e-business. Figure 15 shows the whole framework to organize ontology languages, ontologies, and semantic applications (Semantic Web and e-business). The primitives in ontology languages organized with hierarchies are used to define ontologies, and the concepts in ontologies organized with hierarchies are used to annotate and process semantic information in Semantic Web pages and e-business.

More concretely, because we organize ontology language with hierarchies, we can automatically use the existing ontologies defined with ontology languages DAML, OIL, and DAML+OIL. Our architecture can help to translate the existing ontologies to ontologies defined with the latest ontology language—OWL. Furthermore, we can use single namespace to refer to all the primitives from different ontology languages, and our ontology language hierarchies can help to translate the namespace to the proper namespaces. The ontology designer need not bear in mind which ontology language the primitive exactly comes from. With these techniques, the efficiency of ontology building will be improved.

We also organize ontologies with hierarchies and we discuss some techniques to process the conflicts in ontology design. Consistent and semantic clear ontologies are very important to semantic information processing. The integrated environment of ontology organizations makes the semantics in a domain clear.

Based on the hierarchy of ontologies, the Web pages of Semantic Web and the agents for e-business partners can be easily annotated, and the semantic information processing can be processed efficiently.

References

Amin, M. A., & Morbach, J. (2005). *The DAML+OIL to OWL converter*. Retrieved July 10, 2005, from http://www.lpt.rwth-aachen.de/Research/OntoCAPE/daml2owl.php

Bray, T., Hollander, D., & Layman, A. (1999). *Namespaces in XML*. World Wide Web Consortium. Retrieved January 14, 1999, from http://www.w3.org/TR/REC-xml-names/

Bray, T., Paoli, J., Sperberg-McQueen, C. M., Maler, E., Yergeau, F., & Cowan, J. (2004). *Extensible markup language (XML) 1.1*. W3C recommendation. Retrieved February 4, 2004, from http://www.w3.org/TR/2004/REC-xml11-20040204/

Brickley, D., & Guha, R. V. (2004). *Resource description framework schema (RDFS) specification 1.0.* W3C Recommendation. Retrieved February 10, 2004, from http://www.w3.org/TR/rdf-schema/

Connolly, D., Harmelen, F. V., Horrocks, I., McGuinness, D., Patel-Schneider, P. F., & Stein, L. A. (2001a). *Annotated DAML+OIL ontology markup.* W3C note. Retrieved December 18, 2001, from http://www.w3.org/TR/daml+oil-walkthru/

Connolly, D., Harmelen, F. V., Horrocks, I., McGuinness, D., Patel-Schneider, P. F., & Stein, L. A. (2001b, March). *DAML+OIL reference description.* W3C Note. Retrieved April 11, 2001, from http://www.daml.org/2001/03/reference.html

Garshol, L. M., & Moore, G. (2004). *Topic maps—XML syntax.* Retrieved March 16, 2004, from http://www.jtc1sc34.org/repository/0495.htm

Gil, Y., & Ratnakar, V. (2002). *A comparison of (semantic) markup languages.* In M. S. Haller & G. Simmons (Eds.), *Proceedings of the 15th International FLAIRS Conference, Special Track on Semantic Web*, Pensacola, FL (pp. 413-418). AAAI Press.

Gomez-Perez, A., & Corcho, O. (2002). *Ontology languages for the Semantic Web. Intelligent Systems, IEEE, 17*(1), 54- 60.

Gruber, T. R. (1992). *Ontolingua: A mechanism to support portable ontologies* (Tech. Rep. No. KSL-91-66). Standford Knowledge Systems Laboratory.

Gruber, T. R. (1993). *A translation approach to portable ontologies. Knowledge Acquisition, 5*(2), 199-220.

Harmelen, F. V., Hendler, J., Horrocks, I., McGuinness, D. L., Patel-Schneider, P. F., & Stein., L. A. (2004). *OWL Web ontology language reference.* W3C Recommendation. Retrieved February 10, 2004, from http://www.w3.org/TR/owl-ref/

Horrocks, I., Fensel, D., Broekstra, J., Decker, S., Erdmann, M., Goble, C., et al. (2001). *The ontology inference layer OIL.* Retrieved December 31, 2001, from http://www.ontoknowledge.org/oil/

Kalfoglou, Y., & Schorlemmer, M. (2003). *Ontology mapping: The state of the art. The Knowledge Engineering Review, 18*(1), 1-31.

Lassila, D. O., & Swick, R. (1999). *Resource description framework (RDF) model and syntax specification.* W3C Recommendation. Retrieved January 5, 1999, from http://www.w3.org/TR/PR-rdf-syntax/

Lee, T. B. (1999). *The Semantic Web homepage.* Retrieved December 31, 1999, from http://www.semanticweb.org

Lee, T. B., Fielding, R., & Masinter, L. (1998, August). *Uniform resource identifiers (URI): Generic syntax.* IETF Draft Standard (RFC 2396). Retrieved August 31, 1998, from http://www.ietf.org/rfc/rfc2396.txt

Ling, T. W., & Teo, P. K. (1993). *Inheritance conflicts in object-oriented systems.* In V. Marík, J. Lazanský, & R. Wagner (Eds.), *Proceedings of Database and Expert Systems Applications* (LNCS 720, pp. 189-200). Prague, Czech Republic: Springer.

Luke, S., & Heflin, J. (2000, April 28). *SHOE specification 1.01.* Retrieved April 28, 2000, from http://www.cs.umd.edu/projects/plus/SHOE/spec.html

MacGregor, R. (1991). *Inside the LOOM description classifier. SIGART Bulletin, 2*(3), 88-92.

Popp, B. (2000). *The DARPA agent markup language homepage.* Retrieved September 1, 2000, from http://daml.semanticweb.org/

Section II

Knowledge Management and Semantic Technology

Chapter X

A Communications Model for Knowledge Sharing

Charles E. Beck, University of Colorado at Colorado Springs, USA

Abstract

An integrative, systems-based model of knowledge sharing can provide a way of visualizing the interrelated elements that comprise a knowledge management system. This original model, building on a rhetorical process model of communication, includes both the objective and subjective elements within the human cognition. In addition, it clarifies the purpose and method elements at the center for any effective knowledge system. The model centers on the purpose elements of intentions and audience, and the method elements of technical tools and human processes. The output of knowledge sharing includes objective products and subjective interpretations. Feedback verifies the timeliness and efficiency in the process of building both information and knowledge.

Introduction

Over the past quarter century, the theme of knowledge management (KM) has appeared among the top five influences in changing how organizations work (Abell, 2000). Various thinkers, however, focus on different concepts under the heading of knowledge. Idealistically considered, knowledge consists of information in use, and wisdom combines knowledge with values (Lloyd, 2000). As a practical aspect of business, successful companies recognize intellectual assets as having an equal significance with the tangible assets. With today's economy driven by connectivity, a fundamental shift in business models is occurring, whereby information, knowledge, and relationships underpin competitive advantage (Braun, 2002), especially information built on new technologies (Orr, 2004).

This chapter paper proposes a *systems model of knowledge sharing* as a way to create knowledge-friendly workplaces. After briefly discussing existing models, the chapter elaborates the communication model that underlies underlying communication. The proposed model begins by clarifying the communication model that underlies both explicit and tacit knowledge. It then elaborates the systems elements of the knowledge sharing model: the input status and assumptions; the purpose elements of intention and audiences; the method elements of technical tools and human processes; the chaos creativity that integrates these elements; the output products and interpretations; and system feedback.

Background: Prior Models and Heuristic Basis

In general, models help organize information, According to Vail (2000), "Models efficiently capture, store, and help communicate enterprise knowledge in many forms, ranging from stories (verbal models) to diagrams (pictorial models) to spreadsheets (quantitative models)" (p. 10). Among the limited existing models for this new field, Leonard (1999) focuses on the individual consultant in the knowledge industry; however, this comprehensive approach results in a complex and somewhat unwieldy model. Luan and Serban (2002) propose a tiered knowledge management model, capturing tacit knowledge within an organization. Malhotra (2004) provides two models, differing by routine or structured information and nonstructured/routine; however, the models focus more on technology than on the human element. The proposed model of knowledge sharing attempts to overcome and provide a comprehensive but simplified model, capturing key relationships in a manageable, visual format (Beck & Schornack, 2005). The proposed model expands on a systems-based

Figure 1. Basic systems model

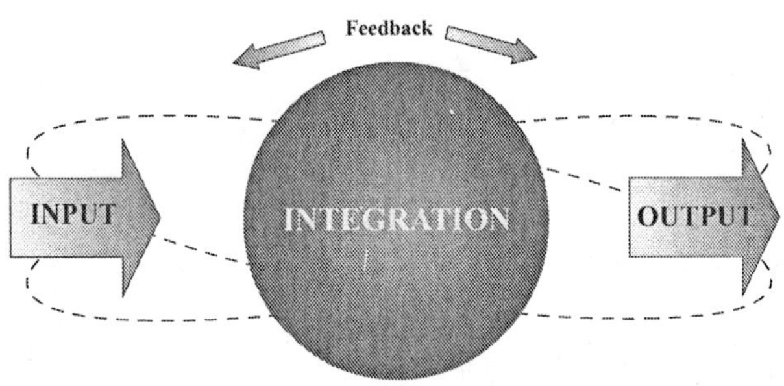

Figure 2. Rhetorical process model (Adapted from Beck, 1999, p. 32)

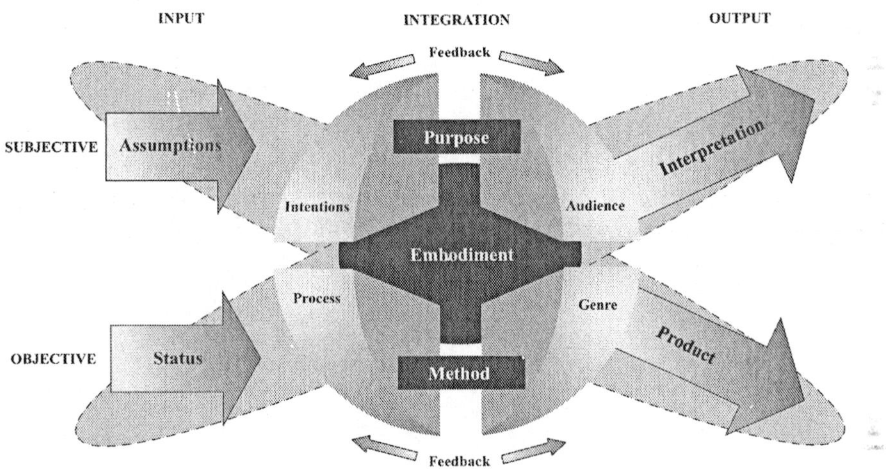

model of communication to identify the elements involved in a knowledge sharing system. The model builds on the underlying systems model (Figure 1).

The rhetorical process model expands this simple system in two dimensions. The horizontal division separates the objective in the subjective parts of the process. Additionally, the integration section is further divided in half, creating four elements within the central integration (see Figure 2).

- The inputs to this process include the objective status and the subjective assumptions. The integration begins at the top center of the model, with the purpose elements of intentions and audiences.

- The integration continues at the lower half of the model with the method elements of genre and process. Rather than following a linear process, these four elements of integration interact, labeled here as embodiment.
- The outputs of the model include both the product and the interpretation. While the products are the objective and observed outputs, the interpretation is more subjective, open to a broader view of the same products, reflected in the nonparallel output arrows.
- The final aspect of the model, feedback, occurs throughout the entire model, rather than just from the outputs back to the inputs.

Proposed Integrative Systems Model: Overview

The systems model of knowledge sharing takes the elements of this rhetorical process and elaborates those aspects that apply to knowledge management sharing. In both the objective and subjective halves of the model, inputs and outputs occur at two levels, that of distinct individuals and that of the organization. The critical integration elements of the model clarify purpose (intentions and audience) and method (technical tools and human processes). The interaction of purpose and

Figure 3. Model of knowledge sharing

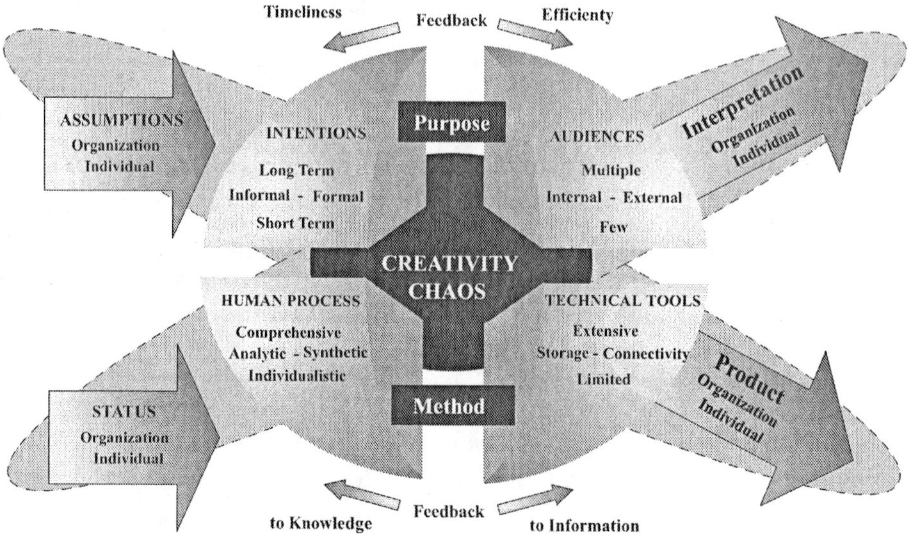

method embody the process labeled *creativity/chaos* in the model. The term *chaos* does not mean confusion but reflects the aspects of chaos theory which recognizes how disparate and random actions may create patterns out of disparate elements. The chaos/creativity interaction of purpose and method results in output products subject to multiple interpretations. Feedback, critical to the process, revises and refines both knowledge and information (Figure 3).

Inputs: Status

The inputs to the model on the left side include the objective status and subjective assumptions. Although inputs to the knowledge sharing system tend to remain rather stable, they may change over time, usually changing rather slowly.

Status, the objective, verifiable elements in any human encounter, consists of two parts: the individual and the organization. All communication begins with the individual, whether a corporate executive or a beginning clerical assistant. At the individual level, status includes both the person's background (education, experience, gender) and their role in the organization (job title, job description, specific responsibilities). Because the knowledge sharing varies by type of organization, the organization itself becomes a significant status element, where organization may include the overall company or a single department. Among numerous ways to classify an organization, two significant aspects include size and diversity. Size indicates the number of people who may need a given type of information or knowledge, based on actual or potential interaction. Increasing numbers raise the challenge of determining how to classify and structure information for both internal and external use (Adams, 2000). Additionally, the diversity of an organization includes the range of backgrounds, types of positions, knowledge requirements, and nature of the tasks.

In clarifying the need for knowledge management systems, organizations must identify the information infrastructure, ranging from the external demographics to the informational literacy competencies of the employees (Oman, 2001). Only then can an organization identify the tools and the technologies through which an organization "knows what it knows," then further clarify the practices and incentives that make the information available to those who need it ("Net Results," 2000). Companies might consider a new position of *chief learning officer* or *chief knowledge officer* who designs, develops, and coordinates new learning initiatives for the organization (Raub & Von Wittich, 2004).

Inputs: Assumptions

The subjective assumptions within any knowledge sharing system also consist of both individual and organizational elements. For individuals, assumptions include underlying values and ethical standards: People act either from an explicit set of values or from an implicit set of behavioral principles, which they follow without much conscious thought. Individual assumptions also appear through the style in which someone completes a task: informal or formal, deductive or inductive, right-brained or left-brained, uptight or laid-back. According to Zuckerman and Buell (1998), rather than technology "it's humans . . . that drive a company and the information management efforts that are crucial to success" (p. X). Ennals (2003) highlights this human face in the process, and White (2004) does so through the implication that KM is neither knowledge nor management.

At the organizational level, culture and climate especially convey assumptions. The organizational culture ranges from family or team styles to dictatorship or even anarchy. The culture may determine whether informal or formal norms will guide activities, including such issues as communication processes and dress codes. As Safdie and Edwards consider knowledge sharing as "a culture, not a system" (1998, p. S2); and this culture must encourage ideas, encourage knowledge sharing, and reward innovation ("Net Results," 2000). The assumptions also include the climate of the organization. An open climate fosters the sense of creativity and innovation among individuals, where people feel free to ask questions, suggest changes, and brainstorm alternatives. In contrast, a closed or defensive climate stifles communication and reduces interaction, as people spend psychic energy protecting themselves from real or perceived threats if they step out of bounds (Beck, 1999). An open environment that stimulates intellectual creativity has been termed an information ecology (Abell, 2000), which increases both individual and corporate capability. Effective knowledge sharing requires an environment that respects individuals (DeTienne & Jackson, 2001) and enhances the information literacy of an organization as essential underpinnings for knowledge sharing and for learning organization practices (Oman, 2001).

Integration Purpose: Intentions

For an organization to capture and leverage the knowledge assets, it must determine its purpose, that is, it must determine what action it intends to take after collecting data. Otherwise, organizations can merely generate data, with little understanding of its significance and what should be done because of it. The systems model of knowledge sharing adapts the concept that all human communication systems must begin with a sense of purpose, by clarifying the specific intentions of the activity and the audience or audiences involved.

Intentions, the objectives an organization wishes to achieve, focus on the extent of the knowledge need and the time frame for the final product. The extent ranges from informal to formal, and the time frame can either be short term or long term. Table 1 presents the quadrants for the purpose element of intentions.

Table 1. Intentions

	Long Term	
	Good Will	Contract
	Adequacy	Strategy
Informal		**Formal**
	Connections	Obligation
	Quick Answer	Tactics
	Short Term	

Using this framework, organizations ask a series of questions:

- Do we need just a single data point or do we need a synthesis of trends?
- Are we answering a simple question for a client or preparing a long-term action strategy?
- Will a quick response fill the need or must we test and verify before creating our recommendations?
- Is our objective to fill a one-time need or to establish a long-term commitment?

The type of information sought will vary depending on the intended use of that information. Overall, a company needs a knowledge-management strategy that reflects its competitive strategy. A company at this point faces a significant challenge: to take unrelated ideas and innovations and bind them together so they have useful application value.

Integration Purpose: Audience

Levine and Pomerol (2001) show how the audience expectation in contracts, forms the starting point for knowledge models, and Ennals (2003) cautions against getting trapped in spreadsheets rather than knowledge for users. To gain strategic advantage, a company must ensure that information-sharing practices become significant at all levels of the organization (Launchbaugh, 2002). In adapting to the information age, organizations must rethink the nature of the workplace: "Workplaces must be understood as social settings of negotiated meanings in which knowledge becomes inextricably and idiosyncraticly embedded within the particular activity system that is generating these meanings" (Porac & Glynn, 1999, p. 583).

As Table 2 indicates, the needs may change if we focus on those external to the organization, ranging from a single user or a narrow market niche to national and international users or government regulators.

Internal audience. Knowledge sharing internally concerns availability and extent of knowledge within an organization. Often described as *information literacy*, this internal focus identifies an individual's ability to recognize when information is needed, then he/she can locate, evaluate, and effectively use the needed information (Oman, 2001). Although some theorists envision information literacy as dependant on individual attributes such as intelligence, education, and experience, any one employee only possesses a subset of the knowledge available and that required by the whole organization ("Knowledge Management," 2000). To enhance the process, organizations could establish a chief knowledge officer (CKO) who develops internal taxonomies of knowledge to help employees find what they are looking for (Friedmann, 20001). The faster rate new knowledge information is changing, thereby increasing the obsolescence of knowledge in individuals; consequently, the audience must constantly change and produce change, or become extinct.

External audiences. The external audience focus involves *competitive intelligence* (CI), which consists of two phases: developing data, then transforming it into information (McGonagle & Vella, 20002). The developing data phase builds usable information from public sources about the competition, competitors, and the wider market. The transformation phase analyzes the data to create usable information to support business decisions. As with the internal audience, information may come from anyone within the organization. Sharing beyond the normal organizational boundaries increases security risks, raising concerns about access to information (Malhotra, 2004). With a more narrow concern, external audiences may focus on creating data bases on most-valued customers. Such initiatives take time and effort—valuable if the organization knows which customers are worth the cost

Table 2. Audiences

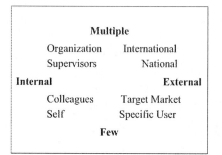

	Multiple	
	Organization Supervisors	International National
Internal		**External**
	Colleagues Self	Target Market Specific User
	Few	

(Davenport, Harris, & Kohli, 20001)—requiring policy makers to clearly define the process of knowledge acquisition.

Integration Method: Technical Tools

The method portion of the model integrates technology and humanity. Although it may use technology, knowledge sharing itself is not a technology (Shaw & Hickok, 2000). Rather, method integrates the two central aspects of information processing: information technology and the human thought process.

The information age has expanded technology to facilitate information processing, using tools ranging from fast computer chips and expanded memory in personal and mainframe computers, to the changing technology for distance communication using phone lines, fiber-optic cable, and satellite transmissions. With such tools changing so rapidly, people can no longer rely solely on their experience, which quickly goes out of date. For technical tools, the model considers the capacity and the connectivity, which range from extensive to limited. The technology merely "enables" the transfer of information, but more significant is "the ability to act on" the information (Lim, Ahmed, & Zairi, 1999, p. 615). Although the area of "technical tools" usually implies electronic systems, the model of knowledge sharing includes manual storage in notebooks and files, along with conversations to obtain knowledge (see Table 3).

The model incorporates storage and connectivity, each addressing different KM objectives. Information management tools attempt to capture and manage explicit product and customer knowledge, then codify and organize it in central repositories ("Net Results," 2000). As a significant limitation, however, the technical tools and techniques selected for looking at problems and situations tend to influence what we find (Duffy, 2001b). Furthermore, the technical tools involved in knowledge

Table 3. Technical tools

	Storage	Connectivity
Extensive	Data Warehouse	WWW
	Mainframe	Internet/LAN
	PC/PalmPilot	Phone/fax
Limited	Notbook/file	Conversation

sharing may represent a fad, including such buzzwords as "expert systems, KM, data mining, intranets, extranets, universal in-boxes, paperless offices, and executive information systems" (Craig & Mittenthall, 2000, p. 38). In contrast to fads, a true focus on knowledge sharing capitalizes on the "best brains" in an organization, regardless of their location or position in that organization (Duffy, 2001a). As an example of integrating the best brains, intranets may consist of four broad categories: (1) internal communication, (2) collaborative/cooperative work, (3) KM, and (4) process redesign (Baker, 2000).

Integration Method: Human Processes

Human cognition, the central processes in the model, encompasses multiple viewpoints: philosophy (epistemology), psychology, and popular culture. For organizations, clarifying these human processes involves asking the right questions (Zuckerman & Buell, 1998). In creating knowledge, cognitive behavior exhibits a broad range, from specific, unique situations to the most comprehensive integration of information. The more comprehensive approach involves theory and wisdom, whereas individualistic processes involve acquaintance with a specific event or a serendipitous one (see Table 4).

Within the knowledge management model, the horizontal elements reflect the analytic and synthetic approaches to knowledge. Alternate labels often characterize the same phenomena: left brain and right brain; classical and romantic; yin and yang; animus and anima; deductive and inductive. As with the other elements in the model, neither approach is "better" than the other; rather, they represent alternate ways of combining ideas to reach knowledge or understanding. The model identifies human categories that apply to any process. However, organizations need to adapt these concepts to the specific conceptual contexts of knowledge used within the organization.

Table 4. Human processes

	Comprehensive	
	Theory	Wisdom
	Explanation	Imagination
Analytic		**Synthetic**
	Description	Intuition
	Acquaintance	Serendipity
	Individualistic	

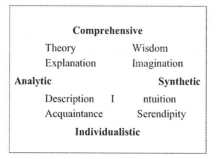

Table 5. Stages for creating and distributing knowledge (Source: Zack, 1999)

Process	Activity
Acquisition	An organization either creates information and knowledge or acquires it from various internal and external sources
Refinement	Before adding captured knowledge to a repository, an organization subjects it to value-adding processes (refining), such as cleansing, labeling, indexing, sorting, abstracting, standardizing, integrating, re-categorizing.
Storage/Retrieval	This stage bridges upstream repository creation and downstream knowledge distribution.
Distribution	This stage comprises the mechanisms an organization uses to make repository content accessible.
Presentation	The context in which an organization uses knowledge pervasively influences its value. Firms must develop capabilities that enable flexibility in arranging, selecting, and integrating knowledge content.

Method of Knowledge Sharing: Technology and Humanity

The combination of technological tools and human processes comprise the overall method portion of the model of knowledge sharing. In any analysis, separating these items proves useful, since machines and humans involve inherently different programming. However, organizations may consider both processes in a unified approach. Zack (1999) identifies a five-stage process that captures the experience of many organizations. Table 5 presents these stages. The people, organization, and activity must operate as one working system. To make this happen all processes must work together.

Chaos-Creativity

The center of the model represents the embodiment of the system. More specifically, the four basic the interaction among the purpose and method elements of intentions, audiences, tools, and process do not have a linear relationship; rather movement occurs within the categories. The terms *chaos* and *creativity* attempt to capture this interaction. Chaos is a richly ambiguous term: at the most popular level it represents an absolute lack of order; on the scientific level, chaos represents the way in which variations and patterns emerge within seemingly random phenomena. "Chaos describes a complex, unpredictable, and orderly disorder in which patterns of behavior unfold in irregular but similar forms. In chaotic systems, order emerges. Structure

Table 6. Key drivers in knowledge management integration (Source: Duffy, 2001a)

Driver	Activity
Managing and leveraging human capital	Capturing, transferring, and reusing what people know is fundamental to maximizing the potential contribution of employees, customers, and suppliers
Achieving operational excellence	Restructuring, reengineering, and improving efficiencies are necessary in today's competitive environment. Capitalizing on lessons learned is a key contributor to eliminating wasted effort.
Fully aligning information technology, business strategies, and actions	Shared knowledge and collaborative processes are vital elements of business and information technology alignment.
Establishing appropriate and valid performance measurement criteria and metrics	As world-renowned management guru Peter Drucker once said, "If you can't measure it, you can't manage it." Understanding what knowledge assets an organization owns is the first step in realizing the value of its intellectual capital.
Designing and implementing fully integrated infrastructures: process, people, and technology	The glue that holds these three key organization components together is the knowledge generated and consumed in everyday activities.
Continuous renewal and innovation	Knowledge innovation, a term created by knowledge management thought leader Debra Amidon, recognizes that knowledge—not technology or finances—is the core component of innovation and that it represents the creation, evolution, exchange, and application of new ideas into marketable goods and services.

evolves. Life is a recognizable pattern within infinite diversity" (Tetenbaum, 1998, p. 24). Thus the term *chaos* itself includes the range of knowledge integration from absolute dispersion to absolute integration. To capture part of theses interrelationships, Duffy (2001a) identifies key drivers in integrating knowledge (Table 6).

Creativity connects in a new way processes that cannot be captured as a single event but result from the interaction of the elements of purpose and method. As an analogy, we are all familiar with an optical illusion in which two lines, or tracks, seem to converge in the distance. We might consider here one track to be information technology (IT) and the other content. Although these two entities have always been interdependent, the emergence of KM and strategic information management brings not merely a convergence but a fusion of the two ("Finding Middle Ground," 2001). Within the model of knowledge sharing, chaos-creativity recognizes the interaction of all the central elements of the model, including both purpose and method.

Table 7. Types of knowledge (Source: Zack, 1999)

Knowledge Type	Knowledge Focus	Knowledge Characteristics
Declarative knowledge	About describing something.	A shared, explicit understanding of concepts, categories, and descriptors lays the foundation for effective communication and knowledge sharing in organizations
Procedural knowledge	About how something occurs or is performed.	Shared explicit procedural knowledge lays a foundation for efficiently coordinated action in organizations.
Causal knowledge	About why something occurs.	Shared explicit causal knowledge, often in the form of' organizational stories, enables organizations to coordinate strategy for achieving goals or outcomes.

Outputs: Product

The outputs of the model of knowledge sharing include the objective products and the subjective interpretations. As with the inputs, the outputs divide among both individuals and organizations, reflecting organizational attempts to move their corporate knowledge from the individual to the wider organization (Gore & Gore, 1999). However, outputs also involve those external to the organization itself.

The products, objective observable phenomena include knowledge—the main focus of the entire model—as well as solutions to perceived needs. Although knowledge happens within individuals, it is not significant for its own sake; rather, it serves to help solve a problem or to provide inputs to further action. For the organization, the outputs include information that serves an organizational need, along with dissemination of that information. In general, knowledge consists of three dominant types, as outlined in Table 7. The actual dissemination involves the various technical tools discussed earlier.

Outputs: Internal Interpretation

Since communication is perception, the interpretation is as significant an aspect of the output as the product itself. People may have multiple and even incompatible interpretations. Furthermore, individuals and the organization have differing primary focal points in interpreting knowledge:

- Individuals focus on usability and simplicity.
- Organizations focus on effectiveness and credibility.

While individuals want to retrieve information quickly to solve a problem, the organization wants information to be effective in meeting wide-ranging goals and credible among all users. Ultimately, organizations must examine how well the information met the need, and did so in the easiest, simplest, and shortest way possible. Unfortunately, many organizations now reward people for doing the opposite. The complexity of knowledge sharing ranges from finding the correct source and managing overload. Interpretation and use of knowledge occurs throughout the organization; however, organizations face an inherent tension when trying to capture information quickly and broadly while maintaining quality (Malhotra, 2004). The size and complexity of organizations by their very nature increase the quantity of information at any level, bringing an inherent risk of overload or "information fatigue syndrome" (Oman, 2001, p. 32). In managing complexity, organizations must recognize that building a knowledge sharing system is costly, with no immediate short-term benefits (Mitchell, 2001).

Outputs: External Interpretation

External KM concerns how our organization interacts with the wider society. The organization must create relevant and accurate information, but others must also see it the same way. The external credibility of the information that goes out reflects the trustworthiness of the organization, its good name and reputation. External KM is also concerned with what our organization can glean from society to aid our efforts. Of particular concern, CI is the process of organizing and gathering information that may benefit our organization, perhaps at the expense of the other. CI gathers bits and pieces of information and feeds it into a systematized structure that collects, organizes, analyzes, and acts on what is learned. Legitimate CI activities pose a particular threat to Internet-driven, knowledge-sharing networks. As a potential problem, however, CI activities may bring potential problems: more knowledge, in more heads, under less control, and in digital form (Erickson & Rothberg, 2000). Ultimately, within the model of knowledge sharing, organizations must contend with both dimensions of external information: maximizing the information it gains from its competition, while minimizing the risk to the organization by others also engaged in such activities.

Feedback

A system is not complete without feedback that permits change throughout the system. In the model of knowledge sharing, feedback from the product itself predominantly involves the development of new knowledge or information within both individual and organization. To represent this feedback simplistically, knowledge returns to the human process, and information returns to the technical tools. From the interpretation, feedback concerns the timeliness of the information and its efficiency in meeting both individual and organizational needs. While these two flows of feedback predominate, the model also recognizes that feedback may impact the inputs to the process. The objective inputs tend to change less frequently, since these are the "givens" within the overall process. However, the subjective inputs or assumptions may change as the result of new knowledge or information. Although assumptions by their very nature are the unquestioned ways of acting, feedback may bring these assumptions into conscious awareness, creating the potential for change both within individuals and organizations.

To use feedback effectively, the organization must recognize the proper value, meaning that efforts toward sharing knowledge must lead to a payoff (Friedmann, 20001). Organizations must distinguish information from knowledge: KM adds actionable value to information by filtering, synthesizing, and developing usage profiles so people can get the kind of information they may need to take action on (Wah, 1999). In such ways, organizations begin to realize that sharing knowledge contributes to an organization's value (Duffy, 2001a), where intellectual capital becomes an institutional asset (Erickson & Rothberg, 2000).

In creating effective KM, organizations must create a culture or an environment for sharing. Organizational efforts require "creating motivation and incentives to share and collaborate" (Friedmann, 2001, p. 57). For instance, organizations may acknowledge or compensate individuals who contribute to the knowledge management system as a way of ensuring timeliness and accuracy of information (Malhotra, 2004). Further, organizations may also need to make knowledge transfer a criterion in the evaluation system, with "high profile rewards and recognition for significant contributions" (DeTienne & Jackson, 2001, p. 7). People do not respond well to big words, 15-step processes, and theories; consequently, the feedback system must be evaluated on its value, based on convincing information used to solve everyday problems. Such considerations play a significant role in the overall organizational feedback within a knowledge sharing system.

Future Trends and Further Research

As currently structured, the systems model of knowledge sharing provides a unified framework for viewing the overall processes involved. However, these processes of knowledge sharing occur at three distinct levels: (1) the specific individual, (2) the organization, and (3) the wider society. The organization may range from a small department to a multi-national corporation. Society includes professional associations, the country involved, technology innovators, industry standards, and even the wider world economy. Accommodating these multiple levels will require an expansion of each element of the model to reflect both the nature of the process at a given level, and to clarify which elements take on a greater significance at the particular level of focus.

Conclusion

The model of knowledge sharing contributes to the dialogue in the field of knowledge management or knowledge sharing. In particular, this model provides an integrative framework that identifies, links, and unifies the major aspects of the knowledge sharing process. It recognizes both the individual and the organizational components, along with both subjective and objective aspects of the processes. While many discussions consider only the system outputs or its technical tools, this model begins with the individual and organizational inputs to the knowledge management system. The critical elements in this model, however, are the central integration of purpose and method. The matrices that describe the intentions, audiences, machine tools, and human processes provide a coherent way to visualize the central elements involved in a knowledge management system.

References

Abell, A. (2000). Skills for knowledge environments. *Information Management Journal, 34*(3), 33-40.

Adams, K. C. (2000, October). My secret life as an ontologist. *American Libraries.*

Baker, S. (2000). Getting the most from your intranet and extranet strategies. *Journal of Business Strategy, 21*(4), 40-43.

Beck, C. E. (1999). *Management communication: Bridging theory and practice.* Upper Saddle River, NJ: Prentice-Hall.

Beck, C. E., & Schornack, G. R. (2005, January). A systems model for knowledge management: A rhetorical heuristic process. In R. H. Sprague, Jr. (Ed.), *Proceedings of the 38th Hawaii International Conference on Systems Sciences* (p. 242 abstract; full text on accompanying CD: 0-7695-2268-8/05). Los Alamitos, CA: IEEE Computer Society.

Braun, P. (2002). Digital knowledge networks: Linking communities of practice with innovation. *Journal of Business Strategies, 19*(1), 43-55.

Craig, D., & Mittenthall, C. (2000). A place to call home. *American Lawyer, 22*(6), 38-39.

Davenport, T. H., Harris, J. G., & Kohli, A. K. (2001). How do they know their customers so well? *MIT Sloan Management Review, 42*(2), 63-73.

DeTienne, K. B., & Jackson, L. A. (2001). Knowledge management: Understanding theory and developing strategy. *Competitiveness Review, 11*(1), 1-12.

Duffy, J. (2001a). Knowledge management and its influence on the records and information manager. *Information Management Journal, 35*(3), 62-65.

Duffy, J. (2001b). The tools and technologies needed for knowledge management. *Information Management Journal, 35*(1), 64-67.

Ennals, R. (2003). Knowledge management with a human face. *Concepts and Transformation, 8*(2), 163-178.

Erickson, S. R., & Rothberg, H. N. (2000). Intellectual capital and competitiveness: Guidelines for policy. *Competitiveness Review, 10*(2), 192-198.

Finding Our New Middle Ground. (2001). *Information Management Journal, 35*(2), 2-3.

Friedmann, R. (2001). Do you know what you know? *American Lawyer, 23*(9), 56-60.

Gore, C., & Gore, E. (1999). Knowledge management: The way forward. *Total Quality Management, 10*(4-5), 554-560.

Knowledge Management: An Overview. (2000). *Information Management Journal, 34*(3), 4-21-27.

Launchbaugh, C. (2002). The writing on the wall. *Information Management Journal, 36*(2), 18-21.

Leonard, A. (1999, August). A viable system model: Consideration of knowledge management. *Journal of Knowledge Management Practice.*

Levine, P., & Pomerol, J. C. (2001). From business modeling based on the semantics of contracts to knowledge modeling and management. In *Proceedings of the 34th Hawaii International Conference on Systems Sciences* (pp. 1-10). IEEE.

Lim, K. K., Ahmed, P. K., & Zairi, M. (1999). Managing for quality through knowledge management. *Total Quality Management, 34*(3), 615-622.

Lloyd, B. (2000). The wisdom of the world: Messages for the new millennium. *The Futurist, 34*(3), 42-46.

Luan, J., & Serban, A. M. (2002). Chapter 6: Technologies, products, and models supporting knowledge management. *New Directions for Institutional Research, 113,* 85-104.

Malhotra, Y. (2004). Why knowledge management systems fail enablers and constraints of knowledge management in human enterprises. In E. D. Michael, Koenig, & T. K. Srikantaiah (Eds.), *Knowledge management lessons learned: What works and what doesn't* (pp. 87-112). Medford, NJ: Information Today Inc. (American Society for Information Science and Technology Monograph Series).

McGonagle, J. J., & Vella, C. M. (2002). A case for competitive intelligence: 90% of the information a company needs to understand its market and competitors and to make key decisions is already public. *Information Management Journal, 36*(4), 35-40.

Mitchell, K. (2001). Introducing the portal. *The Public Manager, 30*(2), 59-60.

Net Results: Effective Use of Information Technology. (2000, April 27). *Marketing*, Supplement p. 7.

Oman, J. A. (2001). Information literacy in the workplace. *Informative Outlook, 5*(6), 32-39.

Orr, B. (2004). Is there an enterprise blog in your future? (2004). *ABA Banking Journal, 96*(12), 54-55.

Porac, J., & Glynn, M. A. (1999). Cognition and communication at work. *Academy of Management Review, 24*(3), 582-585.

Raub, S., & Von Wittich, D. (2004). Implementing knowledge management: Three strategies for effective CKOs. *European Management Journal, 22*(6), 714-724.

Sadie, E., & Edwards, R. (1998, January 12). Knowledge is power for government and business alike. *Government Computer News.*

Tetenbaum, T. (1998). Shifting paradigms: From newton to chaos. *Organizational Dynamics, 26*(4), 21-32.

Vail, E. (2000). Using models for knowledge management. *Knowledge Management Review, 3*(1), 10-11.

Wah, L. (1999). Behind the buzz. *Management Review, 88*(4), 17-27.

White, M. (2004). Knowledge management involves neither knowledge nor management. *EContent, 27*(10), 39-40.

Zack, M. H. (1999). Managing codified knowledge. *Sloan Management Review, 40*(4), 45-57.

Zuckerman, A., & Buell, H. (1998). Is the world ready for knowledge management? *Quality Progress, 31*(6), 81-84.

Chapter XI

Semantic Knowledge Transparency in E-Business Processes

Fergle D'Aubeterre, The University of North Carolina at Greensboro, USA
Rahul Singh, The University of North Carolina at Greensboro, USA
Lakshmi S. Iyer, The University of North Carolina at Greensboro, USA

Abstract

This chapter introduces a new approach named semantic knowledge transparency, *which is defined as the dynamic on-demand and seamless flow of relevant and unambiguous, machine-interpretable knowledge resources within organizations and across inter-organizational systems of business partners engaged in collaborative processes. Semantic knowledge transparency is based on extant research in e-business, knowledge management (KM), and the Semantic Web. In addition, theoretical conceptualizations are formalized using description logics (DL) and ontological analysis. As a result, the ontology will support a common vocabulary for transparent knowledge exchange among inter-organizational systems of business partners of a value chain, so that* semantic interoperability *can be achieved. An example is furnished to illustrate how semantic knowledge transparency in the e-marketplace provides critical input to the supplier discovery and selection decision problem while reducing the transaction and search costs for the buyer organization.*

Introduction

Business partners, in this digital economy, perform large numbers of transactions in open, dynamic, and heterogeneous environments. Inter-organizational information systems and communication technologies are considered as key factors for improving communication and reducing coordination costs among business partners in a value chain—we consider virtual organizations as an extension of a traditional value chain, where business partners must coordinate resources and activities to effectively achieve common goals. Emerging Internet technologies have led to e-business processes that aim to achieve business goals where information and knowledge exchange enables and facilitates the execution of inter-organizational business activities and supports decision making that is underlying these activities. Information sharing among partners in e-business is conceived to be the key to alleviate problems related to demand volatility and capacity planning and is critical for efficient workflows (Bellini, Gravitt, & Diana, 2001). Even more critical for achieving efficiency in e-business workflows is transparency in information (availability of information in an unambiguously interpretable format) through effective integration of information flows across a supply chain (Singh, Salam, & Iyer, 2005).

In executing processes across inter-organizational systems, human and software agents perform activities that require access to organizational knowledge resources. In this respect, cooperation in the form of knowledge sharing may increase each partner's knowledge base and therefore their competitiveness (Loebecke, Van Fenema, & Powell, 1999; Lorange, 1996). Knowledge is considered a source of competitive advantage (Drucker, 1992; Simon, 1992) and it has emerged as the most strategically significant resource of the firm (Grant, 1996). Knowledge sharing in the context of supply chain has been recognized to enhance competitive advantage of the supply chain as a whole (Holland, 1995). We posit that in order to achieve such advantages *knowledge transparency* must exist. We define semantic knowledge transparency as the dynamic on-demand and seamless flow of relevant and unambiguous, machine-interpretable knowledge resources within organizations and across inter-organizational systems of business partners engaged in collaborative processes. Current systems integration models suffer from a lack of knowledge transparency (Singh, Iyer, & Salam, 2005). Integrating knowledge resources across collaborating organizations requires knowledge integration for global, inter-organizational, access to knowledge resources. A process view of semantic knowledge integration incorporates management of component knowledge and process knowledge for integrated inter-organizational systems that exhibit semantic knowledge transparency.

Nevertheless, to fully realize the benefits of semantic knowledge transparency several issues must be addressed. The main problem is how to determine how much and what knowledge should be shared, when, with whom, and under what conditions (Loebecke et al., 1999). The effective standardizations and adaptability afforded by integrative technologies that support the transparent exchange of information and knowledge make inter-organizational e-business relationships viable. This is increasingly prevalent through efforts such as ebXML (www.ebXML.org), Business Process Execution Language (BPEL) (www.oasis-open.org) and the Web Services Architecture (WSA) standards. These allow for standardized content representation for enterprise applications integration by defining the standards for adaptability and standardization. These technologies provide businesses with great opportunities to integrate e-business processes throughout their value chain. Such integration creates inter-organizational information systems where participant firms integrate their information technologies in architecture with transparent information exchange (Choudhury, 1997). Implementing and managing the integration of value chain activities over distributed and heterogeneous information platforms such as the Internet, is a challenging task with large potential benefits. Although technical integration of systems is essential, a common language to express context-specific constructs and relevant business rules to assist autonomous system entities and decision makers to solve specific business problems is essential (Stal, 2002). Disparate technical systems need the ability to share data, information, and knowledge. A common and shared understanding of the domain-specific concepts and the relations between them is critical for creating integrative views of information and knowledge in e-business processes. However, there is paucity in research on distributed information and knowledge sharing that provides a unifying process perspective to share information and knowledge (Oh & Park, 2003) in a seamless manner.

The Semantic Web is a key component for realizing the vision of semantic knowledge transparency in e-business processes. The Semantic Web provides the technical foundations to support the transparent flow of semantic knowledge representation to automate, enhance, and coordinate collaborative inter-organizational e-business processes (Singh, Iyer, et al., 2005). The Semantic Web vision comprises *ontologies* for common semantics of representation and ways to interpret ontology; *knowledge representation* for structured collections of information and inference rules for automated reasoning in a single system; and *intelligent agent* to collect content from diverse sources and exchange data enriched with semantics (Berners-Lee, Hendler, & Lassila, 2001). This vision provides the foundation for the semantic framework proposed in this research.

This chapter is structured as follows. First, we conduct a review and analysis of the relevant literature in the areas of e-business, KM, and the Semantic Web. Second, the conceptualization of the e-business process universe of discourse and its description logic are developed. Third, we use an intelligent infomediary-based e-marketplace as a scenario to illustrate how semantic knowledge transparency can be used to achieve the coordination of activities and resources across inter-organizational systems. Finally, future research issues and conclusions are stated.

Background

Based on existing research in e-business, KM and the Semantic Web, an innovative approach to achieve semantic knowledge transparency is developed. We use a process perspective to integrate *knowledge of resources* involved in a process and *process knowledge* including process models and workflows used in process automation. In order to achieve semantic knowledge transparency, we develop theoretical conceptualizations using ontological analysis that will be formalized using DLs. The ontology will support a common vocabulary for transparent knowledge exchange among inter-organizational systems of business partners of a value chain, so that semantic interoperability can be achieved. The foundations of the proposed approach are conceptually represented in Figure 1 and explanations follow.

E-Business

Electronic data interchange (EDI) is an information technology that allows business partners to send and receive commercial documents in an electronic format (Hansen

Figure 1. Conceptual representation of semantic knowledge transparency and integration.

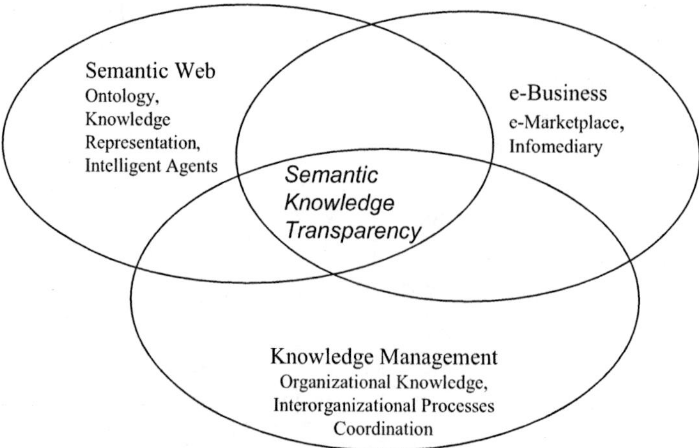

& Hill, 1989). Under EDI proprietary value-added networks data disclosure and information transparency were not a concern. Interestingly, EDI by itself does not provide market transparency (Zhu, 2004).

Nowadays, businesses are moving from EDI to Web-based systems. In fact, many firms have adopted e-business models to improve their collaborative capabilities (Segars & Chatterjee, 2003). Regarding business processes, they are typically modeled as deterministic, action-event sequences in workflow-based information systems and workflow automation systems. Workflows establish the logical order of execution between individual task units that comprise intra-organizational and inter-organizational business processes. The Workflow Management Coalition (www.wfmc.org) describes business process as "a sequence of activities with distinct inputs and outputs and serves a meaningful purpose within an organization or between organizations" (Dustdar, 2004 p. 460).

A process definition is the representation of a business process in a form which supports automated manipulation, such as modeling, or enactment by a workflow management system (WfMS). The process definition consists of a network of activities and their relationships, criteria to indicate the start and the termination of the process, and information about the individual activities, including participants and data (www.wfmc.org). Business processes can thus be generalized as having a "begin" and an "end" point and a series of intermediate tasks that are performed in sequence on some entity, object, or activity. In its simplest case, an e-business process may have each workflow activity performed within a single organization; while in the most general and extensible case, each individual activity may be performed by a different partner organization. Most inter-organizational workflows would fall somewhere in between these end points.

Singh, Iyer, et al. (2005) explain that e-business processes require transparent information and semantic knowledge transparency among business partners. The consequent lack of transparency in information flow across the value chain continues to hinder productive and collaborative partnership among firms in e-marketplaces. Moreover, the lack of transparency in business-to-business (B2B) e-marketplaces increases the uncertainty and perceived risks and hampers trusted relationships among business partners.

E-Marketplace

The main roles of e-marketplace are: (1) *discovery* – of buyers and suppliers that meet each other's requirements; (2) *facilitation* – of transactions to enable information flows leading to the flow of good and services among buyers and suppliers; and (3) *support* – of decision process leading to the development of collaborative relationships between e-marketplace participants (Bakos, 1998). The value added to the process by the e-marketplace is in providing information to buyers and suppliers about each others' capabilities and requirements. E-marketplace is a mechanism to streamline information flow in supply chain and re-balance the information asymmetry (Zhu, 2002). E-marketplaces offer value-added services by leveraging industry-specific knowledge through deciphering complex information and contribute to transaction cost reduction. However, the lack of integration of information and knowledge across the e-value chain continues to hinder productive and collaborative partnerships among firms in e-marketplaces.

Infomediary

In e-marketplaces a new kind of intermediaries has emerged: *Infomediary.* Grover and Teng (2001) define infomediary as "e-commerce companies leveraging the [power of] the Internet to unite buyers and suppliers in a single, efficient virtual marketspace to facilitate the consummation of a transaction" (p. 79). In this chapter, we argue that in the context of e-marketplaces, intermediaries have evolved into infomediaries that add value to their stakeholders by deciphering complex product information and matching buyers' needs with sellers' products and/or services. Grover and Teng focus on the critical information-providing role of the market and identify the roles played by electronic intermediaries, or infomediaries. An infomediary is an emergent business model adopted by organizations in response to the enormous increase in the volume of information available and the critical role of information in enabling processes in electronic markets. Infomediaries perform an indispensable function by matching buyers' needs with suppliers' products and services to facilitate transactions. There is a wealth of market information exchanged through the infomediaries as they perform these functions. As a result, Infomediaries become vital resources of knowledge about the nature of exchanges in the e-marketplace.

An analysis of the infomediary business model shows that individual buyers and suppliers seek distinct goal-oriented information capabilities from the infomediary—they provide decision parameters through their individual demand or supply functions. This is essentially a discovery activity with buyers and suppliers searching for a match of their requirements through infomediaries. This discovery process is influenced by historical information including the past experiences of other buyers' reliability and trustworthiness of the supplier. The infomediary business model can provide valuable information to this decision process through its role as the repository of experiential knowledge of transactional histories for both buyers and suppliers. This information can be used to develop knowledge that informs discovery of buyers and suppliers for subsequent transactions. A realization of the need for greater collaboration among trading partners is fueling the growth of KM to help identify integrative and interrelated elements to enable collaborations.

Knowledge Management

KM can be defined as "a process that helps organizations find, select, organize, disseminate, and transfer important information and expertise necessary for activities such as problem solving, dynamic learning, strategic planning, and decision making" (Gupta, Iyer, & Aronson, 2000, p. 17). KM, including the codification, storage, retrieval, and sharing of knowledge, transpires in the context of a process-scientific, governmental or commercial. Explicit knowledge, declarative enough to be represented using standards-based knowledge representation (KR) languages allows for knowledge to be interpreted by software and shared using automated reasoning mechanisms to reach useful inferences. While all knowledge cannot be explicated and be effectively represented and reasoned with using decidable and complete computational techniques; it is useful to focus on explicit, declarative KR using computationally feasible KR languages to build effective and useful knowledge-based systems. Hamel (1991) identifies that knowledge transparency is directly related to ease of transfer. In line with the notion of firms as repositories of productive knowledge (Demsetz, 1998), where knowledge resources are primary concern, managing cooperative relationships is frequently a process of managing knowledge flows (Badaracco, 1991).

Furthermore, transparency is critical to business partnerships, lowering transaction costs between firms and enabling collaborative commerce (Tapscott & Ticoll, 2003). We focus on two specific types of knowledge in this research:

1. **Component knowledge:** Component knowledge includes descriptions of skills, technologies, tangible and intangible resources and is amenable to knowledge exchange (Hamel, 1991; Tallman, Jenkins, Henry, & Pinch, 2004).
2. **Process knowledge:** Process knowledge is typically embedded in the process models of workflow management systems or exists as coordination knowledge among human agents to coordinate complex processes.

Component and process knowledge are central to activities of human and software agents in inter-organizational e-business processes; therefore, the standard representation of both type of knowledge is fundamental to achieve semantic knowledge transparency. Newell (1982) regards knowledge as "whatever can be ascribed to an agent, such that its behavior can be computed according to the principle of rationality" (p. 105). This definition forms a basis for functional KM using agents, human, and software when using explicit, declarative knowledge that is represented using standards-based knowledge representation languages that can be processed using reasoning mechanisms to reach useful inferences.

Inter-Organizational Process Coordination

Inter-organizational processes allow collaborating organizations to provide complementary services through networks of collaborating organizations (Dyer, 2000; Sawhney & Parikh, 2001). Here, the resource-based view of firms with focused capabilities is replaced by a network of organizations with a *focal enterprise* that coordinates resources of collaborating organizations to execute processes (Sawhney & Parikh, 2001). Complexities of coordinating inter-organizational processes require knowledge-driven coordination structures to determine decision authority and knowledge sources (Anand & Mendelson, 1997). The knowledge-integrated system incorporates the coordination mechanism and offers authorized resource matching in processes. Processes are decomposed into activities organized by generalization-specialization hierarchies and require coordination mechanisms to manage dependencies (Malone & Crowston, 1994). Coordination of activities is embedded in process workflows and WfMS since they essentially deal with issues of task-task and task-resource dependencies and their coordination (Kishore, Sharman, Zhang, & Ramesh, 2004). Coordination constructs used in this proposed research are based on Malone, Crowston, and Herman (2003) and are similar to those in Van der Aalst and Kumar (2003).

The complexity of coordinating e-business processes and the increasing demand by customers for *complete solutions* over single products requires knowledge-driven coordination to provide intelligent support to determine decision authority and knowledge sources in a value network. Alliances are seldom forged to co-produce single products; they increasingly entail developing complex systems and solutions that require resources of multiple partners (Doz & Hamel, 1998). This requires integrative architecture with reasoning ability using knowledge about business processes within a value network. The integrated information system as an integral part of the coordination structure can offer enhanced matchmaking of resources and coordination of activities to allow the value network to respond to dynamic customer demand efficiently and effectively. As organizations become increasingly global and distributed in nature, their reliance on inter-organizational information flows with partner organizations is integral to e-business processes.

Integrating knowledge resources across collaborating organizations requires knowledge transparency for global, inter-organizational, access to knowledge resources. Here, semantic knowledge transparency refers to the dynamic on-demand and seamless flow of relevant and unambiguous, machine-interpretable knowledge resources within organizations and across inter-organizational systems of business partners engaged in collaborative processes. A process view of knowledge integration incorporates management of component knowledge and process knowledge for integrated inter-organizational systems that exhibit knowledge transparency. The effective standardizations and adaptability afforded by integrative technologies that support the transparent exchange of information and knowledge make inter-organizational e-business relationships viable.

Semantic Web

Another theoretical foundation of the semantic knowledge transparency in e-business processes is the concept of the Semantic Web. The Semantic Web is an extension of the current Web in which information is given "well-defined meaning" to allow machines to "process and understand" the information presented to them (Berners-Lee et al., 2001, p. 35). According to Berners-Lee, the Semantic Web comprises and requires knowledge representation, ontologies, and agents in order to function (Figure 2 shows the different layers of the Semantic Web architecture):

- **Knowledge representation:** Structured collections of information and sets of inference rules that can be used to conduct automated reasoning. Knowledge representations must be linked into a single system.
- **Ontologies:** Systems must have a way to discover common meanings for entity representations. In philosophy, ontology is a theory about the nature of existence; in systems, ontology is a document that formally describes classes of objects and defines the relationship among them. In addition, we need ways to interpret ontology.
- **Agents:** Programs that collect content from diverse sources and exchange the result with other programs. Agents exchange "data enriched with semantics." Intelligent software agents can reach a shared understanding by exchanging ontologies that provide the vocabulary needed for discussion. Agents can even

Figure 2. Semantic Web representation layers (Berners-Lee et al., 2001)

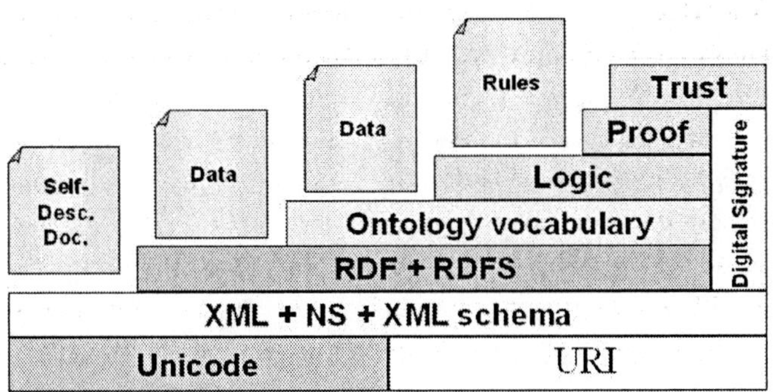

> "bootstrap" new reasoning capabilities when they discover new ontologies. Semantics makes it easier to take advantage of a service that only partially matches a request. (Lee et al. 2001, p. 37)

Given the importance of the Semantic Web components to achieve processes integration and automation, we analyze in more detail relevant work in the areas of ontologies, DLs, and intelligent agents in the next two subsections.

Ontologies and Description Logics

Ontologies provide a shared and common understanding of specific domains that can be communicated between disparate application systems, and therein provide a means to integrate the knowledge used by online processes employed by organizations (Klein, Fensel, Van Harmelen, & Horrocks, 2001). Staab, Studer, Schnurr, and Sure (2001) describe an approach for ontology-based KM through the concept of knowledge metadata, which contains two distinct forms of ontologies that describe the structure of the data itself and issues related to the content of data. Jasper and Uschold (1999) identify that ontologies can be used for: (1) knowledge reuse; (2) knowledge specification; (3) common access of heterogeneous information; and (4) search mechanisms. We refer the reader to Kishore et al. (2004) for a more comprehensive discussion of ontologies and information systems.

Ontology documents can be created using Foundation of Intelligent Physical Agents (FIPA)-compliant content languages like business process execution language (BPEL), resource description framework (RDF), Web ontology language (OWL), and DARPA agent markup language (DAML) to generate standardized representations of the process knowledge.

The structure of ontology documents will be based on DLs. DLs are logical formalisms for knowledge representation (Gomez-Perez, Fernandez-Lopez, & Corcho, 2004; Li & Horrocks, 2004). DLs are divided into two parts: (1) TBox, which contains intentional knowledge in the form of a terminology and is built through declarations that describe general properties of concepts; and (2) ABox, which contains extensional knowledge, which is specified by the individual of the discourse domain (Baader, Calvanese, McGuinness, Nardi, & Patel-Schneider, 2003; Gomez-Perez et al., 2004).

In this study, we adopt the SHIQ DLs presented by Li and Horrocks (2004). They argue that SHIQ's expressive power made it to be equivalent to DAML+Ontology Inference Layer (OIL). In addition, OWL is based on the SH family of description logics which supports Boolean connectives, including intersection, union, and complements, restrictions on properties transitive relationships and relationship hierarchies. Standardized by the World Wide Web Consortium (W3C), OWL is the leading approach to Semantic Web ontologies using DL as its fundamental KR mechanism. Ontological analysis results in ontology descriptions that are presented formally through DL for theoretical soundness; and in machine-readable format using OWL and OWL-DL to provide practicality for the model. In addition, software reasoners, such as Racer, support concept consistency checking, TBox reasoning, and ABox reasoning on models developed using SHIQ-DL translated into OWL-DL. These provide the basis for semantic knowledge transparency to support the e-business processes.

Intelligent Agents

An intelligent agent is "a computer system situated in some environment and that is capable of flexible autonomous action in this environment in order to meet its design objectives" (Jennings & Wooldridge, 1998, p. 8). The agent paradigm can support a range of decision-making activity including information retrieval; generation of alternatives; preference order ranking of options and alternatives; and supporting analysis of the alternative-goal relationships. The specific autonomous behavior expected of intelligent agents depends on the concrete application domain and the expected role and impact of intelligent agents on the potential solution for a particular problem for which the agents are designed to provide cognitive support. Criteria for application of agent technology require that the application domain should show *natural distributivity* with autonomous entities that are geographically distributed and work with distributed data; require *flexible interaction* without a priori assignment of tasks to actors; and be embedded in a *dynamic environment* (Muller, 1997). Papazoglou (2001) provides a complete discussion of the use of intelligent agents to support e-business.

A fundamental implication is that knowledge must be available in formats that allow for processing by software agents. Intelligent agents can be used for KM to support semantic e-business activities. The agent abstraction is created by extending an object with additional features for encapsulation and exchange of knowledge between agents to allow agents to deliver knowledge to users and support decision-making activity (Shoham, 1993). Agents work on a distributed platform and enable the transfer of knowledge by exposing their public methods as Web services using Simple Object Access Protocol (SOAP) and Extensible Markup Language (XML). In this respect, the interactions among the agents are modeled as collaborative interactions, where the agents in the multi-agent community work together to provide decision support and knowledge-based explanations of the decision problem domain to the user.

A recent extension of the Semantic Web is the vision of semantic e-business. Singh, Iyer, et al. (2005) define semantic e-business as "an approach to managing knowledge for coordination of e-business processes through the systematic application of Semantic Web Technologies" (p. 20). Semantic e-business leverages Semantic Web technologies and concepts to support the transparent flow of semantically enriched information and knowledge and enables collaborative e-business processes within and across organizational boundaries. In addition, the Semantic Web aids intelligent agents to organize, store, retrieve, search, and match information and knowledge for effective collaboration among semantic e-business participants. It has been recognized that candidates for applications of semantic e-business include supply chain management and e-marketplaces (Singh, Iyer, et al., 2005). In this study, we apply the vision of semantic e-business in conjunction with the other theoretical foundations to explain how semantic knowledge transparency can be achieved in the context of intelligent, infomediary-based e-marketplace.

Conceptualization of the E-Business Process Universe of Discourse

Ontology represents structured and codified knowledge of the conceptualizations, including concepts, relationships, and constraints, for a domain of interest (Kishore et al., 2004). Fox, Barbuceanu, Gruninger, and Lin (1998) explain that organizations are a set of constraints on the activities performed by organizational agents, which can play one or more roles. At the same time, each role is designed with a set of goals and authorization levels that allow the agent to achieve the predefined goals. In an e-business process, a human or software agent represents a business enterprise and performs activities on its behalf. Agents perform the individual business activities that comprise the e-business process. Business activities require access to resources of the organization in order to perform the e-business process. Activities are operations performed by agents on individual resources owned by a business enterprise. Resources, owned by various owner organizations or business enterprises, coordinate activities that are performed on them. In the e-business process universe of discourse, *information* and *knowledge* are central resources. They are used by actors in business enterprises to perform their assigned tasks (activities) in order to accomplish their goals. In this chapter, we utilize a pragmatic definition of knowledge that is explicit and declarative enough to be represented by a standards-based knowledge representation language or formalism. Additionally, we constrain this declarative knowledge as amenable to being processed through some reasoning mechanism to reach useful inference.

The essential set of concepts fundamental to model e-business processes are: *business enterprise, agent, business activity, resource, coordination, information,* and *knowledge*. These concepts are similar to those proposed by Malone and Crowston (1994). The conceptualization of the e-business process universe of discourse for an intelligent infomediary-based e-marketplace is:

In an e-business process, a business enterprise is represented by an agent to perform activities which are coordinated by resources.

Description Logic Model for Knowledge Representation of E-Business Processes

The elementary descriptions of the atomic concepts in the intelligent, infomediary-based e-Marketplace problem domain include:

i. *Business enterprise (BE)*
ii. *Agent (Ag)*
iii. *Business activity (Ac)*
iv. *Resource (Rs)*

Elementary descriptions of the atomic relationships in the intelligent, infomediary-based e-marketplace problem domain include:

i. *Represents* ($\equiv$ *IsRepresentedBy* $^{-}$)
ii. *Performs* ($\equiv$ *IsPerformedBy* $^{-}$)
iii. *Coordinates* ($\equiv$ *HasCoordination* $^{-}$)

Here, if R is a relationship between two concepts in the problem domain, then R^{-} denotes the inverse of the relationship R. DL derives its descriptive power from the

Figure 3. E-business process universe of discourse for an intelligent, infomediary-based, e-marketplace

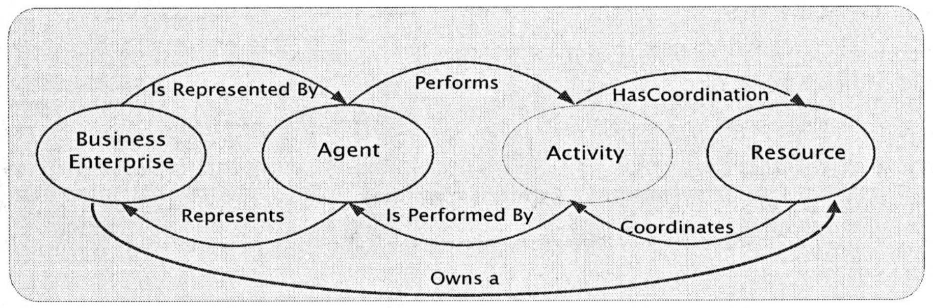

ability to enhance the expressiveness of the atomic descriptions by building complex descriptions of concepts using concept constructors. These *terminological axioms* make statements about how concepts or roles are related to each other.

This develops a set of terminologies, comprised of definitions, which are specific axioms that define the inclusions ($\subseteq$) or the equivalence ($\equiv$). The increased expressive power of the language is manifested in a range of additional constructors, including:

$\exists R.C$ (full existential value restriction)

$\neg C$ (atomic negation of arbitrary concept)

$\leq n\ R$ (at-most cardinality restriction)

$\geq n\ R$ (at-least cardinality restriction)

$= n\ R$ (exact cardinality restriction)

$\leq n\ R.C$ (qualified at-most cardinality restriction)^{o}

$\geq n\ R.C$ (qualified at-least cardinality restriction)

$= n\ R.C$ (qualified exact cardinality restriction)

$\leq_n R$ (concrete domain max restriction)

$\geq_n R$ (concrete domain min restriction)

$=_n R$ (concrete domain exact restriction)

Given the aforementioned concepts and relationships in the problem domain, we can begin to define the relationships between the concepts in the domain. Here, we define the terminology for the intelligent, infomediary-based e-marketplace problem domain using the following terminological axioms. This forms the knowledge representation *terminology,* or *TBOX,* for the problem domain and the basis for the machine-interpretable representation of the ontology in OWL-DL.

A *BE* concept is defined as a *Thing*, the top concept in OWL-DL, which is represented by at least one *Ag* in the problem domain.

$$\begin{aligned}
&BusinessEnterprise \subseteq \\
&\quad (\geq 1\ IsRepresentedBy \cdot Agent) \wedge \\
&\quad (= 1\ HasID \cdot StringData) \wedge \\
&\quad (\geq 1\ HasAddress \cdot Address) \wedge \\
&\quad (\geq 1\ HasDescription \cdot StringData) \wedge \\
&\quad (\geq 1\ HasReputation \cdot StringData) \wedge \\
&\quad (\geq 1\ HasTransactionSatisfactionHistory \cdot StringData)
\end{aligned}$$

An *Ag* concept is defined as a Thing that represents a *BE* and performs activities for the *BE*.

$$Agent \subseteq$$
$$(= 1\ HasID \cdot StringData) \wedge$$
$$(= 1\ Represents \cdot BusinessEnterprise) \wedge$$
$$(\geq 1\ Performs \cdot BusinessActivity)$$

A *Business Activity* defined as a Thing that is performed by an *Ag*, has a coordination relationship with *Rs*, and has a *Begin Time* and an *End Time*.

$$Business\ Activity \subseteq$$
$$(= 1\ hasLabel \cdot StringData) \wedge$$
$$(\geq 1\ isPerformedBy \cdot Agent) \wedge$$
$$(\geq 1\ hasCharacteristics \cdot StringData) \wedge$$
$$(\geq 1\ HasDescription \cdot StringData) \wedge$$
$$(\geq 1\ HasCoordination \cdot Resource) \wedge$$
$$(= 1\ hasBeginTime \cdot DateTimeData) \wedge$$
$$(= 1\ hasEndTime \cdot DateTimeData)$$

Each *Rs* is defined as a Thing that is owned by exactly one *BE* and coordinates *Business Activities.*

$$Resource \subseteq$$
$$(= 1\ hasID \cdot StringData) \wedge$$
$$(\geq 1\ hasOwner \cdot Business\ Enterprise) \wedge$$
$$(\geq 1\ Coordinates \cdot BusinessActivity)$$

We utilize a novel and theoretically grounded, activity-resource, coordination mechanism for capturing the relationships between activities and resources. This allows for the explicit modeling of the coordination of individual business activities, and the e-business process itself, using the information and knowledge resources in inter-organizational e-business processes over virtually integrated business enterprises. Business Activities depend on resources and require coordination mechanisms to resolve these dependencies in an e-business process. A resource is related to an activity through a *Coordinates* relationship, where the resource coordinates business activities through various coordination mechanisms.

$$Resource \ \exists \ (Coordinates \cdot BusinessActivity)$$

$$BusinessActivity \ \exists \ (HasCoordination \cdot Resource)$$

Description logic allows for the specification of generalization-specialization hierarchies of relationships. We use the notion of *activity-resource* dependency where activities have a sharing, flow or fit dependency with a resource (Malone et al., 2003) to specify the relationships between activities and resources. Here we assume that the *Coordinates* relationship between resource and activity is an abstract, general relationship, which materializes in the form of the specialized relationships where a resource may coordination activities through a *CoordinatesFlow, CoordinatesFit,* or *CoordinatesSharing* relationship.

$$Coordinates \subseteq$$

$$CoordinatesFlow$$

$$CoordinatesFit$$

$$CoordinatesSharing$$

$$CoordinatesFlow \subseteq$$

$$CoordinatesFlowProducedBy$$

$$CoordinatesFlowConsumedBy$$

In addition, the *CoordinatesFlow* is further specialized to capture the activity-resource coordination where the resource coordinates the flow of activity by either being produced by or consumed by a business activity.

We utilize the previous inheritance hierarchy of the *Coordinates* relationship to develop a complex description of the relationship between *Rs* and *Business Activities,* as expressed in the following terminological axiom.

$$Resource \ \exists$$

$$(\geq 0 \ CoordinatesFlowProducedBy \cdot BusinessActivity)$$

$$(\geq 0 \ CoordinatesFlowConsumedBy \cdot BusinessActivity)$$

$$(\geq 0 \ CoordinatesFit \cdot BusinessActivity)$$

$$(\geq 0 \ CoordinatesSharing \cdot BusinessActivity)$$

Information and knowledge are the primary resources pertinent to the problem domain we consider in this chapter. We utilize the concept definitions:

$$Resource \subseteq \quad Information \quad Knowledge$$

These complex descriptions of concepts, built from atomic descriptions, describe classes of objects in the problem domain and their inter-relationships. The terminological axioms presented previously make statements about how concepts and relationships are related to each other. The set of terminological axioms, including definitions, provide the terminology, or the TBox, for a problem domain. The aforementioned definitions comprise the terminology for the intelligent, infomediary-based e-marketplace problem domain, including the defined and primitive concepts and the binary relationships between them. This provides the meta-level ontology and knowledge representation for the knowledge base in an intelligent, infomediary-based e-marketplace.

The other component of the knowledge base, in addition to the terminology or TBox, is the *world description,* or *ABox* that includes descriptions of individuals in the problem domain. Together, the TBox and the ABox comprise the knowledge representation system based on description logics. The knowledge representation system provides the knowledge base and facilities to reason about the content.

Proposed Semantic Knowledge Representation for Supplier Selection for Infomediary-Based E-Marketplace

An e-procurement, supplier selection, e-business process in an infomediary-based e-marketplace requires information of attributes that describe the buyer's requirements, such as price, quantity, and the date by which the item is required. The selection of a supplier, from a set of suitable suppliers entails the buyer's preferences of specific supplier characteristics, including supplier capabilities for product quality and production capacity. This is a *discovery activity* that comprises customers and suppliers searching for a match of their requirements in the infomediaries. The result of this activity is the discovery of a set of suppliers capable of meeting their needs. Typically, customers will then engage in internal decision making activity to select a supplier, from the discovered set, that best meets their needs. Such a decision process may be influenced by historical information such as past experiences of customers' reliability and trustworthiness of the supplier. In addition, the decision is influenced by market dimensions including suppliers' reputation, logistics providers, warehousing providers, and other entities represented in the e-marketplace. Together, these lead to the selection of a supplier, from a set of discovered suppliers that satisfy the buyer requirements.

The infomediary business model can provide valuable information to this decision processes by serving as the knowledge repository of transactional histories for both customers and suppliers. Once a supplier is identified, the infomediary performs a transaction facilitation role and enables the flow of information between the customer and suppliers, which leads to the flow of tangible goods or services and the completion of the trade. The agents' communications in an intelligent-agent, infomediary-based e-marketplace and its architecture are shown in Figure 4. The architecture of the intelligent-agent infomediary-based e-marketplace consists of buyer and supplier agents that represent the behaviors of buyers and suppliers business enterprises respectively. A common repository of information/knowledge for sharing and reusing relevant knowledge. Moreover, the infomediary functions (i.e., discovery, facilitation of transaction, and support of knowledge intensive decisions) are accomplished through three agent types: (1) discovery agents, (2) transaction agents, and (3) authenticated monitoring agents. Here, buyer and seller agents must register with the infomediary to be allowed to execute transactions. The monitoring agent is responsible for the coordination of discovery agents across multiples e-marketplaces. The interested reader is referred to Singh, Salam, et al. (2005) for a complete discussion about intelligent-agent, infomediary-based e-marketplace.

Semantic knowledge transparency in the e-marketplace provides critical input to the supplier discovery and selection decision problem while reducing the transaction and search costs for the buyer organization. Infomediaries coordinate and aggregate information flows to support e-business processes and provide value-added services to enhance the information processes of the e-marketplace through deciphering complex product information and providing independent and observed assessment of the commitment of individual buyers and sellers. Infomediaries play a vital role in the exchange of knowledge and information in these knowledge networks embedded within inter-organizational value chains. The transparent flow of information and problem-specific knowledge across collaborating organizations, over systems that exhibit high levels of integration, is required in order to enable such inter-organizational, e-business process coordination. Otherwise, the transaction cost for each buyer organization would include costs of evaluating individual suppliers; logistics and transportation companies; warehousing providers; among other organizations. In addition, the buyer organization would incur costs of setting up ad hoc coordination structures that integrate across these companies while optimizing the decision problem on an individual basis. An e-marketplace that provides knowledge-based services reduces buyer search costs and buyer transaction costs by providing knowledge about the complete e-business process.

Coordinating complex inter-organizational e-business processes requires an integrated view of the complete inter-organizational e-business process and requires knowledge-driven coordination with intelligent support to determine decision authority and knowledge sources (Anand & Mendelson, 1997). This requires integrative knowledge-based semantic architecture with reasoning and inference mechanisms to reason with knowledge about business processes. Integrative systems, as integral parts of coordination structures, offer enhanced matchmaking of resources and coordination of activities for inter-organizational e-business process and allow organizations to respond to dynamic customer demand efficiently and effectively. Intelligent agents have been shown to support the processing of complex information and help reduce the cognitive load of decision makers. An agent enabled infomediary-based e-marketplace incorporates intelligence in the discovery of buyers and suppliers and in the facilitation of transactional roles (Singh, Salam, et al., 2005). Such an e-marketplace provides the basis for creating ad hoc coordination structures and collaborative mechanisms for transactions through the e-marketplace mechanism, thereby allowing for the flexibility and dynamics in business processes required to compete in a dynamic competitive environment (Iyer, Singh, & Salam, 2005).

Figure 4. Agent communications in an intelligent-agent infomediary-based e-marketplace

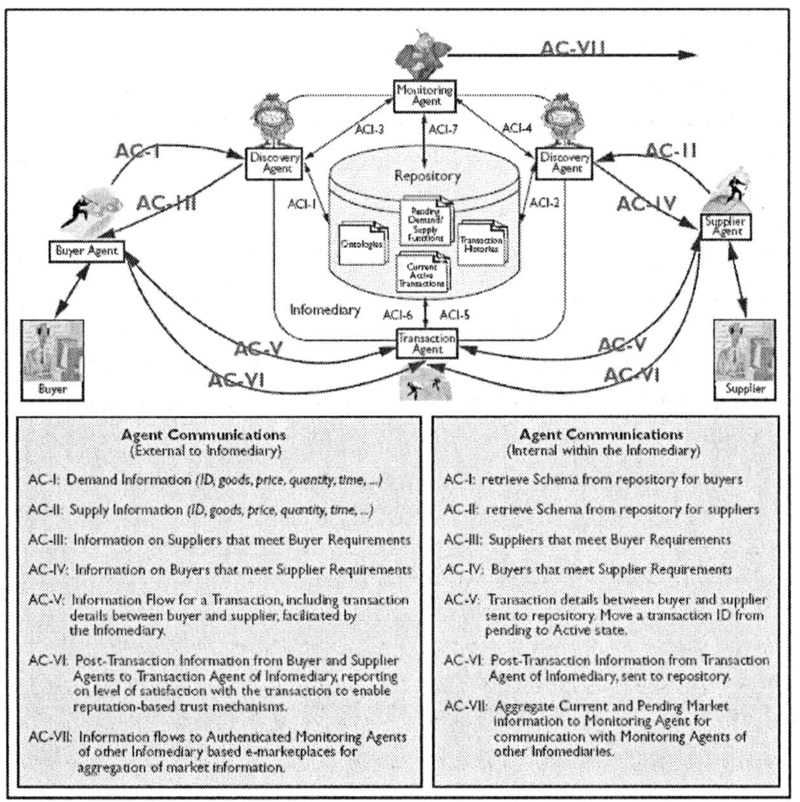

Moreover, semantic knowledge transparency allows for cross e-marketplace semantically enriched communication, so that dynamic and transparent planning of demand and supply requirements through real-time information integration across trading partners of the value chain can optimally occur. This information flow contains key market conditions; potential volatile aggregate demand volume; product information represented in standard ontologies; and market participant reputation information based on transaction histories and reported levels of satisfaction that can be "understood" by the intelligent agent to make decisions on behalf of their business enterprises (buyers/suppliers). In addition, this relevant information from a single e-marketplace can be made available to authorized participants in related e-marketplaces. As a result, suppliers in downstream e-marketplaces in the value chain can integrate their production plans with market-supplied, upstream demand and, at the same time, generate demand functions for downstream e-marketplaces. Subsequently, the DLs for all the software agents of the e-marketplace are developed.

In the context of the intelligent, infomediary-based e-marketplace, buyer, supplier, and infomediary are each a business enterprise described as

$$
\begin{aligned}
&\mathit{Buyer} \subseteq \\
&\quad (\mathit{BusinessEnterprise}) \wedge \\
&\quad (=1\ \mathit{HasID} \cdot \mathit{StringData}) \wedge \\
&\quad (\geq 1\ \mathit{HasAddress} \cdot \mathit{Address}) \\
&\quad (\geq 1\ \mathit{HasDescription} \cdot \mathit{StringData}) \wedge \\
&\quad (\geq 1\ \mathit{HasReputation} \cdot \mathit{StringData}) \wedge \\
&\quad (\geq 1\ \mathit{IsRepresentedBy} \cdot \mathit{BuyerAgent}) \wedge \\
&\quad (\geq 1\ \mathit{Has\ TransactionSatisfactionHistory} \cdot \mathit{StringData}) \wedge
\end{aligned}
$$

$$
\begin{aligned}
&\mathit{Supplier} \subseteq \\
&\quad (\mathit{BusinessEnterprise}) \wedge \\
&\quad (=1\ \mathit{HasID} \cdot \mathit{StringData}) \wedge \\
&\quad (\geq 1\ \mathit{HasAddress} \cdot \mathit{Address}) \\
&\quad (\geq 1\ \mathit{HasDescription} \cdot \mathit{StringData}) \wedge \\
&\quad (\geq 1\ \mathit{HasReputation} \cdot \mathit{StringData}) \wedge \\
&\quad (\geq 1\ \mathit{IsRepresentedBy} \cdot \mathit{SupplierAgent}) \wedge \\
&\quad (\geq 1\ \mathit{Has\ TransactionSatisfactionHistory} \cdot \mathit{StringData}) \wedge
\end{aligned}
$$

$Infomediary \subseteq$

$(\ BusinessEnterprise\ ) \wedge$

$(= 1\ HasID \cdot StringData) \wedge$

$(\geq 1\ HasDescription \cdot StringData) \wedge$

$(\geq 1\ HasAddress \cdot\ Address) \wedge$

$(\geq 1\ IsRepresentedBy \cdot RegistrationAgent) \wedge$

$(\geq 1\ IsRepresentedBy \cdot DiscoveryAgent) \wedge$

$(\geq 1\ IsRepresentedBy \cdot TransactionAgent) \wedge$

A buyer agent represents a buyer business enterprise in the infomediary-based e-marketplace.

$BuyerAgent\ \subseteq$

$(\ SoftwareAgent) \wedge$

$(=1\ Represents.Buyer) \wedge$

$(\geq 1\ Performs.ObtainsOntology) \wedge$

$(\geq 1\ Performs.CommunicateBuyerNeeds) \wedge$

$(\geq 1\ Performs.ReceiveDiscoverdSuppliers) \wedge$

$(\geq 1\ Performs.CommunicateContract) \wedge$

$(\geq 1\ Performs.ReceiveContract) \wedge$

$(\geq 1\ Performs.AuthorizesTransaction) \wedge$

$(\geq 1\ Performs.CommunicatesSatisfactionLevel) \wedge$

A supplier agent represents a supplier business enterprise in the infomediary-based e-marketplace.

$SupplierAgent\ \subseteq$

$(\ SoftwareAgent) \wedge$

$(=1\ Represents.Supplier) \wedge$

$(\geq 1\ Performs.ObtainsOntology) \wedge$

$(\geq 1\ Performs.CommunicatesSupplierCapabilities) \wedge$

$(\geq 1\ Performs.ProvideSupplierAgreement) \wedge$

$(\geq 1\ Pe\ rforms.CommunicatesSatisfactionLevel) \wedge$

The discovery agent and the transaction agents represent the infomediary business enterprise in the transactions presented in the following examples:

$$\begin{aligned} &DiscoveryAgent \subseteq \\ &\qquad (SoftwareAgent) \wedge \\ &\qquad (=1\ Represents.Infomediary) \wedge \\ &\qquad (\geq 1\ Performs.DiscoverSuppliers) \wedge \\ &\qquad (\geq 1\ Performs.RequestSupplierAgreement) \wedge \\ &\qquad (\geq 1\ Performs\ ReceiveSupplierAgreement) \end{aligned}$$

$$\begin{aligned} &TransactionAgent \subseteq \\ &\qquad (SoftwareAgent) \wedge \\ &\qquad (=1\ Represents.Infomediary) \wedge \\ &\qquad (\geq 1\ Performs.InitiateTransaction) \end{aligned}$$

In addition to the previous ontologies for the buyer and supplier business enterprise, the infomediary organization maintains product ontologies. We do not explicitly model the product ontologies in this chapter. Standardized XML-based product ontologies may be based upon the emergent global standards such as the UN/CEFACT ebXML (www.ebxml.org) standard for Global Electronic Commerce thereby ensuring standardization in the information interchange and interoperability among global partners.

In the following section, we provide the ontological engineering using DL-based definitions for the activity resource coordination. We utilize the aforementioned discovery and supplier selection process in infomediary-based e-marketplaces as examples of e-business processes problem domains to illustrate the process knowledge and the activity resource coordination mechanism. We utilize DL as the knowledge representation formalism for expressing structured knowledge in a format that is amenable for intelligent software agents to reason with it in a normative manner. Understanding the inherent relationships among business processes within and between organizations is a key topic of the information systems field. The use of standard DL in developing semantic models allows this approach to be a truly implementable framework using W3C's OWL and OWL-DL without loosing theoretical robustness.

Ontological Engineering for Infomediary-Enabled Buyer/ Supplier Discovery Process

As it can be seen in Figure 4, buyer agents present buyer needs to the e-marketplace by communicating the buyer requirements and buyer preferences. The discovery agent uses the buyer needs to discover a set of suppliers that are able to meet buyer requirements and match the buyer preferences. The set of discovered suppliers are communicated to the buyer enterprises through the buyer agent. It is noteworthy to mention that the process of supplier discovery is an iterative process that culminates with the buyer's selection of a supplier. This is represented in the use-case diagram in Figure 5.

Using the use-case diagram shown in Figure 5 as a model, the DL descriptions to represent the buyer's needs, including buyer requirements and buyer preferences, supplier capabilities, and supplier reputation are presented next. It is important to highlight that these demand requirement characteristics are intended to serve as examples, and they are not exhaustive.

Figure 5. Use-case diagram for supplier discovery based on buyer needs

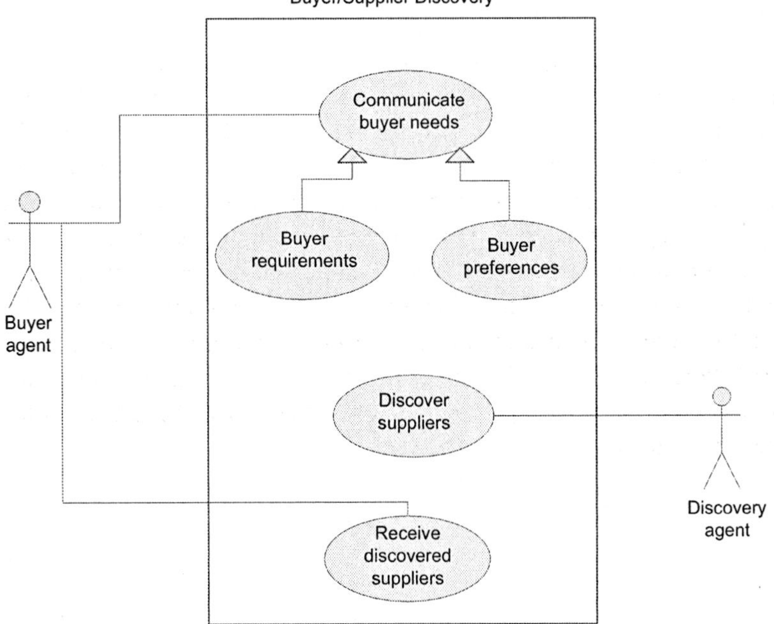

1. Buyers communicate their needs to the e-marketplace using standardized ontology for specifying the buyer needs.

$$BuyerNeeds \subseteq (Resource) \wedge$$
$$(= 1\ hasCharacteristics\ .\ BuyerID) \wedge$$
$$(= 1\ CoordinatesFlowProducedBy\ .\ ComunicateBuyerNeeds) \wedge$$
$$(= 1\ CoordinatesFlowConsumedBy\ .\ DiscoverSuppliers)$$

a. The *BuyerNeeds* resource abstracts the specialized buyer requirements and buyer needs as shown in Figure 6. This inheritance hierarchy of buyer needs illustrates the ability to specify meta-knowledge of processes and instantiate the individual workflows using multiple types of resources that inherit from the same parent resource used in the process knowledge specification.

$$BuyersNeeds \subseteq (\ Resource)$$
$$BuyersRequirements \subseteq BuyerNeeds$$
$$BuyerPreferences \subseteq BuyerNeeds$$

b. *BuyersRequirements* are buyer needs that specify buyers' demand function.

Figure 6. Buyer needs is an abstraction for the buyer requirements and buyer preferences involved in the supplier selection e-business process

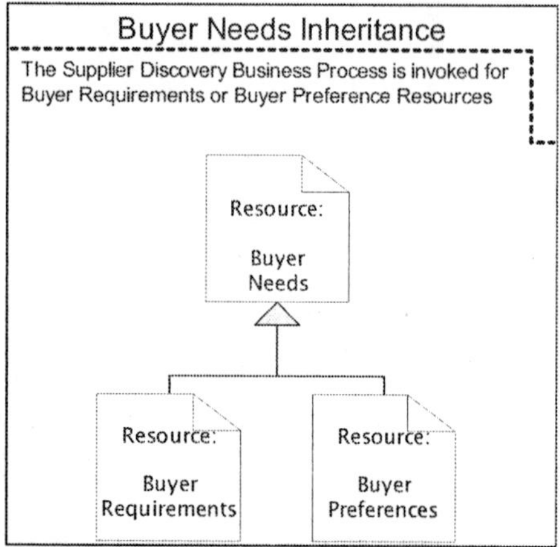

$$BuyersRequirements \subseteq BuyerNeeds$$
$$(= 1\ hasCharacteristics\ .\ ProductName) \wedge$$
$$(= 1\ hasCharacteristics\ .\ ProductType) \wedge$$
$$(= 1\ hasCharacteristics\ .\ PriceType) \wedge$$
$$(= 1\ hasCharacteristics\ .\ Currency) \wedge$$
$$(= 1\ hasCharacteristics\ .\ Quantity) \wedge$$
$$(= 1\ hasCharacteristics\ .\ Quality)$$

c. *Buyer Preferences* specify buyer preferences of suppliers and additional preference criteria for the buyer enterprise.

$$BuyerPreferences \subseteq BuyerNeeds$$
$$(\geq 0\ hasCharacteristics\ .\ PreferredSupplierReputation) \wedge$$
$$(\geq 0\ hasCharacteristics\ .\ PreferredDeliveryMethod) \wedge$$
$$(\geq 1\ hasCharacteristics\ .\ PreferredMinPrice) \wedge$$
$$(\geq 1\ hasCharacteristics\ .\ PreferredMaxPrice)$$

2. The *Buyer Agent* communicates *Buyer Needs* to the e-marketplace to coordinate the supplier discovery activity.

$$CommunicateBuyerNeeds \subseteq (BusinessActivity) \wedge$$
$$(= 1\ IsPerformedby.BuyerAgent) \wedge$$
$$(= 1\ HasCoordinationFlowProduces.BuyerNeeds)$$

3. *Communicating Buyer Needs* by the *Buyer Agent* has a coordination flow relationship with the *Buyer Needs* resource by producing the *Buyer Needs* to the *Discovery Agent*. The *Discovery Agent* is performs the *Discover Suppliers* activity.

$$DiscoverSuppliers \subseteq (BusinessActivity) \wedge$$
$$(= 1\ IsPerformedby.DiscoveryAgent) \wedge$$
$$(= 1\ HasCoordinationFlowConsumes.BuyerNeeds) \wedge$$
$$(= 1\ HasCoordinationFlowProduces.DiscoveredSuppliers)$$

4. The *Discover Suppliers* activity produces a set of discovered suppliers that meets buyer needs.

$$DiscoveredSuppliers \subseteq (Resource)$$
$$(\geq 0\ hasCharacteristics\ .\ Supplier) \wedge$$
$$(=1\ CoordinatesFlowProducedBy\ .\ DiscoverSuppliers) \wedge$$
$$(=1\ CoordinatesFlowConsumedBy\ .\ ReceiveDiscoverdSuppliers)$$

5. The Discovered suppliers resource is produced by the *Discover Suppliers* activity and coordinates the *Receive-Discovered-Suppliers* activity of the buyer agent.

$$ReceiveDiscoverdSuppliers \subseteq (BusinessActivity) \wedge$$
$$(= 1\ IsPerformedby\ .\ BuyerAgent) \wedge$$
$$(= 1\ HasCoordinationFlowConsumes\ .\ DiscoveredSuppliers)$$

Future Research

Information and knowledge resources are inherently distributed within and across organizations. Innovation and discovery rest upon the ability of the organizations to share and use information that are owned and made available by partner organizations in the information and knowledge sharing network. In this context, research that helps with knowledge integration and knowledge management is critical. The development of semantic knowledge integration architecture from the business process perspective brings the added benefit of a much needed knowledge integration framework for e-business process implementations that incorporate semantic management of knowledge in inter-organizational e-business processes.

Several e-marketplaces have failed in spite of the tremendous prospects for growth predicted by reputed research groups including the Gartner Group, Forrester, and e-Marketer.com. A survey by Davenport, Brooks, and Cantrell (2001) on B2B e-marketplaces identified lack of trust as a primary barrier for e-marketplace growth. This lack of trust is essentially due to poor real-time information about trading partners, such as collective feedback from multiple companies, third-party approvals, and availability of product information. Much of the risk associated with lack of trust can be reduced "as information becomes more codified, standardized, aggregated, integrated, distributed, and shaped for ready use" (Davenport, et al., 2001, p. 9).

Therefore, research aims at designing and developing semantic reputation-based trust mechanisms for e-Marketplaces is needed.

Conclusion

Recent advances in Semantic Web-based technologies offer virtual and traditional organizations the means to exchange knowledge in a *meaningful* way. It has been recognized that integrative technologies that support the transparent exchange of information and knowledge make it easier for the development of collaborative e-business relationships through enhanced adaptability and standardization of content representation. In this study, we present business models and architecture that demonstrate the potential of technical advancements in the computer and engineering sciences to be beneficial to businesses and consumers. We use a process perspective to integrate knowledge of resources involved in a process and process knowledge including process models and workflows used in process automation.

We develop theoretical conceptualizations using ontological analysis that are formalized using DLs to attain semantic knowledge transparency. In addition, we apply fundamental work done in Semantic Web technologies, multi-agent systems, semantic e-business, and Web services, to develop a semantic architecture that supports transparent knowledge flows, including content and know-how, to enable semantically enriched e-business processes. We provide an example of how semantic knowledge transparency in the e-marketplace provides critical input to the supplier discovery and selection decision problem while reducing the transaction and search costs for the buyer organization. Moreover, it is important to mention that semantic knowledge transparency allows for collaborative enriched communication, so that dynamic and transparent planning of demand and supply requirements through real-time knowledge integration across trading partners of the value chain can optimally occur. In this work, we are concerned with knowledge representations and semantic architecture for KM for automated inter-organizational e-business processes over seamlessly integrated information systems; however, the concept of semantic knowledge transparency can be applied to automate the coordination of resources and activities in the areas of supply chain management, healthcare information systems, and e-government applications to just name a few.

References

Anand, K. S., & Mendelson, H. (1997). Information and organization for horizontal multi-market coordination. *Management Science, 43*(12), 1609-1627.

Baader, F., Calvanese, D., McGuinness, D., Nardi, D., & Patel-Schneider, P. F. (Eds.). (2003). *The description logic handbook: Theory, implementation and applications.* UK: Cambridge University Press.

Badaracco, J. L. (1991). *The knowledge link.* Boston: Harvard Business School.

Bakos, Y. (1998). The emerging role of electronic marketplaces on the Internet. *Communications of the ACM, 41*(8), 35-42.

Bakos, Y. (1991). A strategic analysis of electronic marketplaces. *MIS Quarterly, 15*(3), 295-310.

Bellini, H., Gravitt, J. P., & Diana, D. (2001, June 20). *The birth of collaborative commerce.* White Paper. NY: Salomon Smith Barney.

Berners-Lee, T., Hendler, J., & Lassila, O, (2001). The Semantic Web. *Scientific American, 284,* 34-43.

Choudhury, V. (1997) Strategic choices in the development of interorganizational information systems. *Information Systems Research, 8*(1), 1-24.

Davenport, T. H., Brooks, J. D., & Cantrell, S. (2001, January). *B2B eMarket survey: Summary of findings.* Working paper from the Accenture Institute of Strategic Change.

Demsetz, H. (1998). The theory of the firm revisited. *Journal of Law, Economics, and Organization, 4*(1), 141-161.

Doz, Y., & Hamel, G. (1998). *Alliance advantage.* Boston: Harvard Business School.

Drucker, P. (1992). The new society of the organizations. *Harvard Business Review, 70*(5), 95-104.

Dustdar, S. (2004). Reconciling knowledge management and workflow management systems: The activity-based knowledge management approach. In *Proceedings of I-KNOW '04* Graz, Austria, (pp. 457-464).

Dyer, J. (2000). *Collaborative advantage: Winning through extended enterprise supplier networks.* New York: Oxford University Press.

Fox, M.S., Barbuceanu, M., Gruninger, M., & Lin, J. (1998). *An organization ontology for enterprise modeling* (pp. 131-152). In M. Prietula, K. Carley, L. Gasser (Eds.), Simulation Organizations: Computational models of institutions and groups, AAA/MIT Press, Menlo Park CA.

Gomez-Perez, A., Fernandez-Lopez, M., & Corcho, O. (2004). *Ontological engineering.* London: Springer.

Grant, R. (1996). Toward a knowledge-based theory of the firm. *Strategic Management Journal, 17,* 109-122.

Grover, V., & Teng, J. (2001). E-commerce and the information market. *Communications of the ACM, 44*(4), 79-86.

Gupta, B., Iyer, L., & Aronson, J. E. (2000). Knowledge management: A taxonomy, practices and challenges. *Industrial Management and Data Systems, 100*(1), 17-21.

Hagel, III, J., & Rayport, J. (1997). The new infomediaries. *The McKinsey Quarterly, 4,* 54-70.

Hamel, G. (1991). Competition for competence and inter-partner learning with international strategic alliances. *Strategic Management Journal, 12,* 83-103.

Hansen, J. V., & Hill, N. C. (1989). Control and audit of electronic data interchange. *MIS Quarterly, 13*(4), 402-413.

Holland, C. P. (1995). Cooperative supply chain management: The impact of interorganizational information systems. *Journal of Strategic Information Systems, 4*(2), 117-133.

Iyer, L. S., Singh, R., & Salam, A. F. (2005). Collaboration and knowledge management in B2B e-marketplaces. *Information Systems Management, 22*(3), 37-49.

Jasper, R., & Uschold, M. (1999). A framework for understanding and classifying ontology applications. *Proceedings of the IJCAI-99 Workshop on Ontologies and Problem-Solving Mehtods*, Stockholm, Sweden.

Jennings, N. R., & Wooldridge, M. (1998). *Agent technology: Foundations, applications, and markets.* London: Springer.

Kishore, R., Sharman, R., Zhang, H., & Ramesh, R. (2004). Computational ontologies and information systems: I. foundations. *Communications of the Association for Information Systems, 14,* 158-183.

Klein, M., Fensel, D., Van Harmelen, F., & Horrocks, I. (2001). The relation between ontologies and XML schemas. *Electronic Transactions on Artificial Intelligence (ETAI), Linköping Electronic Articles in Computer and Information Science, 6*(4).

Li, L., & Horrocks, I. (2004). A software framework for matchmaking based on Semantic Web technology. *International Journal of Electronic Commerce, 8*(4), 39-60.

Loebecke, C., Van Fenema, P., & Powell, P. (1999). Co-opetition and knowledge transfer. *Database for Advances in Information Systems, 30*(2), 14-25.

Lorange, P. (1996). Strategy at the leading edge—Interactive strategy—Alliances and partnership. *Long Range Planning, 29*(4), 581-584.

Malone, T., & Crowston, K. (1994). The interdisciplinary study of coordination. *ACM Computing Surveys, 26*(1), 87-119.

Malone, T., W., Crowston, K., & Herman, G. (Eds.). (2003). *Organizing business knowledge:The MIT process handbook.* Cambridge, MA: MIT Press.

Muller, H. J. (1997). Towards agent systems engineering. *Data and Knowledge Engineering, 23,* 217-245.

Newell, A. (1982). The knowledge level. *Artificial Intelligence, 18,* 87-127.

Oh, S., & Park, S. (2003). Task-role-based access control model. *Information Systems, 28*(6), 533-562.

Papazoglou, M. P. (2001). Agent oriented technology in support of e-business: Enabling the development of intelligent business agents for adaptive, reusable software. *Communications of the ACM, 44*(4), 71-77.

Pollock, J., & Hodgson, R. (2004). *Adaptive information: Improving business through semantic interoperability, grid computing, and enterprise integration.* Hoboken, NJ: John Wiley & Sons.

Sawhney, M., & Parikh, D. (2001). Where value lies in a networked world. *Harvard Business Review, 79*(1), 79-86.

Segars, A. H., & Chatterjee, D. (2003). *An overview of contemporary practices and trends.* In Transformation of the enterprise through e-business, society for information management.

Shoham, Y. (1993) Agent oriented programming. *Journal of Artificial Intelligence, 60*(1), 51-92.

Simon, H. A. (1992). *Models of bounded rationality: Behavioral economics and business organization.* Cambridge, MA: MIT Press.

Singh, R., Iyer, L. S., & Salam, A. F. (2005). Semantic e-business. *International Journal of Semantic Web and Information Systems, 1*(1), 19-35.

Singh, R., Salam, A. F., & Iyer, L. S. (2005) Agents in e-supply chains. *Communications of the ACM, 48*(6), 109-115.

Staab, S., Studer, R., Schnurr, H. P., & Sure, Y. (2001). Knowledge processes and ontologies. *IEEE Intelligent Systems, 16*(1), 26-34.

Stal, M. (2002). Web services: Beyond component-based computing. *Communications of the ACM, 45*(10), 71-76.

Tallman, S., Jenkins, M., Henry, N., & Pinch, S. (2004). Knowledge, clusters, and competitive advantage. *Academy of Management Review, 29*(2), 258-271.

Tapscott, D., & Ticoll, D. (2003) *The naked corporation: How the age of transparency will revolutionize business.* New York: Free Press.

Van der Aalst, W., & Kumar, A. (2003). XML based schema definition for support of inter-organizational workflow. *Information Systems Research, 4*(1), 23-46.

Zhu, K. (2002). Information transparency in electronic marketplaces: Why data transparency may hinder the adoption of B2B exchanges. *Electronic Markets, 12*(2), 92-99.

Zhu, K. (2004). Information transparency of business-to-business electronic markets: A game-theoretic analysis. *Management Science, 50*(5), 670-686.

Terms and Definitions

ABox. ABox contains extensional knowledge, which is specified by the individual of the discourse domain. An ABox describes specific situations or scenarios of the application domain in terms of the *instances* of concepts and their relationships. The ABox contains *concept assertions* on instances of concepts, and *role assertions,* on role-filler instances, which describe the individual relationships between concept assertions (Baader et al., 2003; Gomez-Perez et al., 2004).

Component knowledge. Component knowledge is knowledge that includes descriptions of skills, technologies, tangible and intangible resources, and is amenable to knowledge exchange (Hamel, 1991; Tallman et al., 2004).

Description logics. DLs are logical formalisms for knowledge-representation. Description logics provide a formal linear syntax to express the description of top-level concepts in a problem domain; their relationships and the constraints on the concepts; and the relationships that are imposed by pragmatic considerations in the domain of interest (Gomez-Perez et al., 2004; Li & Horrocks, 2004). DL is divided into two parts: TBox and ABox.

Electronic marketplaces. Electronic marketplaces are defined as interorganizational information systems that facilitate the exchange of information about price and product offerings between buyers and sellers that participate in the marketplace (Bakos, 1991).

Infomediary Infomediary is defined as "a business whose sole or main source of revenue derives from capturing consumer information and developing detailed profiles of individual customers for use by selected third-party vendors" (Hagel & Rayport, 1997, p. 56). In addition, "infomediary is an emergent business model adopted by organizations in response to the enormous increase in the volume of information available and the critical role of information in enabling processes in electronic markets" (Grover & Teng, 2001, p. 79).

Intelligent agent. Intelligent agent can be defined as "a computer system situated in some environment and that is capable of flexible autonomous action in this environment in order to meet its design objectives" (Jennings & Wooldridge, 1998, p. 8).

Ontology. Ontology is defined in philosophy as a theory about the nature of existence; in systems, ontology is a document that formally describes classes of objects and defines the relationship among them.

Process knowledge. Process knowledge is knowledge embedded in the process models of workflow management systems or exists as coordination knowledge among human agents to coordinate complex processes.

Semantic interoperability. Semantic interoperability "is a dynamic enterprise capability derivate from the application of special software technologies (such as reasoners, inference engines, ontologies, and models) that infer, relate, and classify the implicit meanings of digital content without human involvement—which in turn drive adaptive business processes, enterprise knowledge, business rules, and software application interoperability" (Pollock & Hodgson, 2004, p. 6)

Semantic knowledge transparency. Semantic knowledge transparency is defined as the dynamic on-demand and seamless flow of relevant and unambiguous, machine-interpretable knowledge resources within organizations and across inter-organizational systems of business partners engaged in collaborative processes.

TBox. TBox contains intentional knowledge in the form of a terminology and is built through declarations that describe general properties of concepts (Baader et al., 2003; Gomez-Perez et al., 2004).

Chapter XII

Application of Semantic Web Based on the Domain-Specific Ontology for Global KM

Jaehun Joo, Dongguk University, Korea
Sang M. Lee, University of Nebraska – Lincoln, USA
Yongil Jeong, Saltlux, Inc., Korea

Abstract

This chapter introduces an application of the Semantic Web based on ontology to the tourism business. Tourism business is one promising area for Semantic Web applications. To realize the potential of the Semantic Web, we need to find a killer application of the Semantic Web in the knowledge management (KM) area. The ontology as a key enabler is deigned and implemented under a framework of the Semantic-Web-driven KM system in a tourism domain. Finally, we discussed the relationship between the Semantic Web and KM processes.

Introduction

There are two important limitations in exploiting the Web as the space for global KM. These limitations are:

- lack of the mechanism for providing information and knowledge that computers or software agents can understand and process and
- information overload owing to keyword-based search modes.

One limitation results from Web documents represented in Hyper Text Markup Language (HTML). In most cases, computers including software agents neither understand or process data or information automatically on the Web, nor integrate them, in particular, in heterogeneous environments. The other occurs in lack of semantics in information retrieval. The more information resources exist on the Web, the more information overload arises out of search results.

The Semantic Web provides the opportunity for global KM by integrating the resources dispersed across the Internet Web as well as other resources including the existing knowledge base. There are many opportunities to apply the Semantic Web to a variety of areas. One very promising area of the Semantic Web is KM. However, there are still no successful application areas of the Semantic Web because it is in its infancy. Ontology is seen as a key enabler for the Semantic Web. Also, ontologies are useful for improving the accuracy of Web searches (Antoniou & Harmelen, 2004). Thus, ontology development in a variety of domains will enable us to realize the potential of the Semantic Web. In addition, there is a need to develop ontology based on widely accepted or de facto standards such as Resource Description Framework (RDF)/RDF Schema (RDFS) and Web Ontology Language (OWL) in order to ensure the easiness of integration among ontologies.

The purpose of this paper is to present a domain-specific ontology, to propose a conceptual model of a Semantic-Web-driven KM system with such components as resource, metadata, ontology, and user and query layers. Finally, we discuss how the Semantic-Web-driven KM systems can support KM process by overcoming the limitations existing in current KM.

This chapter is organized as follows: after this introductory section, "Relevant Liturature and Scenarios" reviews related literatures and presents two scenarios in the tourism business domain. "Ontology Design for Tourism Business" designs the ontology providing answers to queries of the scenarios. The fourth section, "Implementation," discusses the result of the implemented system. The fifth section, "Global Knowledge Management Based on the Semantic Web," presents a conceptual model of the Semantic-Web-driven KM systems, and discusses the relationship between the Semantic Web technology, KM systems, and the KM process. The final section presents "Conclusion and Future Trends."

Relevant Literature and Scenarios

Capabilities of the Semantic Web come from semantics and machine-processable ability. It resolves information overload problem and offers opportunities to semantic integration across heterogeneous and distributed systems as well as business process automation. There are a number of areas to which the Semantic Web technology can be applied (Antoniou & Harmelen, 2004). One very promising application area of the Semantic Web is KM. Figure 1 shows research areas on the Semantic Web for KM. The studies are classified into four areas: (1) developing infrastructure and architecture, (2) killer applications, (3) business management issues, and (4) other social issues.

The most surprising research area is technical issues related to architecture design and building of infrastructure for KM based on the Semantic Web. According to Berners-Lee, Hendler, and Lassila (2001), the Semantic Web, as an extension of the current Web, enables knowledge representation by using extensible markup language (XML), RDF, and ontologies including rules to make inferences. They also

Figure 1. Research areas of the Semantic Web in KM

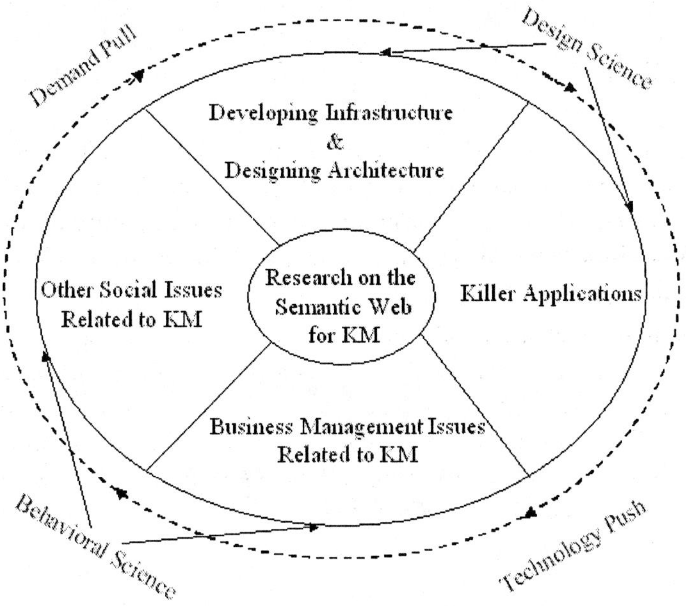

insist that the real power of the Semantic Web will be realized by agents collecting Web content as knowledge, processing it and exchanging the results with others. D'Aquin, Bouthier, Brachais, Lieber, and Napoli (2005) presented an architecture of the systems for knowledge representation, reasoning and visual editing relying on Semantic Web principles, in the domain of oncology, providing support for the medical treatment of people with cancer. Ontology itself facilitates knowledge sharing in organization or inter-organizational context. Edgington, Choi, Henson, Raghu, and Vinze (2004) discussed how to adopt ontology to facilitate knowledge sharing. Maedche, Motik, Stojanovic, Studer, and Voltz (2003) suggested an architecture of ontology management systems enabling ontology mapping and its evolution. The architecture shows how to support multiple ontologies and manage ontology evolution, not in global context such as the Internet Web, but in enterprise wide. The studies on extension of organizational KM systems to the Internet Web have been conducted. Tiwana and Ramesh (2001) discussed how to integrate knowledge on the Web. The Internet Web has been recognized as a medium of access and connection to integrate distributed applications and information before the advent of the Semantic Web. The Semantic Web enables knowledge representation and allows organizations to manage Web contents as knowledge resources with inference abilities.

Recently, a few projects for killer applications as well as building infrastructure have been conducted. On-To-Knowledge project as a typical example aimed at developing an ontology-based tool suit that efficiently processes the large numbers of heterogeneous, distributed, and semistructured documents. The following tools from this project were developed:

- OntoBuilder extracts machine-processable metadata from documents in RDF formats. It consists of two modules, OntoExtract and OntoWraper. OntoExtract extracts information from unstructured free text while OntoWraper does information from structured sources.
- Sesame stores RDF and RDFS data extracted by OntoBuilder and provides query facilities.
- OntoShare facilitates and encourages the sharing of information between communities of practice.
- OntoEdit is a graphical editing tool enabling knowledge engineers to codify and manage an ontology.
- QuizRDF (or RDFferret) is a search engine that combines full-text search with an ability to exploit RDF data in searching.
- Spectable personalizes information as a content presentation platform featuring custom-made information presentations.

Although the project contributed to build an infrastructure for applications of the Semantic Web to KM as well as development of tools, it did not deal with business issues associated with being considered as strategic relationships between information technology (IT) and management. Also, it is at an early stage to claim that such tools can become killer applications. The realization of the Semantic Web capabilities requires a killer application. According to Chen (2004), developers need to build applications available to the public because there is no killer application. KM is a very promising area of killer applications for the Semantic Web. Developing research agendas on killer applications is necessary for the realization of the potential for the Semantic Web through its application to KM. The view that widespread adoption of IT is dependent on the development of a killer application has widely been recognized (Meyer, 1998). According to Middleton (2003), in particular, it is important to develop the killer applications in user-centric view rather than provider-centric view.

As Orlikowski and Iacono (2001) pointed out, it is necessary to study the complex ensemble of people, culture, and technology embedded in social contexts as well as a specific organizational level. However, there are no such studies in the area of KM applying the Semantic Web because the Semantic Web itself is in its infancy.

According to Hevner, March, Park, and Ram's (2004) dichotomy of the research on management information systems, studies on the infrastructure and architecture and the killer applications refer to design science while two other issues in Figure 1 do behavioral science. The former has more characteristics of technology push than the latter. The dotted circle with arrows in Figure 1 shows the interactive relationship between technology push and demand pull. Research in aspect of demand pull in the stage of introduction of the Semantic Web can contribute to improve the performance of IT investment like prototyping improves productivity of waterfall model in system development methodology. Such research is important under the environment of a rapid advance of IT.

This study focuses on tourism area as a killer application of the Semantic Web for KM and deals with two research areas together: killer application and business management issues.

The tourism industry is one of the more successful application areas of the Semantic Web as well as e-commerce because it is a consumer-oriented industry where services and information play a large part in transaction processes (Cardoso, 2004; Dell'Erba, 2004; Fodor & Werthner, 2004; Joo, 2002; Joo & Jeong, 2004). Figure 2 shows an overview of the business model for an electronic tourism market. The electronic tourism market is a marketplace allowing the players to electronically interact and mutually coordinate their benefits. It also provides an infrastructure of e-commerce with its applications to players and becomes a single interface for customers. According to Cardoso (2004), the development of a suitable ontology

Figure 2. Overview of the business model for an electronic tourism market

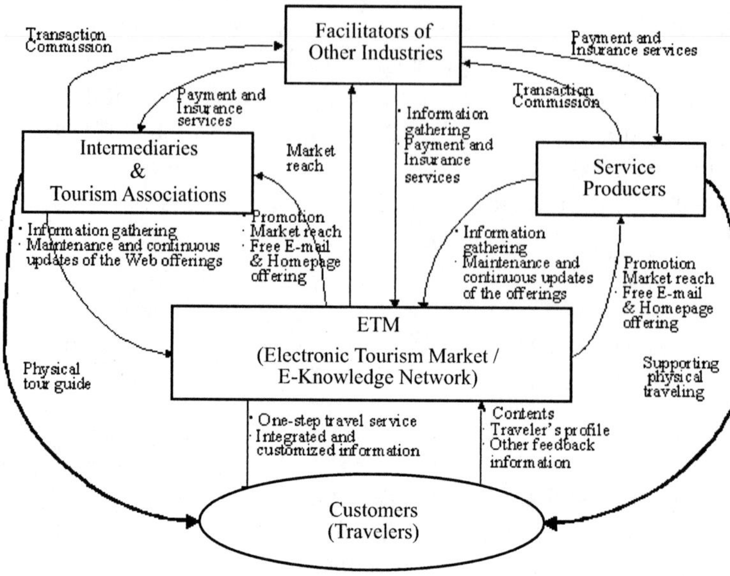

for the tourism industry serves as a common language for travel-related terminology and a mechanism for promoting the seamless exchange of information across all players such as service producers; intermediaries and tourism associations; facilitators; and travelers, as shown in Figure 2. Thus, the tourism market is one of the most promising areas enabling automation of business and transaction processes by applying the Semantic Web.

Consider the situation where tourists are planning to visit Gyeongju (an old imperial city of Shilla Dynasty in Korea). The tourists need information based on their tour schedule, individual preferences, and budget. Let us consider the following two scenarios:

Scenario 1. Accommodation recommendation for tourists

"Recommend an appropriate accommodation for the knapsack tourist who plans to visit Gyeongju city"

Scenario 2. Search for sightseeing spots in nearby regions

"Find attractive sightseeing sites near Kolon Hotel in Gyeongju for the tourist who has about four hours of tour time"

Consider the case as we use Web search services such as Google or Yahoo. In each of the previous scenarios, appropriate keywords are critical to extract good search results. Although desired keywords may be selected, limitations of a keyword-based search cannot be overcome.

Ontology Design for Tourism Business

It is necessary to build ontologies to get answers for the tourist in the two scenarios. Figure 3 shows some of the major classes and properties representing the relations among them in the tourism domain. For example, both GroupTour and IndividualTour are subclasses of the class Tour and the class SchoolJourney is that of the class Grouptour. There are classes of concepts which constitute a hierarchy with multiple inheritances such as the class BusinessTour and the class KnapsackTour as depicted in Figure 3.

Figure 3. Tour package ontology for tourism business

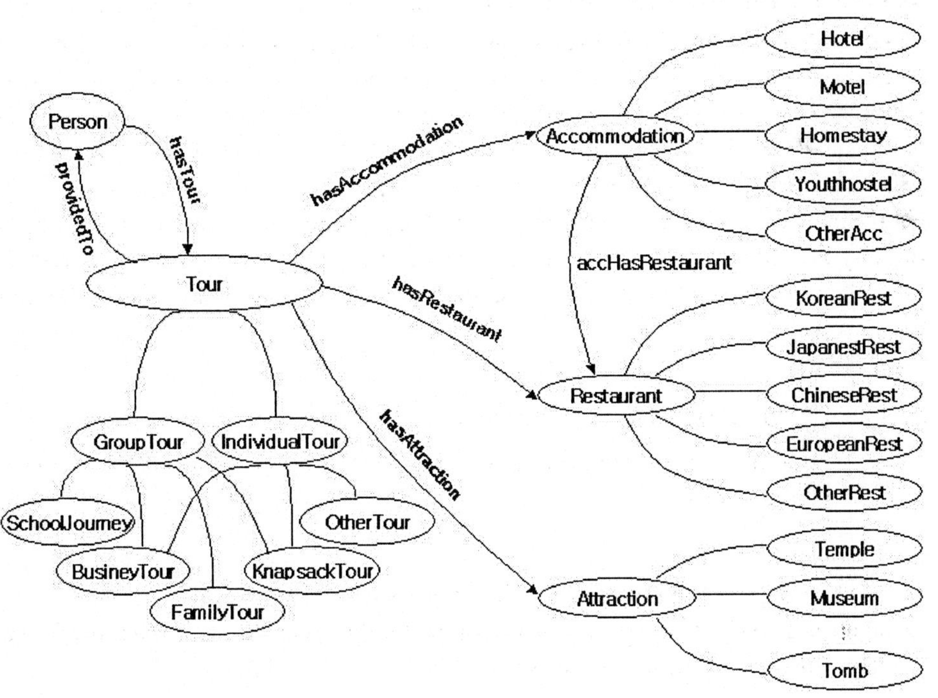

Figure 4. Region-distance ontology

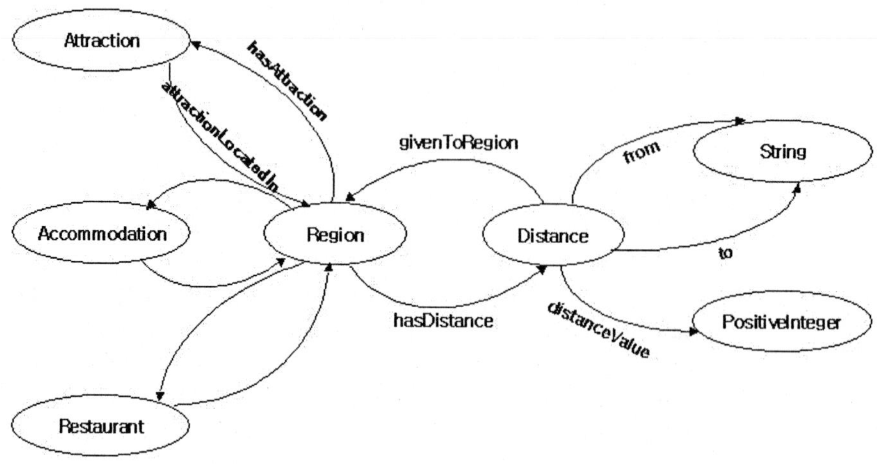

The property hasTour relates the class Person to the class Tour. In other words, resources have properties associated with them. For example, Person has Tour. In the relationship between the class Person and the class Tour, the reverse is true. Thus we can say "the Tour is provided to the Person."

Figure 4 presents the extended ontology to that of Figure 3 by adding the class Region and the class Distance. The relation between the class Attraction and the class Region makes it infer that a region may have some tourism attraction sites. Inversely, we can infer that an attraction site is located in a region. For example, the relation allows software agents to infer that TombOfKingMunmu is located in only one place. To get the answer for query of scenario 2, we need an ontology enabling the system to identify the terminology, "nearby." The region-distance ontology shown in Figure 4 is used to represent knowledge about distance between two regions.

Figure 5 describes the ontology of Figure 4 as a semantic graph form. RDFS defines a property's domain—resources that can be subjects of the property, and a property's ranges—resources that can be objects of a property. For example, the property hasDistance may have a class Region as its domain and a class Distance as its range.

In OWL, there are two types of properties: object property and datatype property. The former relates objects to other objects. The latter relates objects to datatype values. OWL provides a powerful mechanism for enhanced reasoning about a property (World Wide Web Consortium, 2004a). Table 1 summarizes property characteristics for those depicted in Figure 4. For example, hasDistance and givenToRegion are ObjectProperty and there is an inverse relation between them. A region have dis-

Figure 5. A semantic network representing region-distance ontology

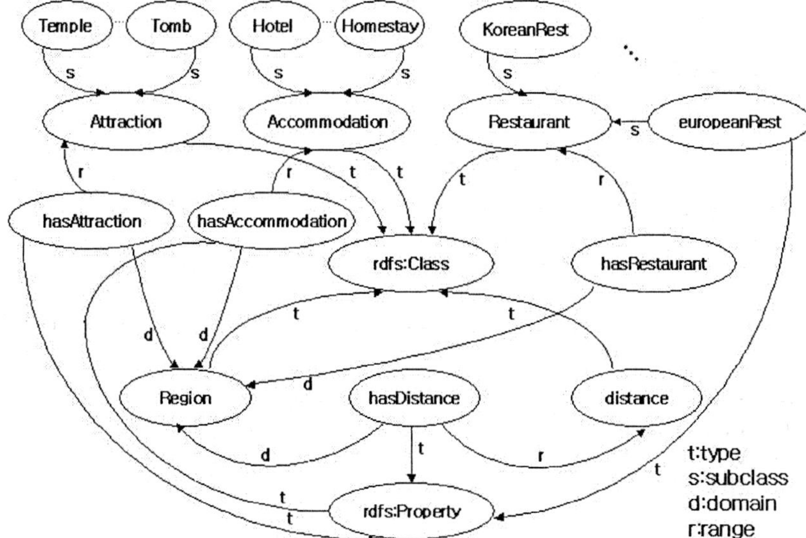

Table 1. Types of property elements in region-distance ontology

Object Property	HasDistance	FunctionalProperty	inverseOf
	GivenToRegion	InverseFunctional Property	
	has Attraction hasReataurant ...		inverseOf
	LocatedIn	TransitiveProperty	
DatatypeProperty	From	String type	
	To		
	DistanceValue	Integer Type	

tance, the distance is given to the region. The relation in either direction is true. The hasDistance property is functional, that is, a region can have at most one distance. The givenToRegion property is inverse functional, that is, a distance must be given to a region. Properties, from, to, and distanceValue are datatype. The property distanceValue takes a positive integer.

We can define tourist as the person who has at least one tour package. In the RDF syntax, for example, Tourist represented in PersonÇTour would be written as:

```
<owl:Class rdf:ID="Tourist">
  <rdfs:subClassOf>
    <owl:Class>
      <owl:intersectionOf rdf:parseType="Collection">
        <owl:Class rdf:about="#Person"/>
        <owl:Class rdf:ID="Tour"/>
      </owl:intersectionOf>
    </owl:Class>
  </rdfs:subClassOf>
</owl:Class>
```

The example defines the class Tourist to be the intersection of Person and Tour. OWL allows us to express the intersection of classes by using owl:intersectionOf.

In general, knapsack tourists do not want to stay in expensive hotels. Following ontology represented in OWL requires only accommodations except hotels to be recommended to them.

```
<owl:Class rdf:about="#KnapsackTour">
  <rdfs:subClassOf>
<owl:Restriction>
<owl:onProperty rdf:ID="#hasAccommodation"/>
<owl:allValuesFrom>
        <owl:Class>
          <owl:oneOf rdf:parseType="Collection">
            <owl:Class rdf:about="#Homestay"/>
            <owl:Class rdf:about="#Motel"/>
            <owl:Class rdf:about="#OtherAcc"/>
            <owl:Class rdf:about="#YouthHostel"/>
          </owl:oneOf>
        </owl:Class>
      </owl:allValuesFrom>
   </owl:Restriction>
  </rdfs:subClassOf>
</owl:Class>
```

As shown in Figure 3, the class KnapsackTour is a subclass of IndividualTour or GroupTour. Both classes, IndividualTour and Grouptour, are subclasses of Tour. The classes Hotel, Motel, Homestay, Youthhostel, and OtherAcc are all subclasses of Accommodation. The hasAccommodation property only has values of a class whose members are the individuals Homestay, Motel, YouthHostel, and OtherAcc. The property hasAccommodation has the domain of Tour and the range of Accommodation. That is, it relates to instances of subclasses of Tour to instances of subclasses of Accommodation.

The example states that the class KnapsackTour is a subclass of an anonymous OWL class that has as its extension a set of all individuals for whom the property hasAccommodation has values in only one class among Homestay, Model, OtherAcc, and Youthhostel. The example defines that Knapsack is subclass of an anonymous class with a property restriction. The element, owl:allValuesFrom is used to specify the class of possible values the property specified by owl:onProperty can take. In other words, the class KnapsackTour has a property called hasAccommodation restricted to have allValuesFrom only in one class among the collection of Homestay, Model, OtherAcc, and Youthhostel. Therefore, the class KnapsackTour never has a value from the instance of the class Hotel.

```
<owl:InverseFunctionalProperty rdf:about="#attractionLocatedIn">
  <rdfs:domain rdf:resource="#Attraction"/>
  <rdf:type rdf:resource="http: //www.w3.org/ 2002/07/ owl#ObjectProperty"/>
  <rdfs:range rdf:resource="#Region"/>
</owl:InverseFunctionalProperty>
```

The owl:InverseFunctionalProperty defines a property for which two different objects cannot have the same value. If two instances of the class Attraction are respectively defined as TombOfKingMunmu and DaewanamUnderwaterTomb, we can infer that these two resources must refer to the same thing in the example.

```
<owl:FunctionalProperty rdf:ID="hasDistance">
  <rdfs:range rdf:resource="#Distance"/>
  <owl:inverseOf>
   <owl:InverseFunctionalProperty rdf:ID="givenToRegion"/>
  </owl:inverseOf>
  <rdfs:domain rdf:resource="#Region"/>
  <rdf:type rdf:resource="http://www.w3.org/2002/07/ owl#ObjectProperty"/>
 </owl:FunctionalProperty>
```

The property hasDistance relates the class Region to the class Distance. The hasDistance defined as owl:FunctionalProperty has at most one unique value for each instance of the class Region.

As shown in Figure 4, the properties from and to defined as Datatype properties have string values and the property distanceValue has a positive integer. We can infer the instances of the class Region having distance values less than a particular value for a given region.

Implementation

We use Jena (n.d.) toolkit to implement the ontology design for the tourism business. Jena is an open-source Semantic Web developer's kit as a set of Java application program interfaces (APIs) for manipulating RDF models. It comprises a number of modules including RDF API, ARP RDF/XML parser, ontology API, RDQL,(World Wide Consortium, 2004b) and storage modules (Jena, n.d.). We used J2SDK 1.4.2 to develop applications of the system.

Figure 6 presents a sequence diagram that displays object interactions arranged in a time sequence. The actor who is user or knowledge engineer may set up environment variables by invoking the object Configurator. The object SearchOwl activates

Figure 6. A sequence diagram of the search system in tourism ontology

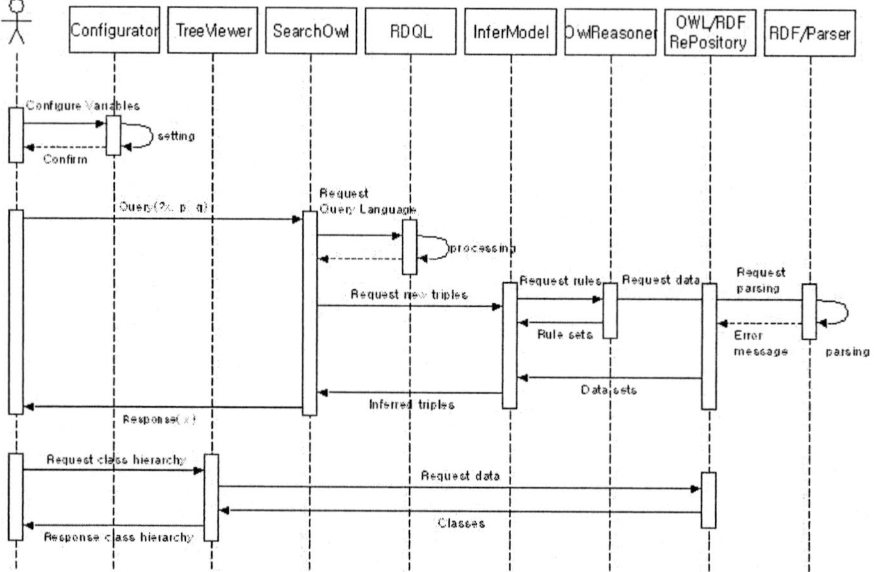

Figure 7. Treeview for the tourism ontology

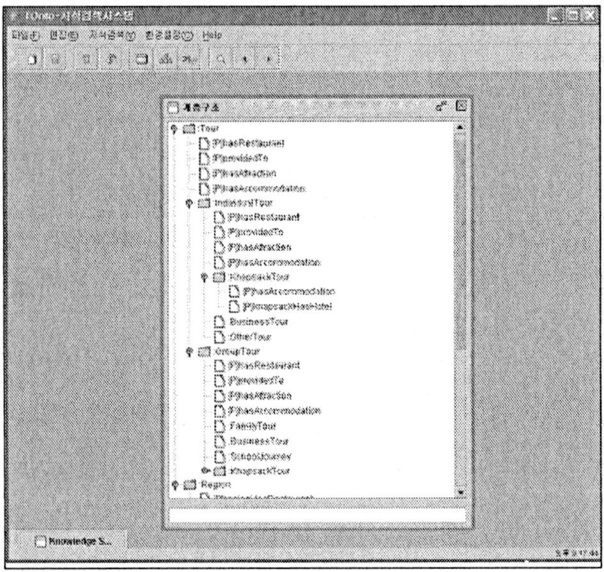

Figure 8. Query result for the scenario 2

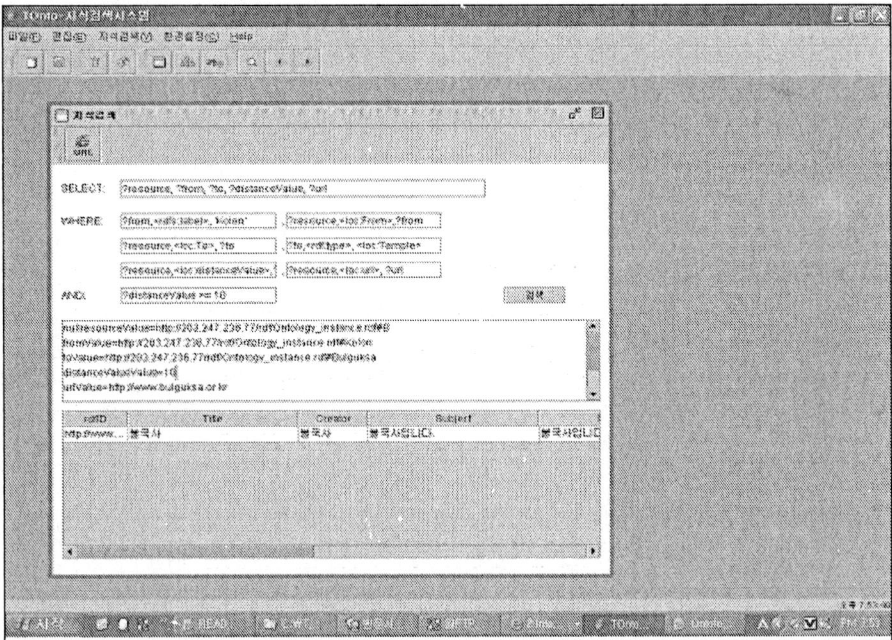

the inference engine to create a new inference model with the query data sets and returns search results of RDF triples by exploiting RDQL (World Wide Consortium, 2004b). The InferModel invokes the OwlReasoner to create a new inference model that is built in triple types (subject, predicate, object) as an extension of the Jena RDF triple. The Reasoner of Jena supports OWL Lite and OWL-DL reasoning (Jena, n.d.). The OwlReasoner provides inference rules based on Description Logics. The OWL/RDF repository stores ontologies represented as OWL language and RDF/RDFS, and allows access and reuse of ontologies.

Figure 7 shows the hierarchy of classes created in the ontology buildings in the tourism business area. Figure 8 shows search results for the query of scenario 2.

Global Knowledge Management Based on the Semantic Web

Conceptual Model of the Semantic-Web-Driven KM Systems

Figure 9 shows a conceptual model for the global KM systems exploiting the Semantic Web technology. The model is composed of four layers. The resource layer refers to a variety of knowledge resources including contents of the Internet Web. The Semantic Web enables us to manage Web contents as organizational knowledge as well as the existing internal knowledge such as database and knowledge base. Also, it allows us to define a part of a document or a sentence as a knowledge piece corresponding to a resource. Thus, system users can find more focused and personalized knowledge and seamlessly integrate knowledge extracted from various resources. The metadata layer includes RDFs as the foundation for processing metadata extracted from the resource layer. The system requires middleware modules or tools to support automatic knowledge extraction from unstructured and semi-structured data in heterogeneous resources. In this layer, we need RDF (World Wide Consortium, 1999) management subsystems including RDF repositories, XML/RDF parser, and RDF APIs which enable the interaction with ontology and resources layers. The ontology layer including RDFS (World Wide Consortium, 2004) and inference engine plays a critical role in the system. Ontology APIs enable Web services or existing KM systems to be integrated into the system. Finally, users can find necessary knowledge through query and semantic search.

Figure 9. Conceptual model for KM based on the Semantic Web

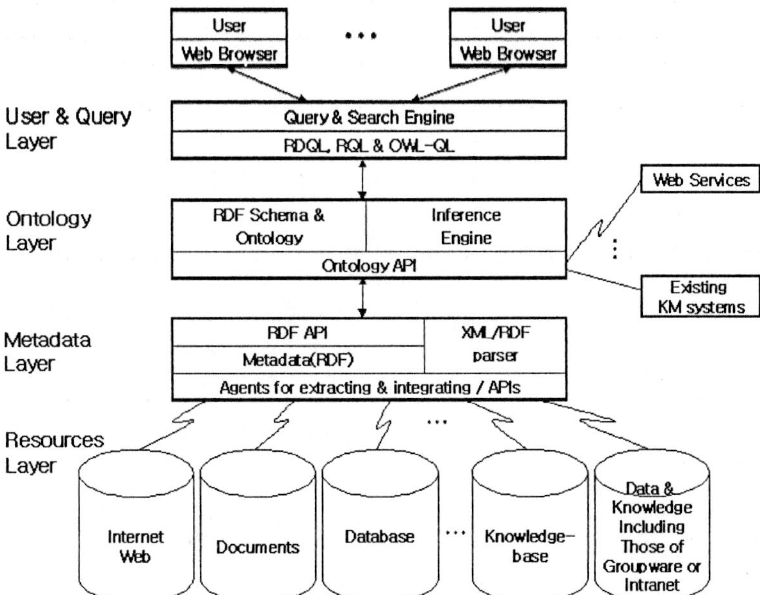

Innovation of KM Process

Recently, many organizations design and use KM systems as specialized information systems into which various technologies such as the Internet Web, groupware, intranet, artificial intelligence, virtual community, and data warehousing are integrated. Although KM systems are helpful for KM and increase organizational effectiveness and competitiveness, they have technical limitations in maximizing objectives of KM due to the following:

- limitations of keyword-based search as well as limited knowledge categorization;
- limitations to integration of heterogeneous systems as knowledge resources and to integration of existing KM systems with Web resources;
- inconvenience of KM systems use resulting from slow response and instability of KM systems; and
- time and space limitation in KM systems use and limitation of access methods in KM systems.

Table 2. Supporting technologies, components, and issues for each layer

Layers	Supporting technologies, components, and issues
User & Query Layer	- There are RDQL, RQL (ICS-FORM, 2005), and OWL-QL (Fikes et al., 2004)as query languages for RDF, RDFS, and ontology. - Users can query knowledge on the Web as well as internal knowledge resources as if they use an integrated database system. - It is necessary to develop tools by which the queries with natural language from users are automatically transformed into the formats of the query language exploited
Ontology Layer	- Ontology editors refer to the system for loading, editing, and storing ontologies. Protégé-2000 (Noy et al., 2001) and OntoEdit are typical GUI-based ontology editors. - Inference engine is a core component of the ontology layer and is used for several tasks like semantic validation and deduction of implicit information. Description Logics (DL) is exploited in reasoning support in OWL. - Ontology layer needs several sets of interfaces such as ontology API ensuring independence between usage and storage of ontologies and APIs for integrating with Web Services or existing KM systems. - It is important to develop the tools for mapping or merging ontologies (Noy & Musen, 2004).
Metadata Layer	- Metadata layer needs components to edit, store, and manage RDFs as metadata. The component should have the ability to test validation of RDF models. RDF/XML parser plays a role as a core component in the metadata layer. Many parsers such as Redland and SiRPAC are available. - One of the important issues in this layer is to develop tools that automatically extract metadata from various resources on the Web. Such tools are necessary to incorporate Dublin Core (dublincore.com) and RSS (RDF Site Summary, web.resource.org/rss/1.0/spec) in order to efficiently build RDF.
Resource Layer	- Resource layer needs the component offering APIs which enable document files, database, knowledge base, or groupware to be integrated into the metadata layer.

In this section, we focus on how to overcome the technical limitations through the Semantic-Web-driven KM systems. Figure 10 shows the relationship between Semantic Web technology, KM systems, and KM process. The capabilities such as semantics and machine-processable, enabled by the Semantic Web technology, allows the Semantic-Web-driven KM systems to have the opportunity to or possibility of semantic integration and thus resolving information overload. Ultimately, the Semantic-Web-driven KM systems support KM process by overcoming the limitations of systems integration and knowledge search embedded in existing KM systems.

All resources in the Semantic Web are represented in RDF as metadata and this representation method makes possible for users to query and get answers as if they use database management systems. The Semantic Web also supports RDFS and ontology which enables semantic analysis on vocabularies contained in query and domains as well as syntactic analysis. Thus, the Semantic Web can provide accurate knowledge suitable to users. Any documents and data being either inside or outside the organization as well as Web resources can be represented as a resource in RDF. This means that a resource of RDF that we call a knowledge object can be searched with an independent knowledge unit as if a user searches a document in document management systems. A specific part or sentence of a Web page or a part of a document may be represented as a knowledge object. This capability allows the Semantic Web-driven KM systems to search for a knowledge object unit rather than a document unit. Therefore, the Semantic Web allows the current KM systems to resolve the problem of knowledge/information overload and duplication.

There are three types of integration: (1) data integration, (2) application integration, and (3) process integration (Giachetti, 2004). The goal of data integration is data sharing where different systems exchange data with each other. The goal of application level is to achieve interoperability between systems. The obstacles of integration arise at syntactic and semantic heterogeneity between different information systems or applications (Giachetti, 2004; Noy, Doan, & Halevy, 2005). Until recently, the approaches to provide interoperability include standardization and middleware or mediators as well as enterprise application integration (EAI). The enterprise knowledge portal (EKP) is a system integrating various tools for KM in the perspective of users. Although the traditional integration approaches such as middleware and standardization easily integrate the structured data extracted from heterogeneous databases, they have limitations when integrating the unstructured data or knowledge from the various knowledge sources such as HTML, word processor files, and spreadsheet files. EKP does not play the role of a content integrator

Figure 10. Relationship between Semantic Web technology, KM systems, and KM process

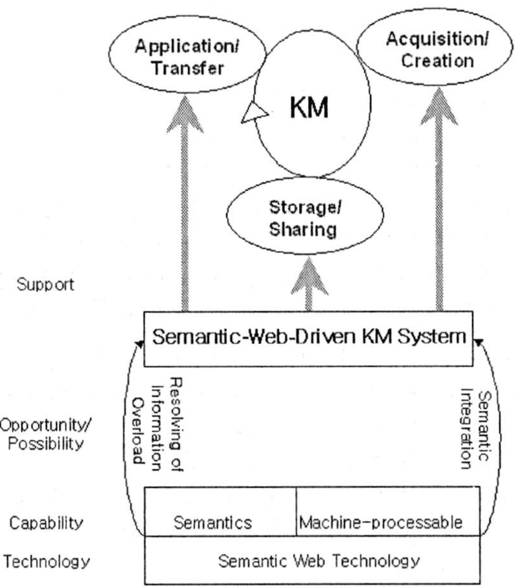

that automatically extracts related knowledge from different knowledge sources and aggregates them, but as an interconnected integrator which integrates different applications and offers one access point for users.

Figure 11 shows the comparison of the traditional integration and semantic integration based on the Semantic Web. Although the traditional approach enables syntactic and structural integration at the application level as well as the data level, it cannot provide the semantic integration. In other words, the traditional approach allows users to share data between different systems and provides them with the interoperability between systems by exploiting the mediator as shown in Figure 11. The traditional approach needs n*(n-1) mediators for mapping and translating between systems in the worst case. However, software agents cannot understand the meanings of the terms differently represented in different systems and also process them without human intervention.

In the integration approach based on the Semantic Web, the software agents understand the meanings of the terms and automatically process them by exploiting the RDF and ontologies as illustrated in the upper and right part of Figure 11. Assume that two different systems have same term, *Lincoln* that actually means different things while the two systems have different terms, *stayed* and *lodged* that mean the

Figure 11. Semantic integration

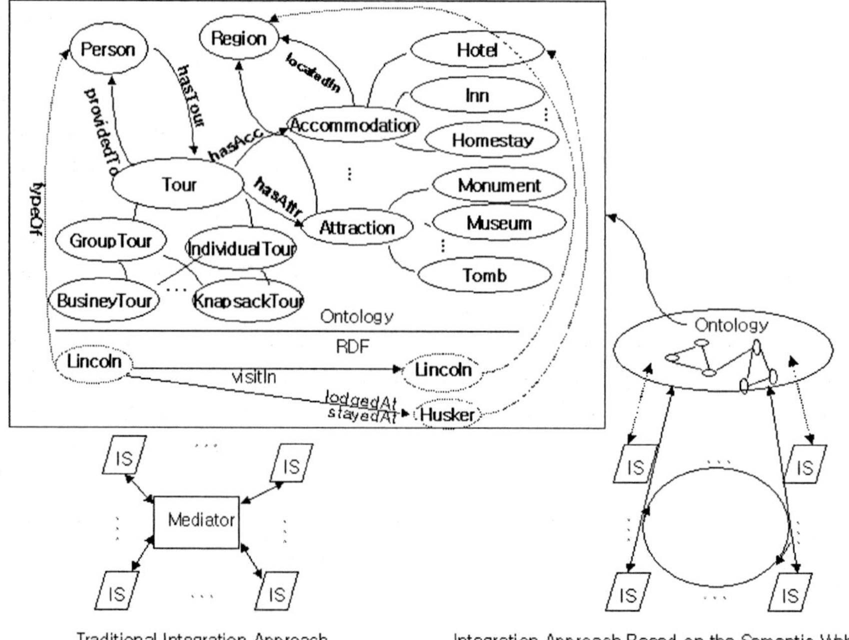

same thing. For example, consider the sentence, "President *Lincoln* visited *Lincoln* and *stayed* (or *lodged*) at *Husker*." The sentence is written in the RDF in the manner as shown in Figure 11. The software agents capture the instance of the RDF and understand the meanings of the terms by referring to ontologies. President *Lincoln* is a type of Person while the other is a type of Region which means the name of a city. *Husker* is a type of Hotel as a subclass of Accommodation and also both stayed and lodged mean the same thing.

In the Semantic-Web-driven KM systems, a software agent can access heterogeneous systems and provide knowledge and information suitable to users. The Semantic Web enables software agents to extract some parts of the related knowledge from different resources including those of resources layer shown in Figure 9 and to automatically aggregate them without the user's intervention.

When the Semantic Web is combined with ubiquitous computing (Chen & Finin, 2004), users can conveniently access KM systems anytime and anywhere. The Semantic-Web-driven KM systems with the support of peer-to peer (P2P) technology (Davies, Fensel, & Harmelen, 2003) can improve personalized KM services. Therefore, the Semantic Web enables the current KM systems to overcome the limitations such as time/space and inconvenience through a combination of ubiquitous networks and P2P technology.

Many researchers define KM process differently. In this chapter, we follow the classification of Alavi and Leidner (2001) with minor modifications as knowledge acquisition/creation, storage/sharing, and application/transfer depicted in Figure 10.

As shown in the resources layer of Figure 9, the Semantic-Web-driven KM systems extends the scope of KM to Internet Web resources beyond those of intra-organization. The Semantic Web-driven KM systems not only broaden the scope of knowledge acquisition but also enhance the quality level of knowledge acquisition through semantics. The Semantic-Web-driven KM systems support knowledge creation through enhancement of connectivity and e-learning. For example, semantic blogging which is a powerful tool for establishing and maintaining an online community by embedding the Semantic Web technology within a blogging framework provides a new way of knowledge creation as well as knowledge sharing and transfer (Cayzer, 2004). The Semantic Web-driven KM systems enable knowledge to be represented as a knowledge object (or granularity of knowledge) rather than a document unit. It facilitates knowledge application by supporting automatic aggregation and integration from the various knowledge resources. Software agents disseminate and transfer knowledge more efficiently so that users can select suitable knowledge according to their preference because of machine-processable representation and semantic search.

Conclusion and Future Trends

Ontologies were designed to support semantic search and solve problems of two scenarios derived from the tourism domain. The ontology will be widely used as a fundamental tool in building a global KM system in the tourism domain. To develop a prototype of the ontology including RDF and RDFS, we used OWL and Jena (n.d.) toolkits. The results of the systems implementation indicated satisfactory search routines.

We developed a conceptual model of the Semantic-Web-driven KM systems with four layers classified into user and query, ontology, metatadata, and resource. The Semantic-Web-driven KM systems support KM process by enabling the current KM systems to overcome their search and integration limitations in several ways.

First, the Semantic-Web-driven KM systems enable global knowledge acquisition and creation by extending the scope of KM to the Internet Web beyond intra-organization. The Semantic-Web-driven KM systems also promote knowledge creation with the extended CoP (Communities of Practice) to the Internet space and support of e-learning. Second, the Semantic-Web-driven KM systems enable us to share global knowledge without making a change in given storage modes whether they are files, documents, or databases, because all knowledge resources are represented as metadata based on RDF. Finally, software agents disseminate and transfer knowledge more efficiently so that users can use knowledge suitable to their preferences because of machine-processable representation and semantic search. This paper sheds new insights on the application of the Semantic Web to KM as an IT innovation and provides a framework of the Semantic Web-based KM systems.

In perspective of the technology push, the Semantic Web will be converged with other IT. For example, the Semantic-Web-driven KMS can be incorporated into ubiquitous computing and P2P technology. The technologies will support context-aware capabilities and personalization of the KM systems. To realize the potential of the Semantic Web, we need to find a killer application of the Semantic Web in the KM area as if the Semantic Web is a killer application of the Internet Web and KM is also a killer application of the Semantic Web. In ensemble view of technology as Orlikowski and Iacono (2001) pointed out, technology should be studied as an evolving system in a complex and dynamic context. Minimization of the gap between technology and the realization of its potential requires research on strategies triggering organizational change through application of the Semantic Web to KM.

References

Alavi, M., & Leidner, D. E. (2001). Review: Knowledge management and knowledge management systems: Conceptual foundations and research issues. *MIS Quarterly, 25*(1), 107-136.

Antoniou, G., & Harmelen, F. (2004). *A Semantic Web prime.* Cambridge, MA: MIT Press.

Berners-Lee, T., Hendler, J., & Lassila, O. (2001). The Semantic Web. *Scientific American, 284*(5), 34-43.

Cardoso, J. (2004). Semantic Web processes and ontologies for the travel industry. *AIS SIGSEMIS Bulletin, 1*(3), 25-28.

Cayzer, S. (2004). Semantic blogging and decentralized KM. *Communications of the ACM, 47*(12), 47-52.

Chen, A. (2004, July 5). Semantic Web is 2 steps closer. *eWeek,* p. 46.

Chen, H., & Finin, T. (2004). An ontology for context aware pervasive computing environments. *Knowledge Engineering, 18*(3), 197-207.

D'Aquin, M., Bouthier, C., Brachais, S., Lieber, J., & Napoli, A. (2005). Knowledge editing and maintenance tools for a semantic portal in oncology. *International Journal of Human-Computer Studies, 62*(5), 619-638.

Davies, N. J., Fensel, D., & Harmelen, F. V. (Eds.). (2003). *Toward the Semantic Web: Ontology-based knowledge management.* Hoboken, NJ: John Wiley & Sons.

Dell'Erba, M. (2004). Exploiting Semantic Web technologies for data interoperability. *AIS SIGSEMIS Bulletin, 1*(3), 48-52.

Edgington, T., Choi, B., Henson, K., Raghu, T. S., & Vinze, A. (2004). Adopting ontology to facilitate knowledge sharing. *Communications of the ACM, 47*(11), 85-90.

Fikes, R., Hayes, P., & Horrocks, I. (2004). OWL-QL: A language for deductive query answering on the Semantic Web. *Web Semantics: Science, Service and Agents on the World Wide Web, 2*(1), 19-29.

Fodor, O., & Werthner, H. (2004). Harmonise: A step toward an interoperable e-tourism marketplace. *International Journal of Electronic Commerce, 9*(2), 11-39.

Giachetti, R. E. (2004). A framework to review the information integration of the enterprise. *International Journal of Production Research, 42*(6), 1147-1166.

Hevner, A. R., March, S. T., Park, J., & Ram, S. (2004). Design science in information systems research. *MIS Quarterly, 28*(1), 75-105.

ICS-FORTH. (2005). *The RDF query language (RQL)*. Retrieved January 24, 2006, from http://139.91.183.30:9090/RDF/RQL/

J2SDK. (2006). *Sun developer network*. Retrieved February 24, 2006, from http://java.sun.com/j2se/1.4.2/download.html

Jena. (n.d.). A Semantic Web framework (Version 2.4) [Computer software]. Retrieved January 24, 2006, from http://jena.sourceforge.net/

Joo, J. (2002). A business model and its development strategies for electronic tourism markets. *Information Systems Management, 19*(3), 58-69.

Joo, J., & Jeong, Y. (2004). *An implementation of the semantic search system based on the ontology for global knowledge management in tourism business domain*. Paper presented KMIS Conference, Seoul, 448-454.

Maedche, A., Motik, B. Stojanovic, L., Studer, R., & Voltz, R. (2003). Ontologies for enterprise knowledge management. *IEEE Intelligent Systems, 18*(2), 26-33.

Meyer, P. (1998, January-March). Killer applications. *Business & Economic Review, 44* (2)13-17.

Middleton, C. A. (2003). What if there is no killer application? An exploration of a user-centric perspective on broadband. *Journal of Information Technology, 18,* 231-245.

Noy, N. F., Doan, A., & Halevy, A. Y. (2005). Semantic integration. *AI Magazine, 26*(1), 7-9.

Noy, N. F., & Musen, M. A. (2004). Ontology versioning in an ontology management framework. *IEEE Intelligent Systems, 19*(4), 6-13.

Noy, N. F., Sintek, M., Decker, S., Crubezy, M., Ferferson, R. W., & Musen, M. A. (2001). Creating Semantic Web contents with Protégé-2000. *IEEE Intelligent Systems*, *16* (2) 60-71.

Oberle, D., Staab, S., Studer, R., & Volz, R. (2005). Supporting application development in the Semantic Web. *ACM Transactions on Internet Technology, 5*(2), 328-358.

OntoEdit. (n.d.). (Version 0.6) [Computer Software]. AIFB, University of Karlsruhe. Retrieved 2005, from http://www.ontoknowledge.org/tools/ontoedit.shtml

Orlikowski, W. J., & Iacono, C. S. (2001). Research commentary: Desperately seeking the "IT" in IT research. A call to theorizing the IT artifact. *Information Systems Research, 12*(2), 121-134.

Protégé. (n.d.). (Version 3.1.1) [Computer software]. Stanford Medical Informatics. Retrieved 2005, from http://protege.stanford.edu/

Tiwana, A., & Ramesh, B. (2001). Integrating knowledge on the Web. *IEEE Internet Computing*, 5(3), 32-39.

World Wide Consortium (W3C). (1999). *Resource description framework (RDF) model and syntax specification.* Retrieved January 24, 2006, from http://www.w3.org/TR19991/REC-rdf-syntax-19990222/

World Wide Consortium (W3C). (2000, March 21). *Resource description framework (RDF) schema specification 1.0.* Retrieved January 24, 2006, from http://www.w3.org/TR/2000/CR-rdf-schema-20000327/

World Wide Consortium (W3C). (2004a, February 10). *OWL Web ontology language overview.* Retrieved January 24, 2006, from http://www.w3.org/TR/2004/REC-owl-features-20040210/

World Wide Consortium (W3C). (2004b, January 9). *RDQL: A query language for RDF.* Retrieved January 24, 2006, from http://www.w3.org/Submission/2004/SUBM-RDQL-20040109/

Chapter XIII

Query Formation and Information Retrieval with Ontology

Sheng-Uei Guan, Brunel University, UK

Abstract

This chapter presents an ontology-based query formation and information retrieval system under the mobile commerce (m-commerce) agent framework. A query formation approach that combines the usage of ontology and keywords is implemented. This approach takes advantage of the tree structure in ontology to form queries visually and efficiently. It also uses additional aids such as keywords to complete the query formation process more efficiently. The proposed information retrieval scheme focuses on using genetic algorithms (GAs) to improve computational effectiveness. Other query optimization techniques used include query restructuring by logical terms and numerical constraints replacement.

Introduction

With the introduction of new technologies such as WAP, HSCSD, GPRS, UMTS, and Bluetooth, it is believed that the e- and m-commerce arena will sooner or later merge its applications with handheld devices to create more opportunities for the birth of a new generation of m-commerce .However, m-commerce is largely unrealized to date because there still does not exist a single application that can attract wireless users to use wireless services. According to a recent survey by Gartner, Inc. (Behrens & McGuire, 2004), besides the importance of coverage of wireless network and pricing issues, the wireless Internet and data services are the next crucial factors that attract users to use wireless services. As such, there is a need to improve the data services over the wireless network. Commonly seen data services include: product brokering, news on demand, stock quotes, stock price alert services, and so forth. One of these services is the information retrieval service.

Information retrieval is an important area of research in information systems and other disciplines such as medicine; library and information sciences; and so forth. Most electronic product information retrieval systems are still not efficient enough to cater to the increasing needs of customers. This is especially serious in the m-commerce arena where the bandwidth of mobile devices is low and large data transfers would not be possible. Thus, the discovery of new information retrieval techniques that would filter through thousands or millions of pages of information and return only minimal, while relevant, information to the users is inevitable.

Semantic Webs can be seen as a huge engineering solution to share and access data. As a globally linked database, it is an efficient way of representing data on the Web such that it is easily processable by machines. In this paper we propose an ontology-based query formation and information retrieval system focused towards use in the e-commerce arena. The system uses the concept of GAs in query modification and is an algorithm that is applicable to a query formation for a knowledge database such as the Semantic Web.

The main objective of this chapter is three-fold: (1) to research the use of ontology to assist the users in shaping up their product enquiries; (2) to study the use of GAs and agents in query restructuring and optimization; and (3) to develop efficient information retrieval services for the m-commerce arena. It proposes a methodology for efficient query formation for product databases and for effective information retrieval systems, which includes the evaluation of retrieved documents to enhance the quality of results that are obtained from product searches.

This chapter discusses the usage of ontology to create an efficient environment for m-commerce users to form queries. The establishment of a method that combines keyword searches with using ontology to perform query formation tasks further allows a more flexible m-commerce environment for users. Also, with the use of GAs, it is hoped that query effectiveness can be achieved, at the same time saving computational time and retrieval time.

Background

Definition of Ontology

In artificial intelligence, ontology is defined as a design of a conceptualization to be reused across multiple applications (Braga, Werner, & Mattosso, 2000; Fensel, 2000; Hendler, 2001). A conceptualization is a set of concepts, relations, objects, and constraints that define a semantic model of some domain of interest. In other words, ontology is like the structure that describes or encodes the conceptualization in any relational aspect (Karp, 2000; McGuinness, 1998). Ontology has been widely used in information retrieval (Aitken & Reid, 2000; Müller, Kenny, & Sternberg, 2004;). In this paper, we illustrate the use of ontology in query formation.

Genetic Algorithms

In this section, a survey of present query formation methods and information retrieval methods will be discussed.

Unlike in e-commerce, query information using keywords alone in m-commerce is unrealistic as mobile devices are too small and keypads are not suitable for typing. Moreover, it may be difficult for the user when the vocabulary of the subject is unfamiliar. Thus, relevance feedback is still the main technique for query modification.

Relevance feedback technique has been investigated for more than 20 years in various information retrieval models, such as the *probabilistic model* and *vector space model* (Boughanem, Chrisment, & Tamine, 1999; Salton, 1989). It is based on randomly changing the set of query terms as well as the weights associated with these terms according to the document retrieved and judged during the initial search.

GAs (Holland, 1973) have been used in a wide variety of applications. It is believed that the use of GAs can help obtain a global optimal solution for a given problem. In the domain of information retrieval too, much research has been done on how GAs can be used in query formation and relevance feedback. (Boughanem et al., 1999; Kouichi, Taketa, & Nunokawa, 1999; Kraft, Petry, Buckles, & Sadasivan, 1994; Yang & Korfhage, 1994). With regards to query formation and effectiveness, one popular approach is query restructuring, which is used to improve the efficiency and effectiveness of the queries formed. In query restructuring, GA actually extends the concepts of relevance feedback. The difference is that GA uses more than one query and compares the fitness among these queries. The fittest query will survive in the end. In this chapter, we extend the concept of query restructuring using GAs and combine it with ontology-based search.

Query Fitness

There are a number of measures of query fitness used in previous works, namely, precision and recall retrieval (Kraft et al., 1994; Salton & McGill, 1983), average search length, and average maximum parse length (Losee, 1991).

Precision is the percentage of documents retrieved that are relevant, while *recall* measures the percentage of the relevant documents retrieved (Kraft et al., 1994; Salton & McGill, 1983). These two tend to be inversely proportional so that one is traded for one another in most situations. *Average search length* is the average number of documents or text fragments examined in moving down a ranked list of documents until arriving at the average position of a relevant document (Losee, 1988, 1996). Evaluating the performance of a filtering or retrieval process with average search length provides a single number measure of performance. *Average maximum parse length* is the average (over a set of sentences) of the largest number of terms in a parse for each sentence. There are also measures that combine both average search length and average maximum parse length.

Typically, present methods had only dealt with the relevance of the document retrieved. This is reasonable but inefficient because it is rather difficult to indicate the relevance of a document when the number of documents could be very large. This chapter measures the relevance of queries instead of documents retrieved. Based on this, efficiency will be improved significantly as the number of queries will be much smaller than the number of documents retrieved, which is ideal for mobile devices.

The Proposed Approaches

Both keyword- and ontology-based approaches have their advantages and disadvantages. Ontology provides the structure, context, and visual aid, while keyword provides a direct search mechanism. Both approaches are relevant for m-commerce because they save time in browsing and searching, which is very much required by mobile users who are always on the move. Thus, by combining keyword queries with ontology, it is possible to achieve a better and more effective query formation. Before ontology terms are accessed to form the queries, there will be a keyword search to find the required ontology term. For example, *ps2* can be hidden in the node "mouse" when presented in the ontology. The user will not be able to know where *ps2* can be found intuitively without eyeballing the ontology. With the help of keyword search, the term *ps2* can be found easily.

In forming queries, there can be a high chance that the vocabulary used by the user to describe a query does not exactly match the vocabulary used by a query system (Preece et al., 1999). This will result in getting insufficient information. Therefore, restructuring dealing with domain ontology relationships might be useful. These relationships involve semantic links such as hyponyms and synonyms (Braga et al., 2000). Here, using synonyms is an adequate option to restructure queries because it correctly broadens the scope of search even to the extent of different languages.

When too little information is retrieved, the use of synonym or hyponym might be necessary in order to relax the constraints of the query. However, this approach has a major disadvantage. By relaxing the constraints of a query using synonym or hyponym to increase the number of documents retrieved, one could actually deface the meaning of the original query such that it could drift away from the user's intention. This concern can be alleviated by having user feedback along the process. Also, we have considered relaxing constraints step-by-step. This option can better eliminate the chances of constructing far-fetched queries from the use of GA.

Main Thrust of the Chapter

Prototype Design and Implementation

Query Formation

Query Formation using Ontology

Query formation will be done with the aid of tree ontology. Following the tree path will help form the requirements of a query. This allows forming queries easily. An illustration of the query formation process is shown in Figure 1. As can be seen from this illustration, using ontology helps the user to save several steps by forming a query using the ontology path that is selected. Thus, it can be claimed that forming queries using ontology is actually more efficient than using keywords.

Combining Keywords and Ontology

The design of parallel combination is rather straightforward. Ontology does not cover everything. Thus, besides having ontology for the user to click on when forming a query, there should be some fields present for the user to fill in. When these fields are being filled in, they can either replace the use of ontology either partially or completely. For a serial combination, keywords are used to look for ontology terms in the ontology. This is necessary because when the ontology is too large, searching for an ontology term by manual clicking becomes difficult. Thus, there would be a field that allows the user to highlight the terms in the ontology itself as shown in

Figure 1. Illustration of using ontology to form queries

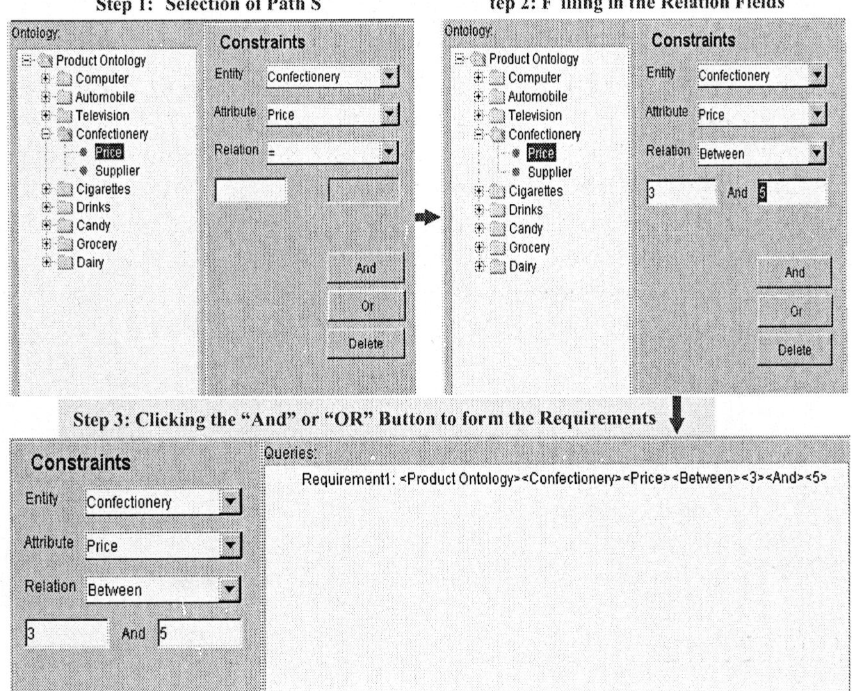

Figure 2. From this illustration, it can be seen that using keywords to search ontology terms in the ontology creates an efficient environment and context for the user.

Information Retrieval

Using the query formed by the query formation application, an application searches the databases to retrieve information. Intuitively, this application would first do a normal search before allowing the user to proceed with a GA search. This is because a GA search would definitely take a much longer time than a normal search because of its expensive iterations. The retrieval results are presented to the user and if he/she is not satisfied, they can then choose to proceed with a GA search.

Figure 2. Illustration of the sequence of events for finding ontology terms

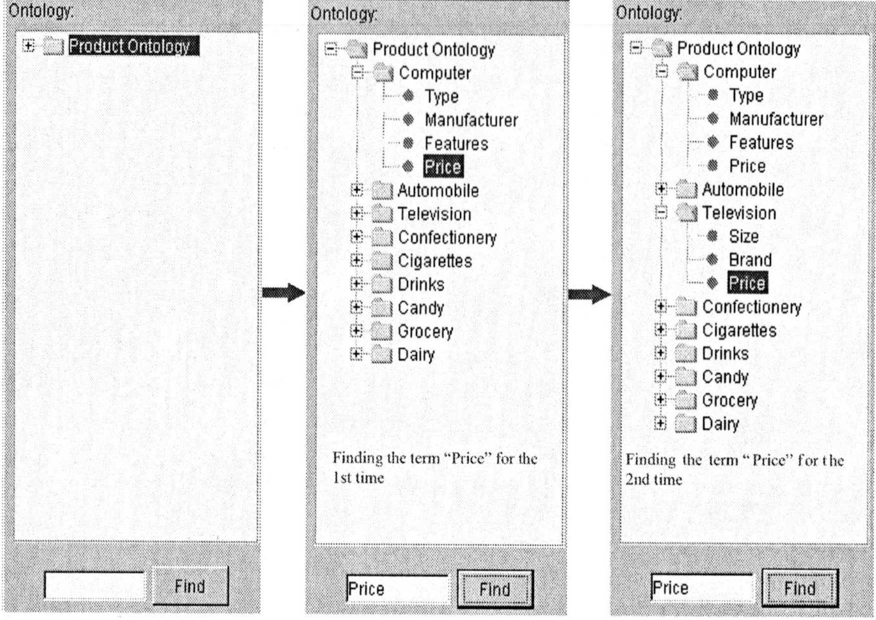

Genetic Algorithm

If the user requests the use of a GA, the system will request for some input from the user to perform GA computation. The system then creates a population of queries from the original query. Basically, GA will mutate the queries according to the synonyms of the terms in the ontology.

The Fitness Function

The main concern of using GA is the design of the fitness function. In this application, three major elements are used to define the fitness function, namely, (1) the fitness of the number of documents retrieved (f_d), (2) the fitness of the average quality of the query results (f_q), and (3) the overall correlation for the query (f_r). The fitness of each chromosome is calculated as follows:

$$Fitness = |f_r \cdot (f_d + f_q)|$$

| . | indicates that the fitness function is normalized to form a population distribution function.

The calculation of the value of f_d is not straightforward. Let *i* be the ideal number of documents specified by the user. If the user does not know the value of *i*, the default value will be 20. Using the value of *i* as the mean value, two "band pass filters"-like functions, namely the triangular and Gaussian functions, are used to create a more flexible mapping from number of documents retrieved *(d)* to f_d. The triangular function gives a constant drop in "gain" (decrease in fitness) from the 'center frequency' (the mean). This function is good when the user wants to give an equal amount of demerits for every document that is away from his expected or ideal number. The Gaussian function is a more robust or high-ordered "band pass" such that its "bandwidth" could be specified by the value of the standard deviation. Thus, this function is useful when the user wants to give heavy demerits to queries that do not fall near his/her expected or ideal number.

Only requirements that are specified by numerical constraints will have the value f_q. Here, it is required that the numerical values are summed up and averaged. Then, they are normalized. The signs < and > formed during the query indicate the direction in which the quality is favored towards.

Another interesting portion that contributes to the fitness function is the correlation of the synonyms (f_r) with the ontology terms. A value from 0 to 1 is assigned to each relation between the ontology terms and their synonyms. When a requirement is <Television><Price><<><2000>, the value or f_r will be the product of all the discrete correlations. Also, the user should be able to edit the correlation values to his/her preference. When there are many requirements in the query, these requirements will be linked with an "OR" or "AND" term.

Mutation and Crossover

The concept of mutation is to replace some terms with synonyms when parsing the results. Basically, the mutants are the terms that are included in each query. These terms are mutated randomly according to the synonyms so that new populations will be formed. Crossover will only be just interchanging the different genes between two different chromosomes. A one-point crossover will be performed. This is also done randomly.

Figure 3. Screenshot of a feedback frame

Feed Back1

Query	Number of Documents	Correlations	Fitness	Good
((Ontology='Product Ontology' AND Category='Grocery' AND Price<3))	9	1	0.096	✓
((Ontology='Ontology' AND Category='Grocery' AND Price<3))	11	0.800	0.088	✓
((Ontology='Product Ontology' AND Category='Grocery' AND Cost<3))	10	0.800	0.096	✓
((Ontology='Product Ontology' AND Category='Grocery' AND Price<3))	9	1	0.096	✓
((Ontology='Product Ontology' AND Category='Grocery' AND Price<3))	9	1	0.096	✓
((Ontology='Product Ontology' AND Category='Instant Food' AND Price<3))	46	0.9	0.060	✓
((Ontology='Product Ontology' AND Category='Condiments' AND Cost<3))	14	0.560	0.089	✓
((Ontology='Product Ontology' AND Category='Sundries' AND Price<3))	3	0.800	0.177	✓
((Ontology='Product' AND Category='Grocery' AND Price<3))	11	0.7	0.106	✓
((Ontology='Product Ontology' AND Category='Grocery' AND Price<3))	9	1	0.096	✓

Continue Stop

Feedback and Selection of Survival

The survivors are selected according to their overall fitness in the roulette-wheel selection manner. However, before this is done, the system will prompt for feedback from the user. The feedback will show the user some quality of each query. From this quality metric, the user may choose to kill queries that do not meet his/her requirements. Figure 3 shows a screenshot of a feedback presented to the user. If the user is satisfied with the results, he/she can choose to end the GA by clicking on the "Stop" button. In this way, he/she can look at the retrieved results immediately.

Prototype Testing and Evaluation of Genetic Algorithm

Effectiveness of the Genetic Algorithm

It is believed that the effectiveness of the GA chosen is mainly determined by its supremacy in query effectiveness amplification. This is because its evolution power allows more retrieval results. The system was tested with a product list database. The effectiveness was measured by testing a series of queries with and without using GA. For example, a query, "<Product Ontology><Grocery><Price><<> <3>", can only retrieve nine items when a normal search was performed but can retrieve 98 items when GA was performed. Table 1 shows the other results obtained by other queries.

Table 1. Results showing effectiveness of GA

Query Formed	Without GA	With GA
<Product Ontology><Drinks><Price><<><2>	25	95
<Product Ontology><Diary><Price><<><3>	3	92
<Product Ontology><Candy><Price><<><3>	13	178
<Product Ontology><Confectionery><Price><<><3>	20	248
<Product Ontology><Confectionery><Supplier> <Contains><Ho>	1	52

By comparing the results shown in Table 1, it is obvious that using GA does, in fact, retrieve more items than using a normal search.

Effect of the Fitness Function

The fitness function in a GA determines how well it can optimize a query. The OntoQuery system tested out various fitness functions to improve the power of the GA. The usage of triangle or Gaussian functions to evaluate the fitness for the number of documents retrieved suggested some ways to counter the "too many or too few retrieved documents" dilemma in typical search engines.

Efficiency of the Genetic Algorithm

Although using GA allows a more flexible and effective platform in retrieving information, there is no doubt that it trades off efficiency due to its expensive iterations. Thus, the only study that can be made here is about its improvement over relevance feedback. In relevance feedback, query expansion is achieved by modifying a query. Similarly, GA extends the relevance feedback techniques with an additional rule, the survival of the fittest.

In this research, the efficiency of the system is measured as follows:

$$\varepsilon \text{ (Efficiecy)} \approx \frac{E}{t}$$

$$\approx \frac{D}{I}$$

where E denotes the effectiveness of the system.

t denotes the time taken for the system.

D denotes the number of relevant documents retrieved.

I denotes the number of iterations.

Efficiency is formulated as shown previously because it is believed that the number of documents retrieved is linearly proportional to the effectiveness of the system. Also, the number of iterations is directly related to the time taken to retrieve the results.

Conclusion and Future Works

In summary, this research work investigated the OntoQuery system within an m-commerce agent framework against current query formation and information retrieval systems from extant work that were not intended for m-commerce.

The prototype implementation results showed that querying formation using an ontology approach is efficient as it provides a friendly environment to the user using mobile devices. In addition, by combining the keyword and ontology approaches, a more efficient and effective way of forming queries could be achieved. Thus, the objective to propose efficient query formation for product databases is successful.

It was found that GA is able to optimize queries effectively. Also, using genetic approaches, we have proposed and tested out various fitness functions for searching product databases. Moreover, adding feedback to the system helps it to cater to the needs of the user more closely.

Considering typical e-commerce or m-commerce users using mobile devices for product enquiry tends to have some time constraints, and they need quick response before making decisions, our work suggests a feasible approach. With the use of ontology, product enquiry can be formed easily and quickly. With the help from GAs and agents and the technique of query optimization such as query restructuring, futile enquiries can be turned into productive ones. And finally, the use of GAs also helps improve the quality of product information retrieved.

However, the algorithm has currently been implemented, not on a Semantic Web structure, but on the World Wide Web structure with focus on e-commerce. It would be necessary to develop an e-commerce-oriented Semantic Web and test the effectiveness of the approach proposed.

References

Aitken, S., & Reid, S. (2000, August 20-25). Evaluation of an ontology-based information retrieval tool. In *Proceedings of ECAI'00 Workshop on Applications of Ontologies and Problem-Solving Methods*, Berlin, Germany.

Behrens, L., & McGuire, M. (2004). *The mobile-wireless Internet glass looks half empty and half full.* Retrieved from http://www.gartner.com

Boughanem, M., Chrisment, C., & Tamine, L. (1999). Genetic approach to query space exploration. *Information Retrieval, 1*(3), 175-192.

Braga, R. M. M., Werner, C. M. L., & Mattosso, M. (2000). Using ontologies for domain information retrieval. In *IEEE Proceedings of 11th International Workshop on Database and Expert Systems Applications* (pp. 836-840). IEEE Press.

Fensel, D. (2000). The Semantic Web and its language. *IEEE Intelligent Systems, 15*(6), 67-73.

Hendler, J. (2001). Agents and the Semantic Web. *IEEE Intelligent Systems, 16*(2), 30-37.

Holland, J. H. (1973). Genetic algorithms and the optimal allocation of trials. *SIAM Journal on Computing, 2*(2), 88-105.

Karp, P. D. (2000). An ontology for biological function based on molecular interactions. *Bioinformatics, 16*(3), 269-285.

Kouichi, A. B. E., Taketa, T., & Nunokawa, H. (1999). An efficient information retrieval method in www using genetic algorithm. In *Proceedings of International Workshops on Parallel Processing* (pp. 522-527). IEEE Press.

Kraft, D. H., Petry, F. E., Buckles, B. P., & Sadasivan, T. (1994). The use of genetic programming to build queries for information retrieval. In *Proceedings of the First IEEE Conference on Computational Intelligence* (pp. 468-473). IEEE Press.

Losee, R. M. (1988). Parameter estimation for probabilistic document retrieval models. *Journal of the American Society for Information Science, 39*(1), 1-16.

Losee, R. M. (1991). An analytic measure predicting information retrieval system performance. *Information Processing and Management, 27*(1), 1-13.

Losee, R. M. (1996). Learning syntactic rules and tags with genetic algorithms for information retrieval and filtering: An empirical basis for grammatical rules. *Information Processing & Management, 32*(2), 185-197.

McGuinness, D. L. (1998). Ontological issues for knowledge-enhanced search. In *Proceedings of the 1st International Conference on Formal Ontology in Information Systems(FOIS'98)*, Trento, Italy (pp. 302-316).

Müller, H. M., Kenny, E. E., & Sternberg, P. W. (2004, November). Textpresso, An ontology-based information retrieval and extraction system for biological literature. *Plos Medicine, 2*(11), 1984-1998.

Preece, A., Hui, K., Gray, A., Marti, P., Bench-Capon, T., Jones, D., et al. (1999). The KRAFT architecture for knowledge fusion and transformation. In M. Bramer, A. Macintosh, & F. Coenen (Eds.), *Research and development in intelligent systems XVI.* (pp. 23-38). Springer-Verlag.

Salton, G. (1989). *The transformation, analysis and retrieval of information by computer.* Reading, MA: Addison-Wesley.

Salton, G., & McGill, M. (1983). *Introduction to modern information retrieval.* New York: McGraw-Hill.

Yang, J. J., & Korfhage, R. R. (1994). Query modification using genetic algorithms in vector space models. *International Journal of Expert Systems: Research and Applications, 7*(2), 165-191.

Terms and Definitions

Crossover. In genetic algorithm, it is the process of combining features of a chromosome with other chromosome(s).

Evolutionary algorithm. An algorithm incorporating aspects of natural selection or survival of the fittest.

Fitness function. In genetic algorithm, it is a measure of how well a chromosome can perform in certain environments (functions).

Genetic algorithm. An evolutionary algorithm which generates each individual from some encoded form known as "chromosomes" or "genome."

Mutation. In genetic algorithm, it is defined as a change in form or qualities of chromosomes.

Ontology. Ontology looks for semantic and ontological primitives and concepts to describe aspects or parts of "the world."

Restructuring. Restructuring is replacing query terms using synonyms so that logical operators and numerical constraints can be restructured.

Roulette-wheel selection. A roulette wheel selects the chromosomes used in reproduction. The wheel is the fitness array, and the marble is a random unsigned integer less than the sum of all fitness in the population. To find the chromosome associated with the marble's landing place, the algorithm iterates through the fitness array; if the marble value is less than the current fitness element, the corresponding chromosome becomes a parent. Otherwise, the algorithm subtracts the current fitness value from the marble and then repeats the process with the next element in the fitness array.

Section III

Semantic Knowledge and Application

Chapter XIV

Utilizing Semantic Web and Software Agents in a Travel Support System

Maria Ganzha, EUH-E and IBS PAN, Poland
Maciej Gawinecki, IBS PAN, Poland
Marcin Paprzycki, SWPS and IBS PAN, Poland
Rafał Gąsiorowski, Warsaw University of Technology, Poland
Szymon Pisarek, Warsaw University of Technology, Poland
Wawrzyniec Hyska, Warsaw University of Technology, Poland

Abstract

The use of Semantic Web technologies in e-business is hampered by the lack of large, publicly-available sources of semantically-demarcated data. In this chapter, we present a number of intermediate steps on the road toward the Semantic Web. Specifically, we discuss how Semantic Web technologies can be adapted as the centerpiece of an agent-based travel support system. First, we present a complete description of the system under development. Second, we introduce ontologies developed for, and utilized in, our system. Finally, we discuss and illustrate through examples how ontologically demarcated data collected in our system is personalized for individual users. In particular, we show how the proposed ontologies can be used to create, manage, and deploy functional user profiles.

Introduction

Let us consider a business traveler who is about to leave Tulsa, Oklahoma for San Diego, California. Let us say that she went there many times in the past, but this trip is rather unexpected and she does not have time to arrange travel details. She just got a ticket from her boss' secretary and has 45 minutes to pack and catch a taxi to leave for the airport. Obviously, she could make all local arrangements after arrival, but this could mean that her personal preferences could not be observed and also that she would have to spend time at the airport in a rather unpleasant area where the courtesy phones are located or spend a long time talking on the cell phone (and listen to call-waiting music) to find a place to stay, and so forth. Yes, one could assume that she could ask her secretary to make arrangements, but this would assume that she does have a secretary (which is now a rarity in the cost-cutting corporate world) and that her secretary knows her personal preferences well.

Let us now consider another scenario. Here, a father is planning a family vacation. He is not sure where they would like to go, so he spends countless hours on the Web, going over zillions of pages, out of which only few match his preferences. Let us note here, that while he will simply skip pages about the beauty of Ozark Mountains—as his family does not like mountains, but he will "have to" go over a number of pages describing beach resorts. While doing this he is going to find out that many possible locations are too expensive, while others do not have kitchenettes that they like to have—as their daughter has special dietary requirements, and they prefer to cook most of their vacation meals themselves.

What do we learn from these two scenarios? In the first case, we have a traveler who, because of her unexpected travel, cannot engage in e-business as she does not have enough time to do it, while she could definitely utilize it. Yes, when in the near future airplanes will have Internet access, she will possibly be able to make the proper arrangements while traveling, but this is likely going to be an expensive proposition. Furthermore, the situation when a traveler is spending time on the plane to make travel arrangements is extremely similar to the second scenario, where the user is confronted with copious volumes of data within which he has to find few pertinent gems.

What is needed in both cases is the creation of a travel support system that would work as follows. In the first case, it would know personal preferences of the traveler and on their basis, while she is flying and preparing for the unexpected business meeting, would arrange accommodations in one of her preferred hotels, make a dinner reservation in one of her favorite restaurants, and negotiate a "special appetizer promotion" (knowing that she loves the shrimp cocktail that is offered there). Upon her arrival in San Diego, results would be displayed on her personal digital assistant (PDA) (or a smart cell phone) and she could go directly to the taxi or to her preferred car rental company. In the second case, the travel support system would act as an interactive advisor—mimicking the work of a travel agent—and would help select a travel destination by removing from considerations locations and accommodations that do not fit the user profile and personalizing content delivery further—by prioritizing information to be displayed and delivering one that would be predicted to be most pertinent first. Both these scenarios would represent an ideal way in which e-business should be conducted.

The aim of this chapter is to propose a system that, when mature, should be able to support the needs of travelers in exactly the previously described way. We will also argue that, and illustrate how, Semantic Web technologies combined with software agents should be used in the proposed system. We proceed as follows. In the next section we briefly discuss the current state of the art in agent systems, Semantic Web, and agent-based travel support systems. We follow with a description of the proposed system illustrated by unified modeling language (UML) diagrams of its most important functionalities. We then discuss how to work with ontologically demarcated data in the world where such resources are practically nonexistent. Finally, we show how resource description framework (RDF) demarcated data is to be used to support personal information delivery. We conclude with a description of the current state of implementation and plans for further development of the system.

Background

There are two main themes that permeate the scenarios and the proposed solution presented previously. These are: *information overload* and need for *content personalization*. One of the seminal papers that addresses exactly these two problems was published by Maes (1994). There she suggested that it will be intelligent software agents that will solve the problem of information overload. In a way it can be claimed that it is that paper that grounded in computer science the notion of a *personal* software *agent* that acts on behalf of its user and autonomously works to deliver desired personalized services. This notion is particularly well matching with travel support, where for years human travel agents played exactly the role that *personal agents* (PAs) are expected to mimic. Unfortunately, as it can be seen, the notion of intelligent personal agent, even though extremely appealing, does not seem to materialize (while its originator has moved away from agent research into a more appealing area of ambient computing).

What can be the reason for this lack of development of intelligent personal agents? One of them seems to be the truly overwhelming amount of available information that is stored mostly in a human consumable form (demarcated using hypertext markup language (HTML) to make it look "appealing" to the viewer). Even a more recent move toward the extensible markup language (XML) as the demarcation language will not solve this problem as XML is not expressive enough. However, a possible solution to this problem has been suggested, in the form of semantic demarcation of resources or, more generally, the Semantic Web (Berners-Lee, Hendler, & Lassila, 2001; Fensel 2001). Here it is claimed that when properly applied, demarcation languages like RDF (Manola & Miller, 2005), Web ontology language (OWL) (McGuinness & Van Harmelen, 2005) or Darpa agent markup language (DAML) (DAML, 2005) will turn human-enjoyable Internet pages into machine-consumable data repositories. While there are those who question the validity of optimistic claims associated with the Semantic Web (M. Orłowska, personal communication, April 2005; A. Zaslavsky, personal communcation, August 2004) and see in it only as a new incarnation of an old problem of unification of information stored in heterogeneous databases—a problem that still remains without general solution—we are not interested in this discussion. For the purpose of this chapter we assume that the Semantic Web can deliver on its promises and focus on how to apply it in our context.

In our work we follow two additional sources of inspiration. First, it has been convincingly argued that the Semantic Web and software agents are highly interdependent and should work very well together to deliver services needed by the user (Hendler, 1999, 2001). Second, we follow the positive program put forward in the highly critical work of Nwana and Ndumu (1999). In this context we see two ways of proceeding for those interested in agent systems (and the Semantic Web). One can wait for all the necessary tools and technologies to be ready to start developing and implementing agent systems (utilize ontological demarcation of resources), or one can start to do it now (using available, however imperfect, technologies and tools)—among others, to help develop a new generation of improved tools and technologies. In our work we follow Nwana and Ndumu in believing that the latter approach is the right one. Therefore, we *do not* engage in the discussion *if* concept of a software agent is anything more but a new name for old ideas; *if* agents should be used in a travel support system; *if* agent mobility is or is not important, *if* JADE (2005), Jena (2005), and Raccoon (2005) are the best technologies to be used, and so forth.. Our goal is to use what we consider top-of-the-line technologies and approaches to develop and implement a complete skeleton of an agent-based travel support system that will utilize semantically demarcated data as its centerpiece.

Here an additional methodological comment is in order. As it was discussed in Gilbert et al. (2004); Harrington et al. (2003); and Wright, Gordon, Paprzycki, Williams, and Harrington (2003) there exists two distinct ways of managing information in an *infomediary* (Galant, Jakubczye, & Paprzycki, 2002) system like the one discussed here (with possible intermediate solutions). Information can be *indexed*—where only references to the actual information available in repositories residing outside of "the system" are stored. Or, information can be *gathered*—where actual content is brought to the central repository. In the original design of the travel support system (Angryk, Galant, Gordon, & Paprzycki, 2002; Gilbert et al., 2004; Harrington et al., 2003; Wright et al., 2003) we planned to follow the indexing path, which is more philosophically aligned with the main ideas behind the Semantic Web. It can be said metaphorically, that in the Semantic Web *everything is a resource* that is located somewhere within the Web and can be found through a generalized resource locator. In this case indexing simply links together resources of interest. Unfortunately, the current state of the Semantic Web is such that there are practically no resources that systems like ours could use. To be able to develop and implement a working system "now" we have decided to gather information. More precisely, in the central repository we will store sets of RDF triples (*tokens*) that will represent travel objects (instances of ontologies). We will also develop an agent-based data collection system that will transform Web-available information into such tokens stored in the system.

Obviously, our work is not the only one in the field of applying agents and ontologies to travel support, however, while we follow many predecessors, we have noticed that most of them have ended on a road leading nowhere. In our survey conducted in 2001 we have found a number of Web sites of agent-based travel support system projects that never made it beyond the initial stages of conceptualization (for more details see Paprzycki, Angryk, et al., 2001; Paprzycki, Kalczyński, Fiedorowicz, Abramowicz, & Cobb, 2001 and references presented there). The situation did not change much since. A typical example of the state of the art in the area is the European Union (EU) funded, CRUMPET project. During its funded existence (between approximately 1999 and 2003) it resulted in a number of publications and apparent demonstrations, but currently its original Web site is gone and it is really difficult to assess which of its promises have been truly delivered on.

Summarizing, there exists a large number of sources of inspiration for our work, but we proceed with development of a system that constitutes a rather unique combination of agents and the Semantic Web.

System Description

Before we proceed describing the system let us stress that what we describe in this chapter is the core of a much larger system that is in various stages of development. In selecting the material to be presented we have decided first, to focus on the parts under development that are finished or almost finished. This means that a number of interesting agents that are to exist in the system in the future and that were proposed and discussed in Angryk et al. (2002); Galant, Gordon, and Paprzycki (2002b); and Gordon and Paprzycki (2005) will be omitted. Furthermore, we concentrate our attention on these parts of the system that are most pertinent to the subject area of this book (Semantic Web and e-business) while practically omitting issues like, for instance, agent-world communication (addressed in Galant, Gordon, & Paprzycki, 2002a; Kaczmarek, Gordon, Paprzycki, & Gawinecki, 2005) and others.

In Figures 1 and 2 we present two distinct top level views on the system. The first one depicts basic "interactions" occurring in the system as well as its main subsystems. It also clearly places the repository of semantically demarcated data in the center of the system. More precisely, starting from right to left, we can see that *content* has been divided into (a) *verified content providers* (*VCP*) that represent sources of trusted content that are consistently available and format of which is changing rarely and not "without a notice" and (b) *other sources* that represents all of the remaining available content. Interested readers can find more information about this distinction in Angryk et al. (2002) and Gordon and Paprzycki (2005).

While the dream of the Semantic Web is a beautiful one indeed, currently (outside of a multitude of academic research projects) it is almost impossible to find within the Web large sources of clean explicitly ontologically demarcated content (in particular, travel related content). This being the case, it is extremely difficult to find actual data that can be used (e.g., for testing purposes) in a system like the one we are developing. Obviously, we could use some of the existing text processing techniques to classify pages as relevant to various travel topics, but this is not what we attempt to achieve here. Therefore, we will, for the time being, omit the area denoted as *other sources* that contains mostly weakly structured and highly volatile data (see also Nwana & Ndumu, 1999, for an interesting discussion of perils of dealing with dynamically changing data sources). This area will become a source

Figure 1. Top level view of the system

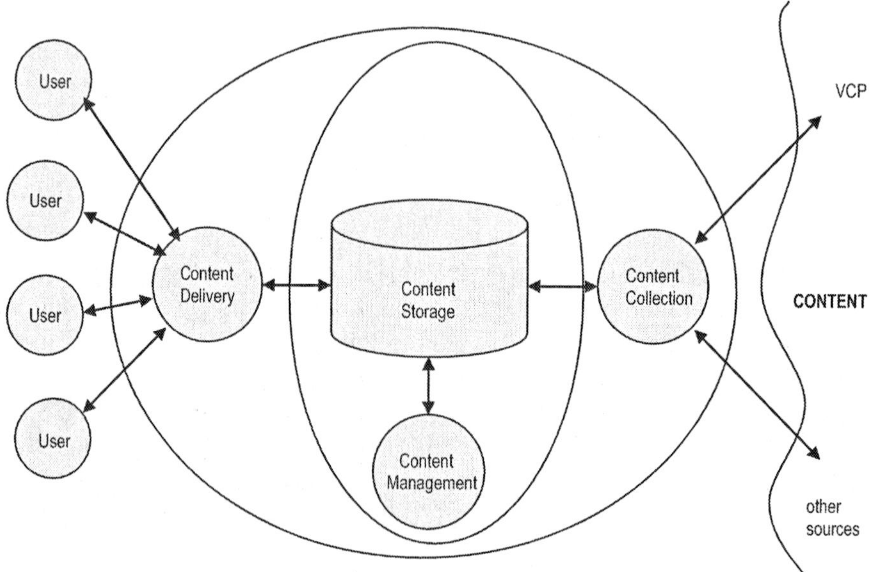

of useful information when the ideas of the Semantic Web and ontological content demarcation become widespread.

Since we assume that VCPs carry content that is structured and rarely changes its format (e.g., the Web site of Hilton hotels), it is possible to extract from them information that can be transformed into a form that is to be stored in our system. More precisely, in our system, we store information about travel objects in the form of instances of ontologies, persisted in a Jena (2005) repository. To be able to do this, in the *content collection subsystem* we use *wrapper agents* (*WA*) designed to interface with specific Web sites and collect information available there (see also Figure 2). Note that currently we have no choice but to create each of the WAs manually. However, in the future, as semantic demarcation becomes standard, the only operation required to adjust our system will be to replace our current "static WAs" with "ontological WAs." This is one of the important strengths of agent-based system design, pointed to in Jennings, 2001 and Wooldridge, 2002.

As mentioned, the *content storage* is the Jena repository, which was designed to persist RDF triples (RDF is our semantic demarcation approach of choice). The *content management subsystem* encompasses a number of agents (considered jointly as a *data management agent* [*DMA*]) that work to assure that users of the system have access to the best quality of data. These agents, among others deal

Figure 2. Top level use case diagram

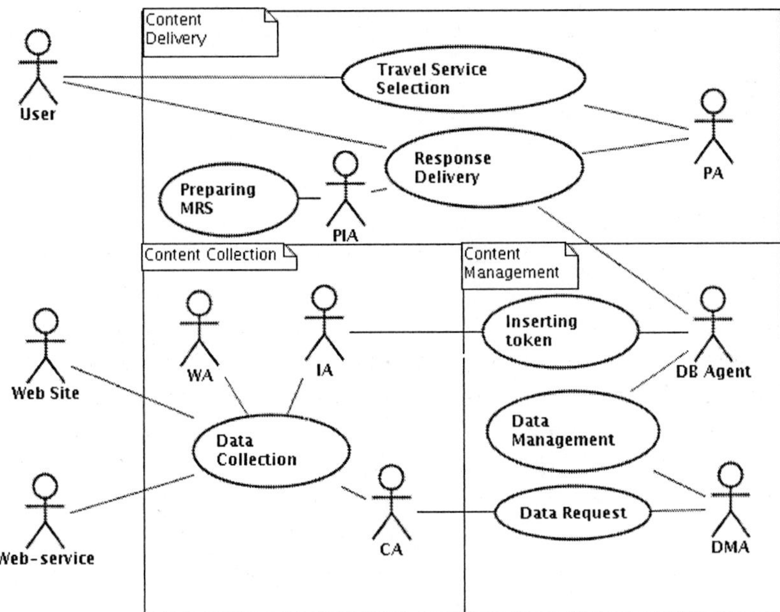

with: time sensitive information (such as changes of programs of movie theaters), incomplete data tokens, or inconsistent information (Angryk et al., 2002; Gordon & Paprzycki, 2005).

Content delivery subsystem has two roles. First it is responsible for the format (and syntax) of interactions between users and the system. However, this aspect of the system, as well as agents responsible for it, is mostly outside of scope of this chapter (more details can be found in Galant et al., 2002a and Kaczmarek et al., 2005). Second, it is responsible for the semantics of user-system interactions. Here two agents play crucial role. First, the *personalization infrastructure agent* (*PIA*) that consists of a number of extremely simple rule-based "RDF subagents" (each one of them is a class within the PIA) that extend the set of travel objects selected as a response to the original query to create a *maximum response set* (*MRS*) that is delivered to the PA for filtering and ordering. Second, the PA that utilizes *user profile* to filter and hierarchically organize information obtained from the PIA as the MRS. It is also the PA that is involved in gathering explicit user feedback (see section "RDF Data Utilization: Content Personalization") that is used to adjust user profile.

In Figure 2 we represent, in the form of a UML use case diagram, the aforementioned agents as well as other agents that are a part of the central system infrastructure. This diagram should be considered together with the system visualization found in Figure 1.

Since we had to abandon, hopefully temporarily, *other sources*, in Figure 2 we depict only Web sites and Web services that belong to the VCP category. They are sources of data for the function *Data Collection* that is serviced by WAs, *indexing agents* (*IA*), and a *coordinator agent* (*CA*). The IA communicates with the *DB agent (DBA)* when performing the *Inserting tokens* function. Separately, the CA receives data requests from the DMA. These data requests represent situations when data tokens were found to be potentially obsolete or incomplete (as a part of the *Data Management* function) and a new token has to be delivered by an appropriate WA to refresh/complete data available in the system. The DMA and the DBA are the only agents that have a direct access to the Jena database. In the content delivery subsystem we have three functions specified. The *Travel Service Selection* function is related to User(s) querying the system (information flow from the User to the central repository), while the *Response Delivery* function involves operations taking place between the time when the initial response to the query is obtained from Jena and when the final personalized response is delivered to the user (information flow from the central repository to the *User*). During this process the PIA performs the *Preparing MRS* function. Let us now discuss in some detail agents and their interactions. Before we proceed let us note that we omit a special situation when the system is initialized for the very first time and does not have any data stored in the Jena repository. While this situation requires agents started in a specific order, since it is only a one-time event it is not worthy of extra attention. We therefore assume that there is already data stored in the system and focus on interactions taking place in a working system.

The WA interfaces with Web sites, mapping XML- or HTML-demarcated data into RDF triples describing travel objects (according to the ontology used in our system [Gawinecki, Gordon, Nguyen, Paprzycki, & Szymczak, 2005; Gawinecki, Gordon, & Paprzycki, et al., 2005; Gordon, Kowalski, et al., 2005]). It is created by the CA on the basis of a *configuration file*. The configuration file may be created by the system administrator and sent to the CA as a message from the *graphical user interface (GUI) agent* or may be contained in a message from the DMA that wants to update one or more tokens. Each completed token is time stamped and priority stamped and send back to the CA. Upon completion of its work the (or in the case of an error) WA sends an appropriate message to the CA and self-destructs. A new WA with the same functionality is created by the CA whenever needed. Note that to simplify agent management we create instances of WA for each "job," even though they may produce tokens describing the same travel resource. For instance, when one WA is working on finding information about *all* Westin Hotels in Central Europe (task assigned by the system administrator), another WA may be asked to find information about Westin Hotel in Warszawa (job requested by the DMA). It is the role of the IA to assure that the most current available token is stored in the repository (see Figure 3). An UML statechart of the WA is contained in Figure 3.

CA manages all activities of the content collection subsystem. When started, it creates a certain number of IA (specified by the system administrator—*Servicing agent management request* function in Figure 4) and enters a listening state. There are six types of messages that may be received: (1) a self-destruction order received from the GUI Agent (send by the system administrator)—resulting in the CA killing all existing WAs and IAs first, and then self-destructing; (2) message from the

Figure 3. Statechart of the WA

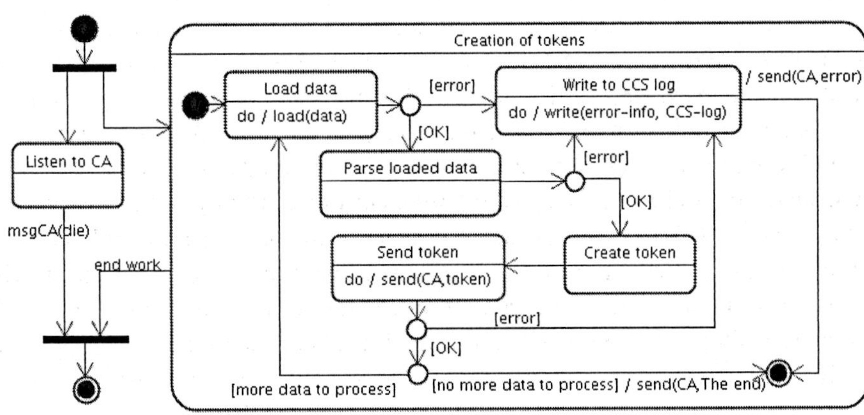

WA that it encountered an error or that it has completed its work and will self-destruct—resulting in appropriate information being recorded; (3) message from the WA containing a token—to be inserted into the priority queue within the CA; (4) message from one of the IAs requesting a new token to be inserted into the repository—which results in the highest priority token being removed from the priority queue and send to the requesting IA. When the queue is empty, a message is send to the IA informing about this fact (as seen in Figure 5, IA will retry requesting token after some delay); (5) message from the DMA containing a request (in the form of a configuration file) to provide one or more tokens—resulting in creation of an appropriate WA (or a number of WAs); and, finally, (6) message from the GUI Agent ordering adjustment of the number of IAs in the system. A complete statechart of the CA is depicted in Figure 4.

IA is responsible for inserting tokens into the central repository as well as initial pre-processing of tokens to facilitate cleanness of data stored in the system. For the time being the IA performs the following simple checks: (1) time consistency of tokens to be inserted—since it is possible that multiple WAs generate tokens describing the same travel resource (see above), the IA compares time stamps of the token to be inserted with that in the repository and inserts its token only when it is newer; (2) data consistency—token to be used to update/append information

Figure 4. Statechart of the CA

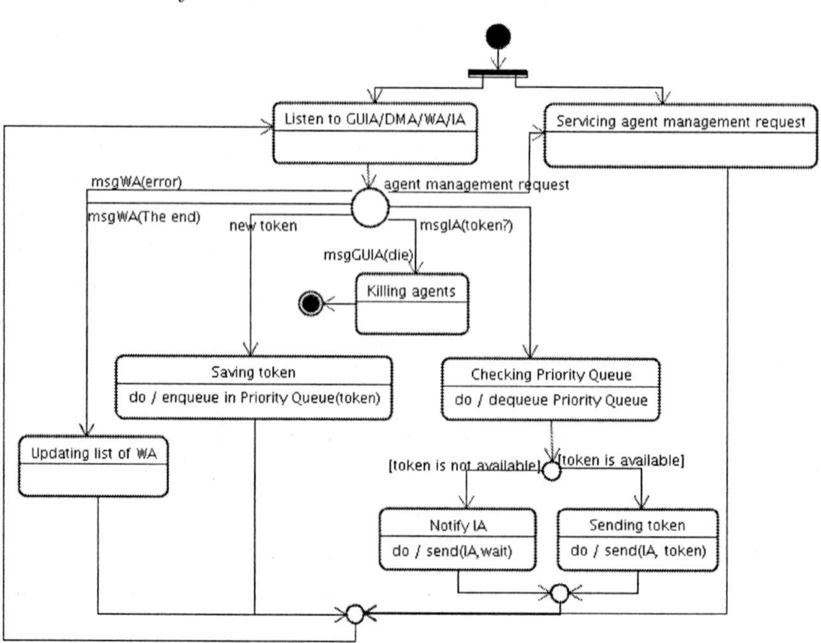

Figure 5. Statechart of the IA

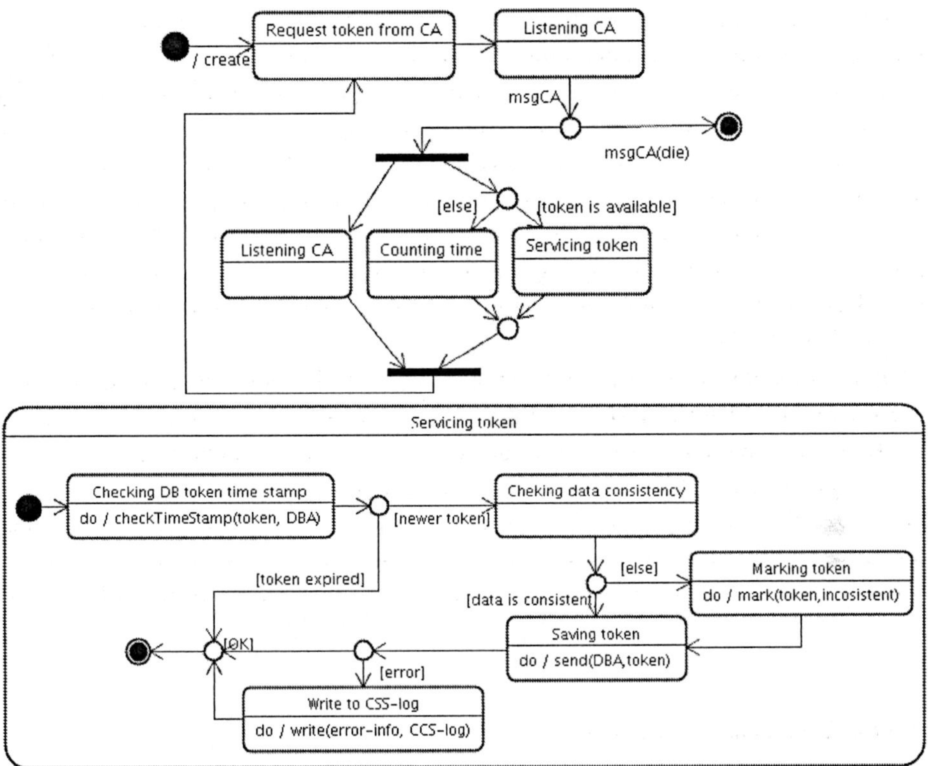

has to be consistent with the token in the repository (e.g., the same hotel has to have the same address); and (3) inconsistent tokens are marked as such and they are to be deconflicted (Angryk et al., 2002). In the case when the priority queue is empty, request will be repeated after delay *T.* The statechart of the IA is represented in Figure 5 (top panel presents the overall process flow, while the bottom panel specifies processes involved in servicing tokens).

Let us now briefly describe the next three agents visible in Figure 2. The DBA represents interface between the database (in our case the Jena repository) and the agent system. It is created to separate an agent system from an "outside technology" in such a way that in case of changes in the repository all other changes will be localized to that agent, while the remaining parts of the system stay unchanged.

In the current system the DMA is a simple one. A number of agents of this type, responsible for different travel objects, are created upon system startup. Their role is to "traverse" the repository to find outdated and incomplete tokens and request new/additional ones to be generated to update/complete information stored in the repository. To achieve this goal DMAs generate a configuration file of an appropriate WA and send them to the CA for processing. In the future DMAs will be responsible for complete management of tokens stored in the repository to assure their completeness, consistency, and freshness.

The PIA consists of a manager and a number of "RDF subagents" (*PIA workers* in Figure 6). Each of these subagents represents one or more of simple rules of the type "Irish pub is also a pub" or "Japanese food is Oriental food." These rules are applied to the set of RDF triples returned by the initial query. Rule application involves querying the repository and is expected to expand the result set (e.g., if the user is asking for a Korean restaurant then other Oriental restaurants are likely to be included). The PIA subagents operate as a team passing the result set from one to the next (in our current implementation they are organized in a ring), and since their role is to maximize the set of responses to be delivered to the user no potential response is removed from the set. Final result of their operation is the MRS that is operated on by the PA. Action diagram of the PIA is depicted in Figure 6.

A separate PA will be created for each user and will play two roles in the content delivery subsystem. First, it is the central coordinator—for each user query it directs it from one agent to the next, constantly monitoring processing progress. Second, it

Figure 6. Action diagram of the PIA

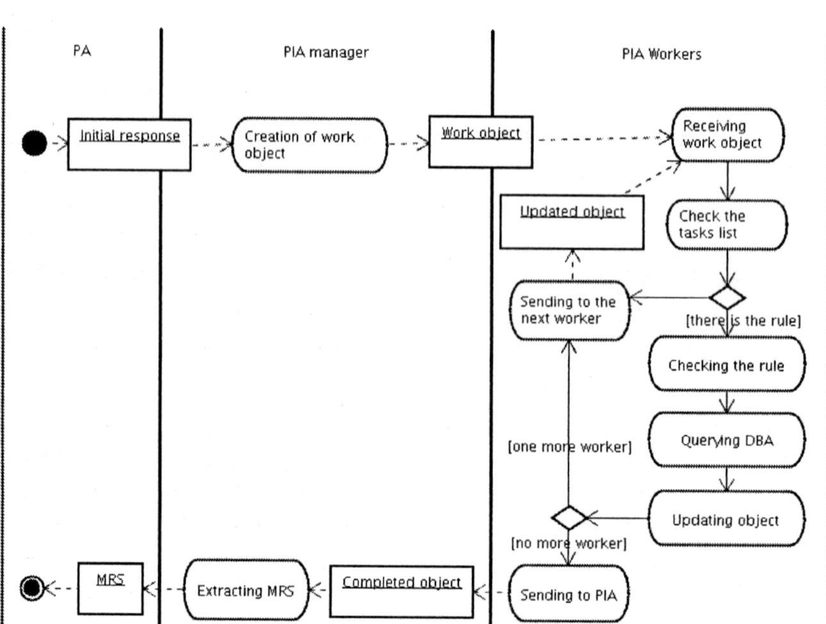

Figure 7. Statechart of the PA

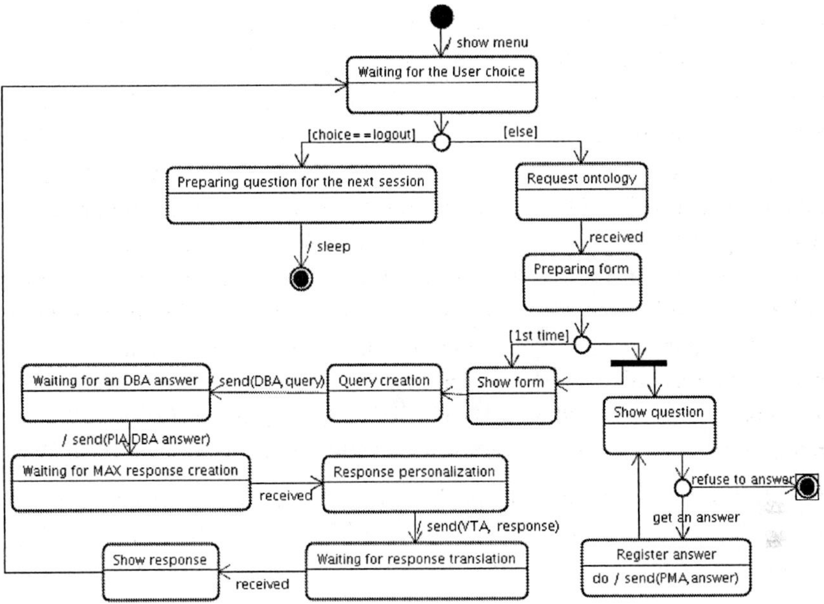

utilizes user profile to filter and order responses that are to be sent to the user. More precisely, the user query, after being pre-processed and transformed into an RDQL query (see Kaczmarek et al., 2005 for more details), is being sent to the DBA. What is returned is the initial response consisting of a number of tokens that satisfy the query. This response is being redirected (by the PA) to the PIA to obtain the MRS. Then the PA utilizes the user profile to: (1) remove from the set responses that do not belong there (e.g., user is known to be adversely inclined toward Italian food, and pizza in particular, and thus all of the Italian food serving restaurants have to be excluded); (2) order the remaining selections in such a way that those that are believed to be of most interest to the user will be displayed first (e.g., if user is known to stay in Hilton hotels, they will be displayed first). The statechart diagram of the PA is contained in Figure 7.

As we can see the PA behaves differently depending if the user is using the system for the first time or if it is a returning user. In the latter case, the PA will attempt at gathering explicit feedback related to the information delivered to the user during the previous session. This will be done through a generation of a questionnaire that will be shown to the user, who may decide to ignore it (see also Galant & Paprzycki, 2002). Obtained responses will be used to adjust the user profile. We can also see how the PA plays the role of response preparation orchestrator by always receiving responses from other agents and forwarding them to the next agent in the processing chain. We have selected this model of information processing so that "worker agents" like the DBA or the PIA know only one agent to interact with (the PA). Otherwise, an unnecessary set of dependencies would be introduced to the system making it substantially more difficult to manage (any change to one of these agents would have to be propagated to all agents that interact with it—while in our case only a single agent needs to be adjusted).

Replacing Semantic Web with a Semantic Database

As noted before, currently the Semantic Web is an attractive idea that lacks its main component—large repositories of semantically demarcated (in particular travel-related) data. This was one of the important reasons to change the design of our systems from data indexing into data gathering. As a result we are able to create our own "mini Semantic Web" (in the form of a semantic database) and store there information that in the future will allow us to extend our system beyond the basic skeleton described here, and start experimenting with its true projected functionalities—like content personalization.

Let us describe how the HTML-demarcated information available on the Web is turned into semantic tokens representing travel objects in our repository. Before proceeding let us discuss briefly ontologies utilized in the system. As reported in Gawinecki, Gordon, Nguyen, et al., 2005; Gawinecki, Gordon, Paprzycki, et al., 2005; and Gordon, Kowalski, et al., 2005, while there exists a large number of attempts at designing ontologies depicting various aspects of the world, we were not able to locate a complete ontology of the most basic objects in the "world of travel" such as a *hotel* and a *restaurant.* More precisely, there exists an implicit ontology of restaurants utilized by the ChefMoz project (ChefMoz, 2005), but it cannot be used directly as a Semantic Web resource, due to the fact that data stored there is infested with bugs that make its automatic utilization impossible without pre-processing that also involves manual operations (see Gawinecki, Gordon, Paprzycki, et al., 2005 and Gordon, Kowalski, et al., 2005 for more details).

This being the case we have proceeded in two directions. First, as reported in Gawinecki, Gordon, and Paprzycki, et al. (2005) and Gordon, Kowalski, et al. (2005) we have reverse engineered the restaurant ontology underlying the ChefMoz project and cleaned data related to Polish restaurants. Separately we have proceeded with designing hotel ontology using a pragmatic approach. Our hotel ontology is to be used to represent, manipulate, and manage hotel information actually appearing within Web-based repositories (in context of travel; i.e., not hotels as landmarks, or sites of historical events). Therefore we have studied content of the 10 largest Internet travel agencies and found out that most of them describe hotels using very similar vocabulary. Therefore we used these common terms to shape our hotel ontology and the results of this process have been reported in Gawinecki, Gordon, Nguyen, et al.

Figure 8. Hilton Sao Paulo Morumbi main page

(2005); Gawinecki, Gordon, Paprzycki, et al. (2005); and Gordon, Kowalski, et al. (2005). As an outcome we have two fully functional, complete ontologies (of a hotel and of a restaurant) that are used to shape data stored in our Jena repository.

In this context, let us illustrate how we transform the VCP featured data into travel tokens. As an example we will utilize the Web site belonging to Hilton hotels (www.hilton.com). More precisely, let us look at some of the information that is available at the Web site of Hilton Sao Paulo Morumbi depicted in Figure 8.

As clearly seen, from this page we can extract information such as the hotel name, address, and phone numbers. This page would also have to be interacted with, in case we planned to utilize our travel support system to make an actual reservation (which is only in very long-term plans and out of scope of this chapter). To find the remaining information defined by the hotel ontology requires traversing the Web

Figure 9. Hilton Sao Paulo Morumbi amenities page

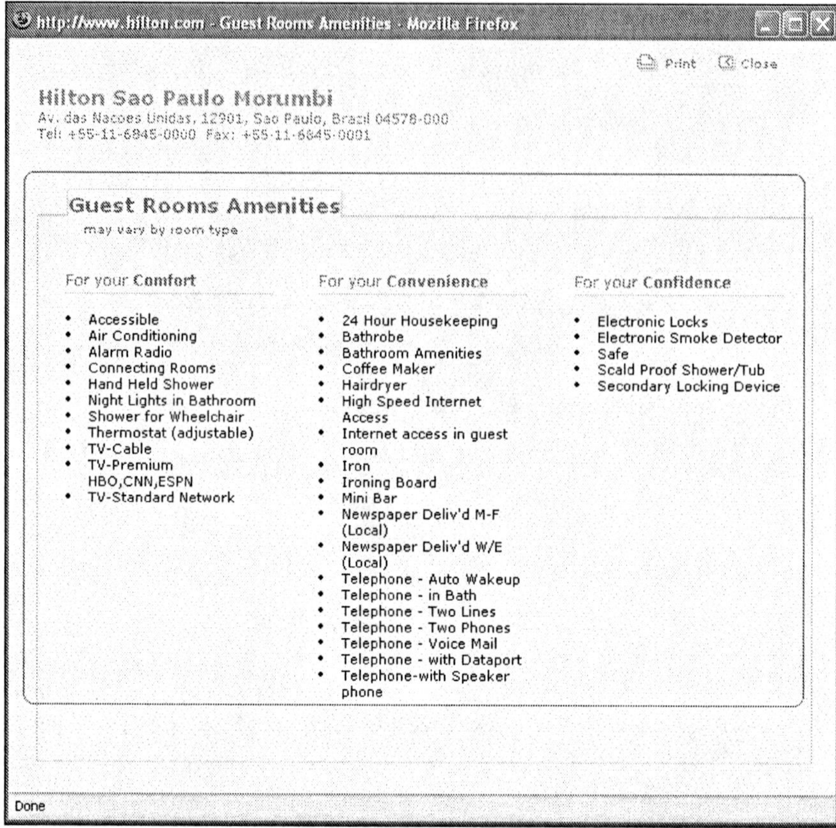

site deeper. Therefore, for instance, the WA has to go to the page contained in Figure 9, to find information about hotel amenities.

As a result the following set of RDF triples (in XML-based notation) will be generated:

```
<rdf:Description
rdf:about="http://www.agentlab.net/travel/hotels/Hilton/SAOMOHI">
  <j.1:roomAmenit rdf:resource="http://.../hotel.rdf#AccessibleRoom"/>
  <j.1:roomAmenity rdf:resource="http://.../hotel.rdf#AirConditioning"/>
  <j.1:roomAmenity rdf:resource="http://.../hotel.rdf#ConnectingRooms"/>
  <j.1:roomAmenity rdf:resource="http://.../hotel.rdf#Shower"/>
  <j.1:roomAmenity rdf:resource="http://.../hotel.rdf#CableTelevision"/>
  <j.1:roomAmenity rdf:resource="http://.../hotel.rdf#CNNavailable"/>
  <j.1:roomAmenity rdf:resource="http://.../hotel.rdf#Bathrobe"/>
```

```
 <j.1:roomAmenity rdf:resource="http://.../hotel.rdf#BathroomAmenities"/>
 <j.1:roomAmenity rdf:resource="http://.../hotel.rdf#Coffee_TeaMaker"/>
 <j.1:roomAmenity rdf:resource="http://.../hotel.rdf#Hairdryer"/>
 <j.1:roomAmenity
          rdf:resource="http://.../hotel.rdf#HighSpeedInternetConnection"/>
 <j.1:roomAmenity rdf:resource="http://.../hotel.rdf#InternetAccess"/>
 <j.1:roomAmenity rdf:resource="http://.../hotel.rdf#Iron"/>
 <j.1:roomAmenity rdf:resource="http://.../hotel.rdf#IroningBoard"/>
 <j.1:roomAmenity rdf:resource="http://.../hotel.rdf#Minibar"/>
 <j.1:roomAmenity rdf:resource="http://.../hotel.rdf#Newspaper"/>
 <j.1:roomAmenity rdf:resource="http://.../hotel.rdf#Wake-upCalls"/>
 <j.1:roomAmenity rdf:resource="http://.../hotel.rdf#Two-linePhone"/>
 <j.1:roomAmenity rdf:resource="http://.../hotel.rdf#VoiceMail"/>
 <j.1:roomAmenity
          rdf:resource="http://.../hotel.rdf#TelephoneWithDataPorts"/>
 <j.1:roomAmenity rdf:resource="http://.../hotel.rdf#SpeakerPhone"/>
 <j.1:roomAmenity rdf:resource="http://.../hotel.rdf#SmokeDetektors"/>
 <j.1:roomAmenity rdf:resource="http://.../hotel.rdf#Safe"/>
</rdf:Description>
```

These RDF triples represent a part of our hotel ontology, but this time they became its instance representing a given Hilton hotel (values of various aspects of the hotel are filled-in). Our WA will then continue traversing the hotel site to find, for instance, information about fitness and recreation as well as check-in and check-out times. An appropriate page belonging to the same hotel is depicted in Figure 10 while the resulting set of RDF triples follows.

```
<rdf:Description
rdf:about="http://www.agentlab.net/travel/hotels/Hilton/SAOMOHI">
 <j.1:recreationService
          rdf:resource="http://.../hotel.rdf#FitnessCenterOnsite"/>
 <j.1:recreationService
rdf:resource="http://.../hotel.rdf#IndoorOrOutdoorConnectingPool"/>
  <j.1:petsPolicy rdf:resource="http://.../hotel.rdf#NoPetsAlowed"/>
 <j.1:additionalDetail
rdf:resource="http://www.agentlab.net/travel/hotels/Hilton/SAOMOHI/CheckIn-CheckOut"/>
</rdf:Description>

<rdf:Description
rdf:about="http://www.agentlab.net/travel/hotels/Hilton/SAOMOHI/CheckIn-CheckOut">
 <j.1:detail>Check-in: 2:00PM, Check-out: 12:00PM</j.1:detail>
</rdf:Description>
```

Figure 10. Hilton Sao Paulo Morumbi fitness and recreation and check-in and check-out information

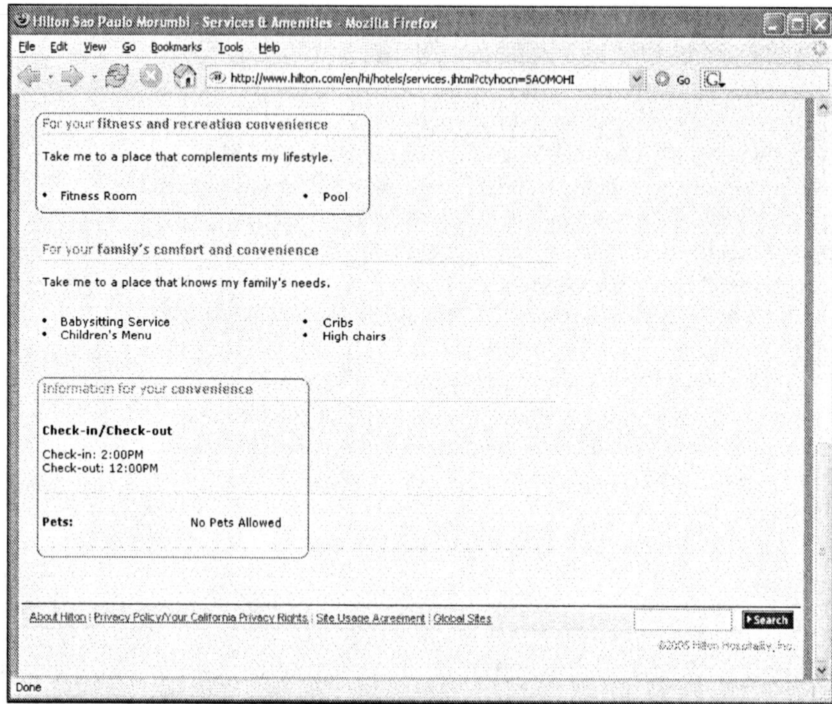

In this way the WA processes all necessary pages belonging to the Hilton Sao Paulo Morumbi and as a result obtains a set of RDF triples that constitute its complete definition (from the point of view of ontology utilized in our system). This set of RDF triples is then time and priority level stamped, packed into an ACL message and send to the CA that inserts it into the priority queue—to be later inserted, by the IA, to the semantic database. Depending on the assignment the WA may continue producing tokens of other Hilton hotels or, if work is completed, it informs the CA about this fact and self-destructs. In this way in our system, by manually creating WAs for a variety of travel information sources, we can collect real-life data representing actual travel objects.

RDF Data Utilization: Content Personalization

Let us now discuss how the data stored in the system is used to deliver personalized responses to the user. While our approach to user profile construction and utilization

Figure 11. Overlay model utilized to represent user profile

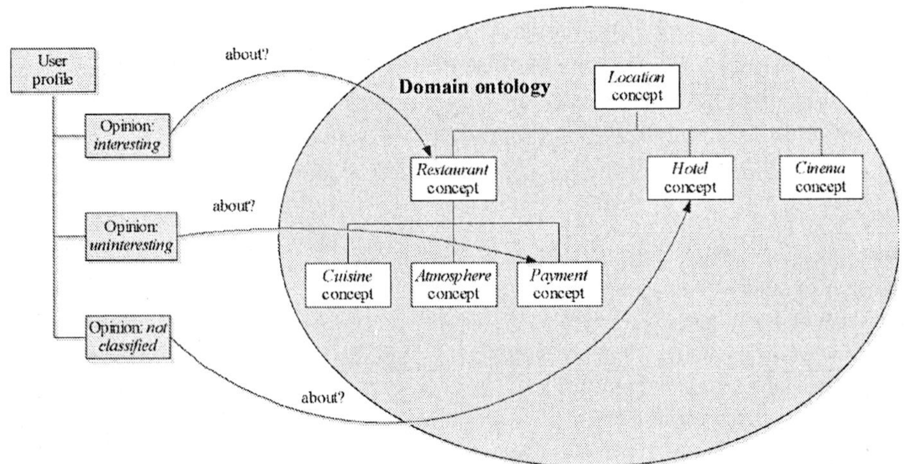

is based on ideas presented in Burke (2002); Fink and Kobsa (2002); Galant and Paprzycki (2002); Kobsa, Koenemann, and Pohl (2001); Montaner, López, and De La Rosa (2003); Rich (1979) and Sołtysiak and Crabtree (1998), however utilization of these methods in the context of ontologically demarcated information is novel and was proposed originally in Gawinecki, Vetulani, Gordon, and Paprzycki (2005).

To be able to deliver personalized content to the user of the system, we have to be able to represent the user in the system first—define user profile. Furthermore, the proposed user profile has to be created in such a way to simplify interactions in the system. Since our system is oriented toward processing of ontologically demarcated data, it is very natural to represent user preferences in the same way. Thus we adapted an *overlay model* of user profile, where opinions are "connected" with appropriate concepts in the domain ontology. This approach is also called a *student model*, since it has been found useful to describe knowledge of the student about specific topics of the domain (Greer & McCalla, 1994). Basic tenets of the overlay model are depicted in Figure 11.

For instance, let us consider our hotel ontology and assume that the user likes to stay in hotels that have both a *pool* and *fitness center*. Both these features are subclasses of the concept *amenities*. We can represent user interest by assigning weight to each amenity (the larger the weight the more important the given feature is to the user). In case of our hypothetical customer, both pool and exercise room will be assigned large weights, while features that user is not particularly interested in (e.g., availability of ironing board—see Figure 9) will be assigned small weight—the lesser the interest is the closer to 0 the value will be. In the case of features about which we do not know anything about users' preferences, no value will be assigned (see

Figure 11). Let us observe that in this approach we are mimicking the notion of probability—all assigned values are from the interval (0, 1). This means that even in the case of strong counter preference towards a given feature we will assign value 0 (there are no negative values available). Proceeding in this described way, we will create a special instance of hotel ontology, one that represents *user-hotel-profile*. The following fragment of an instance of hotel ontology (this time represented in an N3 notation) depicts user (Karol) profile as it is represented in our system:

```
:KarolOpinions    a sys:OpinionsSet;
 sys:containsOpinion
  [sys:about hotel:Pool;
   sys:hasClassification sys:Interesting;
   sys:hasNormalizedProbability 0.89].
  [sys:about hotel:ExerciseRoom;
   sys:hasClassification sys:Interesting;
   sys:hasNormalizedProbability 0.84].
  [sys:about res:AirConditioning;
   sys:hasClassification sys:Interesting;
   sys:hasNormalizedProbability 0.89].
  [sys:about hotel:BathroomAmenities;
   sys:hasClassification sys:Interesting;
   sys:hasNormalizedProbability 0.73].
  [sys:about hotel:IroningBoard;
   sys:hasClassification sys:NotInteresting;
   sys:hasNormalizedProbability 0.11].
  [sys:about hotel:Iron,
   sys:hasClassification sys:NotInteresting;
   sys:hasNormalizedProbability 0.15].
```

The previous hotel profile of Karol, tells us that he likes to stay in hotels with swimming pool and exercise room, while the availability of an iron and ironing board is inconsequential to him.

Obviously, somewhere in the system we have to store, in some form, information about the user. To assure consistency across the system, this is done in the form of a simplistic user ontology. Next, we present a fragment of such ontology:

```
:hasDress a rdf:Property ;
   rdfs:range :Dress ;
   rdfs:domain :UserProfileData.

:hasAge a rdf:Property ;
       rdfs:range :Age ;
       rdfs:domain :UserProfileData .
```

```
:hasWealth a rdf:Property ;
      rdfs:range :Wealth ;
      rdfs:domain :UserProfileData .

:hasProfession a rdf:Property ;
      rdfs:range :Profession ;
      rdfs:domain :UserProfileData .
```

Let us now assume that Karol is a 24-year-old painter, who has enough money to feel rich and whose dressing style is a natural one, then his profile would be represented as:

```
:KarolProfile a sys:UserProfile;
  sys:hasUserID 14-32-61-3456;
  sys:hasUserProfileData :KarolProfileData;
  sys:hasOpinionsSet :KarolOpinions.

:KarolProfileData a sys:UserProfileData;
  sys:hasAge 24;
  sys:hasWealth sys:Rich;
  sys:hasDress sys:NaturalDress;
  sys:hasProfession sys:SpecialistFreeLancer.
```

Rather than keeping them separate, we combine instances of user ontology with the previously described user profile into a complete ontological description—a comprehensive user profile. This user profile is then to be stored in the Jena repository.

One of the important questions that all recommender systems have to address is, how to "introduce" new users to the system (Galant & Paprzycki, 2002). In our system we use stereotyping (Rich, 1979). Obviously, we represent stereotypes the same way we used to represent user profiles, with the difference that instead of specific values representing preferences of a given user, we use sets of variables of nominal (to represent categories—e.g., profession), ordinal (e.g., low income, medium income, high income), and interval (e.g., age between 16 and 22) types. For values of nominal and ordinal types we have established sets of possible values, while for the values of interval types, we defined borders of intervals considered in the system. Using results of a survey and expert knowledge, we were able to create restaurant-related stereotypes (one instance of restaurant ontology of each identified stereotype). To illustrate such a case, here is a fragment of artistic profile in the area of restaurants:

```
:ArtistStereotypeOpinions    a sys:OpinionsSet;
 sys:containsOpinion
  [sys:about res:CafeCoffeeShopCuisine;
   sys:hasClassification sys:Interesting;
   sys:hasNormalizedProbability 1.0].
  [sys:about res:CafeteriaCuisine;
   sys:hasClassification sys:Interesting;
   sys:hasNormalizedProbability 0.75].
  [sys:about res:TeaHouseCuisine;
   sys:hasClassification sys:Interesting;
   sys:hasNormalizedProbability 0.9].
  [sys:about res:WineBeer;
   sys:hasClassification sys:Interesting;
   sys:hasNormalizedProbability 0.8].
  [sys:about res:WineList;
   sys:hasClassification sys:Interesting;
   sys:hasNormalizedProbability 1.0].
  [sys:about res:HotDogsCuisine;
   sys:hasClassification sys:NotInteresting;
   sys:hasNormalizedProbability 0.0].
```

In this stereotype we can see, among others, that an *artist* has been conceptualized as a person who likes *coffee houses* a bit more than *tea houses* and is willing to eat in a *cafeteria*, likes *wine* (a bit more than *beer*), but does not like *hot dogs* (*fast food*). Other stereotypes have been conceptualized similarly and their complete list and a detailed description of their utilization can be found in Gawinecki, Kruszyk, and Paprzycki (2005).

When a new user logs onto the system he/she will be requested to fill out a short questionnaire about age, gender, income level, occupation, address (matching user features defined by the user ontology), as well as questions about travel preferences. While the basic user ontology-based data will be required, answering questions about travel preferences will be voluntary. Personal data collected through the questionnaire will be used to match a person to a stereotype. More precisely, we will calculate a distance measure between user-specified characteristics and these appearing in stereotypes defined in the system and find one that matches his/her profile the closest. To achieve this we will use the following formula:

$$d\left(\hat{S},\hat{u}\right)=\frac{\sum_{f=1}^{k} w^f \delta^f_{\hat{S}\hat{u}} d^f_{\hat{S}\hat{u}}}{\sum_{f=1}^{k} w^f \delta^f_{\hat{S}\hat{u}}}$$

Table 1. Calculating closeness between user profile (Karol) and a stereotype (artist)

Attribute (f)	Attribute weight (w^f)	Data of artist stereotype (comma means OR relation): (S)	Karol's Data: (u)	Distance between value of attribute: ($d^f_{S,u}$)	Weighted distance: ($w^f * d^f_{S,u}$)
Age	2	20-50	24	0.00	0.00
Wealth	4	Not Rich, Average Rich	Rich	0.33	1.33
Dress	1	Naturally, Elegantly	Naturally	0.00	0.00
Profession	2	Student/Pupil, Scientist/ Teacher, Specialist/ FreeLancer Unemployed/WorkSeeker	Specialist/ FreeLancer	0.00	0.00
			COMBINED		1.3(3) / (2+4+1+2)= 0.14(6)

Where: w^f – weight of attribute, $d^f_{S,u}$ – distance between values of the attribute in the stereotype S and user's data u, $\delta^f_{S,u}$ – Boolean flag that informs whether attribute f appears in both: stereotype's data (S) and user's data (u).

To illustrate this, let us consider Karol, the painter, again. In the Table 1 we present Karol's data and the artist stereotype data and show how the closeness between Karol and that stereotype is calculated.

The same process is then repeated comparing Karol's data against all other stereotypes to find the one that fits him the best. In the next step this stereotype is joined with his user data to become his *initial profile*. In the case when he answers any domain-specific questions (recall, that he may omit them), this data will be used to modify his user profile. For example, let us assume that he has been identified as student stereotype, but he has also specified that he does not like coffee houses (while in the student stereotype coffee houses have been assigned a substantial positive weight). Obviously, in his profile, this positive value will be replaced by zero—as explicit personal preferences outweigh these specified in the stereotype (see also Nistor, Oprea, Paprzycki, & Parakh, 2002):

```
:KarolOpinions a sys:OpinionsSet;
  sys:containsOpinion
   [sys:about res:CafeCoffeeShopCuisine;
    sys:hasClassification sys:Interesting;
    sys:hasNormalizedProbability 0.0].
```

Observe that as soon as the system is operational we will be able to store information about user behaviors (Angryk et al., 2003; Galant & Paprzycki, 2002; Gordon & Paprzycki, 2005). These data will be then used not only to modify individual user profiles, but also mined (e.g., clustered) to obtain information about various group behaviors taking place in the system. This information can be used to verify, update, or completely replace our initial stereotypes. Such processes are based on the so-called implicit relevance feedback (Fink & Kobsa, 2002; Kobsa et al., 2001). As described earlier (see Figure 7) we will also utilize explicit feedback based on user responses to subsequent questionnaires. Currently as explicit feedback we utilize only a single question: "Did you like our main suggestion presented last time?" but a more intricate questionnaire could also be used. Specifically, at the end of each user system interaction, on the basis of what was recommended to the user, a set of questions about these recommendations could be prepared. When the user returns to the system, these questions would be then asked to give him/her opportunity to express his/her direct opinion. Both implicit and explicit feedbacks are used to adjust user profile (see also Gawinecki, Vetulani, et al., 2005). Note here, that in most recommender systems stereotyping is *the* method of information filtering (demographic filtering); thus making such systems rather rigid—in this case individual user preferences cannot be properly modeled and modified (Kobsa et al., 2001). In our system we use stereotyping only to solve the cold-start problem—and modify them over time—and thus avoid the rigidity trap.

User profile is utilized by the PA to rank and filter travel objects. Let us assume that after the query, the response preparation process has passed all stages and in the last one the PIA agent has completed its work and the MRS has been delivered to the PA. The PA has now to compute a *temperature* of each travel object that is included in the MRS. The temperature represents the "probability" that a given object is a "favorite" of the user. This way of calculating the importance of selected objects

Figure 12. Construction of final response: Interactions between features

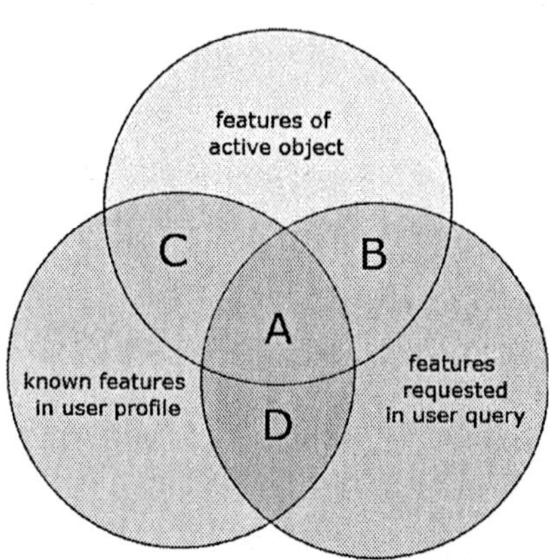

was one of the reasons for the way that we have assigned importance measures to individual features (as belonging to the interval [0,1]). Recall here that the DBA and the PIA know nothing about user preferences and that the PIA uses a variety of general rules to increase the response set beyond that provided as a response to the original query.

To calculate the temperature of a travel object (let us name it an *active object*) three aspects of the situation have to be taken into account. First, features of the active object. Second, user interests represented in the user profile—if a given feature has no preference specified then it cannot be used. In other words, for each token in the MRS we will crop its ontological graph to represent only these features that are defined in user profile. Third, features requested in user query. More specifically, if given keywords appear in the query (representing explicit wishes of the user), for example, if the query was about a restaurant in Las Vegas, then such restaurants should be presented to the user first. Interactions between these three aspects are represented in Figure 12.

Here we can distinguish the following situations:

A. Features explicitly requested by the user that appear in the active object as well as in the user-profile;
B. Features requested by the user and appearing in the active object;
C. Features not requested that are a part of the user profile and that appeared in the active object; and
D. Features that do not appear in the active object (we are not interested in them).

Ratings obtained for each token in the MRS represent what the system believes are user preferences and are used to filter out these objects temperatures of which are below a certain threshold and rank the remaining ones (objects with highest scores will be displayed first). We will omit discussion of a special case when there is no object above the threshold. The MRS is processed in the following way:

1. Travel objects are to be returned to the user in two groups (buckets)
    a. Objects requested explicitly by the user (via the query form) – Group I
    b. Objects not requested explicitly by the user but predicted by the system to be of potential interest to the user – Group II

    Thus, for each active object we divide features according to the areas depicted in Figure 11. Objects for which at least one feature is inside of either area A or B belong to Group I, objects with all features inside area C belong to Group II, while the remaining objects are discarded.

Table 2. Computing temperature of a restaurant

Restaurant N3 descriptions (bold – requested by the user, underlined – in the user profile; could be conjunctive)	Calculations
:RestaurantX a res:Restaurant; res:cuisine **res:ItalianCuisine**; res:cuisine res:PizzaCuisine; res:cuisine res:CafeCoffeeShopCuisine; res:feature <u>res:Outdoor</u>.	+0.5 (=1-0.5) requested; B +0 -0.49 (=0.01-0.5) profile -0.45 (=0.05-0.5) profile **= -0.44**
:RestaurantY a res:Restaurant; res:cuisine **res:ItalianCuisine**; res:smoking **res:PermittedSmoking**.	+0.5 (=1-0.5) requested; B +0.5 (=1-0.5) requested; B **= 1**
:RestaurantZ a res:Restaurant; res:cuisine <u>res:WineBeer</u>; res:smoking <u>res:PermittedSmoking</u>.	+0.3 (=0.8-0.5) not requested; profile; C +0.5 (=1-0.5) not requested; profile; C **= 0.8**

2. Inside of each bucket travel objects are sorted according to their temperature computed in the following way: for a given object O its temperature

$$temp(0) = \sum_{f \in O} temp(f)$$

where $temp(f) = 1$ if $f \in A \cup B$, or $p_n(f)$ if $f \in C$, while $temp(f)=temp(f) - 0.5$. This latter calculation is performed to implicate that these features that are not of interest to the user (their individual temperatures are less than 0.5) reduce the overall temperature of the object. Function $p_n(f)$ is a normalized probability of feature f, based on the user profile.

Let us consider Karol, who is interested in selecting a restaurant. In his query he specified that this restaurant has to serve Italian cuisine and has to allow smoking. Additionally, we know, from Karol's profile, that he does not like *coffee* (weight 0.1) and *outdoor dining* (weight 0.05). Thus for the restaurant X:

```
:RestaurantX a res:Restaurant;
        res:cuisine res:ItalianCuisine;
        res:cuisine res:PizzaCuisine;
        res:cuisine res:CafeCoffeeShopCuisine;
        res:feature res:Outdoor.
```

Figure 13. Content delivery agents and their roles

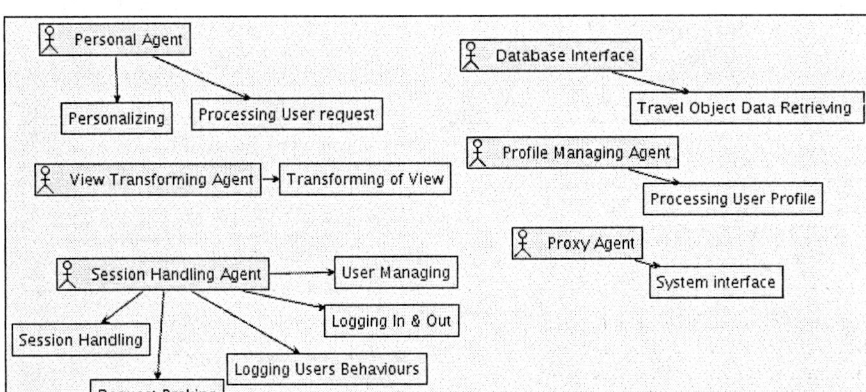

the overall score will be decreased due to the influence of *Outdoor* and *CafeCoffeeShopCuisine* features, but will receive a "temperature boost" because of the *ItalianCuisine* feature (explicitly specified feature). However, the restaurant X it won't be rated as high as the restaurant Y:

```
:RestaurantY a res:Restaurant;
        res:cuisine res:ItalianCuisine;
        res:smoking res:PermittedSmoking.
```

which serves *ItalianCuisine*, where smoking is also permitted. To be more specific, let us consider these two restaurants and the third one described by the following features:

```
:RestaurantZ a res:Restaurant;
        res:cuisine res:WineBeer;
        res:smoking res:PermittedSmoking.
```

Then Table 2 represents the way that temperatures of each restaurant will be computed.

As a result, restaurants X and Y belong to the first bucket (to be displayed to the user as they both have features that belong to area B). However, while restaurant Y has high temperature (1) and definitely should be displayed, restaurant X has very low temperature (-0.44) and thus will not likely be displayed at all. Interestingly, restaurant Z, which belongs to the second bucket (belongs to area C), has an overall

Figure 14. Content delivery action diagram

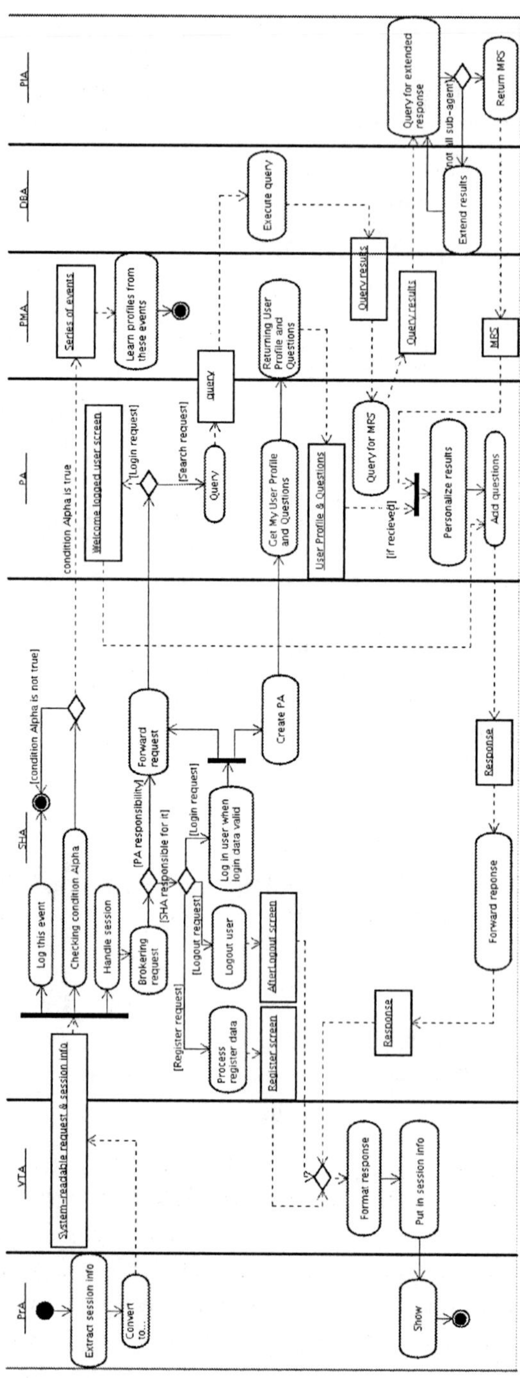

score of 0.8 and is likely to be displayed. This example shows also the potential adverse effect of lack of information (e.g., in the ChefMoz repository; but more generally, within the Web) on the quality of content-based filtering (at least done in a way similar to that proposed previously). Simply said, what we do not know cannot decrease the score, and thus a restaurant for which we know only address and cuisine may be displayed as we do not know that it allows smoking on the premises (which would make it totally unacceptable to a given user).

RDF Data Utilization: Content Delivery

Let us now present in more detail how the delivery of content to the user is implemented as an agent system. To be able to do this we need to briefly introduce additional agents (beyond these presented in Figure 2) and their roles (using Prometheus methodology [Prometheus, 2005])—as represented in Figure 13.

In addition to the PA (described in details in Figure 7) and the DBA, we have also: (1) *view transforming agent* (*VTA*) responsible for delivering response in the form that matches the user I/O device; (2) *proxy agent* (*PrA*) that is responsible for facilitating interactions between the agent system and the outside world (need for these agents as well as a detailed description of their implementation can be found in Kaczmarek et al. (2005); (3) *session handling agent* (*SHA*), which is responsible for complete management and monitoring of functional aspects of user interactions with the system; and (4) *profile managing agent* (*PMA*) which is responsible for (a) creating profiles for new users, (b) retrieving profiles of returning users and (c) updating user-profiles, based on implicit and explicit relevance feedback. Let us now summarize processes involved in content delivery through a UML action diagram. While rather complex, descriptions contained in Figure 14 represent a complete conceptualization of actions involved in servicing user request from the moment that the user logs on to the system, to the moment when he/she obtains response to their query.

State of the System

As indicated earlier in this chapter, we have concentrated on these features of our system that are currently being implemented and close to being ready, while omitting the features that we would like to see developed in the future. While the interface to the system is still under construction, it is possible to connect to it from a browser. Furthermore, we have emulated WAP-based connectivity. As of the day this chapter is being written, we have implemented a function-complete content collection subsystem consisting of: (1) a number of hotel wrappers (WA) that allow us to feed hotel data into the system; (2) CA and IA agents that collaborate with the WAs to

Figure 15. System query screenshot

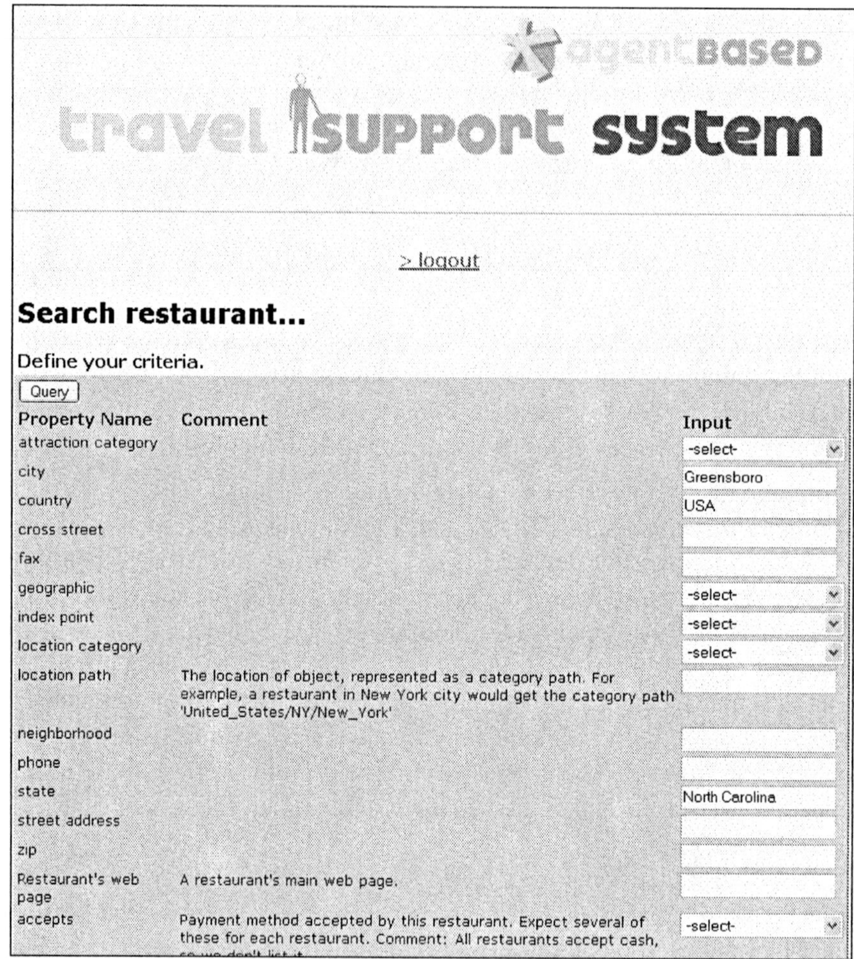

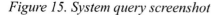

insert data into Jena-based repository; and (3) an initial version of the DMA and the PIA. For the CCS we have semi-automatically cleaned-up subsets of ChefMoz data, describing selected restaurants. We have also a relatively complete content delivery subsystem. In particular, (1) the PrA, the SHA, and the VTA that facilitate user-system interactions have been implemented and tested; (2) the PA is working as described in this chapter (with the PIA working in the case of restaurants only); (3) the PMA has only limited capacity, it is capable of creating and managing a single user profile; (4) while the existing set of stereotypes involves only restaurants. Let us briefly illustrate the work of the system, by screen-shots of the query (Figure 15) and the response (Figure 16). The query was a general query about restaurants in

Figure 16. System response screenshot

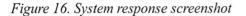

> logout > back to search form

May I ask you about...
- Restaurant "Bistro Sophia" ? [> go]

My recommendation for you...

Check it, please:

1. Biancas' An Italian Eatery [> see address]

   Small, cozy restaurant. Menu switches each week between two basic menus, in addition to various additional special dishes. Small establishment, few tables, quaint ambiance.

   Features: vegetarian dishes, private parties, offsite catering
   Accepts: cash, Visa, MasterCard/Eurocard
   Smoking: section
   Dress: dressy casual
   Alcohol: wine / beer, wine list, extensive wine list
   Reservations: recommended
   Parking: own parking lot
   Handicapped Access: completely accessible

2. Steak Street Restaurant [> see address]

   A New Orleans-style steak and seafood house with the street cafe atmosphere of "outdoor dining inside." With balcony, garden and semi-private seating, Steak Street can accommodate over 200 guests. In addition to an array of hand cut steaks, fresh seafood, pastas and more, Steak Street provides service from a full bar as well as choices from a selected wine list.

   Features: kids' menu, Sunday brunch, takeout, private room, private parties, internet access, phone ahead seating, kid friendly, large groups ok, outdoor/patio dining, nice view, television, entertainment / live music
   Accepts: cash, gift certificates, Visa, Discover, MasterCard/Eurocard, American Express
   Smoking: only at bar

Greensboro, NC; note the box that attempts at asking a question about *Bistro Sophia* that was suggested to the user in the previous session (Figure 16).

One of the biggest problems related to testing our system is the fact that, being realistic, no user would be interested in a system that only provides a few hotel chains and restaurants (e.g., in Poland). This being the case we can ourselves test features of the system like: (1) is the user query handled correctly, that is, do the returned results represent the correct answer taking into account the current state of the system; (2) do the WAs correctly deliver and the CA and IAs accurately insert tokens into the system; and (3) are agent communication and interactions proceeding without deadlocks and does the system scale. Unfortunately, it is practically impossibie to truly test adaptive features of the system. Without actual users utilizing the system to satisfy their real travel needs, all the work that we have done implementing the system cannot be practice verified.

This is a more general problem of the chicken-and-egg type that is facing most of Semantic Web research (regardless of its application area). Without real systems doing real work and utilizing actual ontologically demarcated data on a large scale (to deliver what users need) it is practically impossible to assess if the Semantic Web, the way it was conceptualized, is the way that we will be able to deal with information overload, or is it just another pipe dream like so many in the past of computer science.

Future Developments

As described previously, it seems to be clear what the future of the development of Semantic Web technologies applied in context of e-business (or in any other context) has to be. It has to follow the positive program put forward by Nwana and Ndumu (1999). The same way as agent systems and a large number of systems utilizing Semantic Web technologies have to be implemented and experimented with. Furthermore, it is necessary to develop tools that are going to speed up ontological demarcation of Web content. Here, both the content that is about to be put on the Web as well as tools supporting demarcation of legacy content need to be improved and popularized. Only then, we will be able to truly assess the value proposition of the Semantic Web. Furthermore, since software agents and the Semantic Web are truly intertwined, the development of the Semantic Web should stimulate development of agent systems, while development of agent systems is likely to stimulate development of the Semantic Web.

To facilitate these processes we plan to continue development of our agent-based travel support system. The first step will be to complete integration and testing of the aforementioned described system skeleton. We will proceed further by: (1) developing ontologies of other important travel objects, for example, movie theaters, museums, operas, and so forth; (2) fully developing and implementing the PIA and the DMA infrastructures—according to the previously presented description; (3) continuing implementing WAs to increase the total volume of data available in the system; (4) adding a geographic information system (GIS) component to the system, to allow answering queries like: which restaurant is the closest one to that hotel?; (5) developing and implementing an agent-based collaborative filtering infrastructure; and (6) investigating the potential of utilizing text processing technologies for developing new generation of adaptive WAs.

References

Angryk, R., Galant, V., Gordon, M., & Paprzycki, M. (2002). Travel support system: An agent based framework. In H. R. Arabnia & Y. Mun (Eds.), *Proceedings of the International Conference on Internet Computing (IC'02)* (pp. 719-725). Las Vegas, NV: CSREA Press.

Berners-Lee, T., Hendler, J., Lassila, O. (2001). The Semantic Web. *Scientific American.* Retrieved May, 2001, from http://www.sciam.com/article.cfm?articleID=00048144-10D2-1C70-84A9809EC588EF21

Burke, R. (2002). Hybrid recommender systems: Survey and experiments. *User Modeling and User-Adapted Interaction, 12*(4), 331-370.

ChefMoz. (2005). *ChefMoz dining guide.* Retrieved November, 2004, from http://chefdmoz.org

Darpa Agent Markup Language (DAML). (2005). *Language overview.* Retrieved October, 2005, from http://www.daml.org/

Fensel, D. (2001). *Ontologies: A silver bullet for knowledge management and electronic commerce.* Berlin: Springer.

Fink, J., & Kobsa, A. (2002). User modeling for personalized city tours. *Artificial Intelligence Review, 18,* 33-74.

Galant, V., Gordon, M., & Paprzycki, M. (2002a). Agent-client interaction in a Web-based e-commerce system. In D. Grigoras (Ed.), *Proceedings of the International Symposium on Parallel and Distributed Computing* (pp. 1-10). Iasi, Romania: University of Iaşi Press.

Galant, V., Gordon, M., & Paprzycki, M. (2002b). Knowledge management in an Internet travel support system. In B. Wiszniewski (Ed.), *Proceedings of ECON2002, ACTEN* (pp. 97-104). Wejcherowo: ACTEN.

Galant, V., Jakubczyc, J., & Paprzycki, M. (2002). Infrastructure for e-commerce. In M. Nycz & M. L. Owoc (Eds.), *Proceedings of the 10th Conference Extracting Knowledge from Databases* (pp. 32-47). Poland: Wrocław University of Economics Press.

Galant, V., & Paprzycki, M. (2002, April). Information personalization in an Internet based travel support system. In *Proceedings of the BIS'2002 Conference* (pp. 191-202). Poznań, Poland: Poznań University of Economics Press.

Gawinecki, M., Gordon, M., Nguyen, N., Paprzycki, M., & Szymczak, M. (2005). RDF demarcated resources in an agent based travel support system. In M. Golinski et al. (Eds.), *Informatics and effectiveness of systems* (pp. 303-310). Katowice: PTI Press.

Gawinecki, M., Gordon, M., Paprzycki, M., Szymczak, M., Vetulani, Z., & Wright, J. (2005). Enabling semantic referencing of selected travel related resources.

In W. Abramowicz (Ed.), *Proceedings of the BIS'2005 Conference* (pp. 271-290). Poland: PoznaD University of Economics Press.

Gawinecki, M., Kruszyk, M., & Paprzycki, M. (2005). Ontology-based stereotyping in a travel support system. In *Proceedings of the XXI Fall Meeting of Polish Information Processing Society* (pp. 73-85). PTI Press.

Gawinecki, M., Vetulani, Z., Gordon, M., & Paprzycki, M. (2005). Representing users in a travel support system. In H. Kwaśnicka et al. (Eds.), *Proceedings of the ISDA 2005 Conference* (pp. 393-398). Los Alamitos, CA: IEEE Press.

Gilbert, A., Gordon, M., Nauli, A., Paprzycki, M., Williams, S., & Wright, J. (2004). Indexing agent for data gathering in an e-travel system. *Informatica, 28*(1), 69-78.

Gordon, M., Kowalski, A., Paprzycki, N., Pełech, T., Szymczak, M., & Wasowicz, T. (2005). Ontologies in a travel support system. In D. J. Bem et al. (Eds.), *Internet 2005* (pp. 285-300). Poland: Technical University of Wrocław Press.

Gordon, M., & Paprzycki, M. (2005). Designing agent based travel support system. In *Proceedings of the ISPDC 2005 Conference* (pp. 207-214). Los Alamitos, CA: IEEE Computer Society Press.

Greer, J., & McCalla, G. (1994). *Student modeling: The key to individualized knowledge based instruction* (pp. 3-35). NATO ASI Series. Springer-Verlag.

Harrington, P., Gordon, M., Nauli, A., Paprzycki, M., Williams, S., & Wright, J. (2003). Using software agents to index data in an e-travel system. In N. Callaos (Ed.), *Electronic Proceedings of the 7th SCI Conference* [CD-ROM, file: 001428].

Hendler, J. (1999, March 11). Is there an intelligent agent in your future? *Nature*. Retrieved March, 2004, from http://www.nature.com/nature/webmatters/agents/agents.html

Hendler, J. (2001). Agents and Semantic Web. *IEEE Intelligent Systems Journal, 16*(2), 30-37.

JADE. (2005). (Version 3.4) [Computer software]. Retrieved from http://jade.tilab.com/

Jena. (2005, March). *A Semantic Web framework* (Version 2.4) [Computer software]. Retrieved from http://www.hpl.hp.com/semweb/jena2.htm

Jennings, N. R. (2001). An agent-based approach for building complex software systems. *Communications of the ACM, 44*(4), 35-41.

Kaczmarek, P., Gordon, M., Paprzycki, M., & Gawinecki, M. (2005). The problem of agent-client communication on the Internet. *Scalable Computing: Practice and Experience, 6*(1), 111-123.

Kobsa, A., Koenemann, J., & Pohl, W. (2001). Personalized hypermedia presentation techniques for improving online customer relationships. *The Knowledge Engineering Review, 16*(2), 111-155.

Maes, P. (1994). Agents that reduce work and information overload. *Communications of the ACM, 37*(7), 31-40.

Manola, F., & Miller, E. (Eds.). (2005). *RDF primer.* Retrieved from http://www.w3.org/TR/rdf-primer

McGuinness, D. L., & Van Harmelen, F. (Eds.). (2005, February 10). *OWL Web ontology language overview.* Retrieved December, 2004, from http://www.w3.org/TR/owl-features/

Montaner, M., López, B., & De La Rosa, J. L. (2003). A taxonomy of recommender agents on the Internet. *Artificial Intelligence Review, 19,* 285-330.

Nistor, C. E., Oprea, R., Paprzycki, M., & Parakh, G. (2002). The role of a psychologist in e-commerce personalization. In *Proceedings of the 3rd European E-COMM-LINE 2002 Conference* (pp. 227-231). Bucharest, Romania: IPA S. A.

Nwana, H., & Ndumu, D. (1999). A perspective on software agents research. *The Knowledge Engineering Review, 14*(2), 1-18.

Paprzycki, M., Angryk, R., Kołodziej, K., Fiedorowicz, I., Cobb, M., Ali, D., et al. (2001) Development of a travel support system based on intelligent agent technology. In S. Niwiński (Ed.), *Proceedings of the PIONIER 2001 Conference* (pp. 243-255). Poland: University of PoznaD Press.

Paprzycki, M., Kalczyński, P. J., Fiedorowicz, I., Abramowicz, W., & Cobb, M. (2001) Personalized traveler information system. In B. F. Kubiak & A. Korowicki (Eds.), *Proceedings of the 5th International Conference Human-Computer Interaction* (pp. 445-456). Gdańsk, Poland: Akwila Press.

Raccoon. (2005). (0.5.1) [Computer software]. Retrieved November 2005, from http://rx4rdf.liminalzone.org/Raccoon

Rich, E. (1979). User modeling via stereotypes. *Cognitive Science, 3,* 329-354.

Prometheus. (2005). *Prometheus methodology.* Retrieved from http://www.cs.rmit.edu.au/agents/prometheus/

Sołtysiak, S., & Crabtree, B. (1998). Automatic learning of user profiles—towards the personalization of agent service. *BT Technological Journal, 16*(3), 110-117.

Wooldridge, M. (2002). *An introduction to multiAgent systems.* John Wiley & Sons.

Wright, J., Gordon, M., Paprzycki, M., Williams, S., & Harrington, P. (2003). Using the ebXML registry repository to manage information in an Internet travel support system. In W. Abramowicz & G. Klein (Eds.), *Proceedings of the BIS2003 Conference* (pp. 81-89). Poland: Poznań University of Economics Press.

Chapter XV

Development of an Ontology to Improve Supply Chain Management (SCM) in the Australian Timber Industry

Jaqueline Blake, University of Southern Queensland, Australia
Wayne Pease, University of Southern Queensland, Australia

Abstract

This chapter proposes an ontology using Web ontology language (OWL) for the Australian timber sector that can be used in conjunction with Semantic Web services to provide effective and cheap business-to-business (B2B) communications. From the perspective of the timber industry sector, this study is important because supply chain efficiency is a key component in an organisation's strategy to gain a competitive advantage in the marketplace. Strong improvement in supply chain performance is possible with improved B2B communication, which is used both for building trust and providing real-time marketing data. Traditional methods such as electronic data interchange (EDI), which are used to facilitate B2B communication, have a number of disadvantages such as high implementation and running costs and a rigid and inflexible messaging standard. Information and communications technologies (ICT) have supported the emergence of Web-based EDI which maintains the advantages of the traditional paradigm while negating the disadvantages. This has been further extended by the advent of the Semantic Web which rests on the fundamental idea that Web resources should be annotated with semantic markup that captures information about their meaning and facilitates meaningful machine-to-machine communication.

Introduction

The Australian forest and wood products industry sector form an important element of the Australian economy, with a turnover exceeding $14 billion per year. The industry contributes 7.5% of the manufacturing output of the gross domestic product (Australian Bureau of Agricultural and Resource Economics, 2003). Overall the industry sector supports 674 hardwood mills and 268 softwood mills along with 30 panel board mills employing 78,400 people in 2000/2001 (Australian Bureau of Agricultural and Resource Economics, 2003). The forestry industry is growing in importance in Australia. The stated aim of the Department of Agriculture, Fisheries, and Forest (1997) according to its 2020 vision document is to triple plantation area by the year 2020.

The business process of supply chain management (SCM) provides an opportunity to improve business efficiency within this industry, increasing profit margins, and thus favourably impacting the Australian economy. The prospect of improving the efficiency of SCM is provided by new information and communication technologies. EDI is an established technology that provides B2B communication within the supply chain but demands rigid agreements between organisations concerning the structure and content of communications. From the widespread use of Internet technologies has arisen new methods for automated B2B exchange of information using Web-based EDI. This paradigm adopts a flexible, nonplatform-specific open standard in which agreement between organisations participating in the supply chain can be more readily brokered.

One of the mechanisms semantic technologies provides for brokering agreements is by providing instruments designed for unambiguous, loosely coupled data sharing. An ontology provides for the explicit specification of domain knowledge external to any one system. An organisation commits to external ontologies which may be in use industry-sector wide providing an open standard for B2B communication.

Semantic technologies use the domain knowledge to provide machine interpretable context-sensitive information which may be shared (Lee, 2004). Semantic search engines using ontologies allow the retrieval of context-sensitive information that may be coupled with intelligent agents to provide brokering and negotiation capabilities (Schoop et al., 2002). Ontologies for domains other than an industry sector are available, for instance, the Web service modelling ontology proposed by Roman et al. (2005) uses semantic technologies to automate tasks of Web service discovery, composition, and invocation.

Information Flows in SCM

A typical business receives inputs from a number of suppliers and may then use a number of channels to sell their goods and services. A supply chain is the flow of information, materials, finances, and services stretching from the procuring of raw materials through the delivery of the finished product to the end user (Turban, King, Lee, & Viehland, 2004). Management of the supply chain is done with the intent of improving customer service levels, cycle time reduction, and increased inventory turnover leading to agile supply chains (Christopher & Towill, 2001). Improvements in these functions increase the effectiveness of business processes leading to improved organisational performance (Power & Sohal, 2002; Prem PremKumar, 2003).

SCM can be defined as a set of tools and techniques applied to coordinate suppliers, manufacturers, warehouses, and retailers so that goods and services are produced and distributed to the required locations within requisite service levels, while minimising logistics costs (Simchi-Levi, Kaminsky, & Simchi-Levi, 2003). Fawcett and Magnan (2002) describe the ideal of supply chain management as managing from "the suppliers' supplier to the customers' customers" (p. 340), with Nurmilaakso, Kettunen, and Seilonen (2002) summing up SCM as being about integration.

Members of any supply chain regularly exchange communication to coordinate business activities (Sánchez & Pérez, 2003) as SCM is an organisational boundary crossing activity (Fawcett & Magnan, 2002). This need for a flow of information across organisational boundaries has made agreement between trading partners on the meaning of exchanged information and interoperability of their information systems important (Dow, 2001; Hasselbring & Welgand, 2001). EDI has been a traditional tool for facilitating the information flow. Internet technologies have had an impact on B2B communication enabling the collaboration process (Pease, 2001) and solving some problems in tools such as EDI.

E-Business Enabling Technologies

The interconnection of devices can expand the scope of business and build stronger vendor relationships by allowing information to cross organisational boundaries (Rahman, 2004). Rahman details how Internet technologies have increased the scope of business particularly in supply chain functions. However small to medium enterprises (SME) may not be aware of the opportunities made available by e-commerce and Internet enabling technologies (Mullins, Duan, & Hamblin, 2001).

Internet technologies provide a reliable and efficient network allowing system-to-system interconnections between suppliers and customers removing technology barriers (Golicic, Davis, McCarthy, & Mentzer, 2002). Organisations that initially used the Internet technologies to provide a visible Web presence have now progressed to moving functions of SCM to the Internet. Internet technologies provide advantages such as greater control, flexibility, and savings in business overheads (Yen & Ng, 2003). Technologies such as EDI and product numbering have provided a means to link information flows with the physical flow of goods and services. In the future Burt and Starling (2002) suggest a tightly integrated mesh-like e-chain consisting of nodes, communications, and seamless information transfer will be an essential part of business.

Towill (1997) states that the making available the undistorted, real-time demand information to every echelon in the supply chains leads to a dramatic improvement in the performance of that supply chain. This improvement in overall supply chain performance is a competitive advantage in a market that Bruce, Daly, and Towers (2004) argue competes on a supply chain to supply chain basis. Rahman (2004) describes this as competing on how well your supply chain is managed.

Mason-Jones and Towill (1998) describe demand information as the catalyst for the whole supply chain with the best way to contract the information flow being to directly feed each echelon in the supply chain demand information. Childerhouse, Hermiz, Mason-Jones, Popp, and Towill (2003) suggest that it is crucial that supply chain members have access to information from processes not under their control.

Mason-Jones and Towill (1998) argue that while information technology is an important driver toward compressing the information flow, the focus must be on fidelity and availability of the actual demand data. Ayers (2001) comments that no information is better than bad information. Kalakota, Stallaert and Whinston (1996) and Singh (1996) agree that in order for information to replace inventory the information must be accurate, timely, available, and unambiguous. Organisations where access to timely demand information is available are able to make an informed decision earlier, dragging the push-pull boundary closer to the start of the supply chain (Mason-Jones & Towill, 1998). Information which is distorted, missing, or not timely leads to disruptions within the supply chain, extra costs, and the bullwhip effect (Childerhouse et al., 2003; Mason-Jones & Towill, 1998).

Collaboration

Emerging technologies for SCM are collaborative commerce, e-markets, and collaborative planning forecasting and replenishment (CPFR) (Turban et al., 2004). Collaborative commerce is made possible by Web commerce and means that any participants in the supply chain may work together regardless of their place in the supply chain. This characteristic of collaborative commerce tends to produce a supply chain which is not necessarily linear but may be more like a mesh network (Turban et al., 2004). Collaboration may be internal to the organisation as well involving external organisations (Barratt, 2004).

Collaboration does not focus purely on the upstream supply chain but considers how to optimise the performance of the entire supply chain, so that decisions throughout the supply chain are driven by the end consumer demand (Ireland & Bruce, 2000). Popp (2000) discusses how collaboration occurs when organisational boundaries are blurred as partnerships are formed with Barratt (2004) adding that collaboration is a move away from an adversarial relationship between trading partners toward a win-win relationship. An adversarial relationship focuses on price while collaborative relationships focus on the performance of the supply chain as a whole (Fawcett & Magnan, 2002). Walker (1994) suggests that it is not until the exchange of in-depth proprietary information such as demand data and forecasts that collaboration takes place.

Forming partnerships with suppliers is a means to obtain best performance from the supply chain (Barratt, 2004; Ireland & Bruce, 2000; Wong, 1999). Wong advocates the forming of a clear vision for the goals of the supply chain, describing cooperative goals as the glue in the relationship between supply partners. Collaboration has as a benefit sisable cost reductions in total supply chain costs but it must be limited to a few trading partners, it is not possible to collaborate with all suppliers as they form partnerships with other trading partners (Barratt, 2004; Walker, 1994). Barratt (2004) adds limiting the number of collaborative partnerships to a few strategically important relationships is important due to the resource intensive nature of the relationships. In true collaboration the supply chain acts as a single unit, with decisions being made for the good of the supply chain (Fisher, 1997; Simatupang & Sridharan, 2004).

For collaboration to succeed it is necessary for the relationships to be built on a basis of trust and commitment (Fisher, 1997; Spekman, Kamauff, & Myhr, 1998). Fliedner (2003) details some obstacles to collaboration and CPFR as being lack of trust in sharing information; availability and cost of technology; and expertise and fragmented information sharing standards. He adds that synchronising how the metrics of the supply chain are captured and methods of compatible data interchange are important issues. Standardisation of electronic connections across a number of trading partners is an important factor in keeping connection costs low adding to success factors of a project (Christiaanse & Markus, 2003). Hasselbring and Welgand (2001) state that for organisations to exchange information they must agree on the form of information messages and define the meaning of the information. Collaboration may be driven by technical partnerships such as EDI (Walker, 1994), which provides a vehicle for integration activities (Sánchez & Pérez, 2003).

Electronic Data Interchange

EDI is one type of B2B e-business which allows the internal system of one business to transact with the internal system of another business for the exchange of electronic documents (Hasselbring & Welgand, 2001). The technology is designed to replace the expenditure, effort, and time incurred by paper-based business transactions (Shim, Pendyala, Sundaram, & Gao, 2000). Senn (1998) describes EDI as a favoured technology for implementing interorganisation systems. EDI has been shown to produce error-free current information, while handling a large volume of transactions eliminating some clerical tasks by automation of those tasks (Lu & Wu, 2004; Strader, Lin, & Shaw, 1999; Turban et al., 2004; Witte, Grunhagen, & Clarke, 2003). The automation of tasks gives EDI the ability of speeding up information transfer (Lu & Wu, 2004). EDI is an important element in allowing B2B e-commerce to take place, with Angeles (2000) declaring that EDI is one of two building blocks the other being electronic payments.

The diffusion rate of traditional EDI has been slow (Angeles, 2000; Senn, 1998) despite its advantages due to the cost of implementation and the balance of power skewed with one organisation dictating trading terms (Angeles, 2000). In Jun and Cai's (2003) study, 66% of respondents indicated that they were forced to adopt EDI by their trading partners, showing a lack of management buy-in to the benefits of EDI. Jun and Cai state that previous studies have shown that the EDI initiator usually obtains the majority of the benefits, however Prem PremKumar (2000) states that in the long term all parties benefit.

Senn (1998) describes the disadvantages of traditional EDI as the need for a large initial resource investment, the need to restructure business processes to work with EDI, the number of agreements that must be made, and ongoing operating costs. Shim et al. (2000) adding that different EDI standards are used dependent on the country of origin, making international transactions complex. While Jun and Cai's (2003) study showed that a lack of organisational readiness for EDI and trust were factors in EDI implementation failures. Mullins et al. (2001) state that costs associated with EDI has been a major barrier to EDI adoption by SMEs with some SMEs viewing EDI as a cost of doing business rather than a strategic advantage (Jun & Cai, 2003). Senn (1998) adding that the full potential of EDI systems will not be realised until a larger proportion of organisations are able to participate. In a survey undertaken in 2005 of a sample of the Australian timber and wood products industry it was found that 92% of the respondents belonged to an organisation consisting of fewer than 100 employees and so can therefore be classed as SMEs (Blake & Pease, 2005b). It can be concluded that cost of traditional EDI has formed a barrier to the adoption of EDI in the industry (Blake & Pease, 2005a).

Traditional EDI requires trading partners to agree on message standards which dictate the structure and content of the message, with two well known standards being ANSI X.12 which is used mainly in North America and UN/EDIFACT used in the rest of the world (Lu & Wu, 2004). Trastour, Bartolini and Preist (2002) describe the necessity for agreement as locking in, as trading terms and conditions were locked in as part of the agreement. Traditional EDI involves the use of a value-added network (VAN), an intermediary communications network, which charges trading partners for the use of the service. A VAN provides a secure environment for transactions, with the ability to translate between standards used by the trading partners (Awad, 2002). This process must be repeated with all EDI trading partners.

Due to the close collaboration needed to generate agreement on the message standards and translation software, EDI has been restricted to trading partners with a high volume of transactions and scale of operation as implementation costs are high (Hasselbring & Welgand, 2001; Senn, 1998; Witte et al., 2003). Hasselbring and Welgand (2001) detail that the rigidity of the agreed upon message standards does not allow for the introduction of new products and services without going through a negotiation phase with trading partners or the introduction of new business rules. The interface between trading partners must remain perfectly synchronised with reliance that changes on one side will be reflected on the other by maintenance staff (Hasselbring & Welgand, 2001). This implies a level of technical expertise and staff availability that may not be available in an SME.

Web-Based EDI

Senn (1998) argues that due to traditional EDI's reliance on formal individual agreements, translation software, and VANs, it is not an enabling technology for long-term interorganisation systems. Barriers to traditional EDI use mean that SMEs and large organisations that do not place a large volume of orders and are not able to justify the amount of resources necessary to use EDI (Fu et al. 1999).

The World Wide Web was developed as a data repository, allowing users in separate locations to collaborate on common undertakings (Berners-Lee, Cailliau, Luotonen, Nielsen, & Secret, 1994). Web-based EDI uses the capabilities of the Web and Internet technology as a low-cost, publicly accessible network with ubiquitous connectivity, which does not demand any particular network architecture (Goldfarb & Prescod, 2004; Senn, 1998). Web-based EDI offers the opportunity to participate in EDI at a cost three to ten times cheaper than traditional EDI (Wilde, 1997). Angeles (2000) describes the utilisation of the Internet as an EDI channel, as leading to the democratisation of e-commerce.

Extensible markup language (XML) has emerged as a flexible efficient language that may be used to exchange information (Shim et al., 2000). XML is used as a platform independent, language neutral (Witte et al., 2003) Web-based language, which maintains the content and structure, but separates business rules from content (Goldfarb & Prescod, 2004). XML identifiers and syntax are used to structure electronic documents, and those documents are sent through the Internet. The use of XML means that messages do not have to be as highly structured, with the length and sequence of attributes able to be varied. This flexibility makes agreement on electronic business standards between trading partners easier to negotiate (Hasselbring & Welgand, 2001). One of the benefits of XML is that every one in the supply chain can work with the original data with no need to reinterpret the data at each echelon of the chain to match individual data types (Dow, 2001).

Downing (2002) found that organisations using Web-based EDI reported a higher degree of improvement in their overall performance when using information technology, and rated long-term commitment with their suppliers as higher than those organisations with no EDI or traditional EDI. Nurmilaakso et al. (2002) study compared traditional EDI with an XML-based integration system designed to support EDI and found that the implementation costs of traditional EDI were much higher, with the cost of establishing a new message type three to four times higher.

Web-based EDI offers an alternative to traditional EDI implementation and also provides the means to compliment current EDI arrangements (Senn, 1998; Shim et al., 2000). XML and Web-based EDI can broaden the scope of supply chain integration by including those organisations that are not willing or able to justify the resources necessary for traditional EDI (Nurmilaakso et al., 2002). The introduction of Web-based EDI offers the opportunity for a mature EDI architecture where current EDI can be integrated with Web-based online transactions (Moozakis, 2001). Those organisations that currently use traditional EDI have the opportunity to save costs using Web-based EDI to bypass the use of a VAN (Angeles, 2000) with Internet technologies providing the necessary interoperability.

Interoperability

In business-to-consumer (B2C) e-commerce the requirement is for the business to interface with a small range of Web browsers so interoperability is not a major concern. However, in B2B e-commerce a business is required to interface with a diverse complex range of technologies making interoperability a priority (Shim et al., 2000). Interoperability is the ability of two or more systems to exchange information and to use the information that has been exchanged (Awad, 2002). Prem PremKumar (2003) states that in order to overcome interoperability problems it is necessary to use third party intermediaries such as VANs adding to the operating cots or establish an open information system architecture that can exchange messages irrespective of hardware and software.

The existence of open standards is a vital factor in promoting interoperability (Department of Communications Information Technology and the Arts, 2004). An answer to the integration problem is the use of Internet technology, protocols such as Hyper Text Transfer Protocol (HTTP), and common data exchange languages such as XML (Dow, 2001; Goldfarb & Prescod, 2004).

Murtaza and Shah (2004) make the point that an organisation which chooses to use XML for its internal systems has already dealt with the need for interoperability. They go on to state that XML-based Web services can provide an uncomplicated path for low-cost, efficient interorganisation systems. General approval of Web services and its associated protocols have meant that this is a well-defined path for interoperability (Murtaza & Shah, 2004).

Common Understanding of Semantics

The development of a common global standard will facilitate and hurry the transition from traditional paper-based or inflexible methods to e-commerce methods (Mulligan, 1998). Hasselbring and Welgand (2001) describe the need for the standardisation of message formats and meanings of the messages as a barrier to the wide-scale adoption of e-business. The use of XML and technologies such as Web services help to solve the technical demands of interoperability but there is a need for descriptions of products and services to share common semantics (Trastour et al., 2002).

Interoperability of information systems does not solve the problem of differences that organisations have in their representation of things in their system, such as products, relationships, and units of sale. An example of this within the Australian timber industry is one organisation defines a pack of timber as a number of linear metres, while another organisation considers a pack to be a set number of pieces of timber leading to semantic heterogeneity (Colomb, 2005). Dow (2001) talks about common vocabularies or ontologies bringing the same benefits to interoperability as the small number of tags whose meanings are known bring to HTML. The ontology provides the means for multiple users or multiple organisations to easily share data and to unambiguously understand that data. In traditional EDI this facility was provided by the use of coding systems such as UN/EDIFACT. The move to Internet-based EDI does not negate the need for the shared understanding of the meaning of data elements and their relationships (Reimers, 2001). An open standard for the Australian timber and wood product industry, consisting of an ontology, provides the means for cross institutional data exchange without having to be concerned with the trading partner's internal representation of products. The organisation will have to commit to the ontology, foregoing some autonomy, but they do not have to commit to mapping to other organisations representations (Colomb, 2005). This provides the means for the organisation to introduce loosely coupled connections between trading partners. These loosely coupled connections remove a dependence on a trading partners information systems and the technical burden of maintaining multiple EDI systems.

Ontology

If a group of systems is going to interoperate and exchange messages, then the organisations responsible for the system must agree on the meaning of words and messages in the interoperation. These agreements are called ontologies. The interoperation of more than one information system requires independent information structures outside the interoperating system.

An ontology is an explicit formal specification of how to represent the objects, concepts, and other entities that are assumed to exist in some area of interest and the relationships that holds among them (Gruber, 1993a).

Berners-Lee (cited in Carvin, 2005) describes the Web as only achieving its full potential when data can be shared and processed by automated tools. To achieve this, the Semantic Web must contain machine-readable metadata describing the data, relationships, and the knowledge domain of trusted sources. Defining metadata of a domain to give a shared understanding of data elements results in a domain ontology (Colomb, 2005).

An ontology can be represented as a hierarchical data structure showing the data entities and their relationships and rules, and this data structure can be represented in a language which is often based on XML, such as Resource Description Framework (RDF) and OWL (Colomb, 2005). The ontology describes each data entities critical properties through an attribute value mechanism. The ontology description languages do not have a standard modelling tool to show a graphical representation of an ontology fragment. As discussed by Colomb (2005) Unified Modelling Language (UML) can be used to provide a visual representation of a portion of an ontology demonstrated in the model of the proposed timber ontology shown in Figure 1.

Figure 1 shows a model of the proposed ontology for the Australian timber industry, showing the classes that will be used for reasoning. This model can be extended and made to fit more enterprises as the ontology is adopted, lowering the level of ontological commitment for the enterprise.

Formal upper ontologies which define general nondomain-specific entities that exist in reality, such as creator and date, are both defined in the Dublin Core Metadata Initiative (DCMI, 2005). Degen, Heller, Herre, and Smith (2001) postulate that every domain-specific ontology must import an upper ontology to use as a framework for concepts which are broader than the domain-specific ontology. The Bunge-Wand-Weber (BWW) system defines a number concepts for data entities such as *Thing*, *Things* have *properties*, *Things* have *states* and *Coupling* (Rosemann & Green, 2000). There are a number of other upper ontologies such as the DOLCE system. Importing these ontologies into an information system using domain-specific ontologies, act to introduce richness into the definition of the world described in the ontology (Colomb, 2005).

Gruber (1993b) introduced the theory that the quality of an ontology could be evaluated using five objective concepts: (1) clarity, (2) coherence, (3) extendibility, (4) minimal encoding bias, and (5) minimal ontological commitment (pp. 201-202).

Figure 1. A model of an ontology for the Australian timber and wood products industry

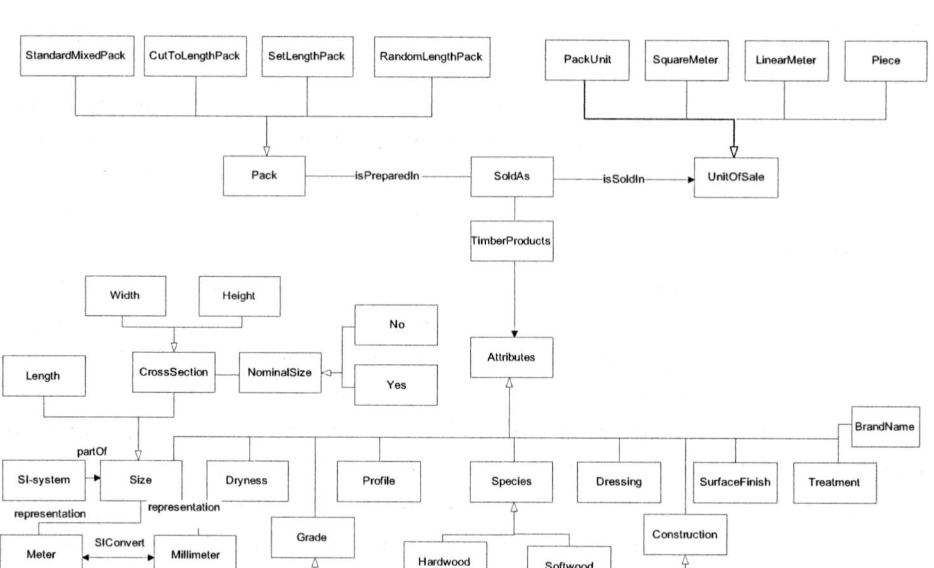

Clarity in an ontology means that the meanings behind the terms defined should be unambiguous and objective so that the organisations sharing the ontology understand the intended meaning of the ontology entities. Definitions should be formal to confine the number of unintended meanings (Gruber, 1993b).

To support clarity, the meaning of the data entities should be able to be understood by means of a formal definition. In the timber industry there is a convention that timber may be referred to in the dimensions that it had before being machined smooth, this is known as its nominal size. So in the timber products ontology the entity of NominalSize should be defined clearly as the dimensions of the premachined timber and not the literal dimensions of the timber.

The explicit associations between data entities can be detailed to support the clarity of the ontology. Associations such as cardinality constraints, part of associations, and coupling can be introduced. Cardinality constraints can be introduced between data entities, for example, between grade and strength. The addition of the cardinality helps to make clear for organisations committing to the ontology that each piece of timber must have one strength grade.

The concept of a *Thing* having a property *part of* derived from the BWW formal upper ontology makes clear the association between data entities. This helps to make the implicit relationship between classes such as **Attributes** and its subclasses such as **Dimension** and **Dryness** explicit. This helps to clarify that the subclasses form *part of* the *whole* that is the class **Attribute**.

It assists the quality of clarity, if in the class hierarchy of an ontology, the subclasses that have been declared, for instance, **Construction** could be defined rather than declared. A defined subclass means that a *Thing* belongs to a subclass because of a predicate on a superclass (Colomb, 2005), in a declared subclass a *Thing* belongs to that subclass through a subjective judgement. In the example of **Construction** an attribute could be created that specified if the construction was solid, finger jointed, or was medium density fibreboard (MDF), and hence the subclass would be defined rather than a declared subclass reducing the number of unintended meanings drawn from the ontology.

Coherence is the consistency of the rules applied in the ontology so that software can carry out the reasoning contained within the ontology. For subclasses such as species, while this is set by the common biological name used for the timber there may be an inconsistency in how people refer to the timber either by its common name, for example, *Slash Pine* or its botanical name *Pinus elliottii*. A reasoning tool may have to be used to map from the common name to the botanical name.

Extendibility is making allowance for an extension of the ontology at some time in the future, this involves eliminating redundancy and trying to isolate future areas of variability, for instance *Price* and *Discount* are areas where there is potential for future variability. Although *Price* and *Discount* are both used in calculating the price of a piece of timber, by separating the entities from each other, flexibility is introduced. This is the same principle as database normalisation (Colomb, 2005).

Minimal encoding bias should exist so that the ontology is implemented at a knowledge level not at the implementation level. As the ontology is for timber products the units used for measuring the dimensions of the timber products, and how a standard pack of timber for that organisation is quantified must be unambiguous. For this ontology to avoid encoding bias a facility must be made for an organisation to specify how the dimensions of the timber are measured and a reasoning tool be used to show equivalence between how each organisation represents their timber. This explicitly implies that the inner workings or implementation is not dictated but left up to the user as long as the correct actions in the environment are produced (Colomb, 2005; Gruber, 1993b).

The last quality concept specified by Gruber (1993b) is minimal ontological commitment. Ontological commitment is the extent to which the agent must give up autonomy in order to make their actions consistent with the ontology. Gruber states that ontological commitment is the agreement to use the ontology in a manner that demonstrates its actions are consistent with the definitions in the ontology. Currently the ontology is restricted to Australia due to restrictions in the Species class and the use of Australian standards to declare classes such as Treatment and Grade. These factors mean that for an overseas timber organisation to commit to this ontology the ontological commitment is high. A way of lessening the level of ontological commitment for this ontology would be to merge a separate species ontology detailing the timber species used in logging with this ontology to cover species outside of Australia.

Representation

The ontology engineering tool Protégé (2005) was used to develop the timber ontology based on the model drawn in UML. Protégé is a free, open source ontology editor developed by Stanford Medical Informatics at the Stanford University School of Medicine. Protégé is based on Java and provides support for both RDF and OWL. Protégé develops the ontology using a hierarchical structure shown in Figure 2.

Figure 3 shows the result of checking for logical consistency in the ontology using a logical reasoning system Racer. Racer and other reasoners are tools that can find new facts from existing data using deductive reasoning. An inconsistent class is one that cannot possibly contain any individuals as members. The reasoner can automatically determine the classification hierarchy which is called an inferred hierarchy.

RDF was developed by the World Wide Web Consortium (W3C) as an XML-based framework for describing and sharing metadata, designed to be applicable for sharing Web metadata, and creating machine-processable data on the Internet (Klyne & Carroll, 2004). To ensure extendibility RDF assumes an open world in which anyone can make statements about any resource. RDF is designed to represent information in a minimally constraining, flexible way.

RDF represents resources in a basic structure called a triple; these consist of a subject, predicate, and object. The RDF triple is used to state that the relationship indicated by the predicate exists between a subject and object. RDF uses Uniform Resource Identifier's (URI) to identify resources. RDF Schema (RDFS) is an extension of RDF that contains supplementary predicates that allows the definition of more structure than RDF (Colomb, 2005). RDFS makes it possible to define a class, subclass, and with an instance being defined using rdfs:Class, rdfs:subClassOF and rdf:type respectively, as shown in Figure 5. RDF can be used in isolated applications, where individually designed formats might be more direct and easily understood, but RDFS generality offer greater value from sharing (Colomb, 2005; Klyne & Carroll, 2004).

OWL is a specialisation of RDF also developed by the W3C designed to be compatible with putting ontologies on the Web. OWL is used when the information is intended to be machine processed and can be used to represent an ontology, (McGuinness &

Figure 2. OWL classes developed in Protégé

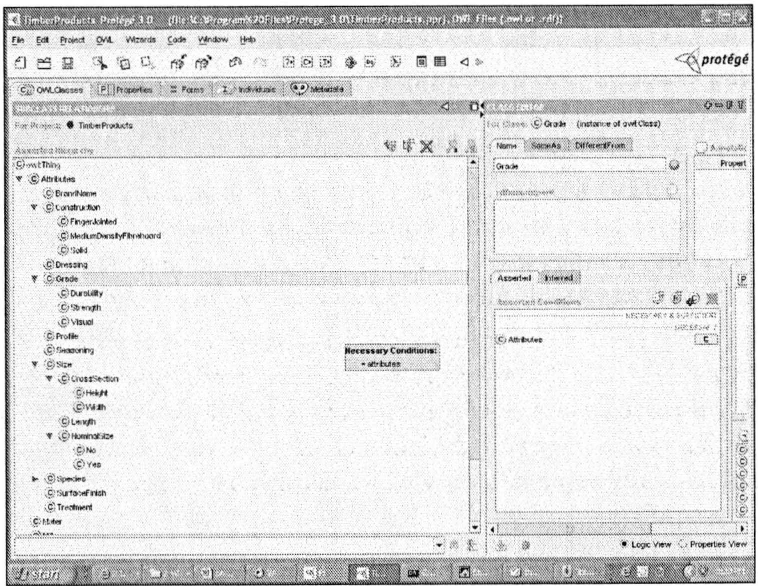

Figure 3. Consistency checking in Protégé using a reasoner

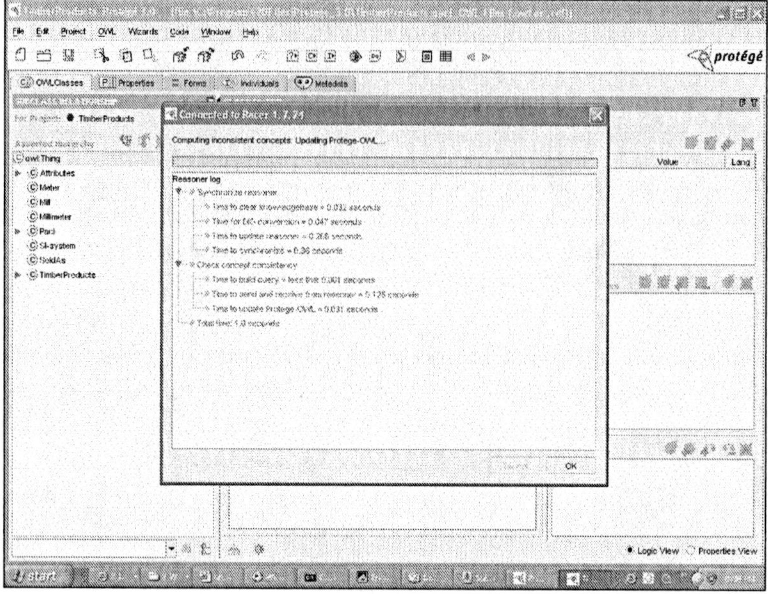

Van Harmelen, 2004) as the RDF structure is unable to support a reasoner (Colomb, 2005). OWL extends RDFS by allowing the defining of complex relationships between different RDFS classes and contains the facility to more accurately place constraints on classes and properties. OWL has been designed to support reasoning with tools such as Racer within Protégé to support this and forms part of the activity surrounding Semantic Web development. Like RDF, OWL makes an open-world assumption, so a class defined in one ontology can be extended in further ontologies (McGuinness & Van Harmelen, 2004).

The ontology described next provides a foundation for an Australian timber and wood product ontology, because of the open-world assumption by both RDF and OWL this ontology can be extended to generalise the ontology to more organisations. The foundation of this ontology is a product listing detailing categories that the organisations 40,000 products fit into. The products are organised into broad categories dependent upon timber attributes, this forms a hierarchy of classes which can be used for machine processing in the Semantic Web or as a basis of an XML document.

The classes, properties, and instances in this model can be explicitly defined by using OWL. As OWL is based on XML it is verbose so that it is not possible to show the whole ontology, examples of a class and the namespace declaration are given using the OWL representation of the model. The OWL shown next was generated by Protègè, used in conjunction with the reasoner Racer.

A standard initial part of an ontology is the namespace declaration as shown in the Figure 4.

The namespace declaration allows for the means to interpret identifiers unambiguously. The line below from within the namespace declaration states that any unprefixed qualified names refer to the current ontology.

```
xmlns=http://www.owl-ontologies.com/australianTimber.owl#
```

Figure 5 gives the OWL representation of the Profile class within the Australian timber ontology, showing that it is disjoint from other classes, a subclass of Attribute and showing how an instance is defined with the rdf:ID syntax.

Figure 4. RDF namespace declaration

```
<?xml version="1.0"?>
<rdf:RDF
  xmlns:rdf="http://www.w3.org/1999/02/22-rdf-syntax-ns#"
  xmlns:rdfs="http://www.w3.org/2000/01/rdf-schema#"
  xmlns:owl="http://www.w3.org/2002/07/owl#"
  xmlns="http://www.owl-ontologies.com/australianTimber.owl#"
 xml:base="http://www.owl-ontologies.com/australianTimber.owl">
```

Figure 5. OWL class definition

```
<owl:Class rdf:about="#Profile">
        < owl:disjointWith>
         <           owl:Class rdf:about="#Size"/>
        </ owl:disjointWith>
        < owl:disjointWith rdf:resource="#Construction"/>
        < rdfs:subClassOf rdf:resource="#Attributes"/>
        < owl:disjointWith rdf:resource="#Grade"/>
        < owl:disjointWith rdf:resource="#Seasoning"/>
        < owl:disjointWith rdf:resource="#Species"/>
        < owl:disjointWith rdf:resource="#SurfaceFinish"/>
        < owl:disjointWith rdf:resource="#Dressing"/>
</owl:Class>
  <Profile rdf:ID="Batten"/>
  <Profile rdf:ID="Fascia"/>
  <Profile rdf:ID="DoubleRebatedSawnNoiseBarrier"/>
  <Profile rdf:ID="Cladding"/>
  <Dressing rdf:ID="DressedOneSide"/>
  <Profile rdf:ID="SingleRebatedSawnNoiseBarrier"/>
  <Profile rdf:ID="Decking"/>
```

Semantic Web

Berners-Lee (cited in Updegrove, 2005) presents the Semantic Web as an evolution of his original vision of the World Wide Web, so that the Semantic Web will exist as a layer upon the existing e-technologies. The goal is to construct an environment where semantically annotated Web sites using ontology-based markup are accessible and readable by machines, for example, intelligent agents and information filters (Decker et al., 2000). The Semantic Web offers not only the ability to search by keyword but also context, moving the World Wide Web away from being a presentation medium for people to enable machine-to-machine interactions (Siorpaes, 2004; Updegrove, 2005).

Taking advantage of the opportunities that semantic technologies generate for improved information technology systems presents a number of challenges to management of the Australian timber and wood products industry. One of these challenges is the need to form strategic alliances with trading partners who accept the need to commit to an external ontology, thereby giving up some autonomy (Colomb, 2005). Semantic technologies make strategic alliances more achievable due to the improved cross organisational information flows allowing the exchange of real-time business data. The increased proficiency in handling information flows has been shown to bring competitive advantage to an organisation (Levy, Loebbecke, & Powell, 2001). Business processes may need to be changed and translation software employed to meet the ontology requirements, but alliance partners internal processes are then no barrier to interoperability. Freedom from the need to have tightly coupled information systems with multiple trading partners offers the potential to reduce maintenance costs, McComb (2005, p. 1) suggests that "corporations typically spend 35 to 65% of their budgets on integration and interoperation."

Semantic Web technologies offer the opportunity of integrating with one external, extendible, and flexible standard, potentially lowering integration costs. A disadvantage to the semantic technology approach is that there must be consensus within the strategic alliance to the same domain-specific ontology. Williams, Krygowski, and Thomas (2002) propose the use of intelligent agents to reach ontology consensus; this may require management to adopt a new way of thinking, planning, and operating focusing on the benefits offered by collaborative commerce (Walters, 2004) and using information systems as an enabler for this co-opetition. Co-opetition is the result of the formation of virtual organizations, partners concurrently cooperating and competing in the same marketplace (Rowe & Pease, 2005).

A focus on collaboration within an industry sector rather than competition is driving the need for the need for a shift in management style and focus. Co-opetition demands a move away from an internally focused approach, for instance focusing on access to and use of resources, rather than ownership of resources (Walters, 2004) to an outwards, customer-focused approach. Managers need to "adopt an entirely different approach to strategic planning and management which can enable them to deploy an extensive infrastructure network based on shared resources with other firms" (Tetteh & Burn, 2001, p. 171). This requires strategic thinking, trust, and a realization of the importance of co-opting or collaboration rather than competition, which typically exists among individual firms within the sector (Rowe & Pease, 2005).

The traditional use of information technology is that of cost reduction, collaboration is a value-added approach. In this approach information technology acts as an enabler for a new business model where management leverages all its assets including its intangible assets of partnerships (Walters, 2004). Levy et al. (2001) describe cooperation and cross institutional information flows providing added value as synergy.

Another management implication of the use of semantic technologies is the need for management to allow time for the evolution of an ontology which represents the domain rather than a single organisation. The development of a representative ontology lowers the level of ontological commitment from any group of organisations encouraging information sharing.

Conclusion

This is the first stage in the development of an open standard domain-specific ontology for the Australian timber and wood product industry. The ontology makes an open-world assumption so that it grows and gains depth with interaction and input from other domain members. The development of an ontology gives the industry a number of options. The ontology provides a path for the industry to be part of the Semantic Web movement, both now and in the future the ontology's extensible ability will allow the ontology to evolve to reflect current needs.

The ontology may also be used in the Web-based EDI paradigm, providing a common set of data elements that an organisation may map to, rather than having to map to individual organisations representations. This gives the ability to maintain a loosely coupled connection between trading partners. This introduces flexibility into the connection so that changes in one organisation's information system or data representations does not impact on the trading partner's information system, thereby increasing maintenance costs. An ontology provides the means to bring the advantages of EDI to SMEs, while lowering the traditional barriers of technical complexity and high implementation and maintenance costs. Web-based EDI provides a path for organisations to exchange real-time data across organisational boundaries bringing the productivity gains and tighter supply chain that this enables.

The adoption of semantic technologies coupled with a flexible open management approach allows an organisation to participate in productive cross institutional information flows. This ability promotes the formation of strategic alliances with trading partners, gaining a competitive advantage for this virtual organisation.

Acknowledgment

We wish to acknowledge the support of the Forestry and Wood Products Research and Development Corporation of Australia (www.fwprdc.org.au) whose interest and financial assistance has made this project possible.

Reference

Angeles, R. (2000). Revisiting the role of Internet-EDI in the current electronic commerce scene. *Logistics Information Management, 13*(1), 45-57.

Australian Bureau of Agricultural and Resource Economics. (2003). *Australian forest and wood product statistics*. Retrieved May 10, 2004, from http://www.abareconomics.com/interactive/foreststatistics_2006/pdf/afps03_march_june.pdf

Awad, E. (2002). *Electronic commerce, from vision to fulfillment*. NJ: Prentice Hall.

Ayers, J. (2001). *Supply chain myths and realities*. Retrieved April 14, 2004, from http://www.itknowledgebase.net/ejournal

Barratt, M. (2004). Understanding the meaning of collaboration in the supply chain. *Supply Chain Management: An International Journal, 9*(1), 30-42.

Berners-Lee, T., Cailliau, R., Luotonen, A., Nielsen, H. F., & Secret, A. (1994). The world-wide Web. *Communications of the ACM, 37*(8), 76-82.

Blake, J., & Pease, W. (2005a). *The e-readiness of the Australian timber and wood sector*. Paper presented at the International Telecommunications Society Africa-Asia-Australasia Regional Conference, Perth, Western Australia.

Blake, J., & Pease, W. (2005b). *An open standard for the exchange of information in the Australian timber sector*. Paper presented at the International Telecommunications Society Africa-Asia-Australasia Regional Conference, Perth, Western Australia.

Bruce, M., Daly, L., & Towers, N. (2004). Lean or agile: A solution for supply chain management in the textiles and clothing industry? *International Journal of Operations & Production Management, 24*(2), 151-170.

Burt, D. N., & Starling, S. L. (2002). *World class supply management.* Paper presented at the ISM 87th Annual International Supply Management Conference, San Francisco.

Carvin, A. (2005). *Tim Berners-Lee: Weaving a Semantic Web.* Retrieved February 24, 2005, from http://www.digitaldivide.net/articles/view.php?ArticleID=20

Childerhouse, P., Hermiz, R., Mason-Jones, R., Popp, A., & Towill, D. R. (2003). Information flow in automotive supply chains—Identifying and learning to overcome barriers to change. *Industrial Management & Data Systems, 103*(7), 491-502.

Christiaanse, E., & Markus, M. L. (2003, January 6-9). *Participation in collaboration electronic marketplaces.* Paper presented at the 36th Annual Hawaii International Conference on System Sciences, Big Island, Hawaii.

Christopher, M., & Towill, D. (2001). An integrated model for the design of agile supply chains. *International Journal of Physical Distribution & Logistics Management, 31*(4), 235-246.

Colomb, R. (2005). *Ontology and the semantic web study book* (Vol. 1). Brisbane: University of Queensland.

DCMI. (2005). *DCMI metadata terms.* Retrieved October 16, 2005, from http://dublincore.org/documents/dcmi-terms/

Decker, S., Melnik, S., Harmelen, F. V., Fensel, D., Klein, M., Broekstra, J., et al. (2000). The Semantic Web: The roles of XML and RDF. *IEEE Internet Computing,* 4(5), 63-74.

Degen, W., Heller, B., Herre, H., & Smith, B. (2001). *GOL: Toward an axiomatized upper-level ontology.* Retrieved October 16, 2005, from http://www.ontology.uni-leipzig.de/Publications/Paper-FOIS-Herre-2001.pdf

Department of Agriculture Fisheries and Forest. (1997). *Plantations for Australia—2020 Vision.* Retrieved May 12, 2004, from http://www.affa.gov.au/content/output.cfm?ObjectID=D2C48F86-BA1A-11A1-A2200060B0A03314

Department of Communications Information Technology and the Arts. (2004). *B2B e-commerce: Capturing value online.* Retrieved June 1, 2005, from http://www.dcita.gov.au/ie/publications/2001/10/b2b_e-commerce/future

Dow, C. (2001). *XML: A common data exchange language for business.* Retrieved June 1, 2005, from http://www.itknowledgebase.net//books/60/Dbm/24-01-60.pdf

Downing, C. E. (2002). Performance of traditional and Web-based EDI. *Information Systems Management, 19*(1), 49-55.

Fawcett, S. E., & Magnan, G. M. (2002). The rhetoric and reality of supply chain integration. *International Journal of Physical Distribution & Logistics Management, 32*(5), 339-361.

Fisher, M. L. (1997). What is the right supply chain for your product? *Harvard Business Review, 75*(2), 105-116.

Fliedner, G. (2003). CPFR: An emerging supply chain tool. *Industrial Management & Data Systems, 103*(1), 14-21.

Fu, S., Chung, J.-Y., Dietrich, W., Gottemukkala, V., Cohen, M., & Chen, S. (1999). *A practical approach to Web-based internet EDI.* Retrieved January 6, 2006 http://www.research.ibm.com/iac/papers/icdcsws99.pdf

Goldfarb, C. F., & Prescod, P. (2004). *XML handbook* (5th ed.). Prentice Hall PTR.

Golicic, S. L., Davis, D. F., McCarthy, T. M., & Mentzer, J. T. (2002). The impact of e-commerce on supply chain relationships. *International Journal of Physical Distribution & Logistics Management, 32*(10), 851-871.

Gruber, T. R. (1993a). A translation approach to portable ontology specifications. *Knowledge Acquisition, 5*(2), 199-220.

Gruber, T. R. (Ed.). (1993b). *Toward principles for the design of ontologies used for knowledge sharing*. Palo Alto, CA: Kluwer Academic.

Hasselbring, W., & Welgand, H. (2001). Languages for electronic business communication: State of the art. *Industrial Management & Data Systems, 101*, 217-226.

Ireland, R., & Bruce, R. (2000). CPFR: Only the beginning of collaboration. *Supply Chain Management Review, 4*(4), 80-87.

Jun, M., & Cai, S. (2003). Key obstacles to EDI success: From the US small manufacturing companies' perspective. *Industrial Management & Data Systems, 103*(3), 192-203.

Kalakota, R., Stallaert, J., & Whinston, A. B. (1996). *Implementing real-time supply chain optimization systems*. Retrieved June 2, 2005, from http://cism.mccombs.utexas.edu/jan/sc_imp.html

Klyne, G., & Carroll, J. J. (2004, February 10). *Resource description framework (RDF): Concepts and abstract syntax, W3C Recommendation.* Retrieved May 19 2005, from http://www.w3.org/TR/rdf-concepts/

Lee, J. (2004). *Introduction to semantics technology.* Retrieved December 20, 2005 http://www.alphaworks.ibm.com/contentnr/introsemantics?Open&ca=dgr-eclpsw02awintrosemantics

Levy, M., Loebbecke, C., & Powell, P. (2001). SMEs, co-opetition and knowledge sharing: The role of information systems. *European Journal of Information systems, 12*(1), 3-17.

Lu, E. J.-L., & Wu, C.-C. (2004). A ReScUE XML/EDI model. *Software: Practice and experience, 34*(3), 315-338.

Mason-Jones, R., & Towill, D. R. (1998). Time compression in the supply chain: Information management is the vital ingredient. *Logistics Information Management, 11*(2), 93-104.

McComb, D. (2005). *The CIO's guide to semantics, version 2.* Semantic Arts, Incorporated. Retrieved October 25, 2006, from http://www.semantic-conference.com/publications.html

McGuinness, D. L., & Van Harmelen, F. (Eds.). (2004, February 10). *OWL Web ontology language overview W3C recommendation.* Retrieved December 20, 2005, from http://www.w3.org/TR/owl-features/

Moozakis, C. (2001). Jupiter: EDIs here to stay. *InternetWeek 849,* 12.

Mulligan, R. (1998). EDI in foreign trade: Case studies in utilisation. *International Journal of Physical Distribution & Logistics Management, 28*(9), 794-804.

Mullins, R., Duan, Y., & Hamblin, D. (2001). A pan-European survey leading to the development of WITS. *Internet Research: Electronic Networking Applications and Policy, 11*(4), 333-340.

Murtaza, M. B., & Shah, J. R. (2004). Managing information for effective business partner relationships. *Information Systems Management, 21*(2), 43-52.

Nurmilaakso, J.-M., Kettunen, J., & Seilonen, I. (2002). XML-based supply chain integration: A case study. *Integrated Manufacturing Systems, 13*(8), 586-595.

Pease, W. (2001, June 19). *E-commerce enabling technologies.* Paper presented at the e-Commerce in Regional Australia Update 2001, Toowoomba.

Popp, A. (2000). Swamped in information but starved of data: Information and intermediaries in clothing supply chains. *Supply Chain Management; An International Journal, 5*(3), 151-161.

Power, D. J., & Sohal, A. S. (2002). Implementation and usage of electronic commerce in managing the supply chain: A comparative study of ten Australian companies. *Benchmarking: An International Journal, 9*(2), 190-208.

Prem PremKumar, G. (2000). Interorganization systems and supply chain management, an information processing perspective. *Information Systems Management, 17*(3), 56-70.

Prem PremKumar, G. (2003). Perspectives of the e-marketplace by multiple stakeholders. *Communications of the ACM, 46*(12), 279-288.

Protégé. (2005). (Version 3.1.1) [Computer software]. Stanford Medical Informatics. Retrieved October 17, 2005, from http://protege.stanford.edu/index.html

Rahman, Z. (2004). Use of Internet in supply chain management: A study of Indian companies. *Industrial Management & Data System, 104*(1), 31-41.

Reimers, K. (2001). Standardizing the new e-business platform: Learning from the EDI experience. *Electronic Markets, 11*(4), 231-237.

Roman, D., Keller, U., Lausen, H., Bruijn, J., Lara, R., Stollberg, et al. (2005). Web service modeling ontology. *Applied Ontology, 1*(1), 77-106.

Rosemann, M., & Green, P. (2000). *Integrating multi-perspective views into ontological analysis.* Paper presented at the Twenty-First International Conference on Information Systems, Brisbane, Queensland, Australia.

Rowe, M., & Pease, W. (2005, July 11-12). *Use of information technology to facilitate collaboration and co-opetition between tourist operators in tourist destinations.* Paper presented to Tourism Enterprise Strategies: Thriving—and Surviving—in an Online Era, Melbourne, Australia.

Sánchez, A. M., & Pérez, M. P. (2003). The use of EDI for interorganisational cooperation and co-ordination in the supply chain. *Integrated Manufacturing Systems, 14*(8), 642-651.

Schoop, M., Becks, A., Quix, C., Burwick, T., Engels, C., & Jarke, M. (2002, June 24-25). *Enhancing decision and negotiation support in enterprise networks through Semantic Web technologies.* Paper presented to XML Technologien für das Semantic Web—XSW 2002, Proceedings zum Workshop, Berlin, Germany.

Senn, J. A. (1998). Expanding the reach of electronic commerce, the Internet EDI alternative. *Information Systems Management, 15*(3), 1-9.

Shim, S., Pendyala, V., Sundaram, M., & Gao, J. (2000). Business-to-business e-commerce frameworks. *IEEE Computer, 33*(10), 40-47.

Simatupang, T. M., & Sridharan, R. (2004). A benchmarking scheme for supply chain collaboration. *Benchmarking: An International Journal, 11*(1), 9-30.

Simchi-Levi, D., Kaminsky, P., & Simchi-Levi, E. (2003). *Designing and managing the supply chain: Concepts, strategies, and case studies* (2nd ed.). New York: McGraw-Hill Higher Education.

Singh, J. (1996). The importance of information flow within the supply chain. *Logistics Information Management, 9*(4), 28-30.

Siorpaes, K. (2004). *On tour: System design.* Retrieved October 17, 2005, from http://e-tourism.deri.at/ont/docu2004/OnTour%20-%20System%20Design.pdf

Spekman, R. E., Kamauff, J. W., Jr., & Myhr, N. (1998). An empirical investigation into supply chain management: A perspective on partnerships. *International Journal of Physical Distribution & Logistics Management, 28*(8), 630-650.

Strader, T. J., Lin, F. R., & Shaw, M. J. (1999). Business-to-business electronic commerce and convergent assembly supply chain management. *Journal of Information Technology, 14*, 361-373.

Tetteh, E., & Burn, J. (2001). Global strategies for SME-business: Applying the SMALL framework. *Logistics Information Management, 14*(1), 171-80.

Towill, D. R. (1997). The seamless supply chain—The predator's strategic advantage. *International Journal of Technology Management, 13,* 37-56.

Trastour, D., Bartolini, C., & Preist, C. (2002, May 7-11). *Semantic Web support for the business-to-business e-commerce lifecycle.* Paper presented at the 11th International Conference on World Wide Web, Honolulu, Hawaii.

Turban, E., King, D., Lee, J., & Viehland, D. (2004). *Electronic commerce 2004.* NJ: Pearson Prentice Hall.

Updegrove, A. (2005). *The Semantic Web: An interview with Tim Berners-Lee.* Retrieved October 19, 2005, from http://www.consortiuminfo.org/bulletins/semanticweb.php

Walker, M. (1994). Supplier-retailer collaboration in European grocery distribution. *Logistics Information Management, 7*(6), 23-27.

Walters, D. (2004). New economy—new business models—new approaches. *International Journal of Physical Distribution & Logistics Management, 34*(3/4), 219-29.

Wilde, C. (1997). *New life for EDI? The Internet may help electronic data interchange finally meet expectations.* Retrieved March 17, 2003, from http://www.informationweek.com/622/22ioedi.htm

Williams, A. B., Krygowski, T. A., & Thomas, G. (2002). *Using agents to reach an ontology consensus. Paper presented to International Conference on Autonomous Agents,* Bologna, Italy.

Witte, C. L., Grunhagen, M., & Clarke, R. L. (2003). The integration of EDI and the Internet. *Information Systems Management, 20*(4), 58-65

Wong, A. (1999). Partnering through cooperative goals in supply chain relationships. *Total Quality Management, 10*(4/5), 786-793.

Yen, B. P.-C., & Ng, E. O. S. (2003). The migration of electronic commerce (EC): From planning to assessing the impact of EC on supply chain. *Management Decision, 41*(7), 656-665.

Chapter XVI

Ontology-Based Spelling Correction for Searching Medical Information

Jane Moon, Monash University, Australia
Frada Burstein, Monash University, Australia

Abstract

There has been a paradigm shift in medical practice. More and more consumers are using the Internet as a source for medical information even before seeing a doctor. The well known fact is that medical terms are often hard to spell. Despite advances in technology, the Internet is still producing futile searches when the search terms are misspelled. Often consumers are frustrated with irrelevant information they retrieve as a result of misspelling. An ontology-based search is one way of assisting users in correcting their spelling errors when searching for medical information. This chapter reviews the types of spelling errors that adults make and identifies current technology available to overcome the problem.

Introduction

Medical terminology includes many words which nonprofessionals find difficult to spell. For novice computer users it can be extremely frustrating when, as a result of misspelling, they cannot find relevant information. The medical implications of errors arising as a result of misspelling a word is well documented in the literature (Lambert, 1997; Lilley, 1995). Reports show that there is a significant error rate observed in patient records—in particular, in discharge letters (Blaser et al., 2004). An intelligent system could provide the users with some suggestions in order to assist in using correct words when dealing with medical information. However; it seems we are still far from reaching this goal.

A word processing program such as Microsoft Word, auto corrects typos and provides advice on whether a word is correctly spelt through a process of "verification and offers users to spell correctly via a process of 'correction'" (Berghel & Andreu, 1998). However, word correction is based on text spelling alone and can cause more problems at the correction stage. For example, Microsoft Word does not distinguish homophones such as *heroin* or *heroine* (Jones & Martin, 1997). The approach it takes in correcting spelling is not context based (Fallman, 2002) or ontology based (Khan, McLeod, & Hovy, 2004; Patel, Supekar, Lee, & Park, 2003; Tijerino & Reza, 2005), it does not recognize blank space which wastes a lot of space (Nix, 1981) and does not exhibit much intelligence. Popular search engines such as Yahoo and Google do provide some spelling correction by prompting a list of words based on keywords. In most cases search method is based on simple word searches and frequency distributions and these do not capture the meaning behind the words. Mauldin (1991) calls this phenomenon *keyword barrier*. Breaking through the keyword barrier will require a system that understands the texts they process.

There have been many attempts to produce spelling correction programs. They focus on various approaches including word concatenation (Berghel & Andreu, 1998), spelling correctors such as *Talisman* (Berghel, 1998), and correcting misspellings that contain a single error form (Pollock & Zamora, 1984). Some of these systems are domain specific and operate in chemistry, such as ChemSpell (Mitton, 1996; Zamora, 1978, 1980).

With the recent explosion of portals and ever expanding health information searching via medical/health portals, the question of the effectiveness of these health portals remains to be answered. Despite major advances and efforts to make portals user friendly, the research shows (Moon, 2005; Moon & Burstein, 2005) that most portals still lack essential functions for assisting users with information retrieval and hence losing potential users from existing portals. Even though the medical portals analyzed had the answers to users' queries, the major problem lay in the portal's inability to handle misspelling, thereby lacking an essential provision for assisting users (Moon & Fisher, 2005).

Another issue is that some major search engines provide a list of words that are not, however, always relevant to the user's query. This is demonstrated in Figures 2-4. Recent advances in ontology-based search is suggested to be overcoming the shortcomings of keyword search (Khan et al., 2004). At least it eliminates lists of words that are not domain specific. It is highly domain specific and context based, thereby eliminating unnecessary retrieval of information. It is an efficient, time-saving method.

In this research we explored the basic patterns of adult spelling errors and researched the spelling error corrector to see what technique has been used. In addition, we present an evaluation of some existing medical spell correctors to test if they meet users' needs. We describe an ontology-based, spell checker architecture that would assist users with medical information retrieval.

Review of Spell Check Approaches

The literature on misspelling is diverse and much of it is based on studies of children. However, very little has been studied on adults. Review of papers show that spelling mistakes in adults are predictable (Yannakoudakis & Fawthrop, 1983). This section describes the types of spelling errors and the existing approaches to their correction.

General Pattern of Spelling Errors

A natural language such as English is not static. The English language is one of the most difficult languages to learn as it has the following properties:

- It is not a phonetic language; there are many words that are not spelled the way they sound.
- It has many borrowed words that are not of English origin.
- It has many suffixes and prefixes that serve the same or similar purposes.

It is natural to make spelling errors in a language as complicated as English. General spelling errors can occur for many reasons, two of which are most common, typographical errors and orthographic errors. These can be described as follows (Peterson, 1980).

Typographic error. The first one occurs when the user knows the correct spelling but enters wrong typing because of fatigue, memory lapse, distraction, carelessness, or inadvertent mistake. This type of error is not consistent but is predictable since it relates to the position of keys on the keyboard and is probably related to finger movements.

There are many different reasons for making typographic spelling errors. One can make mistakes due to keyboard dualities. For example, one may use a keyboard for more than one language where key settings vary; for example, the keyboard can be used for English as well as Spanish and could lead to some sort of confusion. Another reason can be forgetting to use shift key characters or forgetting to undo the capital locks. Phonetic similarities such as "ka" and "ga," which are similar in Japanese could lead to confusion. Visual similarity could also lead to mistakes. For instance if two letters are similar then one may mistype the character without realizing it.

Cognitive/Orthographic errors. This relates to the writer's knowledge, and to the difference between how a word sounds and how it should be spelled. The words with different forms, for example, verbs or nouns can be confusing depending on what context they are used, for example, *effect* and *affect.*

Consistent human spelling error is related to a systematic break of rule rather than exception. Examination of performance errors in spelling seems to indicate the spelling errors are random, but closer study of individual performers invariably reveals a pattern. Across individual spelling, errors are often idiosyncratic, but often there is a substantial degree of intra-individual consistency in the types of errors being made. Most of the spelling errors occur because of some type of systematic errors due to "logical" though incorrect reasoning.

Most spelling errors can be generated from correct spelling by a few simple rules. Damerau (1964) indicates that 80% of all spelling errors are the result of:

- transposition of two letters,
- insertion of a letter,
- missing a letter, or
- one wrong letter.

Yannakoudakis and Fawthrop (1983) confirmed that there are patterns in spelling errors; and continued Damerau's (1964) study and found that:

- many errors are made in the use of vowels;
- many errors are made in the use of the letters "H," "W," and "Y;"
- doubling and singling of any letters is common;
- few errors are made in the first character of a word;

- transposition of any two adjacent characters is common;
- missing or adding a character is common; and
- certain consonants are more frequently interchanged than others.

Based on Damerau's (1964) simple method, a SPELL check program can be written as in Figure 1.

Spelling Correctors

There are two types of spelling programs: *spell checkers* and *spell correctors*. Spell checkers simply look at the entered words and check whether they are correctly spelled. Spell correctors detect misspelled words and try to correct them. A spell corrector uses elements of pattern matching, appropriate algorithms, and coding theory.

Much work has been done on spelling correction algorithms, some based on phonetics, others are algorithms, clustering, and measuring distances which will be described in the following paragraphs.

Error Detection

The two most widely used error detection methods are n-gram analysis (Morris & Cherry, 1975; Zamora, Pollock, & Zamora, 1981) and dictionary look up (Aho and Corasick, 1975; Knuth, 1973; Peterson, 1980). These two approaches can be summarized as follows:

Trigram analysis is a method used to correct spelling by analyzing parts of words in three-letter sequences. It identifies three possible candidates for representing meaningful words. N-gram is used to perform trigram analysis.

- An *n-gram* is an n-letter sequence, extracted from a word, where *n* is usually 1, 2, or 3. In general, n-gram analysis techniques check each n-gram in an input string against a precompiled table of n-gram statistics to determine whether the n-gram can occur in a word. If it does, its frequency of occurrence in the words of the language is computed. Strings containing n-grams that do not occur in words or occur very infrequently are considered to be possible misspellings. For instance, the word HEPATITIS contains the trigrams: -HE, HEP, EPA, PAT, ATI, TIT, TIS, IS- where hyphen (-) represents the word boundary (Yannakoudakis & Fawthrop, 1983).

Figure 1. Show Damerau's simple "arithmetic at" system based on deletion, insertion, transposition, and addition using ORD as example (Damerau, 1964)

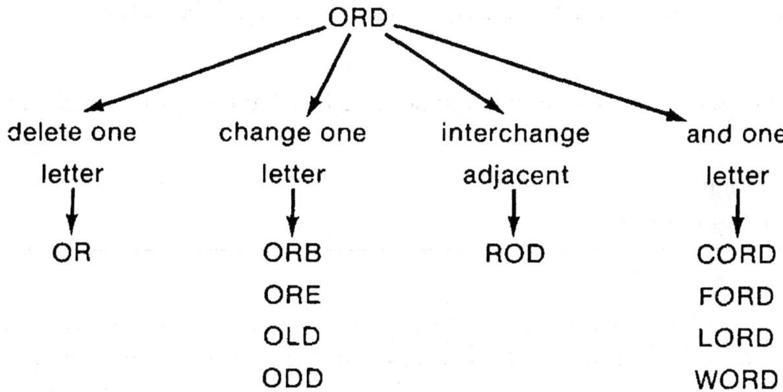

- *Dictionary lookup techniques* check whether an input string appears in a dictionary. It can be regarded as a special case of n-gram analysis where variable length n-grams delimited by blanks or punctuations are used (Zamora et al., 1981). Response time may become a problem as the size of the dictionary grows. To save the search time, most often the suffix is stripped before analysis. This could also present a problem, as meaning could sometimes be changed or lost without a suffix.

Error Correction

There has been much advance in the last decade on spelling error correction. Calculating the distance between strings has been a widely used method for error correction with a degree of success. Some of the error correction methods based on *distance between strings* are the *minimum edit distance, Hamming distance,* and *Levenshtein distance.* Another method of error correction that are based on learning from user's errors and improving and adapting from user's mistakes is called the *neural net technique.* The following paragraph describes approaches to error correction in detail.

Calculating distance between strings has been a commonly used option for modern spell checkers and seems to work well at least in English. In English spell correction word boundary problems such as in the word *forgot* (forgot – for got), run-ons such as in *form – inform,* or short words such as prepositions (to, or, at) are difficult. N-gram is used to correct context-independent problems. However, Asian languages such as Japanese and Chinese consist of run-on words, which are context dependent.

The latest word processor programs are capable of suggesting a replacement for a mistyped word. Spell checkers "know" how to evaluate distance between a misspelled word and the words in its files. Words whose evaluated distance is the smallest are suggested as candidates for replacement.

The minimum edit distance technique was first developed by Damerau (1964), to compute the minimum number of editing operations (such as insertion, deletion, transposition, and substitution) that are required to fix misspelled strings.

Hamming distance (H) is defined only for strings of the same length. Hamming distance is named after Richard Hamming; it is an algorithm that measures the number of *substitutions* required to change one string to the other. For strings s and t, H(s, t) is the number of places in which the two strings differ, have different characters.

For example (http://en.wikipedia.org/wiki/Hamming_distance):

- The Hamming distance between **10*1*1*1*01** and **1001001** is 2.
- The Hamming distance between **2*14*3*8*96** and **2233796** is 3.
- The Hamming distance between "***toned***" and "**roses**" is 3.

Hamming distance is used in telecommunications, signal distance, and cryptography. For more sophisticated systems where addition, subtraction are required, Levenshtein distance is more appropriate.

Levenshtein distance (or edit distance) is more sophisticated. It is defined for strings of arbitrary length. It counts the differences between two strings, where we would count a difference not only when strings have different characters but when one has a character and the other does not. It is the smallest number of insertions, deletions, and substitutions required to change one string or tree into another. An H(m x n) algorithm computes the distance between strings, where m and n are the lengths of the strings (http://www.nist.gov/dads/HTML/levenshtein.html).

The *simple correlation matrix technique* is a correlation technique. Each misspelled word is represented by an n-dimensional feature where Hamming distance of strongly correlated matches the most probably correct word (Cherkassky, Vassilas, Brodt, Wagner, & Fischer, 1974).

The *singular value decomposition* (SVD): Correlation Matrix Technique to apply matrix transformation techniques to simple correlation matrices in an effort to improve spelling correction accuracy (Deerwester, Dumais, Furnas, Landauer, & Harshman, 1990). The goal of SVD is to find the most relevant similarity in lexical space.

The correction of words rests on the basis of three common phenomena: nonword error detection, isolated word error correction, and context-dependent word correction (Kukich, 1992).

The *neural net technique* has the potential to adapt to specific error patterns of their user community, thus maximizing their correction accuracy for that population. This can have a user—adaptable chip that continuously monitors and learns from specific users or groups of users to improve spelling errors (Kukich, 1988).

Kukich did experiments to compare the effectiveness of spelling of the available three techniques to see the effects for different size word lexicons.

As can be seen from Table 1, slight improvements were noted with the neural network of approximately 15%. There was very little difference in performance regardless of numbers of words in the dictionaries.

In the past two decades there has been a lot of exploration of new techniques in word spelling errors (Nagata, 1996; Jones & Martin, 1997; Yannakoudakis & Fawthrop, 1983). There have also been many spelling corrector programs produced based on various algorithms. Table 2 lists some of such products and gives an overview of the strategies and characteristics of those products.

Impact of Spelling Errors on Medical Information Seeking

Medical terms are usually very hard to spell. Typing incorrectly or spelling phonetically can yield to inappropriate or irrelevant results, which causes a waste of time, resources or, at times, can give a false alarm if the users are not aware of the error. Blaster et al. (2004) found that spelling errors caused significant errors in patient discharge letters. Through earlier usability testing on Australian medical portals we found that the users did not want to come back to the sites that did not have spelling error correction facilities to assist their search (Moon & Burstein, 2005). In many instances the users could not find the information they were looking for from such portals. We have concluded then that spelling correction facility is one of the essential characteristics of an intelligent portal.

Table 1. Comparison of three spelling correction methods (Adopted from Kukich, 1992)

Techniques	521-Word Lexicon	1,142-Word Lexicon	1,872-Word Lexicon
Minimum Edit Distance	64%	62%	60%
Simple Correlation Matrix (Hamming Distance)	69%	68%	67%
Neural Network	75%	75%	?

Table 2. Some spelling correction programs

Name of the product	Strategies	Advantages	Disadvantage	Reference
Spell	Based on addition, deletion, insertion and transposition. The list is matched against the dictionary	Short words correct well.	High percentage errors on long strings. Many orthographical errors fall outside of the scope of SPELL	Peterson, 1980
Speecop	Strings are converted to similarity keys. These similarity keys are blurred to mimic original words. The keys found within certain target keys are considered possible corrections.	Frequent problem of doubling, undoubling and transposition are all seen as original words.	Dependence on first few consonants. This causes problems especially on omission of words. Good with frequent typological errors.	Pollock & Zamora, 1984
Talisman	Designed for typing and knowledge errors.	In built to the system i.e. Microsoft.	Logic based (programmed to system) not semantic based.	Berghel & Andreu, 1988
Trigram Analysis	Use of trigrams to correct misspelling.	Works well on long words. Error position is not important.	Single error may disturb all or virtually all trigrams in a short word. Transposition disturb trigrams and thus difficult to correct.	Van Berkel and De Smedt, 1988
Spell Therapist	Linguistic method for correction of orthographical errors. Combines phonological code and checks dictionary for phonemic words.	Works well for words that are homophonous spellings.	Not suitable for typological errors and does not work for hard phonological differences, i.e., 'managable', 'recommand' doesn't correct.	Van Berkel and De Smedt, 1988
The Penguin	Grammar and Spell Checking	Takes into account of idioms, colloquialism, names, and slang expressions. Dynamic, rather than prescriptive such as Microsoft Word.	Not contextual.	Fallman, 2002

Most of the spelling correction techniques mentioned previously are developed for general English language. However, most of these techniques can be applied in a medical context too. In this chapter we investigate how a generic technique, such as Damerau (1964) method, can be suitably applied to medical settings to improve the system, to make a system more "intelligent" in assisting users in seeking information. Before looking at the generic architecture we analyze the functionality of two popular existing commercial medical spell checkers. The problem with using commercial products is high cost and lack of flexibility, which can be achieved with customized development.

Analysis of Medical Spell Checkers

We studied medical spell checkers to see how useful they were in dealing with correcting spelling errors in medical portals. The following two commercial products are available in assisting users with difficult medical terminology and names of medications. Spellex (www.spellex.com) and MediSpell (www.medispell.com) were identified as the most popular and comprehensive packages. Spellex searches for medical words of 670,000 words while MediSpell searches 170,000 words.

We compared the two products against the misspelling of medical terms to see what help the users would get. The words tested were chosen from the usability testing done in an earlier study of the effectiveness of Australian government medical portals (Moon & Burstein, 2005; Moon & Fisher, 2005). Heuristic usability terms were chosen as they are closer to natural language processing, that is, the users are dynamic and unpredictable in the way they spell the words especially when the word is long and difficult.

Figure 2. MediSpell search on "schizophrenia"

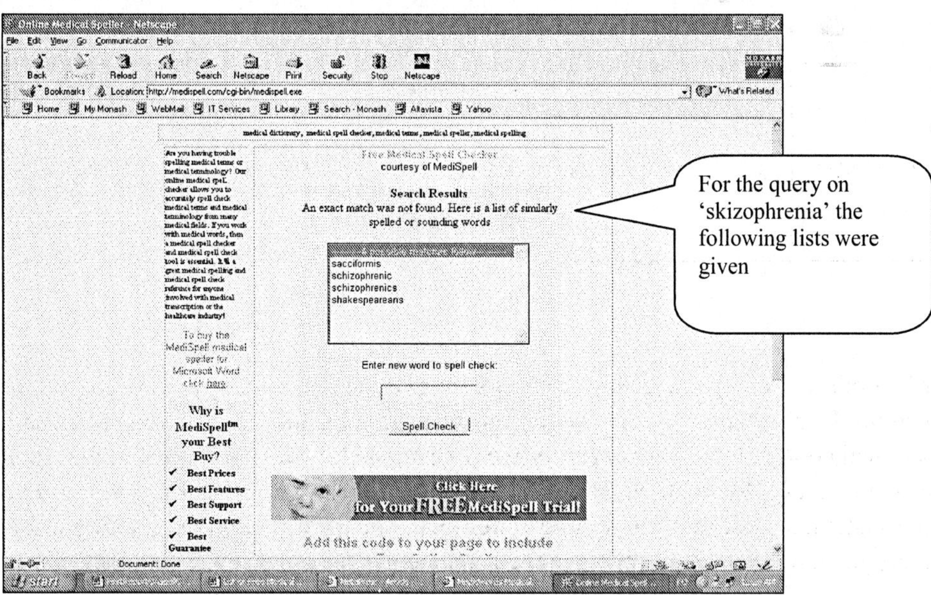

Figure 3. Spellex search on "Tamoxifen"

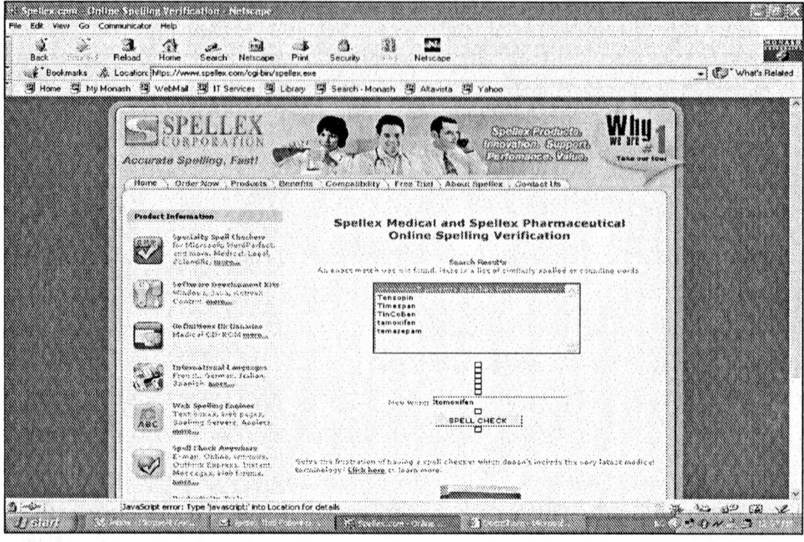

We have chosen words such as *schizophrenia, methotrexate,* and *Tamoxifen*. Schizophrenia is a common mental disease, Methotrexate is a common drug for sufferers of rheumatoid arthritis, and Tamoxifen is a common drug for breast cancer. These terms were chosen because of their wide usage in the community as found from usability testing (Moon & Fisher, 2005).

Both products give a list of synonyms as a pop-up box as seen in Figures 2-4.

A search for the query on skizophrenia produced the following lists:

- Sacciformis
- Schizophrenic ◄――――――
- Schizophrenics
- Shakespeareans

As can be seen, there were four words prompted and they were matched according to the sounds. The word *Shakespeareans* seems rather inappropriate in this list.

It would also be useful if those hits offered a description of what each word meant. For instance, what is sacciformis? Upon looking it up in a medical dictionary with-

Figure 4. Spellex search on "Methotrexate"

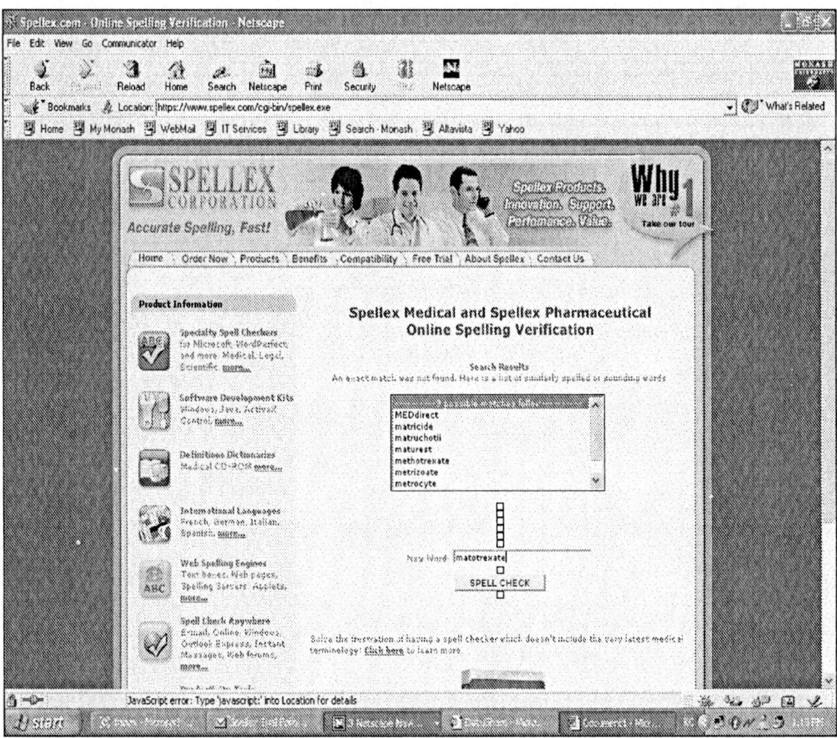

out suffix, *sacciform* is "bag-shaped" or "like a sac" (Davis, 1981), which is also useless in medical context.

Typing a common drug for breast cancer "Tamoxifen" spelled as "Tomoxifen" gave out the following options:

- Tensopin
- timespan
- TinCoBen
- Tamoxifen ←
- Temazepan

An intelligent guess is required to select Tamoxifen as the correct word, as there is no description of definition of any of the options offered. Tensopin is a drug for hypertension, TinCoBen is a skin protectant for skin disease, temazepan is a cannabis. Timespan is an unreasonable list of words for selection.

In another search, typing Methotrexate, a common drug for arthritis, misspelt as "Metatrexate" gave the following options (www.spellex.com/cgi-bin/spellex.exe):

As the result the following list of drug names was produced:

- MEDdirect
- Matricide
- Matruchoti
- Maturest
- Methotrexate ←
- Metrizoate
- metrocyte

From the previous list, one could choose more than one selection as there is a lot of similarity with keywords Methotrexate.

- Matricide is a term used for killing a mother
- Matruchoti a type of species of Bacteria represented as *Bacterionema matruchoti*
- Maturest is an English word being a mature
- Metrizoate is a diagnostic radiopaque that usually occurs as the sodium slat
- Metrocyte refers to a neuron.

As can be seen from the list of words offered as alternatives for Methotrexate they have a completely different meaning for the users to choose. Offering words spelled on the basis of phonology as an alternative choice can be risky and at times dangerous, especially when dealing with large ethnic backgrounds. For instance, in Vietnamese the ending letter "t" is often not pronounced. If the user spells phonetically the user could easily type Methotrexate as Methotrax or Mesotrax.

As can be seen from Figures 2, 3, and 4 of screen dumps, phonetically based spelling alone is not very useful and can be extremely time consuming for the users to select individual choices and check on the Internet for their meaning. However, if the descriptions of words are provided to the users so they could select what they need rather than checking individually. Equally, if the list of words is domain specific, that is, for Rheumatoid Arthritis the hit list returns drugs pertaining to the field would be helpful. The ontology-based search is aiming to solve this problem.

The following section describes steps that can be taken to improve current medical portals in particular correcting spelling mistakes and giving the users hit lists that are relevant to their field of search thereby reducing the time spent for searching, improving the user satisfaction by proving the choice for their selection, and helping them to find the relevant information.

Spelling Correction for Medical Information Retrieval

Generic spelling error detecting tools have been described in the earlier section of this article and their advantages and disadvantages described (Table 2). A few different types of error detection techniques, such as string-string edit distances, statistical packages such as SVD, Hamming distance, and the Levenshtein method have been described. These as well as statistic-based algorithms, where the search is based on probability cannot recognize the search domain. What is lacking in these spell checkers is that the searches are not context based. Spelling error correction based on phonetics combines with context-specific retrieval would eliminate the unnecessary list of words that are offered but not relevant to the user. In addition, ontology-based search can be utilized for searching words specific to the domain thus eliminating words that are not within the specific domain. In this section we consider a few approaches for dealing with phonetic errors in medical contexts, which have proven to be the most frequently encountered misspellings identified from our prior usability study of medical portals. We propose a system architecture, which is based on these approaches. The main advantage of this system is the ability to recognize terms relevant to the users' context as well as provide definitions for these terms.

The following section describes the phonetic and semantic-based search for such a system.

Damerau's Simple Detection Method

By using Damerau's (1964) simple method we can see that 80% of all spelling errors are the results of the following four methods. Damerau's method was developed for English but it can be applied in medical terms as in the following example. The word for liver disease *cirrhosis* can be wrongly written as follows:

1. insertion of a letter: cirrhossis;
2. deletion of a letter; cirhosis;

3. replacement of a letter by another one: cirrhocis; or
4. transposition of two adjacent letters: cirhrocis

In order for a medical portal to recognize these terms as related to the same word, the following methods can be used. These methods combine phonetic and context-based search to achieve more efficient information retrieval.

Phonetic-Based Spell Correction and Aspell

Lawrence Philips' Metaphone Algorithm is an algorithm which returns a rough approximation of how an English word sounds (http://aspell.net/metaphone). The original metaphone method was developed in 1990 for the C language, with more later upgrades to 4GI and for Perl, Java, and now Visual C++ and PHP. This method is used widely by Linux as an open source and matches English words phonetically rather than contextually (Jones & Martin, 1997). Lawrence Philips' methods superceded Soundex (developed by Robert Russell and Margaret Odell and was patented in 1918 and 1922) (http://patft.uspto.gov/netacgi/nph-Parser?patentnumber=1,262,167). Lawrence Philip's Metaphone combines the metaphone algorithm based on phonology and Aspell's open source. Aspell's open source spell checker is an advanced version of Ispell's which uses the basic strategy of inserting a space or hyphen, one letter deletion, one letter addition, and interchanging two adjacent letters when used for a correct term. It is an open source and it is free requiring only a little effort to download it.

Figure 5. Ontology-based spelling correction architecture

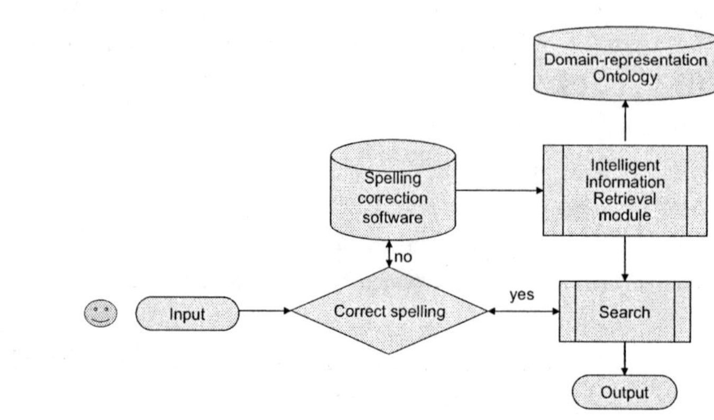

Semantic-Based Search

Kukich (1992) mentioned, in her much quoted review of technologies for automatic word correction, that research on context-based search was still in its infancy and that the task of fixing context-dependent text was an elusive one. She mentioned that 40-45% of spellings are contextual errors (Kukich, 1992a, 1992b). Natural language is complex and according to Zipf's law, "most events occur rarely and a few very common events occur most of the time" (Pedersen, 1996, p. 1). Indeed there has been much progress in parsing technology and grammar checking in English (Bernth, 1997). One example of analysis that incorporate semantic search is *latent semantic analysis (LSA)*.

The LSA proposed by Jones and Martin (1997) promises to be a step further from traditional spelling methods. In traditional spelling methods, the emphasis has been correcting the spelling rather than providing words that are relevant to contexts. Since many words are polysemous (have many meanings) and have many synonyms (words with similar meanings), trying to find the right word that matches the context has not been easy. LSA, with its use of a SVD matrix, has to some extent be able to correct the spelling errors in confusion sets (words such as *principle* and *principal*). However, it does not work yet on unedited texts (Jones & Martin, 1997).

Part of speech (POS). (Ruch, 2002) POS is about an experiment combining string-to-string distance, POS word + word language and found that POS word + word language improved search. Also spelling corrections using both left and right context outperformed the use of the left context.

Ontology-based query expansion using Unified Medical Language System (UMLS). UMLS is a full set of knowledge sources for the medical domain and is hierarchy based. The research shows that users often use the users use scenario-specific queries for information retrieval. The search terms are not keywords such as *hepatitis* or *cancer* but scenario-based search terms such as *lung, cancer treatment,* and *lung excision.* This is different to query expansion, which sought to search keywords in various documents and tried to link the words with documents. However, ontology-based query would look for keywords as well as the words in context. For instance, *lung excision* not only looks for *lung cancer* but also searches for *smoking, cigarette,* and *lymph node* (Liu & Chu, 2005).

System Design

In the system we propose that the user-entered term is first analyzed using phonetic approach as part of a spelling correction software. The terms that this process identifies as possible options are then compared with the domain ontology model. As a result of such comparison those not relevant to the user are excluded, the remaining terms are defined clearly using the definitions stored as part of the ontology. Such search procedure not only increases the relevance of the final results but improves the level of user satisfaction.

Future Trends

In general, medical terminology is very challenging. Understanding the general spelling error patterns of adults and thus creating a system that understands the general algorithm of adult spellers could improve the system. For years scientists have worked on improving systems for information retrieval. Clearly a better system is required if users' needs are to be satisfied. Agent theory, use of artificial intelligence via fuzzy logic, artificial neutral networks, and Semantic Web-based systems are all being researched and refined. Ontology-based search has potential in that the listed hits are relevant to specific domain, thereby reducing the retrieval of irrelevant word lists.

Conclusion

Natural language processing is complicated, and English is a challenging language when it comes to spelling. Adult spelling errors are either typological or orthographical, and many different types of error detection and error correction methods have been developed. Although these studies have been done on English generally, the same techniques can be applied specifically to medical information retrieval. However, the challenge is that medical terminology or jargon often involves difficult, non-English words. From the usability study it was seen that users often spell phonetically and often use a scenario-based search rather than a keyword search.

Current spelling aid systems which are built on a phonetic basis might have high recall but are low in precision. Combinations of phonetic-based systems with a knowledge-based search are seen to improve searches by 5-10% (Liu & Chu, 2005). What is more, Liu and Chu suggest that user queries are often scenario-based rather than keyword based. Ontology-based searches using a medical corpus such as UMLS narrows the search to the medical context thereby reducing irrelevant information, that is, nonmedical information. With the use of query expansion it could prove to be more efficient.

References

Aho, A. V., & Corassick, M. J. (1975). Efficient string matching: An aid to bibliographic search. *Communications of the ACM, 18,* 333-340.

Berghel, H. (1998). Talisman: A prototype expert system for spelling correction. *Proceedings of the 1998 ACM SIGSMALL/PC Symposium on ACTES.*

Berghel, H., & Andreu, C. (1998). Talisman: A prototype expert system for spelling correction. *Proceedings of the 1998 ACM SIGSMALL/PC Symposium on ACTES* (pp. 107-113).

Bernth, A. (1997). EasyEnglish: A tool for improving document quality. *Proceedings of the Fifth Conference on Applied Natural Language Processing.*

Blaser, R., Schnabel, M., Mann, D., Jancke, P., Kuhn, K. A., & Lenz, R. (2004). Potential prevention of medical errors in casualty surgery by using information technology. *Proceedings of the 2004 ACM symposium on Applied computing* (pp. 285-290).

Cherkassky, V., Vassilas, N., Brodt, G. L., Wagner, R. A., & Fischer, M. J. (1974). The string-to-string correction problem. *Journal of ACM, 21,* 168-178.

Damerau, F. J. (1964). A techniques for computer detection and correction of spelling errors. *Communications of the ACM, 7,* 171-176.

Davis, F. A. (1981). Sacciformis. *Taber's Cyclopedic Medical Dictionary.* Davis Company.

Deerwester, S., Dumais, S. T., Furnas, G. W., Landauer, T. K., & Harshman, R. (1990). Indexing by latent semantic analysis, *JASIS, 41,* 391-407.

Fallman, D. (2002). The Penguin: Using the Web as a database for descriptive and dynamic grammar and spell checking. *CHI 2002* (pp. 616-617). Minneapolis, MN.

Goyal, R. D., & Nagaraja, G. (2002). Generalized brain-state-in-a-box based associative memory for correction words and images. *Proceedings of the 9th International Conference on Neural Information Processing (ICONIP'02), 1,* 291-295.

Jones, P. M., & Martin, H. J. (1997). Contextual spelling correction using latent semantic analysis. *Proceedings of the 5th Conference on Applied Natural Language* (pp. 166-173). Washington, DC.

Khan, L., McLeod, D., & Hovy, E. (2004). Retrieval effectiveness of an ontology-based model for information selection. *The International Journal on Very Large Data Bases, 13,* 71-85.

Kukich, K. (1988). Variations on a back-propagation name recognition net. *Proceedings of the Advanced Technology Conference 2*(2), 722-735.

Kukich, K. (1992). Spelling correction for the telecommunications network for the deaf. *Communications of the ACM, 35,* 80-90.

Liu, Z., & Chu, W. W. (2005). Knowledge-based query expansion to support scenario-specific retrieval of medical free text. *ACM,* 1076-1083.

Mauldin, M. L. (1991). *Conceptual information retrieval.* Kluwer Academic.

McKemmish, S., Burstein, F., Manaszewicz, R., & Fisher, J. (2002). *Towards meeting the decision support needs of a community via an "Intelligent portal": Breast cancer knowledge online.* Retrieved May 21, 2002 from http://sims.edu.au/research/eirg

Mitton, R. (1996). *English spelling and the computer.* Addison-Wesley.

Moon, J. (2005). Discussing health issues on the Internet. In S. Dasgupta (Ed.), *Encyclopedia of virtual communities and technologies.* Hershey, PA: Idea Group Inc.

Moon, J., & Burstein, F. (2005). Intelligent portals for supporting medical information needs. In A. Tatnall (Ed.), *Web portals: The new gateways to internet information and services.* Hershey, PA: Idea Group Inc.

Moon, J., & Fisher, J. (2005). *The effectiveness of Australian medical portals: Are they meeting the health consumers' needs?* Working paper.

Morris, R., & Cherry, L. L. (1975). Computer detection of typographical errors. *IEEE Transactions on Professional Communication, 18,* 54-63.

Nix, R. (1981). Experience with a space efficient way to store a dictionary. *Communications of the ACM, 24,* 297.

Patel, C., Supekar, K., Lee, Y., & Park, E. K. (2003). OntoKhoj: A Semantic Web portal for ontology searching,

ranking and classification. *Proceedings of the 5th ACM international workshop on Web information and data management* (pp. 58-61). New Orleans.

Peterson, J. (1980). Computer programs for detecting and correcting spelling errors. *ACM, 23,* 676-687.

Pedersen, T. (1996). Fishing for exactness. *Proceedings of the South-Central SAS Users Group Conference.*

Pollock, J. J., & Zamora, A. (1984). Automatic spelling correction in scientific and scholarly text. *Communications of the ACM, 27,* 358-368.

Ruch, P. (2002). Information retrieval and spelling correction: An Inquiry into lexical disambiguation, *ACM,* 699-703.

Tijerino, Y. A., & Reza, S. (2005). OntoTEMAS: An ontology based teaching materials search engine. *Journal of Computing Sciences in Colleges, 20,* 177-182.

Yannakoudakis, E. J., & Fawthrop, D. (1983). The rules of spelling errors. *Information Processing Management, 19,* 87-99.

Zamora, A. (1978). Control of spelling errors in large data bases. *The Information Age in Perspective, Proceedings of the ASIS, 15,* 364-367.

Zamora, A. (1980). Automatic detection and correction of spelling errors in a large data base. *Journal of the ASIS, 31,* 51-57.

Zamora, E. M., Pollock, J. J., & Zamora, A. (1981). The use of trigram analysis for spelling error detection. *Information Processing Management, 17,* 305-316.

Terms and Definitions

Dictionary lookup techniques. Dictionary lookup techniques check whether an input string appears in a dictionary. Response time may become a problem as the size of the dictionary grows. To save the search time most often suffixes are stripped, and this can cause some problems.

Hamming distance H. H is defined only for strings of the same length. For strings s and t, H(s,t) is the number of places in which the two string differ, or have different characters.

Levenshtein distance (or edit) distance. Levenshtein distance is more sophisticated. It is defined for strings of arbitrary length. It counts the differences between two strings, where we would count a difference not only when strings have different characters but when one has a character whereas the other does not. The smallest number of insertions, deletions, and substitutions required to change one string or tree into another. A H(m x n) algorithm to compute the distance between strings, where m and n are the lengths of the strings (http://www.nist.gov/dads/HTML/levenshtein.html).

Minimum edit distance. Minimum edit distance is based on calculating the distance between a misspelled word and eh words in its files. Words whose evaluated distance is the smallest are offered as candidates for replacement.

n-gram is an n-letter subsequence of a string, where *n* is usually 1,2, or 3. In general, n-gram analysis techniques check each n-gram in an input string against a precompiled table of n-gram statistics to determine whether the n-gram can occur in a word. If it does, its frequency of occurrence in the words of the language is computed. Strings containing n-grams that do not occur in words or occur very infrequently are considered to be possible misspellings.

Phoneme. Phoneme is the smallest unit of sound in a language which can distinguish two words, that is, *pan* and *ban* differ in that *pan* begins with /p/ and *ban* begins with /b/.

Simple correlation matrix technique. Simple coorelation matrix technique is a correlation technique. Each misspelled word is represented by an n-dimensional feature where Hamming distance of strongly correlated matches the most probably correct word (Cherkassky et al., 1974).

Trigram analysis. Trigram analysis is a method used to correct spelling. It simply means three possible candidates for representing words where n-gram is used to apply the analysis.

Chapter XVII

Semantic Web Standards and Ontologies in the Medical Sciences and Healthcare

Sherrie D. Cannoy, The University of North Carolina at Greensboro, USA
Lakshmi Iyer, The University of North Carolina at Greensboro, USA

Abstract

This chapter will discuss Semantic Web standards and ontologies in two areas: (1) the medical sciences field and (2) the healthcare industry. Semantic Web standards are important in the medical sciences since much of the medical research that is available needs an avenue to be shared across disparate computer systems. Ontologies can provide a basis for the searching of context-based medical research information so that it can be integrated and used as a foundation for future research. The healthcare industry will be examined specifically in its use of electronic health records (EHR), which need Semantic Web standards to be communicated across different EHR systems. The increased use of EHRs across healthcare organizations will also require ontologies to support context-sensitive searching of information, as well as creating context-based rules for appointments, procedures, and tests so that the quality of healthcare is improved. Literature in these areas has been combined in this chapter to provide a general view of how Semantic Web standards and ontologies are used, and to give examples of applications in the areas of healthcare and the medical sciences.

Introduction

"One of the most challenging problems in the healthcare domain is providing interoperability among healthcare systems" (Bicer, Laleci, Dogac, & Kabak, 2005). The importance of this interoperability is to enable universal forms of knowledge representation integrate heterogeneous information, answer complex queries, and pursue data integration and knowledge sharing in healthcare (Nardon & Moura, 2004). With the recent emergence of EHRs and the need to distribute medical information across organizations, the Semantic Web can allow advances in sharing such information across disparate systems by utilizing ontologies to create a uniform language and by using standards to allow interoperability in transmission. The purpose of this article is to provide an overview of how Semantic Web standards and ontologies are utilized in the medical sciences and healthcare fields. We examine the healthcare field as the inclusion of hospitals, physicians, and others who provide or collaborate in patient healthcare. The medical sciences field provides much of the research to support the care of patients, and their need lies in being able to share and find medical research being performed by their colleagues to build upon current work. Interoperability between these different healthcare structures is difficult and there needs to be a common "data medium" to exchange such heterogeneous data (Lee, Patel, Chun, & Geller, 2004).

Decision making in the medical field is often a shared and distributed process (Artemis, 2005). It has become apparent that the sharing of information in the medical sciences field has been prevented by three main problems: (1) uncommon exchange formats; (2) lack of *syntactic* operability; and (3) lack of *semantic* interoperability (Decker et al., 2000). Semantic Web applications can be applied to these problems. Berners-Lee, Hendler, and Lassila (2001), pioneers in the field of the Semantic Web, suggest that "the semantic web will bring structure to the meaningful content of web pages". In this article published in *Scientific American*, they present a scenario in which someone can access the Web to retrieve information—to retrieve treatment, prescription, and provider information based on one query. For example, a query regarding a diagnosis of melanoma may provide results which suggest treatments, tests, and providers who accept the insurance plan with which one participates. This is the type of contextually based result that the Semantic Web can provide. The notion of ontologies can be utilized to regulate language, and standards can be used to provide a foundation for representing and transferring information. We will focus on the lack of semantic and syntactic interoperabilities in this article. The semantic interoperable concept will be utilized in the context of ontologies, and syntactic interoperabilities are referred to as standards of interoperability.

Background

The Semantic Web is an emerging area of research and technology. Berners-Lee (1989) proposed to the Centre Europeen pour la Recherche Nuclaire (CERN) the concept of the World Wide Web. He has been a pioneer also in the concept of the Semantic Web and has expressed the interest of the healthcare field to integrate the silos of data that exist to enable better healthcare (Updegrove, 2005). He has been involved with the World Wide Web Consortium (W3C) Web site (http://www.w3.org), which offers a vast array of Semantic Web information in a variety of subject areas, including the medical sciences and healthcare. Miller (2004) states that the Semantic Web should provide common data representation to "facilitate integrating multiple sources to draw new conclusions;" and to "increase the utility of information by connecting it to its definitions and context". Kishore, Sharman, and Ramesh (2004) wrote two articles which provide detailed information about ontologies and information systems.

The concept of the Semantic Web is to extend the current World Wide Web such that context and meaning is given to information (Gruetter & Eikemeier, 2004). Instead of information being produced for machines, information will be produced for human consumption (Berners-Lee et al., 2001). There are two main aspects of Semantic Web development: (1) ontologies for consistent terminology and (2) standards for interoperability.

Ontologies

Ontologies have been defined in many ways through the areas of philosophy, sociology, and computer science. For the Semantic Web context, ontology is the vocabulary, terminology, and relationships of a topic area (Gomez-Perez, Fernandez-Lopez, & Corcho, 2004). Ontology gives the meaning and context to information found in Web resources (databases, etc.) for a specific domain of interest, using relationships between concepts (Singh, Iyer, & Salam, 2005). According to Pisnalli, Gangemi, Battaglia, and Catenacci (2004), ontologies should have:

1. *logical consistency* and be expressed in a "logical language with an explicit formal semantics.
2. *semantic coverage* such that it covers "all entities from its domain."
3. *modeling precision* and represent "only the intended models for its domain of interest."
4. *strong modularity* for the domain's "conceptual space. . .by organizing the domain theories."
5. *scalability* so that the language is expressive of intended meanings.

The domain of an ontology should include a taxonomy of classes, objects, and their relations, as well as inference rules for associative power (Berners-Lee et al., 2001). This shared understanding of the concepts and their relationships allows a means to integrate the knowledge between disparate healthcare and medical science systems. Much of the Semantic Web research in the medical sciences area has been specific in either generating more efficient and effective information searching or to the interoperability of the EHR. Health information is inherently very tacit and intuitive, and the terminology often implies information based on physical examinations and expressions of the patient. While it uses standardized terminology, the difficulty lies in the expression of this tacit knowledge to others, especially across a network of computers. The two great needs in the medical sciences and healthcare that can be fulfilled by Semantic Web are to standardize language and to provide a consistent foundation for transferring EHR information (Decker et al., 2000).

Standards

While ontologies represent the conceptual basis for the information to be transmitted, standards allow for consistent transmission of the data between disparate systems. The data in different clinical information systems silos are in multiple formats, and relevant medical and healthcare knowledge must be accessible in a timely manner. This can be performed through interoperability standards which can enable information integration, "providing transparency for healthcare-related processes involving all entities within and between hospitals, as well as stakeholders such as pharmacies, insurance providers, healthcare providers, and clinical laboratories" (Singh et al., 2005, p. 30). The main standard for interoperability in the Semantic Web is Resource Description Framework (RDF), which is recommended by the W3C. RDF is an object-oriented based standard, which provides reusable components for data interchange over the web (Decker, Mitra, et al., 2000). It is unique in that every concept represented in RDF has a universal unique identifier (the Uniform Resource Identifier [URI]), which identifies every e-mail address, Web page, and other Web elements. This ensures no semantic ambiguity. RDF also enables knowledge representation through a series of concepts such as class, data type, and values. In order to express representations of ontologies for context, RDF allows for extensions such as the DARPA Agent Markup Language +Ontology Inference Layer (DAML+OIL) standard, which is the basis for the Web Ontology Language (OWL) standard that has recently gained popularity (Nardon & Moura, 2004).

Semantic Web Applied Standards and Ontologies in the Medical Sciences and Healthcare

"The semantic web initiative has resulted in a common framework that allows knowledge to be shared and reused across applications" (Health Level 7, 2004) and organizations. An infrastructure of common transmission standards and terminology will enable an interconnected network of systems that can deliver patient information. There have been various calls for the decrease of medical errors via utilization of information technology, and the increase of medical information accessibility and Semantic Web technology has a critical role to play. Besides the delivery of patient information, the Semantic Web can also assist medical sciences research in providing greater accessibility and the sharing of research. In the search for information, the Semantic Web can impart a context and meaning to information so that queries are more efficient in producing results more closely related to the search terms.

Table 1 displays only a few of the main standards currently used for interoperability in the Semantic Web. The affiliated organizations are listed, showing that there are many grassroots efforts involved in generating standards. There are three main organizations that are involved in international standards for EHRs. These include the International Organization for Standardization (ISO), Committee European Normalization (CEN), and Health Level 7 (HL7)—U.S. based (HL7, 2004). Standards are also important to develop on an international basis because countries also report national health status statistics to the world community (Cassidy, 2005).

A list of ontologies in the medical domain is listed in Table 2. For clarification, a logical association to an ontology is that of the ICD-9 (ICD-10 is the new version) coding for diseases. When a patient visits the physician, the physician records a standard ICD-9 code for the diagnosis of the patient and a CPT code for the procedure that was performed on a patient. These are standardized codes that are found in manuals for medical coders; and they allow insurance companies and other medical affiliates to understand information from many different sources. For example, if a patient is seen for a mole, the mole can have many particular qualities. Is it to be removed for cosmetic purposes, or is the mole potentially cancerous? The location of the mole will be important to know, as well, because the treatment may be de-

Table 1. Sample standards for interoperability

Name	Purpose	Associated Organization	Source
XML	eXtensible Markup Language; creation of tags		Decker et al, 2000
RDF	Standardized technology for metadata; for interpreting meaning	W3C	Nardon, 2004 Gruetter, et al, 2004
Clinical Document Architecture CDA	Leading standard for clinical and administrative data exchange among organizations	HL7	Nardon, 2004 Hooda et al 2004
Guidelines Interchange Format (GLIF)	specification for structured representation of guidelines	InterMed Collaboratory	Nardon, 2004 www.glif.org
CORBAmed	Provides interoperability among health care devices	Object Management Group	McCormack, 2000
HL7	Messaging between disparate systems	HL7	www.hl7.org

Table 2. Sample ontologies (is a terminology coding scheme and would be subsumed by an ontology)*

Name	*Purpose*	*Associated Organization*	*Source*
OIL	Oil Interchange Language; representation and inference language	European Community (IBROW and On-To-Knowledge)	Decker et al, 2000 http://www.ontoknowledge.org/oil/oilhome.shtml
Ontology Web Language (OWL)	Aim is to be the Semantic Web standard for ontology representation	W3 Consortium	Nardon, 2004
DAML	Extension of RDF which allows ontologies to be expressed; formed by DARPA Markup	DAML Researcher Group	Nardon, 2004 http://www.daml.org/
Arden Syntax	Standard for medical knowledge representation	HL7	Nardon, 2004 http://cslxinfintcs.csmc.edu/hl7/arden/
Riboweb Ontology	Facilitate models of ribosomal components and compare research results	Helix Group at Stanford Medical Informatics	Hadzic et al, 2005 http://smi-web.stanford.edu/projects/helix/riboweb.html
Gene Ontology	To reveal information regarding the role of an organism's gene products	GO Consortium	Hadzic et al, 2005 http://www.geneontology.org/index.shtml
LinkBase	Represents medical terminology by algorithms in a formal domain ontology	L&C	Hadzic et al, 2005
GALEN	Uses GRAIL language to represent clinical terminology	OpenGALEN	Gomez-Perez, 2004
ADL	Formal language for expressing business rules	openEHR	www.openEHR.org
SNOWMED*	Reference terminology	SNOMED Int'l	Cassidy, 2005
LOINC (Logical	Database for universal names and codes for lab and clinical observations	Regenstrief Institute, Inc.	McCormack, 2000 Gillespie, 2003
UMLS—Unified Medical Language	Facilitates retrieval and integration of information from multiple sources; can be used as basic ontology for any medical	US National Library of Medicine	Nardon, 2004 Hadzic, 2005 Gomez-Perez, 2004
ICD-10*	Classification of diagnosis codes; is newer version after ICD-9	National Center for Health Statistics	Gillespie, 2003
CPT Codes*	Classification of procedure codes	American Medical Association	Gillespie, 2003

termined by the location. The difference in the context may determine whether the insurance company will pay for the treatment of the mole. A cancerous melanoma on the nose would have the diagnosis code of 172.3 and a benign neoplasm would be coded as 238.2. If a tissue sample were taken so that the lab could test the mole for cancerous cells, the diagnosis would be 239.9, which is unspecified until the lab results return for a firm diagnosis. The CPT procedure code for the treatment would be applied and would be determined by a number of factors including the location of the mole, amount of tissue excised, whether a modifier needs to be added to the code if the services is charged with an office visit, and the type of excision utilized. While we have CPT and ICD-9 as a vocabulary for procedure and diagnosis codes, they function only as a part of ontology's purpose. An ontology gives context to the patient's medical history and allows the diagnosis and procedure to be automatically linked, possibly with appropriate medications, lab tests, and x-rays. The next section discusses ways that the Semantic Web has been applied in the medical sciences field.

Semantic Web Applications in Medical Science

Table 3 lists only a few of the sample projects being conducted in the medical science and healthcare field. Previous research in this area has dealt with two main

Table 3. Sample medical Semantic Web projects

PROJECTS			
Name	***Purpose***	***Associated Organization***	***Source***
Good European Health Record Project	To produce a comprehensive multi-media data architecture for EHRs	CHIME	Nardon, 2004 http://www.chime.ucl.ac.uk/work-areas/ehrs/GEHR/index.htm.
Brazilian National Health Card	Aimed at creating infrastructure for capture of encounter information at the point of care		Nardon, 2004
Artemis	Semantic Web Service-based P2P Infrastructure for the Interoperability of Medical Information Systems	Six participating entities from	Bicer et al., 2005 http://www.srdc.metu.edu.tr/webpage/projects/artemis/
Active Semantic Electronic Patient Record	Development of populated ontologies in the healthcare (specially cardiology practice) domain; an annotation tool for annotation of patient records, and decision support algorithms that support rule and ontology based checking/validation and evaluation.	LSDIS (large Scale Distributed Information Systems and AHC (Athens Heart Center)	http://lsdis.cs.uga.edu/projects/asdoc/
MedISeek	Allows users to describe, store, and retrieve medical images; metadata model		Carro et al., 2003

topics: (1) efficient and effective searches of medical science information and (2) the interoperability of EHRs. Our purpose is to provide a comprehensive review of this research to understand the current status of the Semantic Web in healthcare and medical sciences and to determine what future research may be performed.

Electronic Health Records

EHRs are comprehensive patient medical records which show a continuity of care. They contain a patient's complete medical history with information on each visit to a variety of healthcare providers, as well as medical tests and results, prescriptions, and other care histories. (Opposed to EHRs, Electronic medical records [EMRs] are typically those which reside with one physician.) Figure 1 shows the main stakeholders in the healthcare industry, and thus, the necessity for enabling these partners to communicate. Physician's, hospitals, Independent Practice Organizations (IPOs), and pharmacies interact to exchange patient information for medical purposes.

The government requires that healthcare organizations report medical data for statistical analysis and so that the overall health of the nation can be assessed. Medical information is aggregated so that patient identifiers are omitted and reported

Figure 1. The coordination of the healthcare industry is very diverse in its information needs

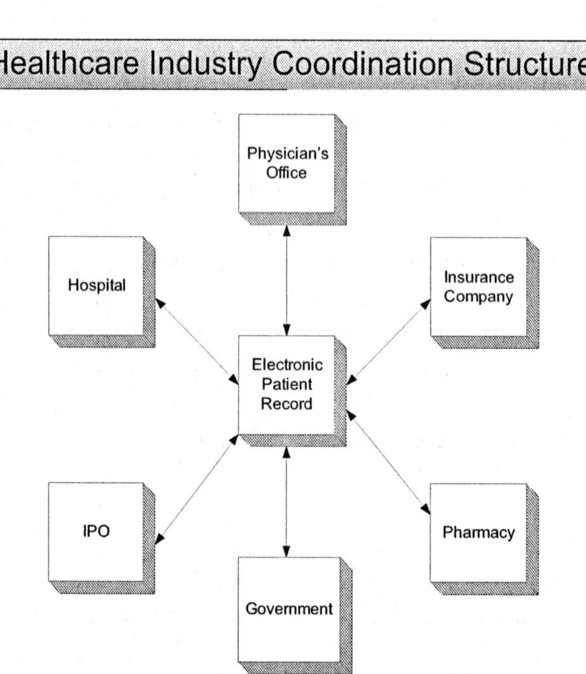

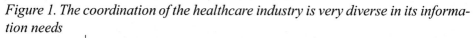

Figure 2. The sharing of information between healthcare entities can enable more efficient and effective quality of care

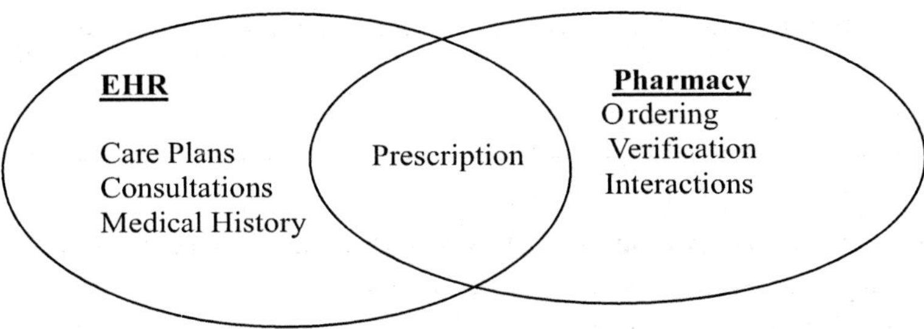

to the government for public health purposes and to catch contagious outbreaks early as well as to determine current health issues and how they can be addressed. For example, cancer registries report specific aggregated cancer information, and healthcare organizations report instances of certain infectious diseases such as the Avian influenza (bird flu), for the welfare of the public. The importance of sharing this information is the improvement of patient safety, efficiency, self-health management (through access of medical information), and effective delivery of healthcare (HL7, 2005). Figure 2 shows how two entities may interact to share information (adapted from HL7).

Indeed, a commission on systemic interoperability has been established through the Medicare Modernization Act of 2003 and recommends product certification, interoperable standards, and standard vocabulary as a way of ensuring that healthcare data is readily accessible (Vijayan, 2005). At a North Carolina Healthcare Information Communications Alliance, one recurring theme was that of interoperable EHRs. Brailler (2005), the first National Health Information Technology Coordinator in the U.S., spoke about standards harmonization for EHRs. The discussion of developing standards for interoperability emphasized the need to "stitch together different efforts" put forth by organizations such as HL7, IEEE, ISO, and SNOMED. Undoubtedly, he recognized that "standards are about economic power" and they need to be analyzed to determine which standards are available for the commercial market. In doing so, the office of National Health Information Technology suggests that there be a compliance certification for EHR based on criteria such as security, interoperability, and clinical standards—basically a seal of approval that if a healthcare organization purchases such a product, it will be "guaranteed" to have specific interoperability certification. Brailler stated "if it's not certified, it's not an EHR." Given this, it has been suggested that the second generation of EHRs is being developed to communicate with structured datasets, middleware, and messaging between systems (Bernstein, Bruun-Rasmussen, Vingtoft, Andersen, & Nohr, 2005).

Perhaps the third generation will provide full scale Semantic Web capabilities in which interoperability is seamless.

Currently, patient information is kept in silos across the aforementioned organizations; the Semantic Web will enable access to these silos through interoperability standards and consistent language. According to a white paper published by HL7 (2004), an organization which has developed HL7 standards for healthcare, improvements in the following five areas can be made through EHR standards: (1) interoperability, (2) safety/security, (3) quality/reliability, (4) efficiency/effectiveness, and (5) communication. To improve these areas, the standards proposed by HL7 include both standardized service interface models for interoperability, but also standardized concept models and terminologies. The current use of the HL7 standard is for the messaging of data to populate other disparate systems. For example, admissions data of a patient is also sent to the billing system. The problem with current messaging systems, such as HL7, is that they duplicate information across systems. Patient demographic information, for example, can be copied from one system to another, and maintenance of such data can create more messaging between systems (usually within an organization).

In Denmark, the examination of EHR use and interoperability has also been an issue of interest (Bernstein et al., 2005). The Danish Health IT Strategy project's goal is to analyze the variety of grassroots models for EHR information modeling and informatics. The National Board of Health is currently analyzing the SNOWMED ontology for use in its EHR. SNOWMED is an ontology that encapsulates classification systems such as ICD9. As a reference terminology, it is much more detailed in the medical concepts that it conveys. This level of detailed information allows the data to be used for quality assurance and resource utilization purposes and allows the EHR to relay more information than ICD9 coding for diagnoses. For example, there are around 13,000 ICD9 codes for diagnoses and SNOWMED contains 365,000 codes (Cassidy, 2005). Similar to the Denmark project, the Artemis project focuses on developing Semantic Web technology such as ontologies as a foundation to interoperability for medical records. Rather than standardizing the actual documents in the EHR, the goal is to standardize the accessibility of the records through wrappers, Web Services Description Language (WSDL) and Simple Object Access Protocol (SOAP) (Artemis, 2005). Bicer et al. (2005) discuss a project with Artemis in which OWL ontologies are used to map information messages from one entity to another.

Partners Healthcare uses RDF to enable medical history from EHRs to be accessible through computer models which select patients for clinical trials (Salamone, 2005). They utilized Semantic Web Rules Language (SWRL) to write decision support rules for this purpose. The advantage in using the Semantic Web approach is that the coding is concise, flexible, and works well with large databases. As Eric Neumann of the pharmaceutical company, Sanofi-Aventis suggests, "with the semantic web, you publish meaning, not just data" (Salamone, 2005).

Information Searching and Sharing

"Ontologies can enhance the functioning of the Web in many ways. They can be used in a simple fashion to improve the accuracy of Web searches" (Berners-Lee et al., 2001). The difficulties and complexities of searching for medical information are discussed by Pisnalli et al. (2004) in their research on medical polysemy. Because polysemy (a word having more than one meaning) can be critical to finding correct medical information, the application of ontologies can be of value in information searching. For example, the ontology of the term *inflammation* can vary depending on the context of its use. As Pisnalli et al. state, inflammation can include the size, shape, evolution, severity, and source. When one searches for the term inflammation, many results may be provided, but time is required to sort through the "hits" for relevance. The ON-9 ontology is utilized by Pisnalli et al. to map contexts for the term inflammation. As Nardon and Moura (2004) emphasize, the relationships among medical terminology is also essential to representation of the information in a logical format. Allowing for specific context to be interpreted through ontologies will enable more efficient and effective searching. Usually, this involves the creation of metadata to identify the relevant data elements and their relationships (Buttler et al., 2002).

Medical vocabularies used to represent data include the Unified Medical Language System (UMLS) from the U.S. National Library of Medicine and Arden Syntax. UMLS is perhaps the most frequently used ontology in the healthcare and medical sciences field. The purpose is to aid in integrating information from multiple biomedical information sources and enabling efficient and effective retrieval. It defines relationships between vocabularies and includes a categorization of concepts as well as the relationships among them. For example, the National Health Card System in Brazil contains an extensive knowledge base of 8 million patients in which complex queries can be run (Nardon & Moura, 2004). Through ontologies and UMLS, mapping of business rules can be applied to medical transactions to infer information and achieve semantic interoperability. For example, if a patient can undergo only a certain procedure once within a 30-day time period, a transaction for a patient setting up an appointment for that procedure can be mapped to business rules to infer that the same person cannot schedule the same procedure within that time period. UMLS would determine the ontology for the appointment and procedures and ensure that the patient is indeed the same, and RDF defines the business rules for sharing the information (Nardon & Moura, 2004).

When querying multiple medical data sources for research purposes, there are many medical science repositories in which data may not be in machine-processable format and stored in nonstandard ways. Most of the interfaces to search and retrieve medical sciences research require human interaction. Data extraction of such large data sources can be very complex and often the data is reused by researchers such as those in Genomics (Buttler et al., 2002). Large databases containing bioinformatics research can be unified through ontologies such as Riboweb, Generic Human Disease Ontology, Gene Ontology (GO), TAMBIS, and LinkBase. These allow a standard vocabulary to exist over disparate ribosomal, disease, gene product, nucleic acid, and protein resources. As an example, the Generic Human Disease Ontology, currently being developed with information from the Mayo Clinic, allows a physician to search by symptom to determine the disease or for type of appropriate treatment, and researchers can search for possible causes of a disorder (Hadzic & Chang, 2005).

MedISeek is an interesting example of using semantic vocabularies to search for medical visual information, such as x-rays and other images (Carro et al., 2003). Biomedical Imaging Research Network (BIRN), a project of the National Institute of Health, examines human neurological disorders and their association with animal models. A significant aspect of their work is through brain imaging. Their goal is to make this information available to others through the Semantic Web via graphical search tools; standard identifiers through ontologies; and cross-referencing of imaging (Halle & Kikinis, 2004). The Semantic Web will enable BIRN, MedISeek, and other healthcare and medical science projects to filter out less appropriate data by searching for a context to the information. RDF is being utilized with MedISeek and BIRN to allow interoperability between metadata patterns.

Conclusion and Future Trends

Sharing of EHR information allows for improved quality of care for patients. Sharing medical science knowledge allows scientists to gather information and avoid redundant experiments. Searching for medical science information on the Semantic Web will be made more efficient and effective by the use of common ontologies and standards for transmissions. "Trusted databases exist, but their schemas are often poorly or not documented for outsiders, and explicit agreement about their contents is therefore rare." The opportunity to share such large amounts of information through the Semantic Web suggests that knowledge management can exist on a comprehensive level with ontology as a unifying resource (Hadzic & Chang, 2005).

While there has been some research in the area of medical sciences information searching on the Semantic Web, there have been few studies on how to better enable healthcare consumers to search for medical information on the Web. Lay terminology of consumers often increases the number of results returned when searching for medical information on the Web. Polysemy creates a multitude of results within which the consumer must further search. The goal should be to use Semantic Web technology to minimize the semantic distance between a search term and its polysemy of translations (Lorence & Spinks, 2004).

The future of the Semantic Web will involve important developments in the emergence of e-healthcare through the use of intelligent agents. Singh et al. (2005) suggest that emerging Semantic Web-based technologies offer means to allow seamless and transparent flow of semantically enriched information through ontologies, knowledge representation, and intelligent agents. Intelligent agents can enrich the information by interpretation on behalf of the user to perform an automated function. The example given at the beginning of this article in which someone queries for melanoma information and receives information regarding treatments, tests, and providers in that person's location which accept his insurance, shows how intelligent agents can be utilized to search the Semantic Web. Agents can also be utilized to verify the source of the information. When sharing of information occurs across the Web and is pulled automatically by agents, the source of the information needs to be verified. This is especially true in healthcare with Health Insurance Portability and Accountability Act (HIPAA) 1996 regulations. If the foundation of ontology and interoperable standards exists, intelligent agents will be able to search the Web for information within the context desired.

Legal issues associated with the dispersion of healthcare information need to be identified. With HIPAA (1996)), healthcare organizations are required to keep patient personally identifiable information secure and private. This means encryption, access control, audit trails, and data integrity must be insured in the transmission process (Jagannathan, 2001). Who has rights to the data and who "owns the data," particularly in EHRs? Similarly, there is an issue of trust involved with sharing medical science and healthcare data, and this is an area ripe for further research. How can authentication be provided so that others know the source of data is trusted and how can it be ensured that the data will be edited by a trusted entity? The area of e-commerce can be a foundation for future research in trust, as well.

Semantic Web technology can function as a foundation for the sharing and searching of information for the healthcare and medical sciences fields. Because of the intuitive nature of patient care, the Semantic Web will enable context and meaning to be applied to medical information, as well as the conveyance of relationships between data. With the generation of standards for transmission of data between disparate systems, the quality of healthcare through better research and the sharing of information between healthcare providers will be a critical step in the evolution of patient care. This will enable the third generation of EHRs to be seamlessly interoperable for more efficient and effective patient care. These innovations can lead to improved work satisfaction, patient satisfaction, and patient care (Eysenbach, 2003).

References

Artemis. (2005). Retrieved November 2005, from www.srdc.metu.edu.tr/webpage/projects/artemis/home.html

Berners-Lee, T. (1989). *Proposal of Semantic Web to CERN.* Retrieved October, 2005 from http://www.w3.org/History/1989/proposal.html

Berners-Lee, T., Hendler, J., & Lassila, O. (2001, May 17). The Semantic Web. *The Scientific American.* Retrieved May 2005, from www.sciam.com

Bernstein, K., Bruun-Rasmussen, M., Vingtoft, S., Andersen, S. K., & Nohr, C. (2005). Modelling and implementing electronic health records in Denmark. *International Journal of Medical Informatics, 74,* 213-220.

Bicer, V., Laleci, G., Dogac, A., & Kabak, Y. (2005, September). Artemis message exchange framework: Semantic interoperability of exchanged messages in the healthcare domain. *SIGMOD Record, 34*(3), 71-76.

Brailler, D. (2005). Keynote address. *NCHICA 11th Annual Conference,* Greensboro, NC. Retrieved November 2005, from www.nchica.org

Buttler, D., Coleman, M., Critchlow, T., Fileto, R., Han, W., Pu, C., et al. (2002, December). Querying multiple bioinformatics information sources: Can Semantic Web research help? *SIGMOD Record, 31*(4), 59-64.

Carro, S., Scharcanski, J., & De Lima, J. (2003). MedISeek: A Web based diffusion system for medical visual information. Workshop on Web information and data management. *Proceedings of the 5th ACM international workshop on Web information and data management,* New Orleans, Louisiana, USA.

Cassidy, T. (2005, September 26). Building a bridge to EHRs: ICD-10 and SNOMED-CT. *Advance for Health Information Professionals.*

Decker, S., Melnik, S., et al. (2000, September/October). The Semantic Web: The roles of XML and RDF. *IEEE Internet Computing.*

Decker, S., Mitra, P., & Melnik, S. (2000, Novmeber/December). Framework for the Semantic Web: An RDF tutorial. *IEEE Internet Computing,* 68-73.

Eysenbach, G. (2003). The Semantic Web and healthcare consumers: A new challenge and opportunity on the horizon? *International Journal of Healthcare Technology and Management,* *5*(3/4/5), 194-212.

Gillespie, G. (2003). NCVHS to extol a standard vocab. *Health Data Management, 11*(5), 50-58.

Gomez-Perez, A., Fernandez-Lopez, M., & Corcho, O. (2004). *Ontological engineering,* London: Springer.

Gruetter, R., & Eikemeier, C. (2004). *Applying the Semantic Web to clinical process.* Retrieved October 2005, from http://www.egms.de/en/meetings/gmds2004/04gmds316.shtml

Hadzic, M., & Chang, E. (2005). Ontology-based support for human disease study. *Proceedings of the 38th Hawaii International Conference on System Sciences.*

Halle, M., & Kikinis, R. (2004). Flexible frameworks for medical multimedia. *Proceedings of the 12th Annual ACM International Conference on Multimedia.* 768-775.

Health Level 7. (2004). HL7 HER system functional model: A major development towards consensus on electronic health record system functionality. White Paper.

Hooda, J. S., Dogdu, E., & Sunderraman, R. (2004). Health level-7 compliant clinical patient records system. *2004 ACM Symposium on Applied Computing,* 259-263.

Jagannathan, V. (2001, May/June). The careflow architecture: A case study in medical transcription. *IEEE Internet Computing,* 59-64.

Kishore, R., Sharman, R., & Ramesh, R. (2004). Computational ontologies and information Systems: I. Foundations. *Communications of the Association for Information Systems, 14,* 158-183.

Lee, Y., Patel, C., Chun, S. A., & Geller, J. (2004). Compositional knowledge management for medical services on Semantic Web. *The Thirteenth International World Wide Web Conference Proceedings,* New York. Retrieved August 2005, from http://www.www2004.org/proceedings/docs/2p498.pdf

Lorence, D., & Spinks, A. (2004). Semantics and the medical Web: A review of barriers and breakthroughs in effective healthcare query. *Health Information and Libraries Journal, 21,* 109-116.

McCormack, J. (2000, May). Standard Bearers cite progress. *Health Data Management, 8*(5). 98-102.

Miller, E. (2004, January). *Weaving meaning: An overview of the Semantic Web.* Paper presented at the University of Michigan, Ann Arbor, Michigan. Retrieved October 2005, from http://www.w3.org/2004/Talks/0120-semweb-umich/

Nardon, F., & Moura, L. (2004). Knowledge sharing and information integration in healthcare ontologies and deductive databases. *MEDINFO,* 62.

Pisanelli, D., Gangemi, A., Battaglia, M., & Catenacci, C. (2004). Coping with medical polysemy in the Semantic Web: The role of ontologies. *MEDINFO,* 416-419.

Salamone, S. (2005, June 8) Semantic Web interest grows. *Bio-IT World.* Retrieved November 2005, from http://www.bio-itworld/archive/microscope/document.2005-06-16.8341855754

Sharman, R., Kishore, R., & Ramesh, R. (2004). Computational ontologies and information systems: II. Formal specification. *Communications of the Association for Information Systems, 14,* 184-205.

Singh, R., Iyer, L., & Salam, A. F. (2005, January-March). Semantic eBusiness. *International Journal on Semantic Web and Information Systems, 1*(1), 19-35.

Updegrove, A. (2005, June) *The Semantic Web: An interview with Tim Berners-Lee.* Retrieved November 2005, from http://www.TheConsotriumInfo.org

Vijayan, J. (2005, November 1). Federal commission looks to push e-health record adoption. *Computerworld.* Retrieved November 2005, from http://www.computerworld.com/securitytopics/security/story/0,10801,105860,00.html

About the Authors

A.F. Salam is an associate professor in the Information Systems and Operations Management Department in the Bryan School of Business, The University of North Carolina at Greensboro (USA). He earned both his MBA and PhD from the School of Management at the State University of New York at Buffalo. His research interests include e-business and emerging technologies, Semantic Web technologies and business, ontology and knowledge representation, secure semantic distributed knowledge management, intelligent multi-agent software systems, business processes and service oriented architecture, trust and exchange relationship in e-commerce, ERP implementation and information technology management. His research has been published or forthcoming in *IEEE Transactions on Systems, Man and Cybernetics (Part A), Communications of the ACM, Information & Management, Information Systems Journal, Communications of the AIS (CAIS), Information Systems Management, International Journal of Semantic Web and Information Systems, eService Journal, Electronic Government and Journal of Information Technology Cases and Applications*. He has been a co-guest editor of the special section of the *Communications of the ACM* on *Semantic EBusiness Vision* and on *Internet and Marketing*. He was also a co-guest editor of the special issue of the *Journal of Electronic Commerce Research* on *Exchange Relationship in the Digital Economy*. He is on the editorial review board of the *International Journal of Semantic Web and Information Systems* and *International Journal of Information Security and Privacy*. He was also a co-chair of the semantic e-business mini-track in AMCIS 2005 and 2006.

Jason R. Stevens earned his BS in computer information systems from the University of Southern Indiana in 2001, and his MS in information systems at the Kelley School of Business at the Indiana University in 2004. Stevens is currently a doctoral student in the information systems PhD program in the Information Systems and Operations Management Department at the Bryan School of Business and Economics, The University of North Carolina at Greensboro (USA). His research interests include Semantic Web technologies and application of these emerging technologies in the extended enterprise. He has published in the *Proceedings of the Americas Conference on Information Systems (AMCIS) 2005* and in the *Proceedings of the Decision Sciences Institutes, 2005.*

* * *

Charles E. Beck is an associate professor of management and communication at the University of Colorado at Colorado Springs (USA). He began his career as an Air Force aircraft maintenance officer, and later taught at the Air Force and Naval Academies, and the AF Institute of Technology. Beck directed the MS in Technical Communication at the University of Colorado before moving to the Business College. He has contributed as an author and editor to numerous journals and proceedings and has published the book *Managerial Communication: Bridging Theory and Practice* (Prentice-Hall). He has served as a consultant to businesses in Dayton, Washington DC, and in Colorado.

Jacqueline Blake is in business management with a private company in the construction industry. In 2003 she accepted a scholarship from the Australian Forestry and Wood Product Research and Development Corporation to complete a Master of Information Technology (research). Her research interests include electronic commerce and its impact on business processes; the Semantic Web and its impact on supply chain management.

Athanasios Bouras graduated in 2003 from the School of Electrical and Computer Engineering of the National Technical University of Athens (Greece). His diploma thesis was in the area of system analysis and design for knowledge management applications. In the past he has worked on the INKASS IST project and on several ATHOC (ATHENS 2004 Olympic Games) projects. He is currently a research engineer at the School of Electrical and Computer Engineering of NTUA. His current research interests include the emerging Semantic Web and business (re-) engineering of media that support application integration, process fusion, and knowledge distribution and transfer in an intra- and inter- organizational level and web services that implement e-business and e-government applications. He is a teaching assistant in Management and Evaluation of Projects.

Frada Burstein is an associate professor at Monash University, Australia. She received her Master of Sciences (computer sciences) in 1978 from Tbilisi State University, Georgia, USSR and doctoral degree in decision support systems at 1984 from the Institute of Cybernetics Georgian Academy of Sciences. At Monash University, Professor Burstein initiated and continues to lead Knowledge Management Research Program. She has been a chief investigator for a number of research projects supported by grants and scholarships from the Australian Research Council and industry. Professor Burstein has published extensively in academic journals and collections of papers. She is an associate editor for the International Journal of Knowledge Management and Journal of Decision Systems and an area editor for the Journal of Decision Support Systems. Her research interests include intelligent decision support, organisational memory, knowledge modelling.

Sherrie D. Cannoy is a doctoral student in the information systems program at The University of North Carolina at Greensboro, USA. Her research interests include health informatics and e-healthcare, security and privacy issues, and the social affects of information systems in organizations. She earned a double-major BS in information systems and business education as well as a master's degree in IT management from UNC Greensboro. Her industry experience has been in both healthcare and educational organizations, including teaching at various levels of the U.S. education system. Her research has been published in the *Encyclopedia of E-Commerce, E-Government, and Mobile Commerce*, the forthcoming *Semantic Web Technologies and eBusiness: Virtual Organizations and Business Process Automation*, and in conference proceedings for the *Decision Sciences Institute, Southern INFORMS, Global Information Technology Management, and Southeast Decision Sciences Institute*, as well as research currently being reviewed with *CACM* and the *Journal of Strategic Information Systems.*

Jorge Cardoso joined the University of Madeira (Portugal) in March 2003. He previously gave lectures at the University of Georgia (USA) and at the Instituto Politécnico de Leiria (Portugal). Dr. Cardoso received his PhD in computer science from the University of Georgia in 2002. In 1999, he worked at the Boeing Company on enterprise application integration. Dr. Cardoso was the co-organizer and co-chair of the First and Second International Workshop on Semantic and Dynamic Web Processes. He has published over 50 refereed papers in the areas of workflow management systems, Semantic Web, and related fields.

Liang-Tien Chia received a BSc and PhD from Loughborough University (1990 and 1994, respectively). He is the director for the Centre of Multimedia and Network Technology and also an associate professor in the division of computer communications, School of Computer Engineering, Nanyang Technological University, Singapore.

His current research interests are in multimedia storage and retrieval, multimedia processing, error concealment techniques, video communication, bandwidth management and wireless Internet. He has published over 70 research papers.

Sumali J. Conlon is an associate professor of MIS at the University of Mississippi, USA. She received her PhD from the Illinois Institute of Technology. Her teaching and research interests include Semantic Web, Web services, Web mining, natural language processing, information retrieval, knowledge management, and database systems. Her work has appeared in the Journal of the American Society for Information Science, Information Processing & Management, Omega, and Decision Support Systems, International Journal of Information and Management Science, among others.

Fergle D'Aubeterre is a doctoral student in the Information Systems and Operations Management Department at The University of North Carolina at Greensboro, USA. He obtained his MBA from Central Michigan University. His research interests include knowledge management, global IT management, Semantic Web and IT security and privacy. He has published papers in journals such as *Information Systems Journal, Electronic Government an International Journal, Encyclopedia of Encyclopedia of E-Commerce, E-Government, and Mobile Commerce ,the Proceedings of Global Information Technology Management, the Proceedings of Americas Conference on Information Systems and the Proceedings of the Decision Sciences Institute.*

Ming Dong received a BS from Shanghai Jiao Tong University, Shanghai, China, in 1995 and a PhD from the University of Cincinnati, Ohio, in 2001, all in electrical engineering. He joined the Faculty of Wayne State University, Detroit, MI, in 2002 and is currently an assistant professor in the Department of Computer Science. He is also the director of the Machine Vision and Pattern Recognition Laboratory. His research interests include pattern recognition, computer vision, multimedia, and semantic web. He is a member of the editorial board of the *International Journal on Semantic Web and Information Systems* and has been a program committee member of various conferences. He is also a board member of the Association for Information Systems SIG on Semantic Web and information systems.

Farshad Fotouhi received his PhD in computer science from Michigan State University, Lansing, in 1988. He joined the Faculty of Computer Science at Wayne State University, Detroit, Michigan in August 1988 where he is currently a professor and chair of the department. His major area of research is databases and Semantic Web, including relational, object-oriented, multimedia/hypermedia systems, and data warehousing. Dr Fotouhi has published over 80 papers in refereed journals and conference proceedings, served as a program committee member of various database related conferences. He also serves on the editorial boards of the IEEE Multimedia Magazine and The International Journal on Semantic Web and Information Systems.

Maria Ganzha works as an assistant professor at the Elblag University of Humanities and Economics in Elblag, Poland and as a senior researcher at the Systems Research Institute of Polish Academy of Science. She obtained MS and PhD degrees in applied mathematics from Moscow State University (1987 and 1991, respectively). After devoting her time to her two daughters she has recently returned to active research and works in the areas of software engineering and agent systems. She is on editorial boards of three journals and a book series and was invited to program committees of over 20 conferences.

Maciej Gawinecki obtained an MS degree in computer science from Adam Mickiewicz University in Poznan, Poland (2005). Currently, Gawinecki works as a senior researcher in the Systems Research Institute of Polish Academy of Science.

Rafał Gąsiorowski obtained an MS degree in computer science from Warsaw University of Technology in Warsaw, Poland (2005).

Panagiotis Gouvas graduated in 2004 from the School of Electrical and Computer Engineering of the National Technical University of Athens (Greece). His diploma thesis was in the area of mobile and personal communications (location based services in wireless LANs). During 2002-2004 he worked as software engineer in the company European Profiles S.A. He has participated in several research IST projects (Healthy-Market, QUALEG) and e-Contect projects (ML-IMAGES). At present he is a PhD candidate in the School of Electrical & Computer Engineering at NTUA. His research interests lie in the field of multi-agent architectures, knowledge management and semantic-grid architectures for efficient process of DNA-genome data (with emphasis in HIV virus).

Sheng-Uei Guan earned his MSc and PhD from The University of North Carolina at Chapel Hill. He is a chair professor with the School of Engineering and Design at Brunel University. Professor Guan has worked in a prestigious R&D organization for several years, serving as a design engineer, project leader, and manager. After leaving the industry, he joined Yuan-Ze University in Taiwan for three and half years. He served as deputy director for the Computing Center and the chairman for the Department of Information & Communication Technology.

Anna Lisa Guido graduated in computer science engineering from the University of Lecce in July 2004. She is a PhD student at SetLab- Software Engineering and Telemedia Laboratory-University of Lecce (Italy). Her research areas include Web information systems. She is oriented to develop a framework light for small-to-medium size companies that allow to manage business processes. The framework will be made both by a methodology and by tools that helps the designer in the design, development and manage of Web information system process-oriented. The methodology will link the know-how of Web application design and the know-how of process design.

Jason G. Hale is an IT manager who has also served in several software development roles in industry and education since 1993. He is currently a PhD student in computer science at the University of Mississippi, USA. His research interests include the Semantic Web, natural language processing, knowledge representation, and e-learning systems.

Wawrzyniec Hyska obtained an MS degree in computer science from Warsaw University of Technology in Warsaw, Poland (2005).

Lakshmi Iyer is an associate professor in the Information Systems and Operations Management Department at The University of North Carolina at Greensboro. She obtained her PhD from the University of Georgia, Athens. Her research interests are in the area of e-business processes, e-commerce issues, global issues in IS, intelligent agents, decision support systems and knowledge management. Her research work has been published or accepted for publication in *CACM, eService Journal, Annals of OR, DSS, International Journal of Semantic Web and Information Systems, Journal of Global Information Technology Management, Journal of Scientific and Industrial Research, Encyclopedia of ORMS, Journal of Information Technology Management, Journal of Data Warehousing* and *Industrial Management and Data Systems.*

Yongil Jeong is an associate research engineer of Saltlux, Inc. in Korea. His research areas include applications of the Semantic Web and natural language processing.

Jaehun Joo is a professor of Dongguk University in Korea. His research has appeared in Information Systems Management, Expert Systems with Applications, International Journal of Industrial Engineering, INFORMS, Journal of MIS Research, Korean Management Reviews, and other publications. His research interests include e-business, e-tourism, u-commerce, knowledge management, and Semantic Web. This work was supported by the research program of Dongguk University.

Bu-Sung Lee received a BSc (Hons.) and a PhD from the Electrial and Electronics Department, Loughborough University of Technology, UK (1982 and 1987, respectively). He is currently an associate professor at the Nanyang Technological University, Singapore. He also holds the position of vice dean of Research in School of Computer Engineering, NTU. He is the technology area director of the Asia Pacific Advance Network (APAN) and an associate with Singapore Research and Education Networks (SingAREN). He has been an active member of several national standards organizations such as the National Infrastructure Initiative (Singapore One) Network Working Group, the Singapore ATM Testbed, and the Bio-Medical Grid (BMG) Task Force. His research interests are in network management, broadband networks, distributed networks, and network optimization.

Sang M. Lee is the university eminent professor, Firstier Bank distinguished professor, chair of the Management Department, CBA, University of Nebraska – Lincoln, USA. He has authored or co-authored 50 books, mostly in the field of management. He has published more than 170 journal articles, and 360 original papers, and has presented over 2,000 speeches. He is currently president of the Pan-Pacific Business Association. He also served as president of the Decision Sciences Institute. He has organized 26 international conferences as the program chair. He is on the editorial board of 23 journals, and has been listed in more than 50 Who's Who publications, including Who's Who in America.

Changqing Li is a PhD candidate in Department of Computer Science, School of Computing, National University of Singapore. He has submitted his PhD thesis. His research interests include ontology modeling, Semantic Web, data integration and data interoperability, XML query and update processing based on labeling schemes, and query of XML changes. During the PhD period, Changqing has published 10 papers in different journals and conferences, including VLDB journal, ICDE06, DASFAA06, CIKM05, DASFAA05, DEXA05, and ER04. In addition, he has published three papers during his master's period in Peking University, China. He is a student member of IEEE.

Tok Wang Ling is a professor with the Department of Computer Science, School of Computing at the National University of Singapore, Singapore. His research interests include data modeling, entity-relationship approach, object-oriented data model, normalization theory, logic and database, integrity constraint checking, semistructured data model, and data warehousing. He has published more than 150 international journal/conference papers and chapters in books, and co-authored a book, mainly in data modeling. He also co-edited 12 conference and workshop proceedings. He organized and served as program committee co-chair of DASFAA'95, DOOD'95, ER'98, WISE 2002, and ER 2003. He organized and served/serves as conference co-chair of Human.Society@Internet conference (HSI) in 2001, 2003, and 2005, WAIM 2004, ER 2004, DASFAA 2005, SIGMOD 2007. He is the honorary conference chair of DASFAA 2006. He serves/served on the program committees of more than 100 international database conferences since 1985. He is the advisor of the steering committee of International Conference on Database Systems for Advanced Applications (DASFAA), a member of the steering committee of International Conference on Conceptual Modeling (ER), and the International Conference on Human.Society@Internet (HSI). He was chair and vice chair of the steering committee of ER conference and DASFAA conference, and was a member of the steering committee of the International Conference on Deductive and Object-Oriented Databases (DOOD). He is an editor of the journal *Data & Knowledge Engineering*, *International Journal of Cooperative Information Systems*, *Journal of Database Management*, *Journal of Data Semantics*, and *World Wide Web: Internet and Web Information Systems.* He is a member of ACM, IEEE, and Singapore Computer Society.

Susan Lukose is a PhD student of computer and information science at the University of Mississippi, USA. Her research interests include information extraction, information retrieval and natural language processing.

Gregoris Mentzas is a professor of information management at the School of Electrical and Computer Engineering of the National Technical University of Athens (NTUA) and director of the Information Management Unit (IMU), a multidisciplinary research unit at the university. During the 2006-2009 period, he will serve on the board of directors of the Institute of Communication and Computer Systems of NTUA. His area of expertise is information technology management and his research concerns the integration of knowledge management, Semantic Web and e-service technologies, collaboration and workflow management, corporate knowledge management in e-government and e-business settings. He has spoken at conferences and guest seminars world wide, and is internationally known for his scholarly work in the area of knowledge management and e-government. Professor Mentzas holds a diploma degree in engineering (1984) and a PhD in operations research and information systems (1988), both from NTUA. During 1996-1997 he was a visiting fellow in the UK, in the area of information management systems in business transformation.

Jane Moon is a PhD candidate at Monash University. She has degrees in medical science (immunology) and an MArts (linguistics) from the University of Melbourne; graduate diploma in health administration, graduate diploma in business studies and MBA from LaTrobe University; graduate certificate in European business studies from ESC-Rouen France; post graduate diploma in immunology and graduate diploma in computer science from Monash University. She has special interest in health informatics and is currently researching factors contributing to effectiveness of medical portals.

Roberto Paiano received a DrEng in electronic engineering from the University of Bologna, Italy. He worked in IBM Italy until the 1996. Since the 1997 he has been at the Department of Engineering, University of Lecce, where he's assistant professor. His research interests include the methodology of Web application design and Web information systems design. He is member of the IEEE and the IEEE Computer Society.

Marcin Paprzycki works as an associate professor at the SWPS University in Warsaw, Poland. He has received his MS in 1986 from Adam Mickiewicz University in Poznan, Poland and his PhD in 1990 from Southern Methodist University in Dallas, Texas. His initial research interests were in high performance computing and parallel computing, and over time they evolved toward distributed systems and Internet-based computing; in particular, agent systems. He has published more than 200 research papers and was invited to program committees of over 200 international conferences. He is on editorial boards of 10 journals and a book series.

Wayne Pease is a lecturer in the Department of Information Systems, Faculty of Business at the Wide Bay Campus of the University of Southern Queensland. His employment background is in senior management with Queensland Health and has worked in higher education since 1998 when he accepted a lecturing position in information systems at the then new USQ Wide Bay Campus. His research interests include electronic commerce and its impact on rural and regional communities; payment and security systems in electronic commerce; web design and web data delivery systems including DBMS integration and query optimisation; and windows application development.

Szymon Pisarek obtained his MS degrees in computer science from Warsaw University of Technology in Warsaw, Poland (2005).

Marc Rabaey holds a Master of Social and Military Science (1984) and a degree of Commercial Engineer (1990). He starts his professional career in the IT-center of the Medical Service. In 1990 he was project manager of replacing the mainframes of the Medical Service by Sun/Sybase/IP-network. In 1993 he became the head of IT of the Command Medical Operations. From 1997 until 2001, he was assigned respectively as deputy chief IT and chief IT medical service. Since 2002 he has been the information system manager of the Department Evaluation of the Belgian Defence. His PhD in applied economics is from the Vrije Universiteit Brussel and Royal Military Academy. Its subject is "Investment in ICT: A holistic approach," aligning IT with the strategy of an organization.

Manjeet Rege has a BS in mathematics from University of Mumbai, India and an MS in computer information systems from Eastern Michigan University, Ypsilanti, Michigan. Currently, he is a PhD candidate in the Department of Computer Science at Wayne State University, Detroit, Michigan. His research interests include image processing, semantic web, multimedia information retrieval and computer vision.

Rahul Singh is an assistant professor in the Information Systems and Operations Management Department at The University of North Carolina at Greensboro, USA. He obtained his PhD in business administration from Virginia Commonwealth University. His research interests are in the area of the design of systems that apply intelligent technologies to business decision systems. Specific interests include intelligent agents, knowledge management systems, data mining and machine learning systems. His research work has been published in journals such as *CACM, eService Journal, Information Resources Management Journal, Journal of Decision Systems, International Journal of Semantic Web and Information Systems, International Journal of Production Engineering Socio-Economic Planning Sciences* and *The Encyclopedia of information Systems.*

Martin Timmerman received a bachelor's degree in telecommunications engineering from the Royal Military Academy (RMA), Brussels, Belgium, and was subsequently awarded a doctorate in applied science from Ghent University (1982). As a specialist in computer engineering, he established, in 1983, the System Development Centre for the Belgian Armed Forces. Today, he is professor and head of Department IT of the Royal Military Academy. Timmerman is best known, however, for Dedicated Systems Experts, an expert company in the field of embedded real-time systems. The company's core competencies can be interpreted as aiming to assist clients to remove ambiguity and confusion from their embedded system design.

Herman Tromp holds an electrical engineering degree (1972), a degree in telecommunications engineering (1973) and a PhD in engineering (1978), all from Ghent University, Belgium. Since 1972 he has been with the Department of Information Technology, Ghent University, Belgium, on leave with McMaster University, Canada in 1974-1975 and the Belgian Military Academy (Telecom Department) in 1975-1976. The main interests of Professor Tromp are currently in research on architectural resources for the revitalisation and integration of legacy IT systems, and on software development methodology in general. He also teaches software engineering to computer science students at Ghent University, Belgium and regularly gives lectures in post-academic programs.

Koenraad Vandenborre holds an electrical engineering degree (1992) obtained at Ghent University. From 1998 until 2001 he was affiliated with the Department of Information Technology, Ghent University, Belgium as a PhD student. In 2001 he became an IT-consultant within Inno.com, a Belgian consulting firm delivering IT architecture and IT strategy services. In 2004 he returned to research at Hogeschool Gent in order to finalize his PhD on information architecture and information management. Vandenborre's main interests are in software engineering in general and in specific in the supportive and / or enabling role of enterprise architecture and information architecture toward business processes and the business strategy.

Eddy Vandijck has been dean of the Faculty of Economic, Social and Political Sciences and Management school Solvay of the Vrije Universiteit Brussel since 2002. In 1972 he started as a researcher for the Belgian ministry of sciences. In 1976 he became VUB administrative data processing department. From 1984 to 1989 he was director of the data Processing Department of the Antwerp University hospital. Since 1989 he was a full-time professor at the Vrije Universiteit Brussel. He is a visiting professor at University of Ghana, Legon and at University of Lisbon, Portugal. His research areas are system methodologies, database systems, knowledge management, ICT-auditing and management information systems in general

Anil Vinjamur is a graduate student of computer and information science at the University of Mississippi.

Chen Zhou received his BE degree in computer science and technology from Shanghai Jiao Tong University, China, 2002. After that he has been working toward a PhD in the School of Computer Engineering, Nanyang Technological University, Singapore. His current research interests include Web services discovery, semantic web, service QoS and middleware distributed systems.

Fangming Zhu received his BS and MS degrees from Shanghai Jiaotong University, China (1994 and 1997, respectively). He is currently with the Institute of Systems Science, National University of Singapore. His research interests include evolutionary computation, pattern classification, and intelligent agents.

Index

D

E

F

G

H

I

J

K

L

M

N

O

P

Q

R

S

T